Indus Script Cipher

Hieroglyphs of Indian linguistic area

S. Kalyanaraman

Sarasvati Research Center

ISBN 9780982897102

Library of Congress Control Number: 2010911331

All rights reserved.

Printed in the USA

First paperback printing, July 2010

The text type was set in Arial Unicode

About the book

This is a path-breaking work as significant as the decipherment of Egyptian hieroglyphs by Champollion.

For nearly130 years, the Indus script has remained a challenging enigma to scholars of languages, writing systems and civilization studies. The script was invented and used over an extensive area of what is called the Indus or Sindhu-Sarasvati civilization. Over 2000 or 80% of archaeological sites are found on the Sarasvati River basin, a river adored in a very old human document called the Rigveda and which dried up due to tectonic and resulting river migration causes. In 1822, history was made when Egyptian hieroglyphs were deciphered by Jean-François Champollion from parts of the Rosetta Stone. Champollion showed that the Egyptian writing system, c.3000 BCE was a combination of phonetic and ideographic glyphs. The Rosetta Stone is dated196 BCE and had a decree in three versions: one in ancient Egyptian hieroglyphs, one in the Egyptian demotic script, and one in ancient Greek. Since alphabets of ancient Greek were known, Champollion used the trilingual inscription to validate his historic decipherment.

Indus Script Cipher makes history recording hundreds of hieroglyphs of India. Absence of a Rosetta Stone which has been the principal impediment in validating any decryption of Indus script cipher is thus overcome. Further validation comes from evidences of the historical periods in India from c. 600 BCE showing continued use of Indus script hieroglyphs which evolved from c. 3300 BCE. This book details a decipherment.of the Indus script using the same rebus method used by Champollion to read ancient phonetic hieroglyphs of Indiat. By demonstrating an Indian linguistic area of cultural and language contacts and history of language changes, this is a landmark contribution to civilization studies of the world and will promote efforts to rewrite the ancient socio-cultural and economic history of a billion people in India and neighboring regions.

Acknowledgments

This book is a dedication to children of present and future generations. The author gratefully acknowledges interactions with and contributions of editor and book designer, Anu Girish, Kiran Girish, cover designer, Prabha Girish, who are Kalyanaraman's daughter and granddaughters, and Girish Venkat. They are all enthused about tracing their cultural roots. The author gratefully acknowledges the contributions made by Asko Parpola and I. Mahadevan, Harappa Archaeological Research Project, in particular –and other compilers of corpus of Indus inscriptions -- and owes a deep debt of gratitude to hundreds of scholars (including Gregory Possehl, BB Lal, Massimo Vidale, Lyle Campbell) who have provided insights into the structure, form and purpose of the script, contact areas and the underlying linguistic area. Figures including those on cover pages of Sarasvati (divinity of vidyā, learning and vāk, language) painting by Raja Ravi Varma (1848-1906), two svastika seals are in the public domain and/or courtesy Archaeological Survey of India, Department of Archaeology and Museums, Govt. of Pakistan, British and other museums of the world.

About the author

Dr. S. Kalyanaraman is Director, Sarasvati Research Center, President, Ramasetu Protection Movement in India and BoD member of World Association for Vedic Studies. His research interests relate to rediscovery of Vedic Sarasvati River, roots of Hindu civilization, decoding of Indus Script, National Water Grid and creation of Indian Ocean Community. He has a Ph.D. in Public Administration from the Universitty of the Philippines. He is a multi-lingual scholar versed in Tamil, Telugu, Kannada, Sanskrit, Hindi. He was a senior financial and IT executive in Asian Development Bank, Manila, Philippines and on Indian Railways. His 15 publications include: *Indian Lexicon* - a multilingual dictionary for over 25 Indian languages, *Sarasvati* in 15 volumes, *Indian Alchemy - Soma in the Veda*. He is a recipient of many awards including Vakankar Award (2000), Shivananda Eminent Citizens' Award (2008) and Dr. Hedgewar Prajna Samman (2008). Website: http://sites.google.com/site/kalyan97

Indus Script Cipher

--Hieroglyphs of Indian linguistic area

Executive summary

Indus Script Cipher achieves a break-through, a successful decryption of the key used in the Indus writing code. The key is rebus method applied to the underlying language of the linguistic area of South Asia. Decryption draws upon the database of 8000 semantic clusters of glosses, from an *Indian Lexicon*, a multi-lingual comparative dictionary of over 25 ancient Indian languages, painstakingly compiled over 20 years.

Decrypted Indus script reveals that artisans – lapidaries, masons, carpenters, miners and smiths -- of the civilization working with stones, wood, ivory, shell, minerals, metals and alloys of metals, created the Indus writing system to record 1) the characteristics of artifacts produced by them and 2) techniques used. The principal thesis of decryption of Indus script cipher is that, in the Indian linguistic area, artisans of proto-Indic language families Indo-Aryan, Munda (Kol) and Dravidian interacted with one another, absorbed many glosses and structural language features from one another. Complemented by recent advances in the method of areal linguistics, rebus method is applied to glyptic elements to decode Indus writing system. Given the fact that the three language families are a *sprachbund* (language union), with cultural contact situations and history of phonetic changes, of semantic expansions, the glosses common to two or more of these language families constitute the Indus language lexicon.

Decrypting the cipher

> "Nobody notices postmen nowadays," says Father Brown. (G.K. Chesterton, 1911, *The Innocence of Father Brown*).

Indus script decipherment is to find a solution to a problem in cryptography (called *mlecchita vikalpa* in Sanskrit), like Chesterton's detective Father Brown; to decipher or, decode the glyphs to understand meanings of the messages conveyed by Indus writing on nearly 5000 inscriptions unearthed so far.

Cipher uses a code and a code key to transform information. Cipher meaning the numeral 0 derives from Arabic صفر (*ṣifr*, nothing). Artisan-traders of ancient times created the cipher (variant spelling of the word, cypher) and their trade associates who received the messages could *securely* decipher the text of coded messages by performing an inverse substitution using the code keys: rebus. The idea of obscuring the message so that it could not be read even if it were intercepted resulted in "cryptography", Greek for "hidden writing". The result was the development of "codes", or secret languages, and "ciphers", or scrambled messages. A "code" is essentially a secret language invented to conceal the meaning of a message. The simplest form of a code is the "jargon code", in which a particular arbitrary phrase or glyph is used to substitute for the real intended message. This is comparable to army codes used to send concealed messages. [Note: Glyph of a device is shown in front of a one-horned heifer in over 1300 inscriptions: **sangaḍa**, 'lathe, portable furnace'; rebus: battle; rebus: **jangaḍiyo** 'military guard who accompanies treasure into the treasury' (Gujarati)]

Let us assume that Indus writing is a cryptographic system using a code (or algorithm or code key) that converts glyphs into text messages. Such a system should be secure even if everything about the system, except for the key, is public knowledge. This is known as "Kerckhoffs' Principle" named after Dutch linguist and cryptographer, Augustte Kerckhoffs von Niewenhof (1835-1903)[1].

The key for the Indus script cipher is rebus using the language of the linguistic area of India. The underlying language whose glosses are used in the key is **mleccha** (meluhha).

At the outset, it is emphasised that no *a priori*

assumptions are made about 1) the direction of borrowings of words from one language family into other language families to prove or disprove the relative antiquity of languages of India; and 2) the theories related to invasions or migrations or chronology of movements of people into or out of ancient India which yielded the majority of Indus script inscriptions. The keys used are: 1) the rebus method attested in Sumerian and Egyptian hieroglyphs and 2) the principle of linguistic area well-attested in world-wide language studies consistent with the historically attested presence of speakers of Munda, Dravidian and Indo-aryan language families, in contact with one another, resulting in a linguistic area of India. The contact resulted in glosses of mleccha. The result of the decipherment of Indus script is the clear identification of Language X; it is mleccha, which included glosses common to two or three language families of the linguistic area.

Hieroglyphs (Greek ιερογλύφος, *hieroglyphos*), "sacred carving" are characters made by graphical figures (glyphs), be it animals, or objects. In the linguistic area of India, a synonym is kundau to turn on a lathe, to carve (Santali); kũdār, kũdāri (Bengali); kudaṛ spade, axe (Go.) ; kotti 'carver' (Malayalam). The Indus artisan who invented or deployed many skills and techniques had also become a writer or engraver using Indus script cipher.

Svastika as hieroglyph

The two svastika seals exhibited in the British Museum[2] represent the quintessence of the form and purpose of Indus script inscriptions. The *magnum opus* by Thomas Wilson[3] of the Library of Congress reviewed the history of this glyph and concluded that it represented an object. The glyph has been decoded rebus as representing zinc ore (zinc sulphide or zinc oxide) which, as an alloying mineral ore, added luster and shine to the brass alloy giving it a golden appearance. The glyph is inscribed on over 50 inscriptions, on seals, molded tablets, metal objects and copper plates. A svastika seal also appears in Altyn-tepe close to the Caspian Sea in a long-distance, archaeologically attested, trading context. The glyph appears in combination with other glyphs such as elephant, tiger, drummer, endless-knot motif, reinforcing the hieroglyphic nature of the script and the rebus reading method used for the decipherment of the Indus script. The glyph had gained great importance as a sacred glyph which, in the Indian tradition, is drawn on a site before constructing a fire-altar for performing yajña and on temple walls. The importance assigned was equaled by the function zinc ore performed in a casting process to lend glean and shine to the brass alloy artifacts such as vessels, cruse or goblets.

Method of semantic clustering to define Indian linguistic area

From the glosses of the comparative Indian lexicon of over 25 ancient languages of India, phonetic variants of proto-Indic glosses or glosses of the Indus language can be clearly identified within semantic clusters which are groups of words with similar vocabulary and similar 'meanings'. These complement the isogloss bundles which reinforce the Indian linguistic area and the language families in contact in the area and provide basic resources for studying history of language changes.

The semantic clusters yield substrates of the Indian linguistic area which are concordant with glosses of jāti bhāṣā or prākṛitam or lingua franca or deśi as in Hemacandra's deśi nāmamālā distinguished from the grammatically correct, literary language, Sanskrit and many languages of Munda and Dravidian families. An Indian Lexicon has been compiled to record entries for word lists containing glosses from two or more language familes of the Indian linguistic

11

area, attesting to early contact among the language families and constituting a substrate repository or mleccha (meluhha) list of glosses, for decoding the Indus script glyphs.

The lexicon is organized in over 8000 semantic clusters. These proto-Indic glosses relate to the underlying language of Indus script glyphs which are composed and written on a variety of materials such as turbinella pyrum (chank), beads, terracotta bangles, copper tablets, ivory objects, metallic objects such as ingots, daggers, gold pendant, seals, tablets, pottery and even on a massive Dholavira sign board on the citadel gateway. Indus script conveyed messages of artisans -- lapidaries, mine-workers, masons, carpenters and smiths. The messags related to the repertoire of techniques and material used by the artisans, constituting veritable professional calling cards of artisan guilds or advertisement bulletin boards (as in the case of Dholavira sign-board) of products and services of their enterprise. Evidence from ancient texts and Mesopotamian documents attest this proto-Indic language as meluhha (mleccha). The artisans who invented lapidary and metallurgical techniques also invented a hieroglyphic writing system.

Rebus method of writing

Examples of Sumerian and Egyptian hieroglyphs[4]

The use of rebus method to match sound values (words, morphemes or phonemes) to glyphs is well-attested in contemporary civilizations of Egypt and Sumer – of periods prior to 2nd millennium BCE.

Sumerian script was phonetized using the rebus principle. Rebus (Latin: by means of things) is a graphemic expression of the phonetic shape of a word or syllable. Rebus uses words pronounced alike (homophones) but with different meanings. Rebus is a variation of the pun. In rebus method of writing, a pun is created by using (writing) pictures to evoke a sound that is identical or similar to a word or word part (morpheme or phoneme) A word in English can be cited as an example of a pun: club. This word, 'club' means a weapon and also a group. In rebus, the word 'group', for example, can be denoted by the picture or glyph of a club, 'weapon'. An example of writing the name of King Narmer in

13

Egyptian hieroglyphs is cited by Schott: Narmer : n'r 'catfish' + mr 'awl'.[5] In Egyptian hieroglyphs, phonetic signs denote consonants. The façade of Narmer's palace is depicted above his head on the palette (c. 3050 BCE). Inside the picture are placed the glyphs of 'catfish' and 'awl'. These two glyphs identify the king's name using the underlying language. Glyphs of catfish + awl connote the rebus reading: Narmer.[6]

A mud jar sealing[7] indicating that the contents came from the estate of the pharaoh Narmer. This depicts the hieroglyphs of 'catfish' and 'awl': nr + mr on the top register of the façade.

The principle of rebus method is adopted in Sumerian, Egyptian hieroglyphs and Indian hieroglyphs, as picture-writing to denote sounds of an underlying language. In the case of Egytian hieroglyphs, the underlying sounds of language are consonant clusters (syllables) but in the case

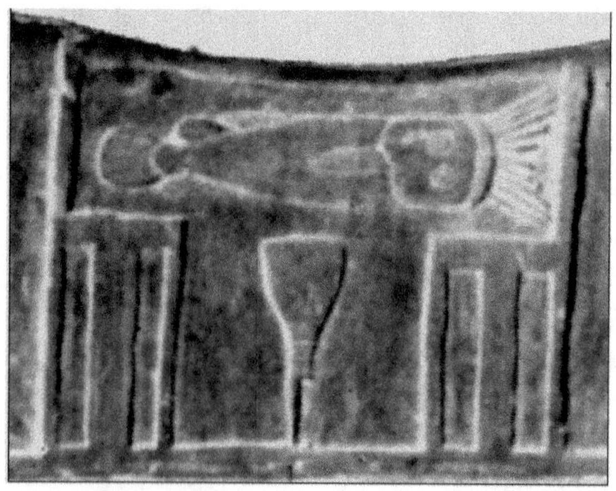

of Sumerian and Indus script hieroglyphs, the underlying sounds of language are mostly words, rendering the Sumerian and Indus scripts logographic.

Narmer in hieroglyphs N'r, Mr. c. 3100 BCE. Narmer's palette.[8]

Given the statistical distribution of glyphs with glyphs like 'rim of jar' and 'heifer' showing very high frequencies of occurrence and given the presence of repetitive messages conveyed through incised or molded tablets, Indus inscriptions do not appear to contain such names of royalty, not even names of places or religious terms (as some decipherment claims had wrongly assumed). Indus inscriptions read rebus the repertoire of artisans as skilled persons organized as guilds or communities of artisans.

Cylinder seal impression. Mesopotamia. ca. 2254-2220 BC (mature); ceramic; cat. 79; two groups in combat. A naked, bearded hero

wrestles with a water buffalo, and a "bull-man" wrestles with a lion. In the center: inscription (unread). Appears to be recut.

The rear of a bovine is ligatured to the bearded horned hero, not unlike the ligaturing method used on Indus script hieroglyphs. Cylinder seal of Ibni-sharrum, a scribe of Shar-kali-sharri and impression, ca. 2183–2159 B.C.; Akkadian, reign of Shar-kali-sharri. Mesopotamia. Cuneiform inscription in Old Akkadian. Serpentine; H. 3.9 cm (1 1/2 in.); Diam. 2.6 cm (1 in.). Musée du Louvre, Département des Antiquités Orientales, Paris AO 22303.

Indus artisans: turners of beads and minerals

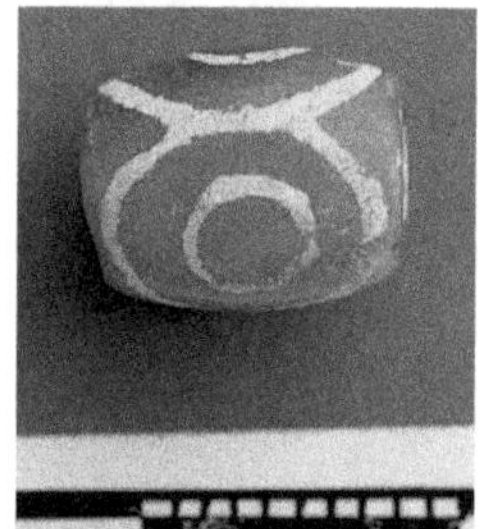

Carnelian beads with white lines. This carnelian bead[9] has been artificially colored with white lines and circles using a special bleaching technique developed by the ancient Harappans. The circle as

a colored white line is a glyph: *po (-t) 'hole'.[10] Rebus: pot 'glass bead' (H.); putti 'small bead' (B.)(CDIAL 8403). An allograph of pot is a group of male animals.

1. A banded agate bead (at left), a long terracotta bead (center) and a cylindrical steatite bead (at right) 2. Different types of beads.

Groups of animals as hieroglyphs: Lapidary workshop, smithy

pōt[11] 'male of animals' (Go.)(DEDR 2441, 4586) Rebus: pot 'glass bead' (H.)(CDIAL 8403).

  M1393, m1394, m1395B, m1405B (tiger, rhinoceros – kol, badhia), m1431B (one-horned heifer, elephant, rhinoceros; 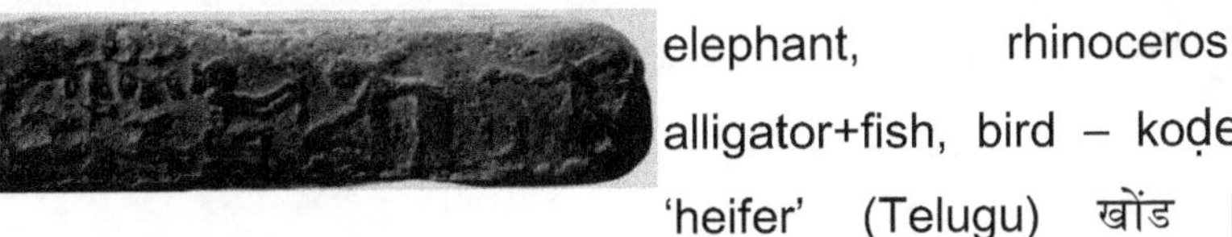 alligator+fish, bird – koḍe 'heifer' (Telugu) खोंड [

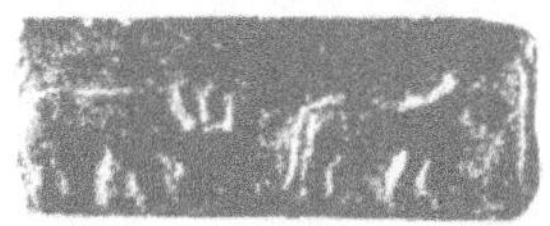 

khōṇḍa] *m* A young bull, a bullcalf. Rebus: कोंडण [kōṇḍaṇa] *f* A fold or pen. (Marathi) (Vikalpa: damṛa), karibha, badhia, khar, kuthāru, baṭa), m1431E (Drilling, goats+tree) -- kuṭi 'tree'; mlekh 'goat'; rebus: milakkhu 'copper' (Pali)

Orthography of the two goats on the prism   tablet is comparable to the glyph on a shell plaque from Ur. mlekh, mṛeka 'goat' (Br.Telugu); rebus: milakkhu 'copper'. डगर

[ḍagara[12]]A slope or ascent (as of a river's bank, of a small hill). A pair is dula; rebus: dul 'cast (metal)'(Santali)Rebus: ḍāṅgar 'blacksmith' (H.) Thus, the glyptic composition is read rebus: dul mlekh ḍāṅgar 'cast copper-smith'.

Shell plaque From Ur, Southern Iraq (c. 2,600-2,400 B.C.) Entwined in the branches of a flowering tree, two goats appear to be nibbling on its leaves. This decorative plaque, which was carved from

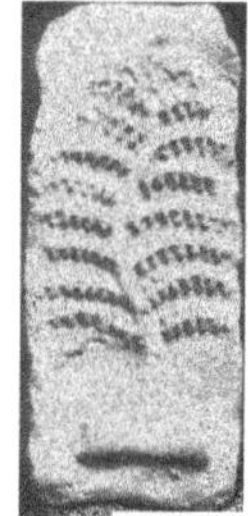

shell and highlighted with bitumen, was also excavated from the Royal Tombs of Ur.

khōṇḍa A tree of which the head and branches are broken off, a stock or stump: also the lower portion of the trunk--that below the branches. (Marathi) Rebus: **koḍ** 'workshop' (G.)

M1431E shows a turner at work, assisted by a person bending on all fours. kunda 'turner' kundār turner (A.); kũdār, kũdāri (B.); kundāru (Or.); kundau to turn on a lathe, to carve, to chase; kundau dhiri = a hewn stone; kundau murhut = a graven image (Santali) kunda a turner's lathe (Skt.)(CDIAL 3295) Glyph: Br. **kōṇḍō** on all fours, bent double. (DEDR 2054a) The seated person is shown wearing knot of hair at back. sūnd gaṭ (Go.) cundī the hairtail as worn by men (Kur.)(DEDR 2670). Rebus: **cundakāra** a turner J vi.339 (Pali) **cundakāra** cognate **kundār.**

A person on all fours bending in front of the bull. Br. **kōṇḍō** on all fours, bent double. (DEDR 2054a) Rebus: kundār turner (A.) Glyph: ḍangar 'bull';

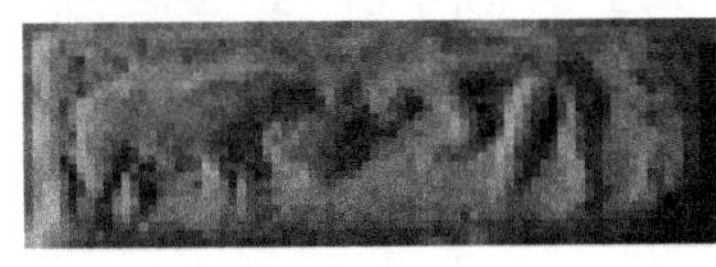

rebus: dhangar 'blacksmith' (H.). The tablet is decoded: kundār dhangar 'turner, blacksmith'.

The rebus readings of the glyphs on these inscriptions can be decoded: **kundār pot koḍ** 'turner bead workshop; **kuṭhāru** 'armourer'; (working in) **milakkhu** 'copper'; **baṭa** 'furnace'; **kuṭhi** 'smelter'; **karb, ib** 'iron'; **baḍhi** 'a worker both in iron and wood'; **khar** 'blacksmith'; **kol** 'working in iron'.

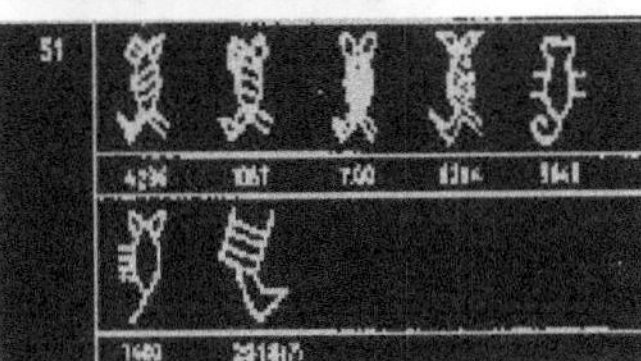

Two glyphs get uniquely ligatured with identical superscripts: leaf, rat. Glyphs (Sign nos. 51 and 52) could be glyphs of a rat considering the sign variant shown on Ur Seal 15A. This variant of Sign 51 shows a seated rat as seen from its back.

urseal15 A rat (?scorpion or, some seated animal seen from the back) is seen as the first sign from left. 9845 Ur Seal impression; UPenn; steatite; bull below a scorpion; dia. 2.4cm.; Gadd, PBA 18 (1932), p. 13, Pl. III, no. 15; Legrain, MJ (1929), p. 306, pl. XLI, no.

119; found at Ur in the cemetery area, in a ruined grave .9 metres from the surface, together with a pair of gold ear-rings of the double-crescent type and long beads of steatite and carnelian, two of gilt copper, and others of lapis-lazuli, carnelian, and banded sard. The first sign to the left has the form of a flower or perhaps an animal's skin with curly tail; there is a round spot upon the bull's back. [The first sign looks like an animal with a long tail – as seen from the back and may have been the model for the orthography of Sign 51 as noted in Mahadevan corpus]. "...the most remarkable sign being the first one to the left (in the impression) having the form of a flower or perhaps an animal's skin with curly tail...the round spot upon the bull's back is also curious."[13]

Vikalpa: kōḍel bandicoot (Pa.) [koḍel = rat (Go.)] Rebus: kole.l = smithy, temple in Kota village (Ko.)

The superscript ligatures can be read as suffixes: -kāra 'artisan'. kāruvu = mechanic, artisan, Vis'vakarma, the celestial artisan (Te.); kāruvu. [Skt.] n. An artist, artificer. An agent . One is a loha-kāra (metalsmith). the other is a cunda-kāra (ivory turner).

Decoding the ligatured Sign 52 (rat glyph + long-linear-stroke). koḍa 'one'; rebus: koḍ 'workshop' (Kuwi). That is, **cunda koḍ** 'ivory workshop'. Vikalpa: midh 'one' (Savara) med. 'iron' (Ho.) mēṛh t iron; ispat m. = steel; dul m. = cast iron; kolhe m. iron manufactured by the Kolhes (Santali); mered (Mun.d.ari); med (Ho.)(Santali.Bodding)

One is a mine-worker (vikalpa: turner who works with ivory cunda); the other is a metal-worker-cum-merchant. One glyph, the bandicoot depicts: kole.l = smithy, temple in Kota village (Ko.); the second glyph, the leaf depicts: pattar 'leaf'; rebus: pattar-ai community; guild as of workmen (Ta.); pattar merchants; perh. vartaka (Skt.) OMarw. pātharī ' precious stone '. (CDIAL 8857)

sunda musk-rat (Ka.)(DEDR 2661). śundi-mūṣikā, śunda-mūṣikā musk-rat (Skt.)(CDIAL 12517). Rebus: sund 'pit (furnace)'; sum, sumbh a mine, a pit, the opening into a mine, the shaft of a mine; sum bhugak the entrance to a mine, pit's mouth (Santali). sundi a semi-hinduised aboriginal caste; this caste are the distillers and liquor sellers; sundi gadi a liquor shop (Santali) cund to boil away (Ko.); sundu to evaporate (Ka.); cundu to be evaporated or dried up (Te.); śunthi to become dry (Skt.)(DED 2662). cunda an artist who works in ivory J vi.261 (Com: dantakāra); Miln 331. cundakāra a turner J vi.339 (Pali)

Glyph: scorpion. Vikalpa: Te. potti, pottiya scorpion; putta-tēlu large black scorpion. Ga. (S.) potte scorpion. (DEDR 4488) Rebus: **pot** 'glass bead' (H.) A pair of scorpions: dula 'pair' (Kashmiri); rebus: dul 'casting' (Santali).

loa = a species of fig tree, ficus glomerata, the fruit of ficus glomerata (Santali) Rebus: lo 'iron' (Assamese, Bengali); loa 'iron' (Gypsy) lauha = made of copper or iron (Gr.S'r.); metal, iron (Skt.) loha-kāra a metal worker, coppersmith, blacksmith Miln 331 (Pali)

Graphemes:

- sūnd gaṭ knot of hair at back (Go.); cundī the hairtail as worn by me (Kur.)(DEDR 2670). m0309 depicts a person seated on a tree branch, wearing a hair-bun (knot of hair at the back).

śuṇḍ = trunk of elephant (Skt.)

Text 2805 Zebu (*bos indicus*) and other glyphs; row of animals in file (a one-horned bull, an elephant and a rhinoceros from right); a gharial with a fish held in its jaw above the animals; a bird (?) at right. Pict-116: From R.—a person holding a vessel; a woman with a platter (?); a kneeling person with a staff in his hands facing the woman; a goat with its forelegs on a platform under a tree. [Or, two goats flanking a tree on a platform, with one antelope looking backwards?]. Tiger looking back, person seated on tree-branch. Bos indicus decoded: adar ḍangar 'zebu'; rebus: aduru ḍangar 'native metal smith'.

Archaeological evidence is replete with finds of tumbled and engraved gemstones and bangles of terracotta or turbinella pyrum (chank). Indus lapidary (lit. 'concerned with stones) is an artisan who formed, turned, engraved stone, mineral, gemstones and other durable resources such as shell, agate, coral, carnelian, ivory, bone, horn. Early workings of stone masons, miners and smiths working with minerals, metals, alloys may also be considered as lapidary or turner arts involving casting, polishing, faceting, drilling holes, carving, engraving and making of jewellery. Another meaning of 'lapidary' is 'of inscriptions'. Inscriptions of Indus artisans – lapidaries and smiths alike – were etched or carved or prepared in mould castings.

Method of areal linguistics

Complementing the use of rebus method of decoding glyphs is the use of the method of areal linguistics which is elucidated by Lyle Campbell succinctly. Lyle Campbell (2006), in a path-breaking monograph and a global survey of

'Areal linguistics' surveys the state-of-the-art of language studies and linguistic methods, starting with a profound quote from Moby Dick : 'It is not down in any map; true places never are.' Lyle Campbell notes that there is no meaningful distinction between borrowing and areal linguistics, or between what was inherited from what was diffused and that it would be necessary to provide a historical account of language changes.

Following upon this insight of Lyle Campbell, decryption of Indus script cipher presented herein is an investigation of the facts of linguistic diffusion in the archaeological context of finds of over 4000 inscriptions over the Sarasvati-Sindhu (Sarasvati-Indus) river basins (which is variously called a 'sprachbund, linguistic area diffusion area, convergence area, or areal type').

Indian linguistic area (also called South Asian linguistic area) shared not just loan words, but also shared phonological, morphological, syntactic traits which are structural features of languages or language families of the geographical area defined by the Indus (also referred to as Sarasvati-Sindhu) civilization. Indian or South Asia linguistic area is composed of languages belonging to the Indo-Aryan, Dravidian, Munda and Tibeto-Burman language families. Examples of shared traits are:

1.   Retroflex consonants, retroflex stops;

2.   Absence of prefixes (except in Munda)

3.   Presence of a dative-subject construction (that is, dative experience, as in Hindi mujhe mālūm thā, 'I knew it' ['to me' + 'know' + PAST]);

4.   Subject-object-verb (SOV) basic word order, including postpositions;

5.   Absence of a verb 'to have';

6.   'conjunctive or absolutive participles' – a tendency for subordinate clauses to have nonfinite verbs;

7.   Morphological causativess;

8.   sound symbolic forms (onomatopoeia) based on reduplication, often with k suffixed (for example, in Kota, a Dravidian language: kad-kadk '[heart] beats fast with guilt or worry' (After Campbell, Lyle 1966, p.455).

The sum of borrowings of structural features (matched by shared glosses) among Indo-Aryan, Dravidian and Munda language families is clearly established in cultural contact situations, and contingent historical events starting from the days of Sarasvati-Sindhu civilization. One such historical, socio-cultural-economic or political-economy event stands out: the continued use of Indus script glyphs on punch-marked coins over the entire Indian linguistic area.

Resolving problems with over 100 decipherment claims and deriving glosses of Proto-Indian speech as Indus language

Claims of decipherment number over 100, but none has found acceptance because of one or more of the following reasons.

1. Possehl (1966) surveyed many claims of decipherment and concluded that the script has not been deciphered. From an archaeological perspective, BB Lal rejects claims of decipherment by SR Rao and Asko Parpola, assuming the underlying language to be Sanskrit or Dravidian. "From the foregoing review of the work of Rao and Parpola et al it would be seen that no case has yet been established to prove that the language used by the Indus people was either Sanskrit or Dravidian. This is not to say that the Inddus language could not have been either of these. Far from it. All that has been demonstrated here is that there are internal inconsistencies in the above-menttioned two attempts, although, as already stated, more has to be seen in the work of Parpola et al, which certainly is on more scientific lines than that of Rao. However, one wonders as to why the Indus language must necessarily be either Sanskrit or Dravidian. Is it impossible that it could have been yet another language which is since dead? After all, what happened in Egypt and Mesopotamia could as well have happened in India."[14]

2. In addition to the arguments advanced by BB Lal, it may be noted that the decipherment claims using the underlying language to be Sanskrit or Dravidian ignore the current status of knowledge advanced by language studies pointing to India, which accounts for the majority of the archaeological sites of the civilization, as an Indian linguistic area. Parpola notes: "Indo-Aryan languages have been spoken in the area once occupied by the Indus civilisation and gradually all over North India since at least 1000 B.C."[15] This is the reason why he seems to exclude Indo-Aryan languages from the linguistic area. This reasoning is, *prima facie*, invalid since Indo-Aryan was NOT evolved on a clean slate after 1000 BCE and since the linguistic area had attested interactions among at least three language families: Indo-Aryan, Munda and Dravidian and hence, there is no reason why Indo-Aryan and Munda should be excluded from being part of the linguistic area which used the Indus script, retaining only Dravidian as the substrate. That the Indus script encodes language is argued by Sukumar Rajagopal et al.[16] This follows up on the work of Massimo Vidale:[17] "The authors (of 'illiteracy hypothesis') would like to throw the ball to their opponents, asking them to refute their views by providing a sound decipherment in linguistic terms. But they have raised the problem, proposing a different interpretation and the first readings, and they have to provide a demonstration of their thesis by interpreting

and explaining to us the symbolic sequences..." Parpola seeks to counter the 'illiterary' argument noting that 'indus script' is a representation of speech and not an arbitrary assemblage of unspoken, unspeakable, arbitrarily selected symbols by 'illiterates'. The 'illiteracy' proponents have to explain some extraordinary glyphs showing bizarre copulation scenes involving crocodile or intercourse *a tergo*, *pudendum muliebre*, scorpions, wild or domesticated animals shown in front of a trough. Such proponents have to explain why the glyphs cannot be simple word-lists and not based on syllabic or alphabetic readings. The onus is on such 'illiterary' proponents to detail and specify how the glyphs relate to heraldry or agriculture or any myths, magic, rituals, religious, socio-political or economic functions of the creators of the glyphs. If explanations have not been offered so far, one can reasonably conclude that the 'illiteracy' claim is 1) simply a cop-out to avoid readings of the glyphs of the script and 2) simply 'throwing the ball to their opponents' as Massimo Vidale observes. A scientific contribution was made by Rajesh Rao et al using Markov model to analyse the structure of the Indus writing system to conclude: "...results provide evidence which, ...given the rich syntactic structure in the script (and other evidence), increases the probability that the script represents language...Given that the Indus script shares... properties with linguistic scripts, we claim that the similarity in conditional entropy of the Indus script to other natural languages provides additional evidence in favor of the linguistic hypothesis... block entropies of the Indus script scale in a manner similar to natural languages, when viewed in conjunction with the other language-like properties of the script as described above, adds further support to the linguistic hypothesis..."[18]

3. Many decipherment claims choose to dismiss or just ignore the language-based importance of pictorial motifs or field symbols and focusing only on 'signs' of the script. Some claim that the pictorial motifs were mere totem symbols without explaining if the pictorial motifs and pictorial glyphs had an underlying basis in the Indus language. The problem with such claims is that the vivid and clearly unambiguous glyphs which occupy a dominant space on an inscribed object remain unexplained in terms of the messaging system of the inscriptions. The debate about the script tends to be polemical because many decipherments ignored the pictorial motifs and focused only on the signs. Any decipherment which does not explain each pictorial motif in context is a failed decipherment.

4. Many decipherment claims assign syllabic or alphabetic values to the glyptic elements of 'signs' and attempt to read the script as names or professions or word with religious or cosmic connotations. For example, Parpola reads the variants of 'fish' glyphs as 'min' connoting

rebus: 'star'. But such a 'religious or cosmis' connotation is not consistently established for the corpus of inscriptions but is based on anecdotal evidences of select inscriptions. The problem concerned the assumptions made about the 'sound' values to be assigned to each glyph (pictorial motif or sign). One group said that the glyphs had syllabic/ alphabetic values. Another said that the values to be assigned were only numeric. A third group said that the values assigned could be a combination of word and syllables with grammatical markers. Heras, an early scholar who treated the script as dravidian, had read entire sentence sequences by assigning phrase-values to the glyphs.

5. Another problem is the understanding of the nature of orthography of the Indus writing system. There have been debates about the distinction between a pictorial motif (also called field symbol) and a sign of the script. For example, two concordance-makers, Parpola and Mahadevan dealt with svastika glyph differently: one called it a sign and the other called it a pictorial motif. There have also been differing opinions about the 'fish' glyph; was it a fish or was it a loop of thread stylized as a sign?

6. Language identification problem

The debate has lasted, nearly 130 years, since 1873 when Alexander Cunningham published a drawing of a seal showing a bull and some other glyphs in Indus script. The debate intensified when some unsubstantiated claims were made that the inventors of the writing system were illiterate and that the writing system did not represent a language at all. The claims were unsubstantiated because the claimants did not prove or demonstrate that the writing system represented something other than language. (Massimo Vidale, 2007).

Added to the problems of understanding why just 5 signs plus a pictorial motif were adequate to communicate a message in writing was the problem of identifying the language of the inventors who invented and used the writing system.

Critique of the decipherment claims of Parpola and Mahadevan and alternative readings of glyphs 'deciphered' by them

Mahadevan, 1997:" Parpola's interpretations rely more on mythology than on textual or linguistic analysis...Granting that the seal-texts are probably only strings of names and titles, and assuming that the writing is mostly logographic, it would still be necessary to employ minimally parts

	SIGN	IDENTI-FICATION	READING	MEANING
a	fish	fish	mīn	1. fish 2. star
b		3 + fish	mu(m) mīn	three stars (Mrigasiras)
c		6 + fish	caru mīn	six stars (Pleiades)
d		7 + fish	elu mīn	seven stars (Ursa Major)

of speech like pronouns, conjunctions and verbal participles and also grammatical morphs to indicate person, number, gender and case."[19]

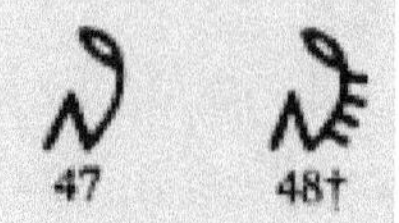 Using the word 'Murukan,' Parpola and Mahadevan read rebus different glyphs for the same word.

	SIGN	IDENTI-FICATION	READING	MEANING
a	⬭	ear/nose rings, bangles	*muruku*	Murukan (god)
b	⬭	bangles + squirrel	*muruku pillay*	Murukan Pillay (god)

Mahadevan identifies these signs as connoting Murukan: "...the seated posture is suggestive of divinity and the skeletal body gives the linguistic clue to the name of the deity. The basic Dravidian word mur (Ta. muri, Ka. muruhu, Pa. & Ga. murg, Go. moorga etc., DEDR. 4977) means 'to bend, contract, fold' etc. Applying the technique of rebus, we get mur (Ta. murunku, murukku; Ma.murukka, Kol., Nk. murk, Malt. murke etc., DEDR 4975) meaning 'to destroy, kill, cut'. etc. Thus the name of the deity muruku and his characteristics 'destroyer, killer' are derived."[20]

Since Parpola and Mahadevan assign the 'Murukan' value to different signs, who is right about the Dravidian identification of a glyph to denote 'Murukan'? Parpola or Mahadevan?

 m0290 Seal impression and seal (Parpola, 2010) Parpola's readings of the first two signs:

kaZutai or "donkey"; rebus: *kaZ(i) / *kaLLar 'saline soil' and *utay 'to kick'.

taaL (from *taaZ, preserved in Old Kannada) '(hind) leg, stem of tree' (whence taaZ 'tree with a prominent stem' > 'wine palm') is in many ways connected with the wild ass.

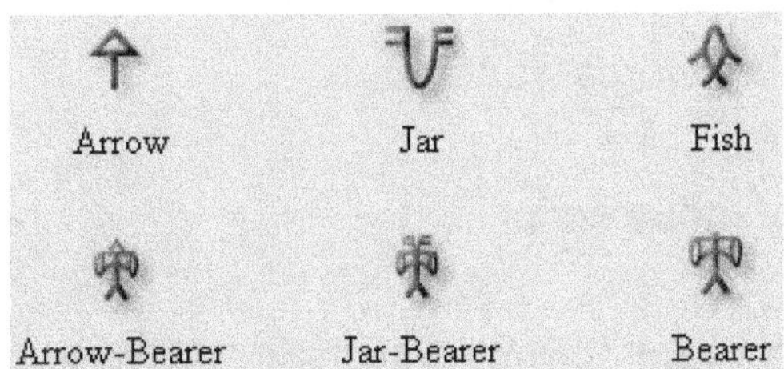

Rebus: ponds are calledtaalaab. This Persian word comes from Indo-Aryan taala 'pond', from Proto-Dravidian *taaZ 'low place, depression.'[21] Critique: So, does the seal explain a location of the seal-maker? What is the significance of the third 'comb' glyph on m0290? What do the tiger and trough in front of the tiger denote? These questions are unanswered, since no pictorial motifs or field symbols has been decoded by Mahadevan and Parpola. This is a surprise and renders any decipherment claim by them a bit too hasty, since pictorial motifs or field symbols dominate the space used for inscriptions as demonstrated by illustrations of inscribed objects in this work.

Since the arrow sign also occurs in sequence with 'fish', Mahadevan discounts the possibility of the signs being grammatical case-markers.

 "The arrow sign in the Indus Script represents pictorially an arrow, and functionally a grammatical morph, the non-masculine singular nominal suffix. Its phonetic value, derived by rebus, is *-(a)mp(u). it follows almost automatically that the JAR sign must be the masculine singular suffix with the phonetic value *(a)nru"[22] Comment: Mahadevan attempts to assign 'syllabic or morphemic' values to the glyphs (signs) and excludes the possibility that the glyphs (signs and field-symbols alike) may connote words, read rebus.

Decoding select glyphs of Indus script

Agreeing with Mahadevan and Parpola on their use of the rebus method but disagreeing on 1. the religious overtones they see in the inscriptions and glyphs and 2. assignment of grammatical morph and phonetic values glyphs, alternative straight-forward rebus decoding of the select glyphs is presented, without indulging in special pleading, but using glosses of the Indian linguistic area which semantically cluster into repertoire -- products and skills of artisans and thus justifies the use of inscriptions directly in a trading context without suggesting occurrence of any names of people, places or deities.

 Text on m0290. The inscription can be decoded rebus as: **kaṇṭ pot kuro kharāḍī** 'bead furnace,

silver, turner' (Glyphs: pot 'calf of hind leg'; **khuru** 'wild ass';

kharedo = a currycomb) Glyptic context (pictorial motif): tiger + trough: kolimi dhangar 'forge, smith'.

khuru 'wild ass' (Kashmiri) **kuro** silver (Kol.Nk.Go.)(DEDR 1782).

Long-linear stroke + wild ass. khuru 'wild ass' (Kashmiri)

Rebus: khura silver (Nk.); kuruku whiteness'; kuru brilliancy (Ta.); kuro silver (Kol.Nk.Go.) (DEDR 1782). koda 'one'(Santali); kod 'workshop' (G.)

Thus, the seal is decoded rebus: khuru koda 'wild-ass, one'; rebus: khura kod 'silver workshop'.

Ko. **kaṇt-po·t**[23] 'flesh of hind thigh of animal (DEDR 1175). Pe. pota calf of leg. Maṇḍ. pata id. Kui pota id. ? (DEDR 4513) Rebus:

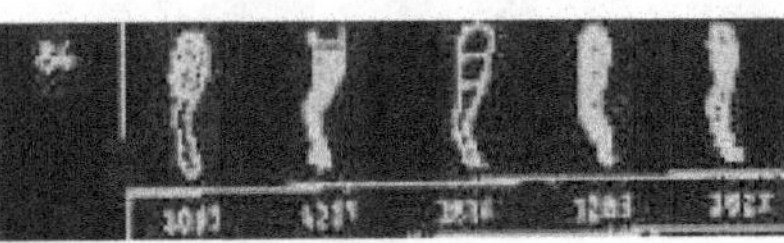

pot[24] 'glass bead' (H.); putti 'small bead' (B.)(CDIAL 8403).

m022, Text 1194 Glyph: **pot** 'thigh' (Ko.); rebus: **pot** 'glass bead' (H.) Glyph: Glyph: ligatured rat: śunda; rebus: **kūdār** 'turner' (B.) Go. **badoṛi** 'bat''. Rebus: **baḍhoe** 'a carpenter, worker in wood'; badhoria 'expert in working in wood'(Santali) The seal m022 thus is decoded as **kũdār pot baḍhoe koḍ** 'workshop of turner (of) beads, ivory, carpenter'.

kharedo = a currycomb (G.) Rebus: **kharādī** ' turner' (G.)

Vikalpa: ḍhagaraam 'thigh' (G.); ḍhangar 'smith' (H.)

kaśēru[25] 'the backbone' (Bengali. Skt.); **kaśēru**ka id. (Skt.)

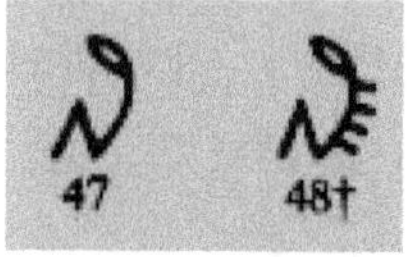

Rebus: **kasērā**[26]' metal worker ' (Lahnda)(CDIAL 2988, 2989) Vikalpa: riṛ 'ridge formed by the backbone' (Santali); rebus: rīti 'brass' (Skt.)[27]

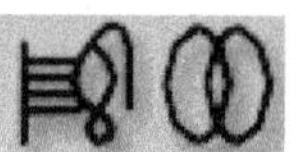

tsāni, tsānye 'squirrel' (Kon.) rebus: śannī a small workshop (WPah)[28]

bangaḍī 'a bracelet of glass, gold or other material, a bangle

worn on the wrist by women (G.) Rebus: bangala 'a goldsmith's portable furnace' (Te.)[29]

Gola dhoro, Gujarat. Unfinished shell circlets with grinding stone in front. The gloss **sēkhā** (Bengali)

may denote such shell circlets produced as bracelets.[30]

shēkh शेंख़ (Kashmiri)[31] Rebus: sekra 'a hindu caste who work in brass and bell metal' (Santali)

Hence, the pair of glyphs can together read: bangaḍī 'a bracelet of glass, gold or other material (G.) Rebus: bangala 'a goldsmith's portable furnace' (Te.)[32]

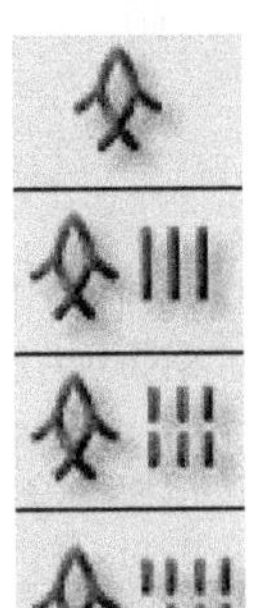

Rebus: bangala sekra 'portable gold furnace.'[33] worker in brass and bell metal.'

ayo 'fish' (Santali); rebus: aya 'metal, iron' (G.)

kolmo 'three' (Mu.); rebus: kolami 'smithy' (Te.) hence, ayo kolmo 'iron smithy'

bhaṭa 'six' (G.); rebus: bhaṭa 'furnace' (Santali)

Four + three strokes are read (since the strokes are shown on two lines one below the other) : gaṇḍa 'four' (Santali); rebus: 'furnace, kaṇḍ fire-altar'; kolmo 'three' (Mu.); rebus: kolami 'smithy' (Te.) Vikalpa: ?ea 'seven' (Santali); rebus: ?eh-ku 'steel' (Te.)

Rim-of-jar glyph

The 'jar' sign is read as 'rim of jar' with accent on the rim. kaṇḍ[34] kanka (Santali); **kaṇḍ** denotes a brass pot; Rebus: kaṇḍ karṇaka 'furnace scribe' (Skt.)[35] The most frequently occurring glyph is thus explained as a 'furnace scribe' and is consistent with the readings of glyphs which occur together with this glyph. Kan-ka may denote an artisan working with copper, ka**n** (Ta.) ka**nn**ār 'coppersmiths, blacksmiths' (Ta.) Thus, the phrase **kaṇḍ karṇaka** may be decoded rebus as a brassworker, scribe. **karṇaka** 'scribe, accountant'.

A splinter glyph – two short strokes -- is ligatured within the rim of jar glyph. **sal** stake, spike, splinter, thorn, difficulty (H.); Rebus: **sal** 'workshop' (Santali)[36]

kanka 'Rim of jar' (Santali); karṇaka rim of jar'(Skt.) Rebus: karṇaka 'scribe' (Te.); gaṇaka id. (Skt.) (Santali)

Glyphs of Indus script are presented in the following segments of analysis:

- Glyptic element

- Mleccha reading glyptic element

- Mleccha reading of homonym

- Glyptic legacy on punch-marked coins

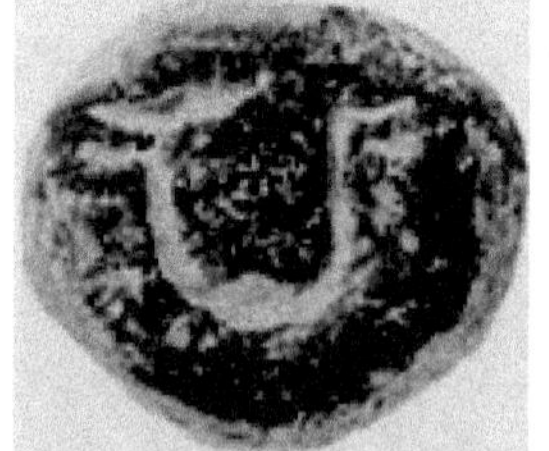 ' Daimabad seal (ca. 1400 BCE)

Frequency of occurrence of sign: 1395

 Text of inscription on m0892. This is one example of the orthographic emphasis on the

38

'rim' or 'handle' of the short-necked jar on two glyphs: one shows the rim and the other shows the rim and ligatures two short-strokes. The two short-strokes are a splinter; rebus: sal 'workshop' (Santali); śāla id. (Skt.). ālai id. (Tamil) The two signs thus read, rebus: furnace scribe, workshop furnace scribe.

•The rim of a jar is **kaṇḍ kan-ka** (Santali)

Hieroglyphs of Indus writing

Gadd notes that the 'water-carrier' seal is is an unmistakable example of an 'hieroglyphic' seal. Seal impression, Ur (Upenn; U.16747); [After Edith Porada, 1971, Remarks on seals found in the Gulf States. Artibus Asiae 33 (4): 331-7: pl.9, fig.5]; water carrier with a skin (or pot?) hung on each end of the yoke across his shoulders and another one below the crook of his left arm; the vessel on the right end of his yoke is over a receptacle for the water; a star on either side of the head (denoting supernatural?). The whole object is enclosed by 'parenthesis' marks. The parenthesis is perhaps a way of splitting of the ellipse (Hunter, G.R., JRAS, 1932, 476).

m1405At Pict-97: Person standing at the center pointing with his right hand at a bison facing a trough, and with his left hand pointing to the sign

The glyptic elements on m1405 are: 1. bison, 2. trough, 3. person lifting up his hand, 4. water-carrier. These are hieroglyphs decoded rebus.

1. bison sal 'bos gaurus'; rebus sal 'workshop' (Santali) śāla[37] 'workshop' (Skt.) ālai 'workshop' (Ta.)

2. bison, trough ḍhangar 'trough'; ḍhangar 'bull'; rebus: ḍhangar 'blacksmith' Vikalpa: pātra 'trough'; patthar 'merchant' sal 'bos gaurus'; rebus: sal 'workshop'.[38]

3. Water-carrier glyph kuṭi 'water-carrier' (Telugu); Rebus: kuṭhi 'smelter furnace' (Santali) kuṛī f. 'fireplace' (H.); krvṛi f. 'granary (WPah.); kuṛī, kuṛo house, building'(Ku.)(CDIAL 3232) kuṭi 'hut made of boughs' (Skt.) guḍi temple (Telugu) [The bull is shown in front of the trough for drinking; hence the semantics of 'drinking'.[39]]

Decryption of Indus script cipher of hieroglyphs of Indian linguistic area, announced in this work, avoids the pitfalls of many past decipherment claims. The work is premised on the Indian linguistic area and consistent with the principle of occam's razor, uses a simple rebus method to read all the glyphs – pictorial motifs with glyptic elements and signs with glyptic elements – as based on words of the Indus language from a repertoire of artisans' work attested archaeologically. The Indus language is independently delineated by the linguistic area' principle and a comparative Indian Lexicon

provides the glosses for matching words with glyptic

elements and identifying homonyms which render the

message content of inscriptions. The set of glosses from the

Indian linguistic area lead to a decipherment of the

messages as representations of the repertoire of artisans –

lapidaries, miners and smiths. The underlying language – for

glosses which render the glyptic elements and concordant

homonyms -- is not exclusive Munda or exclusive Sanskrit

or exclusive Dravidian but the lingua franca which included

glosses from all three language families – with glosses

borrowed from one another. Evidence for the decipherment

comes from the cultural continuum including punch-marked

coins and sculptural glyphs of the historical periods which

continued to use the glyphs of Indus script. Evidence is also

provided to equate the Indus language with a language

category called mleccha (cognate: meluhha) attested in

Mesopotamian texts, in an

archaeological context and attested in ancient Indian texts

which point to mleccha as a language with shared super-set

of glosses, as lingua franca clearly distinguishable from

literary language – just as Prākṛtam is distinguishable from Sanskrit. Thus, mleccha is construed as the set of glosses shared in the Indian sprachbund in contact situations and the context of history of changes in phonetic forms and/or semantic expansions of glosses. Seals m1118 and Kalibangan032

Blacksmith guild making excellent iron (metal)

Decoding epigraphs on seals, Mohenjodaro1118 and Kalibangan 032 : ayaskāṇḍa (of) aḍar ḍhangar khuṭ 'native-metal-blacksmith community (guild)(making) excellent metal'.

Excellent metal

Ayo 'fish' (Mu.) + gaṇḍa 'set of four' (Santali)

Ayo 'fish' (Mu.) + kaṇḍa 'arrow' (Skt.)

Rebus: ayaskāṇḍa 'a quantity of iron, excellent   iron' (Pāṇ.gaṇ) aya = iron (G.); ayah, ayas = metal (Skt.)

Brahmini or Brahmani bull is also called the zebu. It has a pronounced hump, long horns, droopy ears and a large dewlap. Scientific name was originally bos indicus; it is called bos taurus indicus adapted to tropical environments, domesticated in India over 10,000 years ago. It is allowed to roam free in many parts of India, considered a sacred bull; this may have led to the name

Brahmani. adar, adar dangra a brahmini bull, a bull kept for breeding purposes and not put to work (Santali) It is also called khũṭ[40] Brahmani bull (Kathiawar G.); khũṭro entire bull used for agriculture, not for breeding (G.)(CDIAL 3899). Decoded rebus: khũṭ 'community' (perhaps, a guild). Cf. Santali gloss: khũṭ[41] a community, sect, society, division, clique, schism, stock (Santali). The zebu (brāhmaṇi bull) is: aḍar ḍangra (Santali); rebus: aduru = gan.iyinda tegadu karagade iruva aduru = ore taken from the mine and not subjected to melting in a furnace (Ka.) dhan:gar 'blacksmith' (Mth.)

Fish + arrow: pair of glyphs and allograph

Glyph (Sign 60) is an allograph of Sign 59 (glyph: fish) + Sign 211 (glyph: arrow).

 m296 seal

 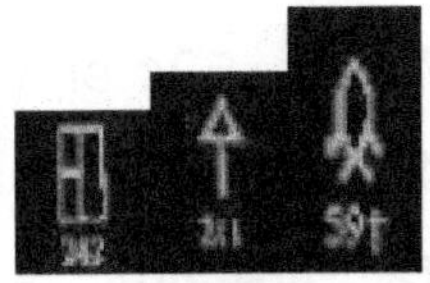 Texts 5477, 1554

Glyptic elements of m296 seal: 1. Two heads of one-horned heifers; 2. ligatured to a pair of rings and a standard device; 3. ligatured to nine leaves. Read rebus:

koḍiyum 'heifer, rings on neck'; rebus: koḍ 'workshop' (Kuwi.G.); dula 'pair' (Kashmiri); rebus: dul 'cast metal' (Mu.) lo, no 'nine' (B.); loa 'ficus religiosa' (Santali); rebus: loh 'metal' (Skt.) sangaḍa 'jointed animals' (Marathi); sangaḍa 'lathe' (G.) The pictorial motif is thus decoded rebus: loh dul koḍ 'metal cast(ing) smithy turner (lathe) workshop '. Part of the inscription is read rebus: **ayaskāṇḍa kole.l** 'smithy, excellent quantity of iron'.

 The last sign on epigraph 5477 and 1554 (m296 seal) is read as: kole.l = smithy, temple in Kota village (Ko.)

 The U sign could be baṭi 'broad-mouthed, rimless metal vessel'; rebus: baṭi 'smelting furnace'. The structural form within which this sign is enclosed may represent a temple: kole.l 'temple, smithy' (Ko.); kolme smithy' (Ka.)

The first sign of epigraphs 5477 and 4604 and the first two signs of epigraphs 1554 and 4604 can be read as: ayas kaṇḍa 'fish, arrow' rebus: metal, fire-altar. **ayaskāṇḍa** is explained in Panini as 'excellent quantity of iron'.

Parpola notes (1994, pp.69-70): "…the four strokes around the 'fish' sign may in fact be understood to be read after it, and that their meaning is close to the sign 'arrow' that is often found in this position." gaṇḍa 'four' (Santali)

Many circumscribed signs occur as the left-most glyph and comparable to the 'rim of jar' sign 342 in position. Similarly, the 'arrow' sign terminates 184 epigraphs (read from right to left) – in a total of 227 arrow-sign occurrences

The rim of jar is: kaṇḍa kanka (Santali); arrow is kaṇḍa

kaṇḍa 'fire-altar (Santali); kan 'copper' (Ta.)

Invention of alloyed metals seems to be matched by the invention of a writing system, read rebus to transact the products of the smithy guild across the extensive civilization area.

Pictorial motifs and signs are part of the writing system.

For example, pictures of animals connote words which can be read rebus to indicate metallurgical repertoire of Indus metalsmiths.

Ibha 'elephant'; rebus: ib 'iron'

adar ḍangra 'zebu'; rebus: aduru 'native metal'; dangar 'smith'

kol 'tiger'; rebus: kol 'alloy of five metals, panchaloha'

pasaramu 'animals'; rebus: pasra 'smithy'

baḍhia = a castrated boar, a hog; rebus: baḍhi 'a caste who work both in iron and wood'

damra 'heifer'; rebus: tam(b)ra 'copper'

koda 'horn'; rebus: koda 'workshop'

kamadha 'penance'; rebus: kampattam 'mint'

kuthi 'vagina'; rebus: kuthi 'smelting furnace'

Since there are over 400 'signs', they cannot merely be either alphabetic or syllabic; they simply represent words.

bata 'pot'; rebus: bata 'furnace'

kanka 'rim of jar'; rebus: kan 'copper'; karṇaka 'scribe'

ayo, hako 'fish'; rebus: ayo, ayas 'metal'

kolom 'cob'; kolami 'forge, smithy'

kolmo 'three'; kolami 'forge, smithy'

meḍ 'body'; rebus: meḍ 'iron'

Body glyph with upraised arm

M1224d,e two sides of a seal Pa. **pot** upper part of back; pottel back; adv. behind. Ga. (Oll.) poṭ, poṭṭel, (S.3) poṭṭu back. (DEDR 4514) Rebus: **pot**[42] 'glass bead' (H.); putti 'small bead' (B.)(CDIAL 8403). [Person ligatured to the back[43] of a bovine on m1224; the person is lifting up his arm.]

3. person lifting up his hand med. 'body'; rebus: meḍ 'iron' 94) er-aka 'upraised arm' (Ta.); rebus: eraka =

copper (Ka.) The body is ligatured to the back of a bovine: **pot** 'back' (Pa.); rebus: **pot** 'glass bead' (H.)The glyph of a body with right-hand raised and ligatured to the back of a bovine is read rebus: kuḍi eraka 'upraised right arm'; rebus: kuṭhi eraka 'copper-furnace'. The body is horned: koḍ 'horns'; rebus: koḍ 'workshop' (Kuwi.G.) Thus, the glyptic composition is decoded rebus: **meḍ pot kuḍi eraka koḍ** 'iron, bead, copper furnace workshop'.

Right hand, water-carrier

kuṭi 'water carrier' (Te.) kuḍi. [Tel. from కూడు food.] n. Eating. కుడుపు. adj. Right, belonging to the right (dexter.) rebus: kuṭhi = kiln (Santali) kūṭi-nīḷḷu. n. Sour water. Water in which boiled rice has been steeped. కుడి⁹ [kuḍi]

Banawali 23A A tall person with an upraised arm in front of a one-horned bull and a markhor with upturned faces (apparently listening to the person); two signs occur: 'fish'

and 'arrow' graphemes, decoded as **ayaskāṇḍa** 'excellent quantity of iron' (Pāṇ.). The sealing is on terracotta. The ten steatite seals and one sealing have only come from the lower town, not the citadel…these seals were generally recovered from houses which on the basis of their contents…have been tentatively attributed to a trader or jeweler (Bisht, R.S., 1982, Excavations at Banawali: 1974-77, in: Gregory L. Possehl, Harappan Civilization, Delhi, p.118). Glyph: miṇḍāl markhor (Tor.wali) meḍho a ram, a sheep (G.)(CDIAL 10120) Rebus: meḍ iron (Ho.) meṛed-bica = iron stone ore, in contrast to bali-bica, iron sand ore (Mu.lex.) koḍiyum 'heifer'; koḍ 'workshop' (G.) The seal impression, with the pictorial motif and inscription, is decoded rebus: **ayaskāṇḍa meḍ   kuḍi eraka koḍ** 'excellent quantity of iron (from) iron smelter, copper workshop'.

Almost every one of the 100 pictorial motifs and over 400 signs can be explained rebus using lapidary and metallurgical repertoire words. This is consistent with the exports from Meluhha related of stone beads, ivory and metals – attested in Mesopotamian texts.

The Indus script writing system was employed on a variety of material: faience seals, terracotta tablets, copper/bronze plates, pottery, terracotta bangles and even on a sign-board which adorned the gateway of the fort at Dholavira. The context was trade attested over long distances upto Mesopotamia, from the 2000-odd archaeological sites along Sarasvati, a Himalayan river which had flowed over 1600 kms. from the Himalayas to the Indian Ocean. The attestation of trade comes from 1) cuneiform records of the bronze age; and 2) seals/tablets of Indus script found at sites like Tell Asmar, Ur along the Tigris-Euphrates rivers across the Persian Gulf. The valuable items of trade included many articles including bronze and metal products. The items were of such value that they had to be authenticated in writing in a language understood by the traders.

Problem of short messages becomes the solution

A vital clue to decode or decipher the writing system is provided by a statistical analysis of the corpus (CISI = Corpus of Indus Seals and Inscriptions). The writing system employed, on each message, a pictorial motif plus an average of 5 signs. The corpus of about 4000 distinct, individual messages, has over 100 pictorial motifs and over 400 glyptic signs to choose from. The short messages, in fact, become the solution. They clearly show that the writing system was not meant to write essays or even paragraphs using alphabets and syllables about heraldry or faith, but to simply list the traded articles of value, lapidary, metal and mineral artifacts of the bronze-age. (cf. Massimo Vidale, 2007).

Examples of pictorial motifs included such glyphs as: bos indicus, bull heifer, buffalo heifer, bull, antelope, tiger, elephant, rhinoceros, alligator, a person seated in penance, a person seated on a tree-branch as a tiger turns its neck backward looking up at the person, a naked woman seated with her legs spread out flanked by two scorpions.

Examples of glyptic signs included such glyphs as: rim of jar, rimless pot, fish, cob of corn, two, three or four short numeral strokes, arrow.

Glyphs with ligatured tail

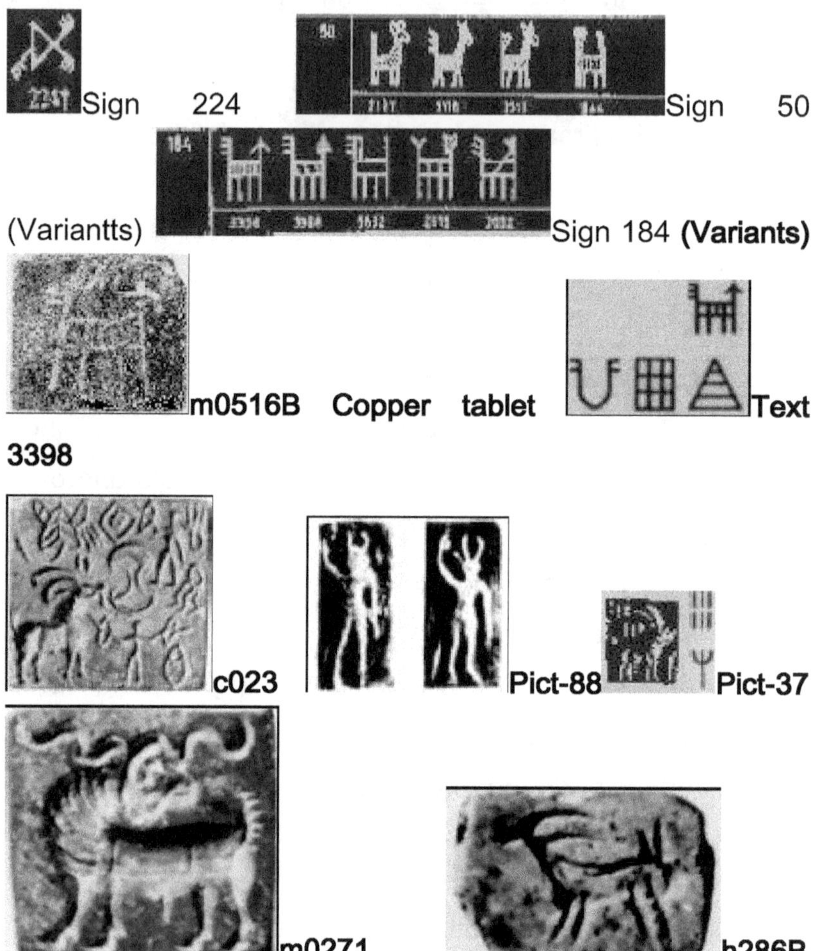

Sign 224   Sign 50

(Variantts)   Sign 184 **(Variants)**

m0516B Copper tablet 3398   Text

c023   Pict-88   Pict-37

m0271   h286B

medho a ram, a sheep (G.)(CDIAL 10120);

kaḍum 'neck-band, ring'

adar ḍangra 'zebu'

ibha 'elephant' (Skt.); rebus: ib 'iron' (Ko.)

kolo 'jackal' (Kon.)

moṇḍ the tail of a serpent (Santali) Rebus: Md. moḍenī[44] ' massages, mixes '. Kal.rumb. **moṇḍ** -- ' to thresh ', urt. maṇḍ -- ' to soften ' (CDIAL 9890) Thus, the ligature of the serpent as a tail of the composite animal glyph is decoded as: polished metal (artifact).

mūhe 'face' (Santali);   mleccha-mukha (Skt.) = milakkhu 'copper' (Pali)

கோடு kōṭu : *நடுநிலை நீங்குகை. கோடிறீக் கூற்றம் (நாலடி, 5). 3. [K. kōḍu.] Tusk; யானை பன்றிகளின் தந்தம். மத்த யானையின் கோடும் (தேவா. 39, 1). 4. Horn; விலங்கின் கொம்பு. கோட்டிடை யாடினை கூத்து (திவ். இயற். திருவிருத். 21).

Ta. kōṭu (in cpds. kōṭṭu-) horn, tusk, branch of tree, cluster, bunch, coil of hair, line, diagram, bank of stream or pool; kuvaṭu branch of a tree; kōṭṭāṉ, kōṭṭuvāṉ rock horned-owl (cf. 1657 Ta. kuṭiñai). Ko. kṛ (obl. kṭ-) horns (one horn is kob), half of hair on each side of parting, side in game, log, section of bamboo used as fuel, line marked out. To. kwṛ (obl. kwṭ-) horn, branch, path across stream in thicket. Ka. kōḍu horn, tusk, branch of a tree; kōṟ horn. Tu. kōḍů, kōḍu horn. Te. kōḍu rivulet, branch of a river. Pa. kōḍ (pl. kōḍul) horn (DEDR 2200)

meḍ 'iron' (Ho.)

khāḍ 'trench, firepit'

aduru 'native metal' (Ka.) ḍhangar 'blacksmith' (H.)

kol 'furnace, forge' (Kuwi) kol 'alloy of five metals, pancaloha' (Ta.)

me~ṛhet, meḍ 'iron' (Mu.Ho.)

mu~hā me~ṛhe~t = iron smelted by the Kolhes and formed into an equilateral lump a little pointed at each of four ends

(Santali)

koḍ = the place where artisans work (G.)

Orthographically, the glytic compositions add on the characteristic short tail as a hieroglyph (on both ligatured signs and on pictorial motifs)

xolā = tail (Kur.); qoli id. (Malt.)(DEDr 2135). Rebus: **kol** 'pañcalōha' (Ta.)கொல் **kol**, n. 1. Iron; இரும்பு. மின் வெள்ளி பொன் கொல்லெனச் சொல்லும்  (தக்கயாகப். 550). 2. Metal; உலோகம். (நாமதீப. 318.) கொல்லன் kollan, n. < T. golla. Custodian of treasure; கஜானாக்காரன். (P. T. L.) கொல்லிச்சி **kollicci**, n. Fem. of கொல்லன். Woman of the blacksmith caste; கொல்லச் சாதிப் பெண். (யாழ். அக.) The gloss kollicci is notable. It clearly evidences that **kol**[45] was a blacksmith. kola 'blacksmith' (Ka.); Koḍ. kollë blacksmith (DEDR 2133). Vikalpa: **dumba**[46] दुम्ब or (El.) duma दुम । पशुपुच्छः m. the **tail** of an animal. (Kashmiri) Rebus: **ḍōmba** ?Gypsy (CDIAL 5570).

Pitfalls of normalising orthography of some glyphs

Parpola (1994) identifies 386 (+12?) signs (or glyphs or graphemes) and their variant forms. Mahadevan (1977) identifies 419 glyphs as signs; out of these 179 have variants totalling 641 forms. [See appended Indus script: Signs and Sign variants]. In addition, there are over 100 pictorial motifs. Each of these motifs has between 3 to 6 glyptic elements on an average. Thus, the glyphs to be decoded number over 600. Parpola observes: "...the grapheme count might be as low as 350...The total range of signs once present in the Indus script is certain to have been greater than is observable now, for new signs have kept turning up in new inscriptions. The rate of discovery has been fairly low, though, and the new signs have more often been ligatures of two or more signs already known as separate graphemes than entirely new signs." (Parpola, 1994, p. 79)

In the process of normalizing the orthography of some glyphs to identify the core 'signs' of the script, some information is lost and at times, the process itself impedes the possibility of decoding the writing system. This can be demonstrated by (1) the 'identification' of a 'squirrel' glyph and (2) the failure to identify 'dotted circle' or 'stars' as glyphs.

It is, therefore, necessary to view the inscribed object as a composite message composed of glyphs: pictorial motifs and signs alike.

Unit of analysis: inscribed object

We have to be very cautious in interpreting the individual signs and individual pictorials; because, given the small size of the corpus, virtually ANY lexemic or phonemic or even artistic (cultural) value may be assigned and ANY language may be read into the inscriptions, if inscriptions they are, 'readable' in a language and do not merely represent artistic extravaganzas. Total objects presented in Parpola pictorial corpuses and Mahadevan concordance are a statistically small population, further fragmented due to the 400 to 500 signs (including variants and ligatures of basic signs) and over 100 (including variants and pictorial ligatures yielding the so-called 'fabulous' animals categories). Thus, statistical stratification techniques assuming a normal distribution of population cannot provide statistically verifiable results. Hence, an inscribed object is the unit of analysis.

Considering that as many as 273 (111 + 42 + 120) inscriptions are communicated using two signs or less (with or without a pictorial motif or 'field symbol'), it may not be appropriate to assign syllabic or alphabetic values to each sign or each pictorial. Each pictorial or each sign may contain a 'word' or 'lexeme'.(Unless, of course, the entire messaging system is cryptographic using 'syllabic' or 'alphabetic' codes; this we think, is unlikely considering the nature of the cylinder seals in Mesopotamia mainly with pictorials used to convey movable property items.) One clue emerges from the fact that there are inscribed object with only pictorials (i.e. without any sign constituting a 'text'): the pictorials are as important as signs and must be 'deciphered' to understand the message conveyed by the inscription on an object.

Another clue may be surmised considering that there are inscribed objects with just a single sign: a sign by itself may constitute a message and hence may be a lexeme.

Many signs of the script are clearly derivatives from pictorial motifs (glyphs). For example, there are over 50 seals depicted in the Parpola pictorial corpus containing the motif, svastika as a field symbol. Similarly there are inscriptions containing the motif of a dotted circle which has not been recognized as a sign of the script by the corpus compilers. Many such pictographic signs (or glyphs/graphemes) may be identified.

Nature of objects with epigraphs

Possessions and objects made could be described on epigraphs on many types of objects, such as: seals, tablets, copper plates, bangles and even on a monumental display-board (like an advertisement hoarding). The frequencies in parenthesis are based on Mahadevan conordance (which excludes objects that do not contain a 'sign'); the actual numbers will be higher based on the more comprehensive Parpola photo corpus which includes inscriptions containing only pictorials.

- Seals (1814)

- Tablets (in bas-relief or inscribed) (511)*[including Seal Impressions]
- Miniature tablets (of stone, terracotta or faience) (272)
- Copper tablets (plates) (135)
- Bronze implements/weapons (11)
- Seal Impressions*
- Pottery graffitii (119)
- Ivory or bone rods (29)
- Inscribed on stone, bracelets (or, bangles), Ivory plaque, Ivory dice, Carnelian tablet, Terracotta ball, Brick (15)
- Display-board (Dholavira or Kotda with 10 signs, possibly atop a gateway) (1)

Almost all the miniature tablets are from Harappa; almost all copper tablets are from Mohenjodaro. An inference is that the miniature tablets served the same function as the copper tablets which evidence repetitive messages or sign sequences. These could have been used as professional identity cards of members of a group or guild of artisans working together in the same workshop.

Many epigraphs could have been recorded only by lapidary or metal-smith-fire-workers.

This classification provides a clue as to the function served by many inscriptions: inscriptions on bronze implements/weapons (11) and copper tablets (135) could perhaps have been done only by a metal-smithfire-worker. There is a reasonable inference here: many messages may relate to the 'economic activity' of metal-smiths. This inference is consistent with the emergence of the Bronze Age in neighbouring civilizations which have also attested to contacts with the Indus civilization sites (witness, for e.g. the finds of cylinder seals in Sarasvati-Sindu civilization (Indus) sites and the finds of closely comparrable 'Indus' seals and artefacts in Mesopotamian sites.)

Duplicate epigraphs

Though the corpus is limited, it is surprising that there is a substantial number of duplicate inscriptions; this has become apparent from the recent report of excavations at Harappa (1993 to 1995 seasons). Obviously, the inscriptions do not represent not 'names' of owners. The inscriptions could simply be 'functions' performed by or the 'professional title' of the person who carried the inscribed object on his wrist (or as a pendant attached to a necklace) or the list of objects he/she was invoicing for trade (as bill of lading) or to list possessions of property items listed). In Indian cultural continuum from Indus civilization, the use of copper plate inscriptions served the purpose of recording property transactions, listing possessions of property items.

This hypothesis gets re-inforced by (1) the finds of inscriptions on copper tablets (again, with many duplicates – all apparently made by a metal-worker and hence may relate to metal objects produced, say, in an armoury); and (2) the presence of over 200 inscribed objects with no sign (only pictorial motif) or just one or two signs. [The signs could hardly have been alphabets or syllables since there are not many 'names' attested in the historical periods with just one or two syllables.]

Allographs

An allograph is a variant shape of a glyph or a combination of glyphs (as in ligatures) that can represent one gloss. An example in English are f and gh which can represent the phoneme /f/. There are allographs within the set of glyphs rendered as pictorial motifs and as signs of Indus script. The presence of allographs may explain the occurrence of over 500 glyphs.

kāṭī 'spinner' (G.)

Rebus: khati 'wheelwright' (H.) kāṭi = fireplace in the form of a long ditch (Ta.Skt.Vedic) kāṭya = being in a hole (VS. XVI.37); kāṭ a hole, depth (RV. i. 106.6) khāḍ a ditch, a trench; khāḍ o khaiyo several pits and ditches (G.) khaṇḍrun: 'pit (furnace)' (Santali)

Kur. kaṇḍō a stool. Malt. kando stool, seat. (DEDR 1179) Rebus: kaṇḍ 'fire-altar, furnace' (Santali) kola 'tiger, jackal' (Kon.); rebus: kolami 'smithy' (Te.) Grapheme as a phonetic determinant of the depiction of woman, kola; rebus: kolami 'smithy' (Te.)

kola 'woman' (Nahali); Rebus: kolami 'smithy' (Te.)[47]

ayo 'fish' (Mu.); rebus: aya 'metal' (G.)

bhaṭa 'six' (G.); rebus: bhaṭa 'furnace' (Santali)

Elamite lady spinner. Musee du Louvre. Paris. An elegantly coiffed, exquisitely-dressed and well fanned Elamite woman sits on a lion footed stool winding thread on a spindle. The stool on which the lovely Elamite lady sits has the legs of a lion or panther; the fish is also placed on a similar stool in front her. This five-inch fragment is dated 8th century BCE[48].

bhaṭa 'six' (G.) Rebus: bhaṭa 'furnace' (G.)

kola 'woman' (Nahali); Rebus: kolami 'smithy' (Te.)

meḍhi, miḍhī, meṇḍhī[49] = a plait in a

woman's hair; a plaited or twisted strand of hair (P.) Rebus: meḍ 'iron' (Ho.) Thus, the glyptic elements of woman, plaited hair and six plaits can be decoded as: **meḍ bhaṭa kolami** 'iron smelter smithy'.

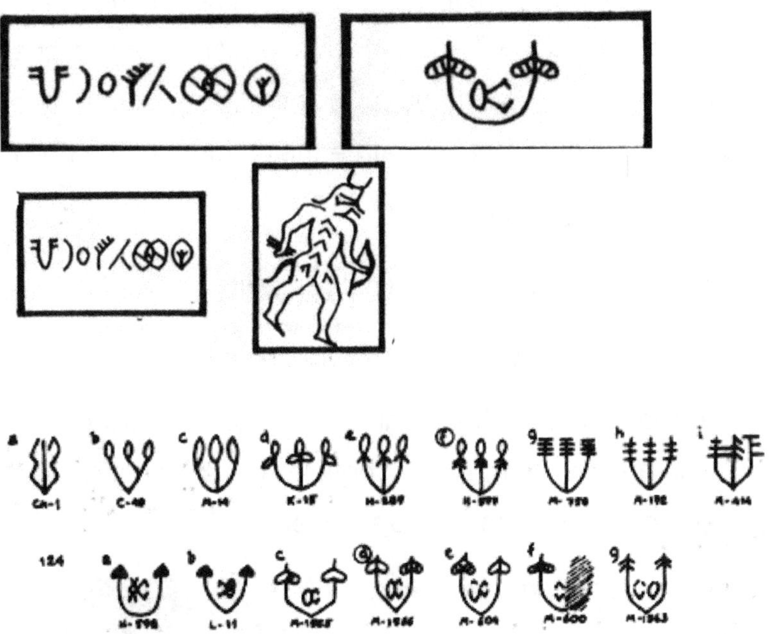

Allographs of a leaf sign, ligature with crab sign [After Parpola, 1994, fig. 13.15] The archer shown on one copper tablet seems to be equivalent to a glyph on another copper plate -- that of ligatured U (rimless wide-mouthed pot) with leaves and crab's claws.

- The archer shown on one copper tablet seems to be a synonym of the leaves ligatured with crab on another copper tablet since the inscription on the obverse of each of the tablets is identical. [cf. Parpola, 1994, fig. 13.13]

This ligatured sign appears on two seals- one from Harappa and another from Lothal. Leaves ligatured with crab is a sign which occurs on these seals and with similar sign sequences. [cf. Parpola, 1994, fig. 13.12]

kamāṭhiyo = archer; kāmaṭhum = a bow; kāmaḍ, kāmaḍum = a chip of bamboo (G.) kāmaṭhiyo a bowman; an archer (Skt.lex.)   Rebus: kammaṭi a coiner (Ka.); kampaṭṭam coinage, coin, mint (Ta.) kammaṭa = mint, gold furnace (Te.)

Allographs (graphemes):

kamḍa, khamḍa 'copulation' (Santali)

kamaṭha crab (Skt.)

kamarkom = fig leaf (Santali.lex.) kamarmaṛā (Has.), kamarkom (Nag.); the petiole or stalk of a leaf (Mundari.lex.) kamat.ha = fig leaf, religiosa (Skt.)

Allographs denoting workshop of artisans

A remarkable glyph (Sign 39) occurs on a few Indus inscriptions depicting a mudhif.

Sign 39 and variants m0702 Text 2206 showing Sign 39.

Text 1330 showing Sign 39. Pictorial motif: Zebu (Bos indicus) This sign is comparable to the cattle byre of Southern Mesopotamia dated to c. 3000

BCE. This is called mudhif in Iraq (Sumerian reedhouse)[50].

Bhoj. ḍāṅgar ' cattle ' (CDIAL 5524) adar ḍangra 'zebu' (Santali) Konḍa (BB.) aḍar herd of cows. Pe. aḍer id. (DEDR 84) Rebus: aduru 'native, unsmelted metal' (Ka.) Vikalpa: khar = a herd, a flock; khar ke khar = in multitudes, flock after flock (Santali.lex.)

Rebus: kanḍ furnace (Santali) gadi a shop (Santali) katai shop, bazaar, market (Ta.); kaṭa market (Ma.)(DEDR 1142). śrēṇi. [Skt.] n. A line, row, range, rank. Regular order. śrēṇika. [Skt.] n. A tent (Telugu) **seṇi** ' row of rafters in a thatched roof, the wooden plates on which the rafters are put crosswise ' (Or.)(CDIAL 12718)

Grapheme: goṭ = the place where cattle are collected at mid-day (Santali); **goṭh[51]** (Brj.)(CDIAL 4336). goṣṭha (Skt.); cattle-shed (Or.) koḍ = a cow-pen; a cattlepen; a byre (G.) कोठी cattle-shed (Marathi) कोंडी [kōṇḍī] A pen or fold for cattle. गोठी [gōṭhī] f C (Dim. of गोठा) A pen or fold for calves. (Marathi) Vikalpa: Interpreting the glyph as a reed-house: kāṛā ' stem of muñja grass (used for thatching) (Bi.) (CDIAL 3023). Rebus: H. kãḍerā[52] m. ' a caste of bow -- and arrow -- makers (CDIAL 3024).

Rebus: koḍ = place where artisan's work (Kur.) कोठी[53] [kōṭhī

] f (कोष्ठ S) A granary, garner, storehouse, warehouse, treasury, factory, bank. (Marathi)

Grapheme: गोटी[54] [gōṭī] f (Dim. of गोटा) A roundish stone or pebble. गोदा [gōdā] m A circular brand or mark made by actual cautery (Marathi)

gōti. [Tel.] n. A woman. (Telugu)

Grapheme: **lohi** (L. 458), a **blanket**. (Kashmiri)

Cattle Byres c.3200-3000 B.C. Late Uruk-Jemdet Nasr period. Magnesite. Cylinder seal. In the lower field of this seal appear three reed cattle byres. Each byre is

surmounted by three reed pillars topped by rings, a motif that has been suggested as symbolizing a male god, perhaps Dumuzi. Within the huts calves or vessels appear alternately; from the sides come calves that drink out of a vessel between them. Above each pair of animals another small calf appears. A herd of enormous cattle moves in the upper field.[55] Cattle and cattle byres in Southern Mesopotamia, c. 3500 BCE. Drawing of an impression from a Uruk period cylinder seal.[56]

Glyph, taberna montana

Ur cylinder seal with taberna montana plant, BM 122947; A soft-stone flask, 6 cm. tall, from Bactria (northern Afghanistan) showing a winged female deity (?) flanked by two flowers similar to those shown on the comb from Tell Abraq.[57] Ivory comb with Mountain Tulip motif and dotted 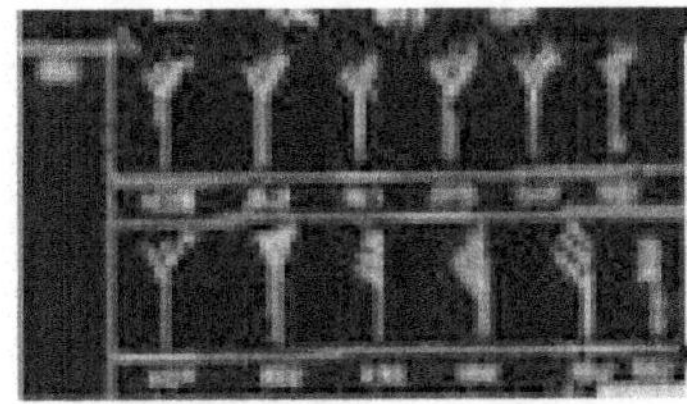 circles. TA 1649 Tell Abraq.[58] tagar = a flowering shrub; a plant in bloom (G.lex.) tagara = the shrub tabernaemontana coronaria, and a fragrant powder or perfume obtained from it, incense (Vin 1.203); tagara-mallika_ two kinds of gandha_ (P.lex.) ṭagara (tagara) a spec. plant; fragrant wood (Pkt.Skt.) tagara = a kind of flowering tree (Te.lex.) This is a flower, tagaraka, used as a hair-fragrance (Skt.) and hence is also depicted on a bonecomb. Signs, 162, 163, 169 sign variants

Rebus: tagromi 'tin, metal alloy' (Kuwi)[59]

ran:ga ron:ga, ran:ga con:ga = thorny, spikey, armed with thorns; edel dare ran:ga con:ga dareka = this cotton tree grows with spikes on it (Santali) ran:ga, ran: pewter is an alloy of tin lead and antimony (añjana) (Santali).

- adar ḍangra 'zebu'; rebus: aduru 'native metal' (Ka.); ḍhangar 'blacksmith' (H.)

A soft-stone flask, 6 cm. tall, from Bactria (northern Afghanistan) showing a winged female deity (?) flanked by two flowers similar to those shown on the comb from Tell Abraq (After Pottier, M.H., 1984, Materiel funeraire e la Bactriane meridionale de l'Age du Bronze, Paris, Editions Recherche sur les Civilisations: plate 20.150)

Tell Abraq comb and axe with epigraph After Fig. 7Holly Pittman, 1984, Art of the Bronze Age: Southeastern Iran, Western Central Asia, and the Indus Valley, New York, The Metropolitan Museum of Art, pp. 29-30].

Wild tulip motif. A motif that occurs on southeast Iranian cylinder seals and on Persian Gulf seals. 1st row: Bactrian artifacts; 2nd row: a comb from the Gulf area and late trans-Elamite seals [After Marie-Helene Pottier, 1984, Materiel funeraire de la Bactriane meridionale de l'age du bronze, Recherche sur les Civilizations, Memoire 36, Paris, fig. 21; Sarianidi, V.I., 1986, Le complexe culturel de Togolok 21 en Margiane, Arts Asiatiques 41: fig. 6,21; Potts, 1994, fig. 53,8; Amiet, 1986, fig. 132]. Bone comb with Mountain Tulip motif and dotted circles. TA 1649 Tell Abraq, United Arab Emirates. Ivory comb with Mountain Tulip motif and dotted circles. TA 1649 Tell Abraq. [D.T. Potts, South and Central Asian elements at Tell Abraq (Emirate of Umm al-Qaiwain, United Arab Emirates), c. 2200 BC—AD 400, in Asko Parpola and Petteri Koskikallio, South Asian Archaeology 1993: , pp. 615-666] The ivory comb found at Tell Abraq measures 11 X 8.2 X .4 cm. Both sides of the comb bear identical, incised decoration in the form of two long-stemmed flowers with crenate or dentate leaves, flanking three dotted circles arranged in a triangular pattern. Bone and ivory combs with dotted-circle decoration are well-known in the Harappan area (e.g. at Chanhu-daro and Mohenjo-daro), but none of the Harappan combs bear the distinctive floral motif of the Tell Abraq comb. These flowers are identified as tulips, perhaps Mountain tulip or Boeotian tulip (both of which grow in Afghanistan) which have an undulate leaf. There is a possibility that the comb is an import from Bactria, perhaps transmitted through Meluhha to the Oman Peninsula site of Tell Abraq.

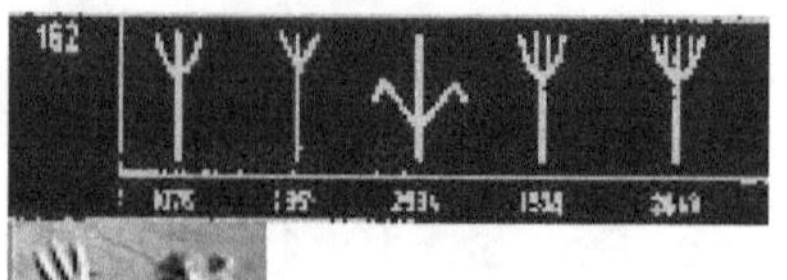
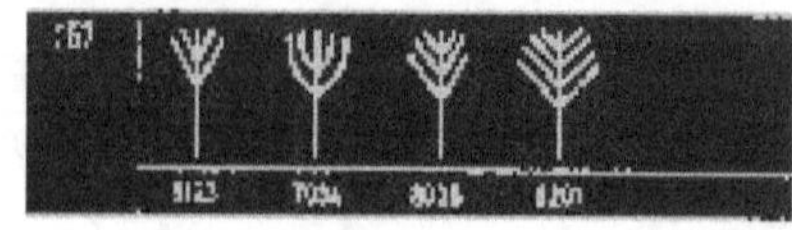

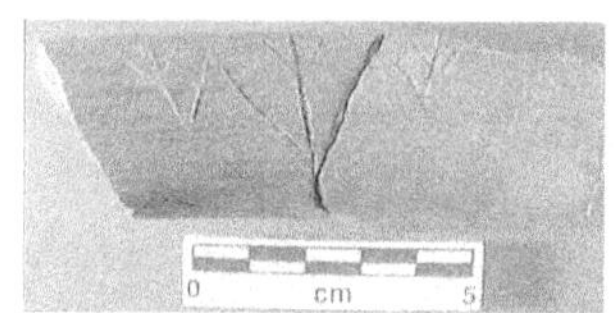 Seal impression from Harappa (Kenoyer, 1998); a woman is carrying a three-petalled flower

Kenoyer Slide 124 Inscribed Ravi sherd (1998 find at Harappa: Kenoyer and Meadow); the sherd contains the same sign (ca. 3300 BCE). The sign on this potsherd (with five petals as in tabernae montana, tagaraka) is stylized as Sign 162 (with three prongs) and Sign 165 (with five petals). Sign 167 shows five petals (and variants show many more branches). The sign also is ligatured to form other signs:

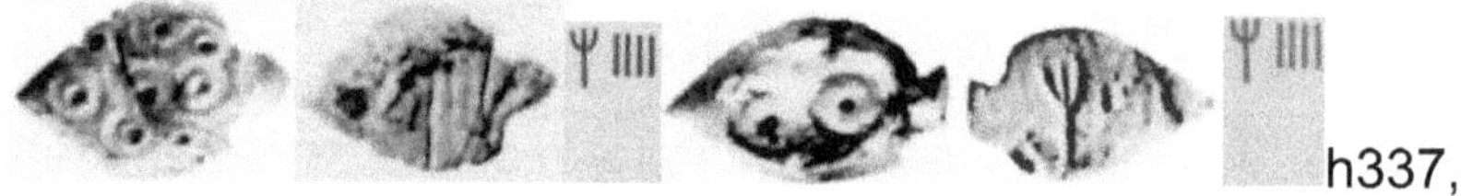h337, h338 Texts 4417, 4426 (les on leaf-shaped tablets)

Altyn-tepe seals with hieroglyphs of Indian linguistic area, attesting trade contacts with Meluhha

Altyn-depe (close to the Caspian sea, in Turkmenistan). Silver seal. Pictograph of ligatured animal with three heads.

sangaḍa 'jointed naimal' (M.) san:gāḍo a lathe (M.); cutting stone, gilding (G.)

Two seals found at Altyn-depe[60]

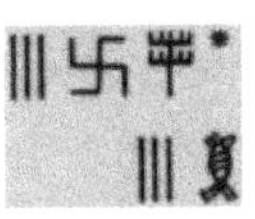

The text on an Altyn-tepe seals compare with an inscription on a miniature tablet, Text 4500 (Incised miniature tablet; not illustrated).

Altyn-tepe seals are decoded: svastika; rebus: jasta 'zinc' (Kashmiri) aḍar 'harrow'; rebus: aduru 'native metal'; kolmo 'paddy plant'; rebus: kolami 'forge, smithy' (Te.) Thus, the two-sign sequence reads: kolmo aduru 'forged native metal'. Harappan weight TA 1356 from Tell Abraq. C. 22nd cent. BCE. Banded chert or flint weight 54.06 g. This is approx. 4 times the unit Harappan weight of 13.63 g.

Finds at Altyn-depe: ivory sticks and gaming pieces (?) obtained from Sarasvati Sindhu civilization; similar objects with dotted circles found in Mohenjodaro and Harappa.

Bhagawanpura is a site located on the right bank of the River Sarasvati_ in Dist. Kuruks.etra. Remains of semi-circular huts leaving behind only post-holes and rammed

floors have been found. From Period IB levels bones of true domesticatd horse, equus caballus have been found. Intersecting dotted circle designs are found on pottery of Painted Grey Ware which overlap the Late Harappan ware.

Mohenjo-daro. Dotted circle decoration on a steatite bowl (DK 3178), DK-B, house 3, room VIII (Jansen and Urban,

1985, RTWH, Aachen).

Vessel fragments with dot-in-circle design from Susa. Louvre Museum. At the Royal Cemetery of Ur, Woolley 1934: 558-59 found a small container with a narrow neck and sides decorated with three dot-incircle designs.

Terracotta female adorned with 'dotted circles'; Period Namazga II; Yalangach Tepe, Geoksyur (Weiner, 1984, Fig. 183)

khaṇḍi = a sari, a full dress for a woman, a piece of cloth twelve cubits long by two in width; khaṇḍa = a piece of cloth suitable for the dress of a woman's sar.i; khaṇḍi bande,

bande = to dress, of women binding round waist (Santali) khand 'ivory' kandhi 'a lump, a piece' (Santali)Rebus: **kandi**[61] 'beads' (Pa.)(DEDR 1215). khaṇḍ 'ivory' (H.) Rebus: khaṇḍaran, khaṇḍrun 'pit furnace' (Santali)

Hence, the depiction of 'dotted circles' (like perforated beads) surrounding a fire-altar and also on ivory objects. काढतें [kāḍhatēṃ] n Among gamesters. An ivory counter &c. placed to represent a sum of money. (Marathi) The dotted circles also adorn the standard device which is a drill-lathe, sangaḍa खंड [khaṇḍa] A piece, bit, fragment, portion.(Marathi) **kandi** 'beads' (Pa.)

Dotted circle glyph: context, vedi glyph, ivory artifacts

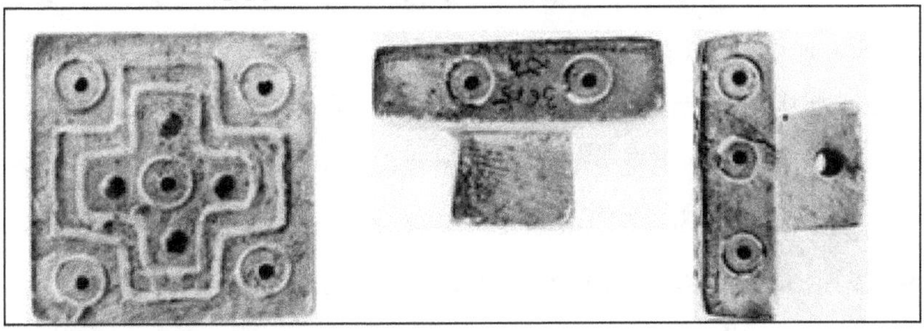

vēdha m. ' hitting the mark ' MBh., ' penetration, hole ' VarBṛS. [√vyadh] Pa. vēdha -- m. ' prick, wound '; Pk. vēha -- m. ' boring, hole ', P. veh, beh m., H. beh m., G. veh m. karṇavēdha -- .(CDIAL 12108) வேதிதம் vētitam , n. < vēdhita. (யாழ். அக.) 1. Perforating, drilling; துளைக்கை. 2. Tube; துளையுடைப்பொருள். வேதை[3] vētai , n. < vēdha. 1. Drilling, boring; துளைக்கை. (Tamil) Vedhin (adj.) [fr. **vidh=vyadh**] piercing, shooting, hitting (Pali) Rebus: **vēdi** f. '

raised piece of ground serving as an altar and usu. strewed with kuśa grass ' RV., ' stand, bench ' MBh., ' platform for wedding ceremony ' Kāv., vēdika<-> m. ' bench ' R., °kā -- f. MBh. [Cf. vēdá -- m. ' bunch of kuśa grass used as broom ' AV.] Pa. vēdi -- , °dī -- , °dikā -- f. ' cornice, ledge, rail '; Pk. vēi -- , vēiā -- f. ' platform '; A. bei ' quadrangular frame of greenery forming platform on which ceremonial bathing of bride and bridegroom is performed '.(CDIAL 12107). Vedi & **Vedī** (f.) [Vedic vedi sacrificial bench] ledge, cornice, rail Mhvs 32, 5; 35, 2; 36, 52 (pāsāṇa°); 36, 103; Vv 8416 (=vedikā VvA 346). -- See on term Dial. ii.210; Mhvs. tsrln220, 296. Vedikā (f.) (& **vediyā**) [fr. vedi] cornice, ledge, railing D ii.179; Vin ii.120; J iv.229, 266; Vv 786 (vediyā= vedikā VvA 304); 8416 (=vedikā VvA 340); VvA 275. Velli [dial.?] is a word peculiar to the Jātaka. At one passage it is expld by the Commentary as "vedi" (i. e. rail, cornice), where it is applied to the slender waist of a woman (cp. **vilāka & vilaggita**): J vi.456. At most of the other passages it is expld as "a heap of gold": thus at J v.506 (verse: **velli** -- vilāka -- majjhā; C.: ettha **vellī** ti **rāsi** vilākamajjhā ti vilagga -- majjhā uttattaghana -- suvaṇṇa -- **rāsi** -- ppabhā c' eva tanu -- dīgha -- majjhā ca"), and vi.269 (verse: kañcana -- velli -- viggaha; C.: "suvaṇṇa -- **rāsi** -- sassirīka -- sarīrā"). At v.398 in the same passage as vi.269 expld in C. as "kañcana -- rūpakasadisa -- sarīrā"). The idea of "golden" is connected with it throughout. (Pali) vēdi [Skt.] n. A terrace, a piece of raised ground, a platform. An altar. (Telugu)

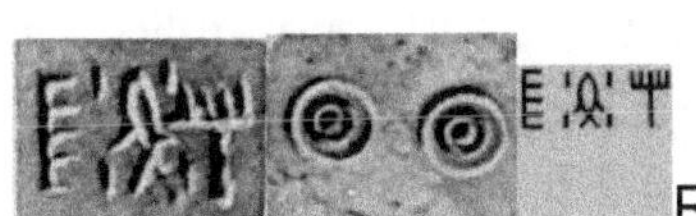 Ropar 1,Text 9021 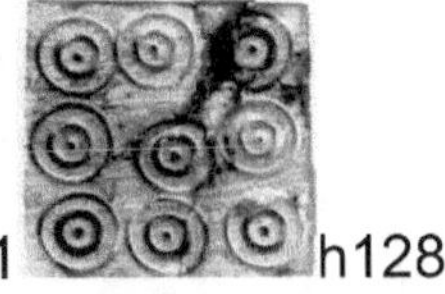 h128

After Vats, Pl.CXIX,.No.6 An ivory comb fragment with one preserved tooth and ornamented with double incised circles (3.8 in. long).

Kalibangan, Ivory comb with three dotted circles; Kalibangan, Period II; Thapar 1979, Pl.XXVII, in: Ancient Cities of the Indus.

Ivory rod, ivory plaque with dotted circles. Mohenjodaro. [Musee National De Arts Asiatiques Guimet, 1988-1989, Les cites oubliees de l'Indus Archeologie du Pakistan.]

h1017ivorystick

The ivory comb found at Tell Abraq measures 11 X 8.2 X .4 cm. Both sides of the comb bear identical,

incised decoration in the form of two long-stemmed flowers with crenate or dentate leaves, flanking three dotted circles arranged in a triangular pattern. Bone and ivory combs with dotted-circle decoration are well-known in the Harappan area (e.g. at Chanhu-daro and Mohenjo-daro), but none of the Harappan combs bear the distinctive floral motif of the Tell Abraq comb. These flowers are identified as

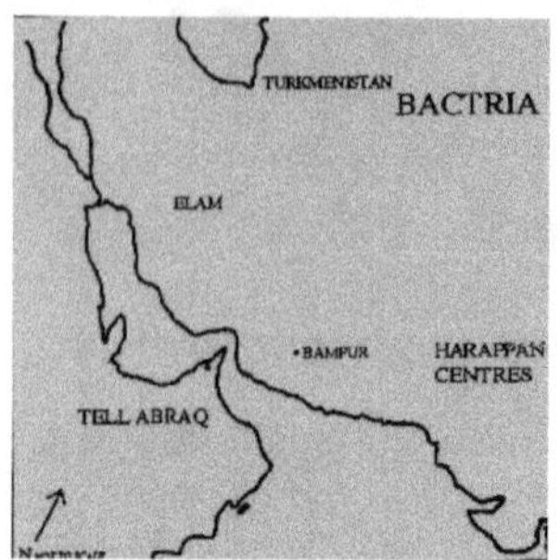

tulips, perhaps Mountain tulip or Boeotian tulip (both of which grow in Afghanistan) which have an undulate leaf. There is a possibility that the comb is an import from Bactria, perhaps transmitted through Meluhha to the Oman Peninsula site of Tell Abraq.

Epigraphs 5477, 1554; 4604, 5477

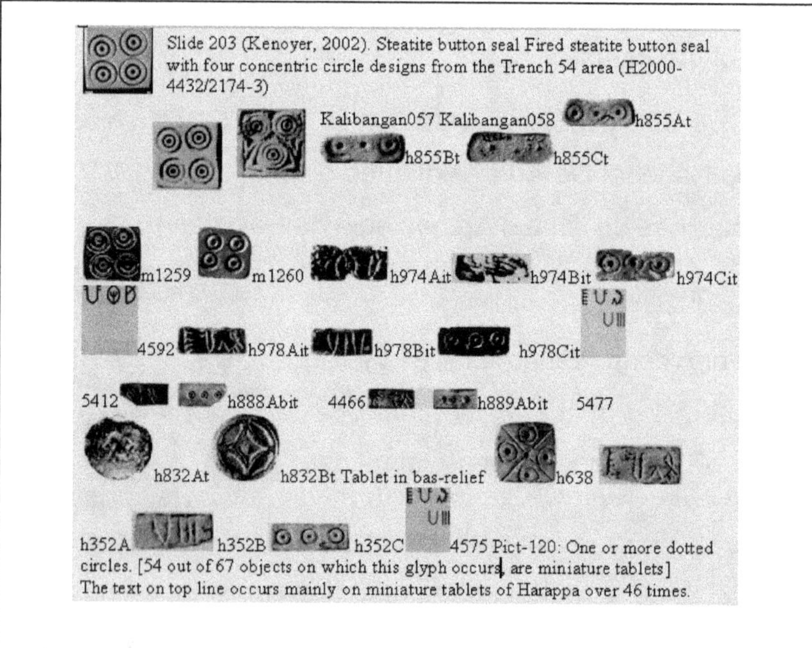

Slide 203 (Kenoyer, 2002). Steatite button seal Fired steatite button seal with four concentric circle designs from the Trench 54 area (H2000-4432/2174-3)

Kalibangan057 Kalibangan058 h855At h855Bt h855Ct

m1259 m1260 h974Ait h974Bit h974Cit

4592 h978Ait h978Bit h978Cit

5412 h888Abit 4466 h889Abit 5477

h832At h832Bt Tablet in bas-relief h638

h352A h352B h352C 4575 Pict-120: One or more dotted circles. [54 out of 67 objects on which this glyph occurs are miniature tablets]
The text on top line occurs mainly on miniature tablets of Harappa over 46 times.

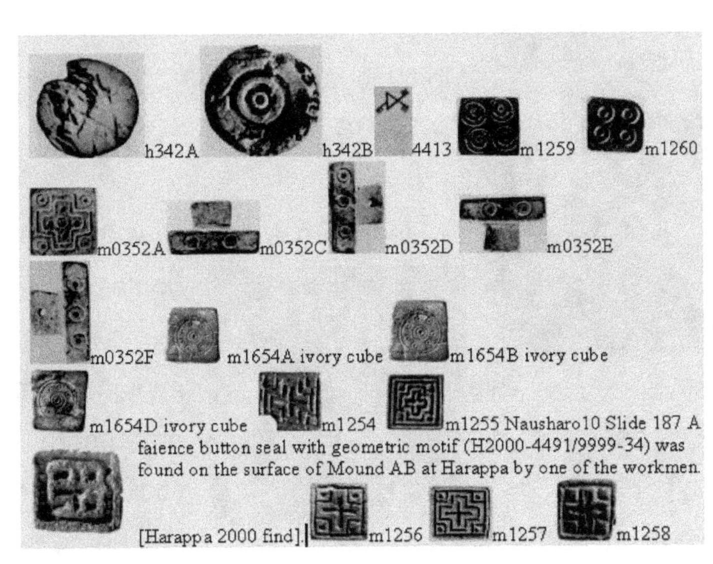

h342A
h342B
4413
m1259
m1260
m0352A
m0352C
m0352D
m0352E
m0352F
m1654A ivory cube
m1654B ivory cube
m1654D ivory cube
m1254
m1255 Nausharo10 Slide 187 A
faience button seal with geometric motif (H2000-4491/9999-34) was
found on the surface of Mound AB at Harappa by one of the workmen.
[Harappa 2000 find].
m1256
m1257
m1258

Monkey hieroglyph and glyphs of interlocked bodies

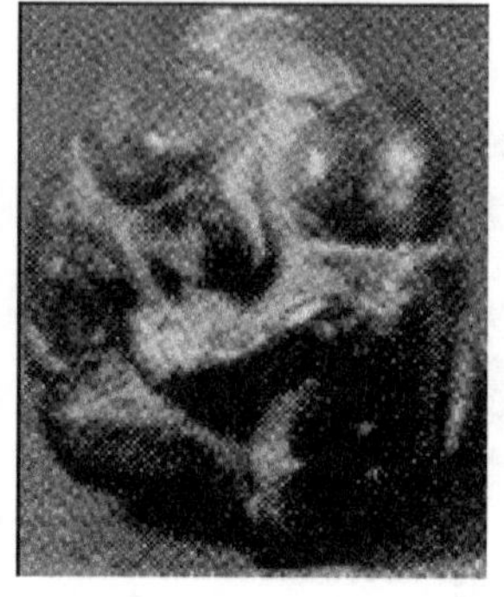

Mohenjodaro FEM, Pl. LXXXVIII, 316

Text 2316

Molded faience figurine with a hole in center. Three ligatured monkeys. This faience bead or pin possibly placed on a stick or cord. Possibly molded and carved. Material: yellow brown glazed faience; 1.6 cm. high and 1.4 cm. dia; Mohenjodaro K 1053. Marshall 1931: pl. CLVIII.5; after Fig. 8.23, Kenoyer, 2000.

kuthāru[62] = a monkey (Skt.lex.) Rebus: kuthāru 'armourer or weapons maker'(metal-worker), also an inscriber or writer. kolmo 'three' (Mu.) Rebus: kolami 'forge' (Te.) Thus, the figurine of 3 monkeys is decoded: kolami kuthāru 'armourer's forge'. Vikalpa: Glyph: gāṛi = a monkey; sakam gāṛī a small species of monkey (Santali) gaḍava = male monkey (Ka.); gaḍḍi, gaḍḍē(Go.); kaṭuvan= (Ta.)(DEDR 1140) [Note a seal where a monkey is shown in lieu of a standard device in front of a one-horned bull].

MS 4602 Indus Valley cylinder seal, ca. 3000 BCE depicting a palm tree and a man between two lions with wings and snakeheads, holding one arm around each, two long fish below, and one fish jumping after one lion's tail or the tail of a sitting monkey above it, facing a quiver of weapons. Seal matrix on creamy stone or shell, Indus Valley, Pakistan, ca. 3000 BC, 1 cylinder seal, diam. 2,0x3,7 cm, in fine execution influenced by the Jemdet Nasr style of Sumer. **khol**[63], lā 'quiver' (B.)(CDIAL 3944) Rebus: **kole·l**[64] smithy, temple in Kota village. (Ko.) kol working in iron, blacksmith (Ta.)(DEDR 2133)

m440AC Two short-horned bulls facing each other on the top register. This glyphs on this tablet are identical to m1395Bt; obverse m1395At shows five intertwined tigers.

m1395Bt Multiple heads of tigers joined/interlocked to a tiger's body in m1395At and

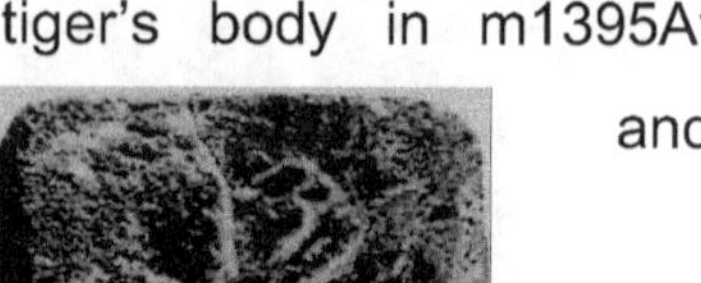

m0441At[65]

sāgaḍa[66] 'jointed animals' (M.) sāgāḍo gilding (G.); lathe (G.) khaṛ = a herd, a flock; khaṛ ke khaṛ = in multitudes, flock after flock (Santali.lex.) Rebus: kaṇḍ furnace (Santali) gadi a shop (Santali) kaṭai shop, bazaar, market (Ta.); kaṭa market (Ma.)(DEDR 1142). Vikalpa: **cāli** Interlocking bodies (IL 3872) Rebus: sal 'workshop' (Santali) śāla 'workshop' (Skt.) kol 'tiger'; rebus: kol 'iron' (Ta.) Thus, the glyptic composition is decoded rebus: **kol śāla** 'iron workshop'.

Parpola notes (1994, pp.103-104): "A comparative study of the allographs provides one important means of identifying the iconic meaning of even fairly abstract shapes...the (allograph) continuum)...Taken together, these signs can be understood as pictures of a single object, namely, 'steps, staircase or ladder'; taken individually, such a conclusion would hardly be possible."

śreṇi i[67] [Skt.] n. A line, row, range, rank. Regular order.
śrēṇika. [Skt.] n. A tent (Telugu) **seṇi** ' row of rafters in a thatched roof, the wooden plates on which the rafters are put crosswise ' (Or.)(CDIAL 12718) Rebus: śreṇi 'guild' (Skt.)

panjĕr 'ladder, stairs'(Bshk.) (CDIAL 7760)

pasra 'smithy' (Santali)

Allograph:

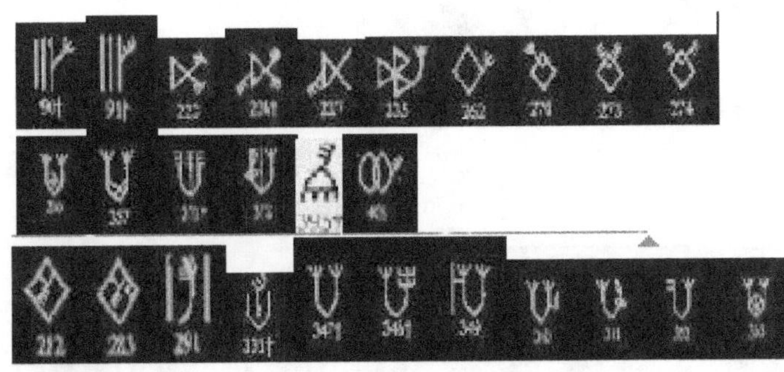

Signs

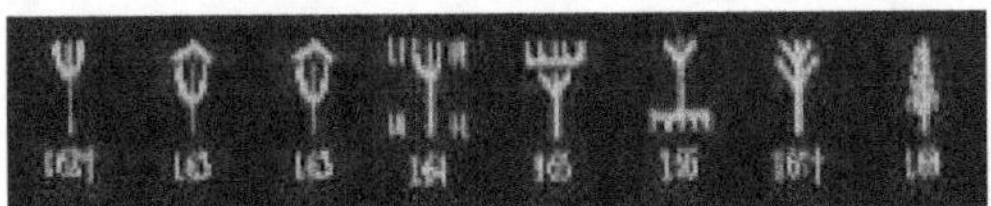

90,91,223,224,227,235.262,270,273,274,282,283,291,331,347-352,355-357, 371,372, 388,390,395,405 [With ligatures of Sign 162 or Sign 169]

Signs 162 to 168 [Orthography: sprout]. As a countable object,the sign represents the rebus of (number of) [brick] kilns, the number (count) being indicated by short linear strokes. A variant lexeme of Sign 167 (because of five petals shown) could be: tagara, tabaernae montana, a flowering, fragrant shrub; rebus: takaram = tin (Ta.lex.)

pajhaṛ = to sprout from a root; pagra = a cutting of sugar-cane used for planting (Santali .lex.)

m1390Bt Text 2868 Pict-74: Bird in flight.m0451A,B Text3235 h166A,B Harappa XCI.255.

Seal; Vats 1940, II: Pl.

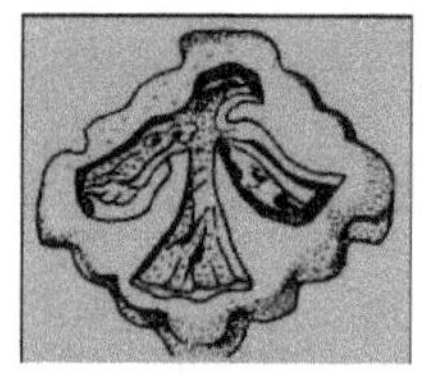

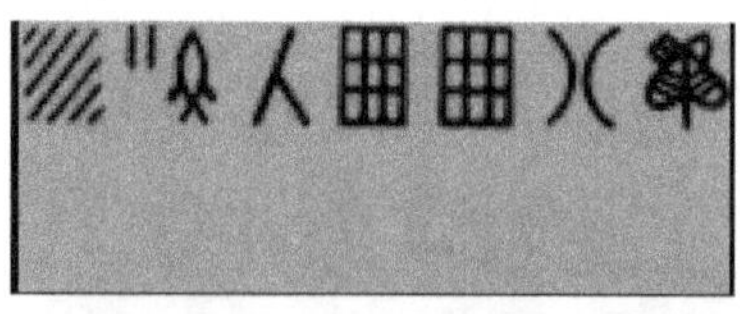

Two seals from Gonur 1 in the Murghab delta; dark brown stone
(Sarianidi 1981 b: 232-233, Fig. 7,8); eagle engraved on one

pajhaṛ 'eagle' (Santali) pajhar. = the Indian tawny , the Indian black eagle, the Indian crested hawk; eagle, buru pajhar.,

the hill-eagle, aquila imperialis; hako sat.i pajhaṛ = a fish-eating eagle (also called dak pajhar.); huru pajhaṛ = the imperial eagle (Santali .lex.)

panji-il = a certain feather in each wing of a vulture (Mundari .lex.) [See the hieroglyph of an eagle ligatured to a tiger on a Nal pot. kol 'tiger' (Santali)]Rebus: kol is pancaloha, alloy of five metals (Tamil); kollan 'smith' (Tamil)

Vikalpa: sen:gel gidi = the male of the Indian king-vulture, ologyps calvus (Santali.lex.)

sen:gel = fire; sen:gel kut.ra = a spark of fire, a burning bit of wood; sen:gel ku_n.d. = a heavy fire (Mundari)

gitil bali = grains of magnetic iron resembling sand (Santali)

sen:gel gidi rebus: sen:gel gitil = (furnace) fire for meteoric iron fragments.

The ligature on the Nal pot ca 2800 BCE (Baluchisan: first settlement in southeastern Baluchistan was in the 4th millennium BCE) is extraordinary: an eagle's head is ligatured to the body of a tiger. In BMAC area, the 'eagle' is a recurrent motif on seals. Ute Franke-Vogt: "Different pottery styles link this area also to central and northern Balochistan, and after about 2900/2800 BCE to southern Sindh where, at this time, the Indus Civilization took shape. The Nal pottery with its particular geometric and figurative patterns painted in blue, yellow, red and turquoise after firing is among the earliest and most dominanstyles in the south."

Griffin, Baluchistan (Provenance unknown); ficus leaves, tiger, with a wing, ligatured to an eagle.

Lentoid seal with a griffin, ca. 1450–1400 B.C.;Late Minoan II Minoan; Greece, Crete Agate; H. 1 1/16 in. (2.7 cm), W. 1 1/16 (2.7 cm), Diam. ½ in. (1.2 cm) It is engraved with an image of a crouching griffin, a powerful mythical creature with the head and wings of a bird and the body of a lion. http://www.metmuseum.org

abru = wing (Akkadian/Assyrian) Rebus: **abāru** = lead; antimony (**annaku** is most unlikely to be lead rather than tin).(cf. CAD A (II): 126; AHw 49) (Akkadian/Assyrian).

Graheme: abaru = enclose, surround; aburru = enclosure (Akkadian/Assyrian) abaru = be strong, powerful; strength, power (Akkadian/Assyrian)

883-59 BCE Mesopotamian, Neo-Assyrian; Limestone;

height 1 m (39 3/8
in.);47.181 Detroit Institute
of Arts, USA.

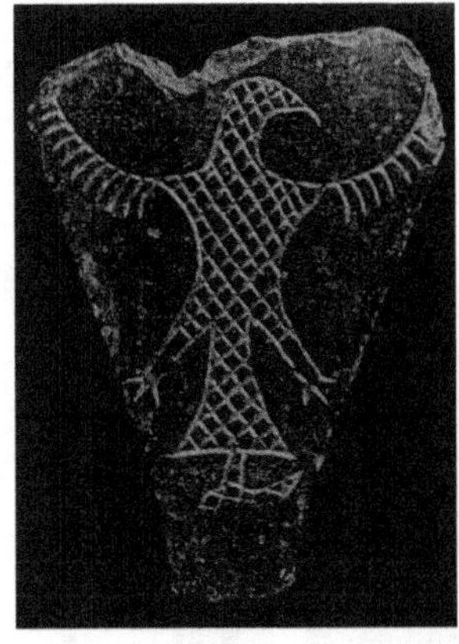

Eagle incised on a ceremonial axe made of chlorite. Tepe Yahya. (After Fig. 9.6 in Philip H. Kohl, 2001, opcit.)

Nippur vessel with combatant snake and eagle motif. Istanbul Museum. The design is raised above the base; the vessel of chlorite was found in a mixed Ur III context at Nippur in southern Mesopotamia.

baroṭi 'twelve'; rebus: **bhārata** 'a factitious alloy of copper, pewter, tin (M.)'

kuṭila 'bent'; rebus: 'bronze (8 parts copper, 2 parts tin)'

lo 'ficus'; rebus: metal

baṭa 'pot' 'quail'; rebus: 'furnace'

khaṇḍ 'division'; rebus: kaṇḍ 'furnace'

kolmo 'seedling'; rebus: kolami 'smithy'

ḍhālako Sign 274; rebus: 'a large metal ingot (G.)'

beḍa 'fish'; rebus: 'hearth'

erako[68] nave; rebus: 'molten cast (copper)'

kuṭi 'eyebrow'; rebus: 'smelter'

meḍ 'body'; rebus: 'iron'

Pure tin ingots (Sarasvati rosetta stones) found in a ship-

wreck, Haifa[69] incised with Sarasvati hieroglyphs

Copper tablet; side B perhaps is a graphemic representation of an antelope; note the ligatured tail comparable to the tail on m273, b012 and k037]

•ran:ku = tin (Santali)

•ran:ku = liquid measure (Santali)

•ran:ku a species of deer; ran:kuka (Skt.)(CDIAL 10559). See middle glyph on copper plates m0522 & m0516

•dāṭu = cross (Te.); dhatu = mineral (Santali) dhātu 'mineral (Pali) dhātu 'mineral' (Vedic); a mineral, metal (Santali); dhāta id. (G.)

H. dhāṛnā 'to send out, pour out, cast (metal)' (CDIAL 6771).

Elephant hieroglyph

Two semantic clusters point to glosses meaning 'iron'. One cluster relates to **karba** and cognates in Indian linguistic area. The second cluster relates to **ib** and cognates in Inddian linguistic area. Both are relatable to homonyms (and related graphemes) of elephant. The rebus words for elephant are: **karin, karabha** and **ibha**

An allograph is *ficus religiosa*: **karibha**[70] -- m. ' Ficus religiosa (?) [Semantics of ficus religiosa may be relatable to homonyms used to denote both the sacred tree and rebus gloss: **loa**, ficus (Santali); **loh** 'metal' (Skt.)]

> karba 'iron' (Ka.)(DEDR 1278) as in ajirda karba 'iron' (Ka.) kari, karu 'black' (Ma.)(DEDR 1278) karbura 'gold' (Ka.) karbon 'black gold, iron' (Ka.) kabbiṇa 'iron' (Ka.) karum pon 'iron' (Ta.); kabin 'iron' (Ko.)(DEDR 1278)

> Ib 'iron' (Santali) [cf. Toda gloss below: ib 'needle'.] Ta. Irumpu iron, instrument, weapon. a. irumpu,irimpu iron. Ko. ibid. To. Ib needle. Koḍ. Irïmbï iron. Te. Inumu id. Kol. (Kin.) inum (pl. inmul)iron, sword. Kui (Friend-Pereira) rumba vaḍi ironstone (for vaḍi, see 5285). (DEDR 486)

Mohenjo-daro. Elephant glyph shown on two copper tablets. **karabha** 'young elephant; **karin** elephant; **ibha**[71] id. (Skt.)

Ligatured tiger to reinforce tiger as hieroglyph

A woman's face and headdress ligatured to a tiger kul 'tiger' (Santali); kōlu id. (Te.) kōlupuli = Bengal tiger (Te.)

kōla = woman (Nahali)   [The ligature of a woman to a tiger is a phonetic determinant; the scribe clearly conveys that the gloss represented is **kōla**] Pk. kolhuya -- , kulha -- m. ' jackal ' < *kōdhu -- ; H.kolhā, °lā m. ' jackal ', adj. ' crafty '; G. kohlũ, °lũ n. ' **jackal** ', M. kolhā, °lā m. **krōṣṭf̄** ' crying ' BhP., m. ' jackal ' RV. = krṓṣṭu -- m. Pāṇ. [√kruś] Pa. koṭṭhu -- , °uka -- and kotthu -- , °uka -- m. ' jackal ', Pk. koṭṭhu -- m.; Si. koṭa ' jackal ', koṭiya ' leopard ' GS 42 (CDIAL 3615). कोल्हा [kōlhā] कोल्हें [kōlhēṃ] A jackal (Marathi) Rebus: **Ta. kol** working in iron, blacksmith; **kollan** blacksmith. **Ma. kollan** blacksmith, artificer. **Ko. kole·l** smithy, temple in Kota village. **To. kwala·l** Kota smithy. **Ka. kolime, kolume, kulame, kulime, kulume, kulme** fire-pit, furnace; (Bell.; U.P.U.) **konimi** blacksmith; (Gowda) **kolla** id. **Koḍ. kollë** blacksmith. **Te. kolimi** furnace. **Go.** (SR.) **kollusānā** to mend implements; (Ph.) **kolstānā, kulsānā** to forge; (Tr.) **kōlstānā** to repair (of ploughshares); (SR.) **kolmi** smithy (**Voc.** 948). **Kuwi** (F.) **kolhali** to forge (DEDR 2133) கொல்² **kol** Working in iron; கொற்றொழில். Blacksmith; கொல்லன். (Tamil)

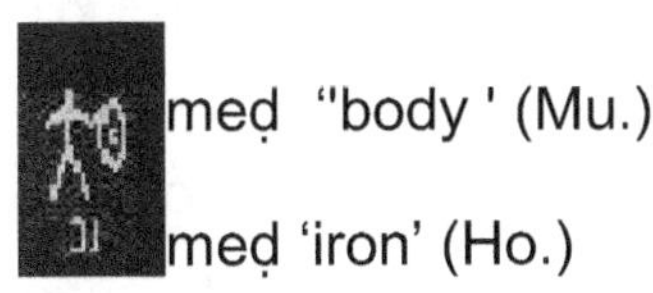

meḍ "body ' (Mu.)

meḍ 'iron' (Ho.)

The orthography of the body glyph shows the legs spread out indicating a man's pace. P. karo, °rū m. ' pace, a man's pace ', karo karo ' at each pace '; kráma m. ' step, series ' AV. ; Pa. kama -- m. ' step, way ', kamēna ' in succession '(CDIAL 3577) Rebus: khar 'blacksmith' (Kashmiri) Thus, the body glyph is decoded: meḍ karo 'man's pace'; rebus: meḍ khar 'iron smith'.

dhālako = a large metal ingot (G.) dhālakī = a metal heated and poured into a mould; a solid piece of metal; an ingot (G.) kol 'tiger'; rebus: kol 'working in iron'; kolami 'forge' (Te.). pattara 'trough'; rebus: vartaka 'merchant'. Hence, the seal is read rebus as: 'forged iron ingot merchant.'

Bos gaurus glyph

Text 2279 Person throwing a spear at a buffalo and placing one foot on the head of the buffalo. 2279 seal impression, Mohenjodaro (DK 8165); after Mackay 1938: pl.88, no.279

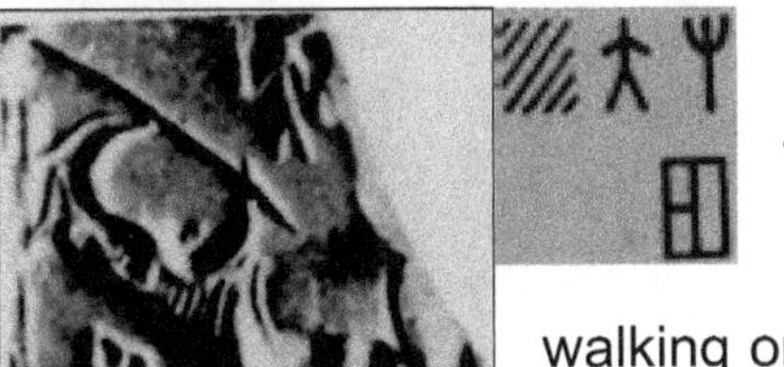

kolsa = to kick the foot forward, the foot to come into contact with anything when walking or running; **kolsa pasirkedan** = I kicked it over (Santali.lex.) **kola** =

killing, e.g. āḍukola = woman-slaying (Te.) Thus, **homa kola** = bison slaying. Rebus: **hom** = gold (Ka.) **kol** =metal (Ta.) **kol sal** 'iron workshop'. This glyhph on line 1 of the inscription on DK 8164 seal impression, could be a phonetic determinant: kwal.el 'smithy, temple in Kota village' (Ko.); kwala.l Kota smithy (To.)(DEDR 2133). Vikalpa: mēṛsa = v.a. toss, kick with the foot, hit with the tail (Santali.lex.) Rebus: mēṛh t iron; ispat m. = steel; dul m. = cast iron (Mu.); meḍ (Ho.) The glyptic scene is decoded rebus: **meḍ kol sal** 'iron, metal workshop'

sal[72] 'the Indian gaur, gaveus gaurus'; sal sakwa 'a horn made from a horn of the gaur' (Santali) சைரிபம் cairipam, n. < sairibha. buffalo; எருமை. (பிங்.) (Skt.Tamil)

m0312

Rebus: **sāl**[73] 'shed, workshop' (B.)(CDIAL 12414) **sal** 'house,

as in school house; shop, as in workshop (Santali)

baṭi[74] trs. To overturn, to overset or ovethrow; to turn or throw from a foundation or foothold (Santali) Rebus: **baṭi, bhaṭi** 'furnace' (H.)

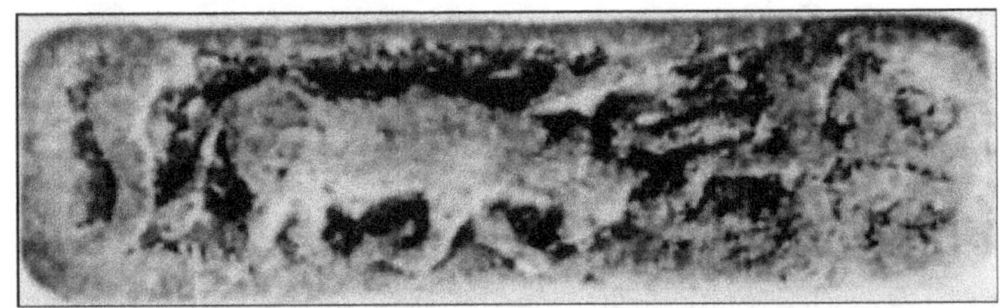

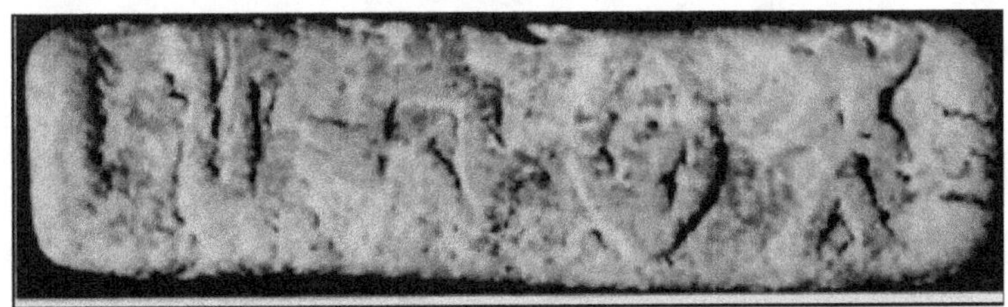

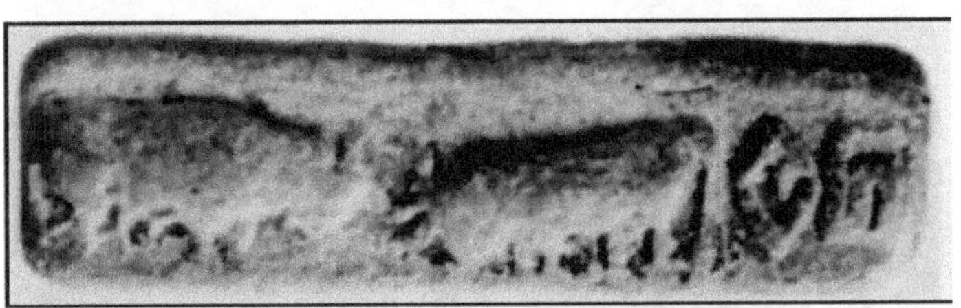

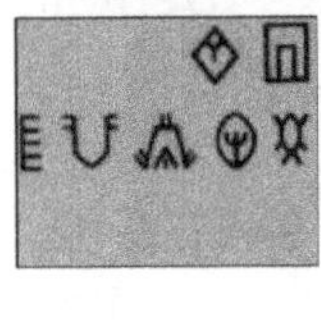

m0492A,B,C Pict-99: Person throwing a spear at a bison and placing one foot on the head of the bison; a hooded serpent at left.Two bisons standing face-to-face. Person spearing bison. A hooded serpent.

saman: = to offer an offering, to place in front of; front, to front or face (Santali) Rebus: **samr.obica**, stones containing gold(Mundari). nāga = snake (Skt.) Rebus: nāga = lead (Skt.)

Allograph

m1406 A, B Drummer, people tumbling over ḍangara, ḍangura public notice by a crier who beats a tom-tom (Ka.); ḍāngorā (M.);ḍangura (Te.);taṇḍora (Ta.); ḍavaṇḍī (M.) (Ka.)Rebus: ḍangar 'blacksmith' (H.) **baṭi** trs. To overturn, to overset or ovethrow (Santali) Rebus: **baṭi, bhaṭi** 'furnace' (H.)

k020 Glyphs: threaded beads + water-carrier. gota 'string'; rebus: **kotti** 'mason' (Ma.); goṭ 'assembly' (Santali) kuṭi 'water-carrier' (Te.); rebus: kuṭi 'smelter furnace' (Santali)

gotao to thread, to string; saire sutamko gotaca they thread

needles (Santali) Rebus: **goṭ**[75], goṭh The place where cattle are collected at mid-day; goṭ.ao, goṭ.hao to collect cattle together for their mid-day rest (Santali) Rebus: **kottan̠** a mason (Ta.) **kotti** pick-axe, stone-digger, carver (Ma.) (DEDR 2091) koḍ Artisans' workplace (G.) gotga.rn treasurer of the village (Ko.)(DEDR 2093) This sequence of chain of beads + rim-of-jar glyph survives on punch-marked coins.

Punchmarked coin. Fifth sign from left is a rimmed, short-necked jar (Sign 342, Daimabad seal, which has the most-frequent, 1,395 occurrences on epigraphs) kanda kanka 'rim of jar' (Santali); rebus: kan.d.a karn.aka 'fire-altar, accountant, family-head' (Skt.Ta.)

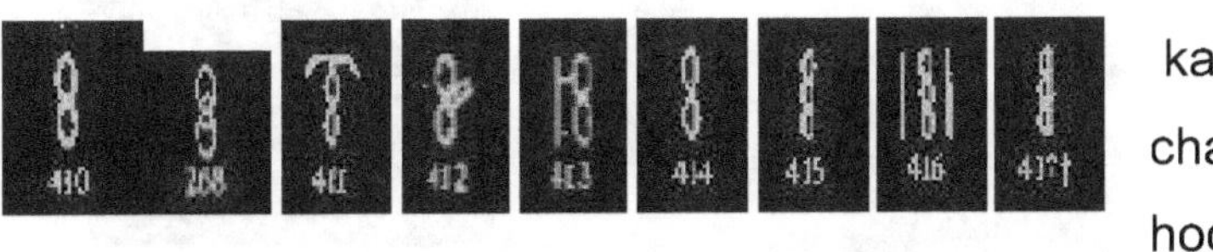

kaḍī a chain; a hook; a link (G.); kaḍum a bracelet, a ring (G.) Rebus: kaḍiyo [Hem. Des. kaḍaio = Skt. sthapati a mason] a bricklayer; a mason; kaḍiyaṇa, kaḍiyeṇa a woman of the bricklayer caste; a wife of a bricklayer (G.)

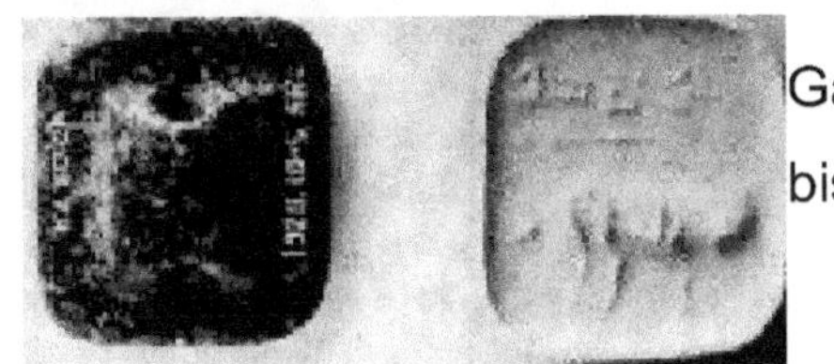

Gadd Seal 1 U7683 with bison & cuneiform

Sag-kusita ? 'Head moneylender' ?

Inscriptions on metal objects

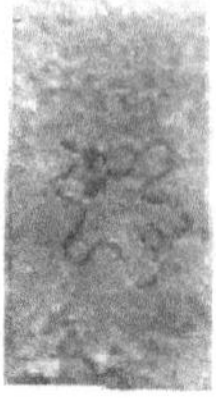

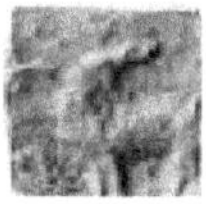

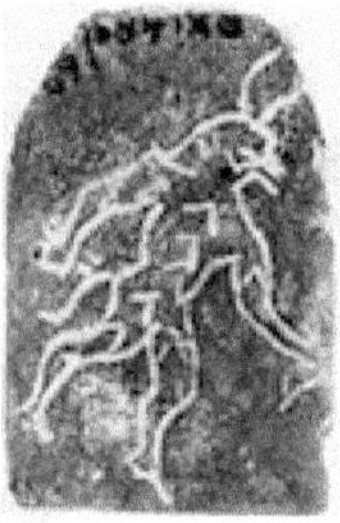

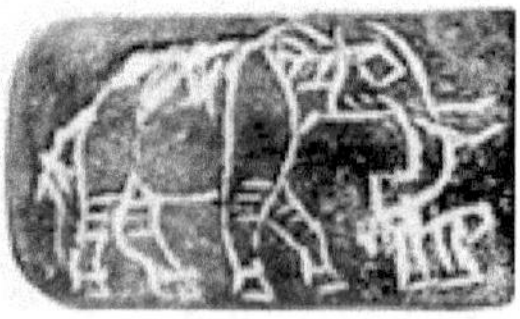

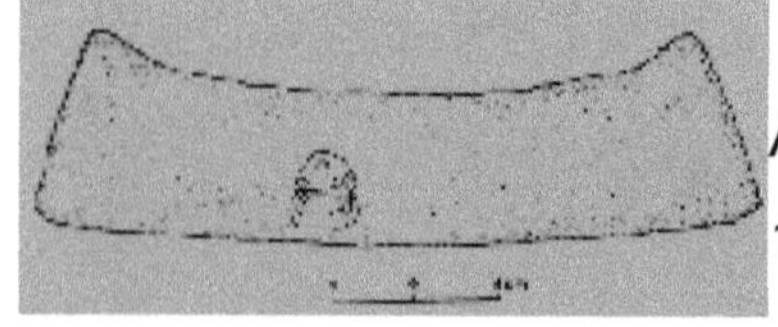

Ax-head or knife of copper, 17.4 cm. long

After Possehl and Raval 1989: 162, fig. 77; 8 cast copper tablets

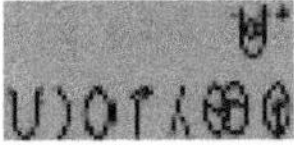

2925 Inscribed bronze implement(MIC Plate CXXVI-5

2903 Incised copper tablet

2923 Inscribed bronze implement(MIC Plat CXXVI-2)

recovered from circular platforms, Harappa (200); m0475; Silver seal 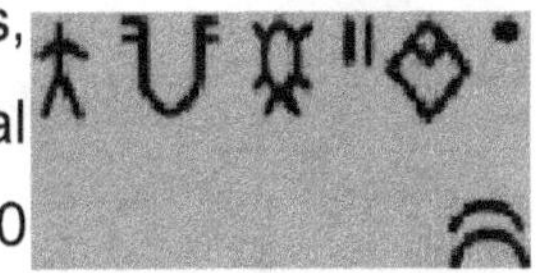 Mackay 1938, vol. 2, Pl. XC,1; XCVI, 520 ; Ras-al-Junayz copper seal; h018; copper seal, Mohenjodaro Indian museum;m0438;; m1449; ; m1452; m1486; m1493; m1498 m1501; m0582 (123 copper tablets)

  Mohenjo-daro. Copper tablet DK 11307 (SC 63.10/262); m0317silver; m1199 silver Harappa. Slide 209 inscribed lead celt

Schoyen collection MS565 copper seal

  h380-381 bronze daggers

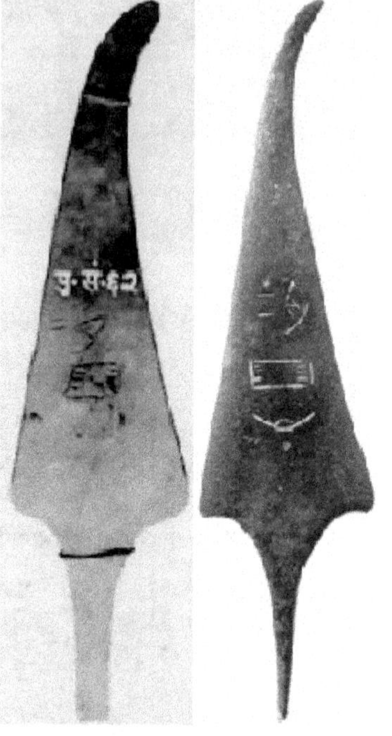

Inscribed weapons are further reported from Harappa Vats 1940: 384ss, Pl. CXX, 5,19), Chanhu Daro (Mackay 1943: 178, Pl. LXXIV, 1-1a,8) and Kalibangan inscribed bronze rod (Mahadevan 1977:7).

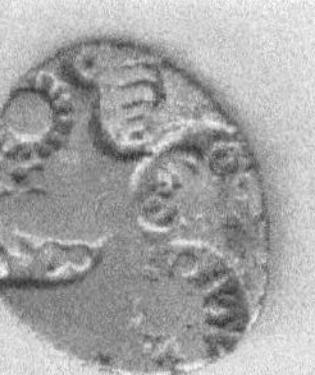 Chanhu-daro, Pl. LXXIV & Mohenjodaro: copper and bronze tools and utensils (an inscription line mirrored on a zebu seal)

 The glyph of sun's rays on an Indus seal continues to be used on punch-marked coins.

arka 'sun' (Skt.) CDIAL 624 Rebus: akka, arka (Tadbhava of arka) 'metal' (Ka.)][76]

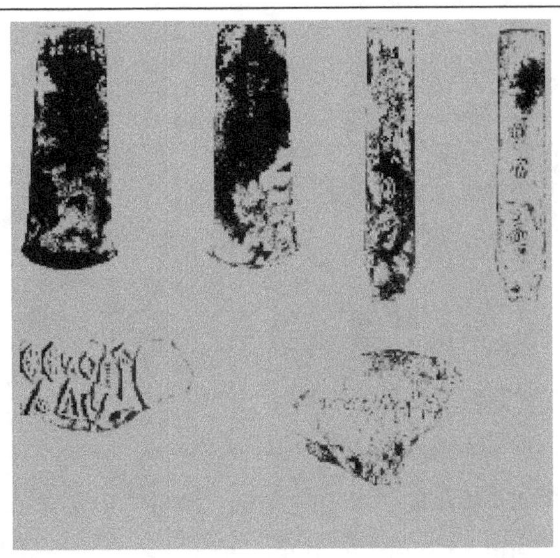

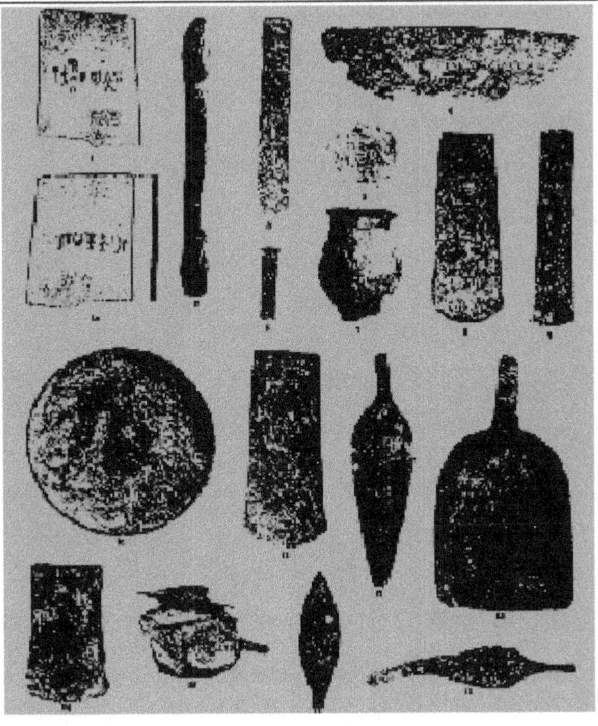

Potsherd from Bhirrana showing dance

Three dancers, m1428C

kolom 'three'(Mu.) meḍ 'body', 'dance' (Santali) மெட்டு¹-தல் meṭṭu-, *v. tr.* cf. நெட்டு-. [K. **meṭṭu**.] To spurn or push with the foot; காலால் தாக்குதல். நிகளத்தை மெட்டி மெட்டிப் பொடிபடுத்தி (பழனிப்பிள்ளைத். 12). (Tamil) meṭṭu 'to put or place down the foot or feet; to step, to pace, to walk (Ka.); meṭṭisu 'to cause to step or walk, to cause to tread on' (Ka.) meḍ 'dance' (Santali); meḍ 'iron' (Ho.)

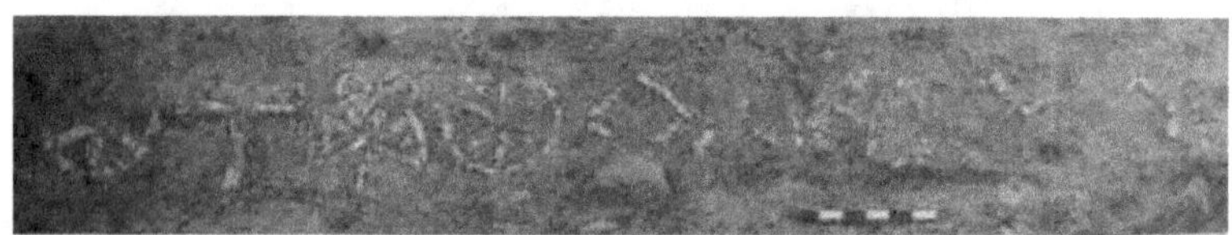

meḍ kolmo 'iron forge'.

Dholavira Sign-board

Dholavira (Kotda) on Kadir island, Kutch, Gujarat; 10 signs inscription found near the western chamber of the northern gate of the citadel high mound (Bisht, 1991: 81, Pl. IX); each sign is 37 cm. high and 25 to 27 cm. wide and made of pieces of white crystalline rock; the signs were apparently inlaid in a wooden plank ca. 3 m. long; maybe, the plank was mounted on the facade of the gate to command the view of the entire cityscape. Ten signs are read from left to right. The 'spoked circle' sign seems to be the divider of the three-part message. (Bisht, R.S., 1991, Dholavira: a new horizon of the Indus Civilization. Puratattva, Bulletin of Indian Archaeological Society, 20: 81; now also Parpola 1994: 113).

Dholavira: Inscribed sign-board found on the floor of a side room in the north gateway (ASI)

Dholavira sign-board on the Gateway of the citadel. Mounted on the façade of the gate, the sign-board would have commanded the entire cityscape.

· Each of the ten signs 37cm. high, is made of crystalline rock.

· The wooden plank is about 3 m. long.

· Bottom: Close up of the first three signs from left to right.

· The 'spoked-wheel' sign seems to be the divider of a

three-part message.

Hypothesis: Three types of metallurgical services are announced.

 This glyph occurs four times on the inscription of Dholavira sign board.

The message, read rebus:

molten

Dholavira Sign board mounted on gate to announce to seafarers: cast furnace, mint, moltencast brass, copperwork, native-metalwork, silver; metal-caster-mineral (metal)-smith

era = knave of wheel; rebus: era = copper; erako = molten cast (G.) eraka, (copper) 'metal infusion'; āra 'spokes'; rebus: āra 'brass' as in ārakūṭa (Skt.)

kund opening in the nave or hub of a wheel to admit the axle (Santali) Rebus: kundam, kund a sacrificial fire-pit (Skt.) kunda 'turner' kundār turner (A.); kũdār, kũdāri (B.); kundāru (Or.); kundau to turn on a lathe, to carve, to chase; kundau dhiri = a hewn stone; kundau murhut = a graven image (Santali) kunda a turner's lathe (Skt.)(CDIAL

 3295) Vikalpa: era, er-a = eraka = ?nave; erako_lu = the iron axle of a carriage (Ka.M.); cf. irasu (Ka.lex.) [Note Sign 391 and its ligatures Signs 392 and 393 may connote a spoked-wheel, nave of the wheel through which the axle passes; cf. ara_, spoke] ஆரம்² āram , n. < āra. 1. Spoke of a wheel. See ஆரக்கால். ஆரஞ்சூழ்ந்த வயில்வாய் நேமியொடு (சிறுபாண். 253) (Tamil)

 kamaḍha = ficus religiosa (Skt.); kamar.kom 'ficus' (Santali) rebus: kamaṭa = portable furnace for melting precious metals (Te.); kampaṭṭam = mint (Ta.) Vikalpa: Fig leaf 'loa'; rebus: loh '(copper) metal'. loha-kāra 'metalsmith' (Skt.).

kana, kanac = corner (Santali); kañcu = bronze (Te.) kan- copper work (Ta.)

aḍaren, ḍaren lid, cover (Santali) Rebus: aduru 'native metal' (Ka.)

goṭ = one (Santali); goṭi = silver (G.) koḍa 'one'(Santali); koḍ 'workshop' (G.)

 A pair of glyphs showing spokes and nave: dula 'pair' (Santali); rebus: dul 'cast (metal)' (Santali) Vikalpa: barea = two (Ka.); baṛea = blacksmith

(Santali)[A pair of glyphs showing nave of wheel, i.e. metal-caster-smith] kundār turner (A.); kũdār, kũdāri (B.); kundāru (Or.); kundau to turn on a lathe, to carve, to chase; kundau dhiri = a hewn stone; kundau murhut = a graven image (Santali) kunda a turner's lathe (Skt.)(CDIAL 3295)

 dato[77] = claws of crab (Santali); dhātu = mineral (Skt.)

 Peg 'khunta[78]'; rebus: kūṭa 'workshop' khu~ṭi = pin (M.) kuṭi= smelter furnace (Santali)

The three-part message is read rebus:

 eraka-aara-kunda 'molten cast copper, brass turner'; pacar 'peg'; pasra 'smithy'; loa 'fig'; loha 'copper' kundār turner (A.); kũdār, kũdāri (B.); kundāru (Or.); kundau to turn on a lathe, to carve, to chase; kundau dhiri = a hewn stone; kundau murhut = a graven image (Santali) kunda a turner's lathe (Skt.)(CDIAL 3295)

1. Copper, brass, molten-cast turner, smithy

 eraka- āra-kunda 'molten cast copper, brass turner'; kanac 'corner'; kancu 'bronze'; adaren 'lid'; aduru 'native metal'; goṭ 'one'; goṭ 'silver'; koḍa 'one'(Santali); koḍ 'workshop' (G.) kundār turner (A.); kũdār, kũdāri (B.); kundāru (Or.); kundau to turn on a lathe,

to carve, to chase; kundau dhiri = a hewn stone; kundau murhut = a graven image (Santali) kunda a turner's lathe (Skt.)(CDIAL 3295) Grapheme (Sign 261): *khuṇṭa2 ' corner '. 2. *kuṇṭa -- 2. [Cf. *khōñca --] 1. Phal. khun ' corner '; H. khūṭ m. ' corner, direction ' (→ P. khūṭ f. ' corner, side '); G. khūṭrī f. ' angle '. <-> X kōṇa -- : G. khuṇ f., khū˘ṇɔ m. ' corner '.2. S. kuṇḍa f. ' corner '; P. kūṭ f. ' corner, side ' (← H.). (CDIAL 3898)

2. Silver, native metal, bronze, copper, brass turner

dula eraka 'pair, nave of wheel'; aara 'spokes'; dul 'cast metal'; eraka-aara 'molten cast copper, brass turner'; daṭo 'claws'; dhatu 'mineral' kundār turner (A.); kũdār, kũdāri (B.); kundāru (Or.); kundau to turn on a lathe, to carve, to chase; kundau dhiri = a hewn stone; kundau murhut = a graven image (Santali) kunda a turner's lathe (Skt.)(CDIAL 3295)

3. Mineral, copper, brass turner

Bird hieroglyph

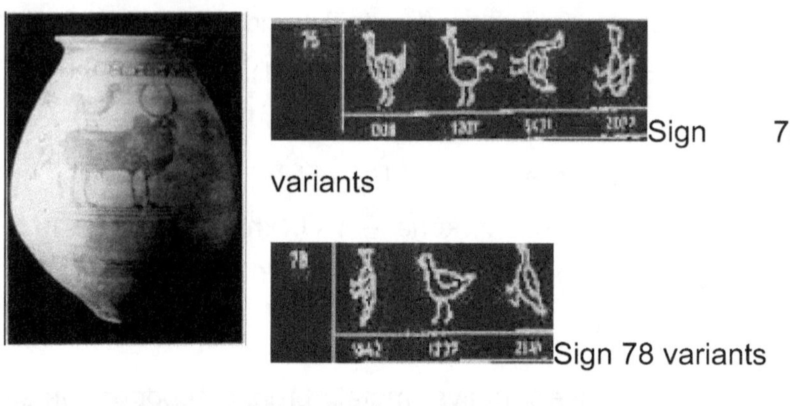

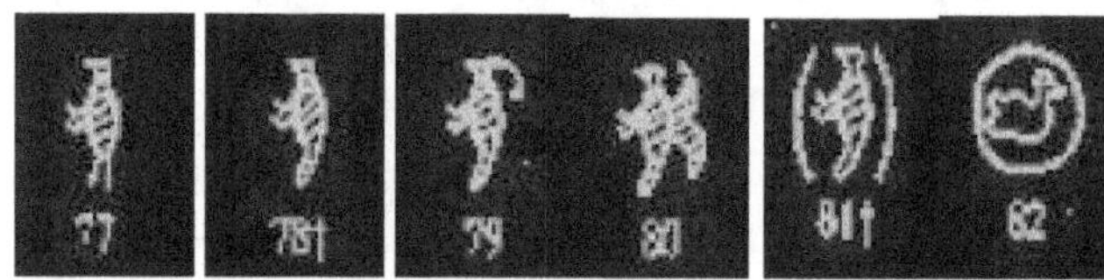Sign 76 variants

Sign 78 variants

A zebu bull tied to a post; a bird above. Large paintedstorage jar discovered in burned rooms at Nausharo, ca. 2600 to 2500 BCE. Cf. Fig. 2.18, J.M. Kenoyer, 1998, Cat. No. 8.

Tell Suleimeh Cylinder seal[79]. A fish over a short-horned bull and a bird over a one-horned bull; cylinder seal impression, (Akkadian to early Old Babylonian).

'Backbone' glyph in context

kaśēru 'the backbone' (Bengali. Skt.); **kaśēru**ka id. (Skt.) Rebus: **kasērā**' metal worker ' (Lahnda)(CDIAL 2988, 2989)

Sign 47 and variants

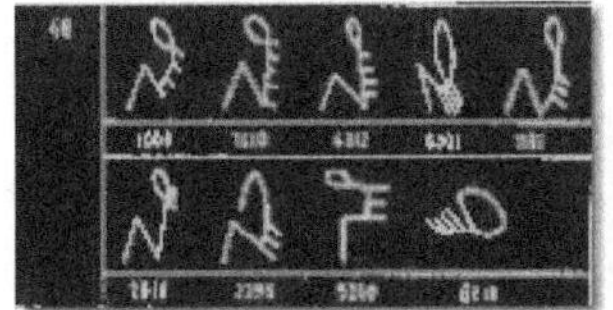

Kalibangan048 Sanur, Tamilnadu Megalithic pottery

Kalibangan 100 potsherd.

Kalibangan

048 "The seated person is facing right (in the original seal), leaning forward. He has a large head and a massive jaw jutting forward. The complete ribcage is shown in clear detail with almost all the ribs in position, curving naturalistically on either side of the backbone. The deity appears to be holding a ladle (?) in his right hand. His knees are drawn up

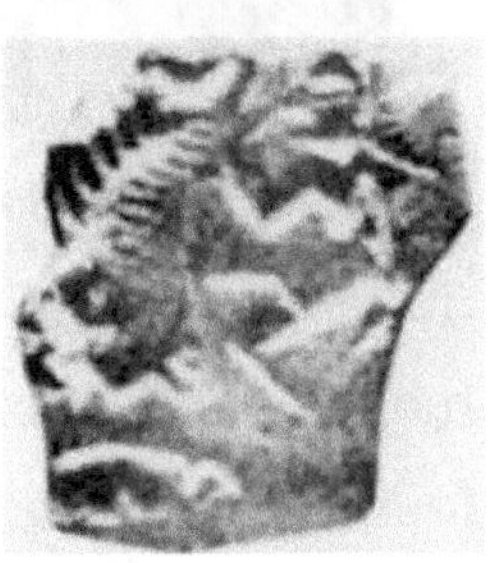

and he seems to be squatting on his haunches.

The details are clearly visible in the highly enlarged photograph of the seal published by Omananda Saraswati.[80]

Inscription on copper plate (one side; the other side shows a bull glyph)

The glyph, third from right, can be distinguished from Sign 47

h1827A This three-sign-sequence tablet is of frequent occurrence, again showing the back-bone glyph.

This sign sequence can also be seen on Slide 205 (harappa.com) faience tablet or standard. This unique mold-made faience tablet or standard (H2000-4483/2342-01) was found in the eroded levels west of the tablet workshop in Trench 54. On one side is a short inscription under a rectangular box filled with 24 dots (or one pair of glyphs with12 dots each). The reverse has a glyptic composition with two bulls face-to-face (or,likeness mirror-imaged) under a thorny, leafless tree.

Side 1: Glyph: ḍhaṁkhara[81]-- m.n. ' branch without leaves or fruit (Pkt.) 'Rebus: ḍangar 'blacksmith' (H.) The leafless tree thus becomes a phonetic determinant of the 'bull' glyph: ḍangar 'bull'. The mirror-reflected reduplication: dula 'pair,

likeness' (Kashmiri); Rebus: dul 'casting (metal)' (Santali) kuṭi 'tree'; Rebus: kuṭhi 'smelter'. kuṭhi'smelting furnace'; **koṭe**[82] forged metal' (Santali) Thus the glyptic composition reads: dul kuṭhi ḍangar 'casting furnace blacksmith'. **saman:** = to offer an offering, to place in front of; front, to front or face (Santali) Rebus: **samr.obica,** stones containing gold(Mundari). It is a lapidary-smith's gold furnace.

Side 2: Glyph on the top register shows a pair of 12 dots. **talka** 'palm of the hand (with twelve phalanges on four fingers); Rebus: **talika** 'inventory, list of articles'. The four glyhphs (signs) in sequence can be read:

ayo 'fish' (Mu.); rebus: **aya** 'metal' (G.)

kōṇṭa corner (Nk.); Tu. **kōṇṭu** angle, corner (Tu.); Rebus: **kōḍā** 'to turn in a lathe' (B.) 'Ligattured glyph read rebus: 'iron turned in lathe'.

- **kaṇḍ kanka** 'rim of jar'; Rebus: **kaṇḍ karṇaka** 'furnace scribe'. Vikalpa: **kaṇḍ** kanaka 'gold furnace'.

- **kāmsako, kāmsiyo** = a large sized comb (G.) Rebus: kaṁsa= bronze (Te.)

Sign 47 shows the spine; Sign 48 shows the ribs of backbone.

Glyph Sign 48: **kaśēru** 'the backbone' (Bengali. Skt.); **kaśēru**ka id. (Skt.) Rebus: **kasērā**' metal worker ' (Lahnda)(CDIAL 2988, 2989)

The arrow sign terminates 184 inscriptions (out of a total of 227 inscriptions in which the sign occurs)

kaṇḍa 'arrow'; kaṇḍ = a furnace, altar (Santali) Text 4129: **kasērā kaṇḍ** metal (brass) furnace.

Grapheme:

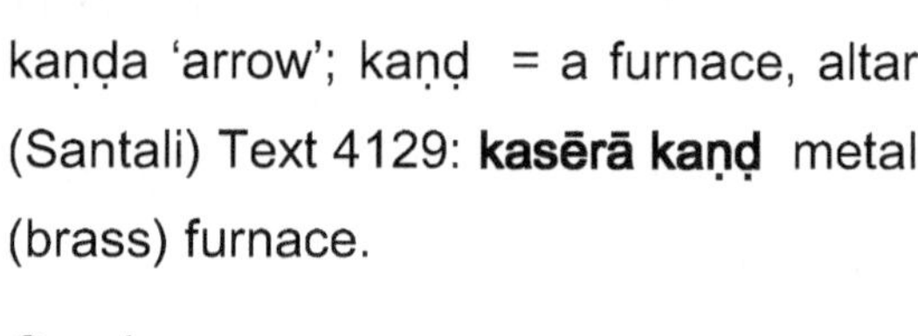

Tepe Yahya. Seal impression. Six-legged lizard and opposing footprints shown on opposing sides of a double-sided steatite stamp seal perforated along the lateral axis. Lamberg- Karlovsky 1971: fig. 2C Six legs of a lizard is an enumeration of six 'portable furnaces' ; rebus: **kakra.** 'lizard'; **kan:gra** 'portable furnace'. That an enumeration is intended is seen from the glyph of a pair of soles depicted on the obverse side of the seal from Tepe Yahya read rebusas : **talika**[83] 'inventory, list of articles'.

Decoding Kalibangan cylinder seal glyphs

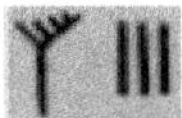 Text 8024 Kalibangan 065a

 A tree; a person with a composite body of a human (female?) in the upper half and body of a tiger in the lower half, having horns, and a tridentlike headdress, facing a group of three persons consisting of a woman (?) in the middle flanked by two men on either side throwing a spear at each other (fencing?) over her head.

Text glyphs: kolmo 'three'; rebus: kolami 'forge, smithy' (Te.) pajhar[84] = to sprout from a root (Santali); Rebus: pasra[85] 'smithy, forge' (Santali)

Glyph: kola 'woman' (Nahali); kolami 'forge' (Te.).**kolhe**[86] 'iron smelter' (Santali) Phonetic determinant glyph: kola[87], kōlu 'jackal, jackal' (Kon.Telugu) dhatu 'scarf'; rebus: dhatu 'mineral' (Santali) Glyph: horns with twig[88]. 'koḍ 'horn' (Pa.); rebus: kod. 'artisan's workshop' (Kuwi) Go. (A.) kōla id.; kōlā (Tr.) a thin twig or stick, esp. for kindling a fire, (DEDR 2237) Thus, kōla 'twig' is also a phonetic determinant to denote kolami 'forge'.

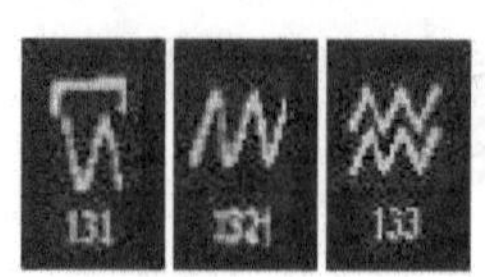 karaṭi[89] 'fencing'(DEDR 1262); Rebus; kharādī[90] 'turner' (G.)

కరడము [karaḍamu] or కరడు or కరుడు karaḍamu. [Tel.] n. A wave. (Telugu) kharaḍakum = a streamlet (G.) Rebus: kharādī = turner (G.) Vikalpa: rītí1 f. ' stream ' RV.[91]

Scarf as a glyptic element

Terracotta tablet, Marshall 1931, Pl. CXVIII,9 scarf (on

 pigtail)

Mohenjo-daro.   A procession depicted on a terracotta tablet. [After Marshall

  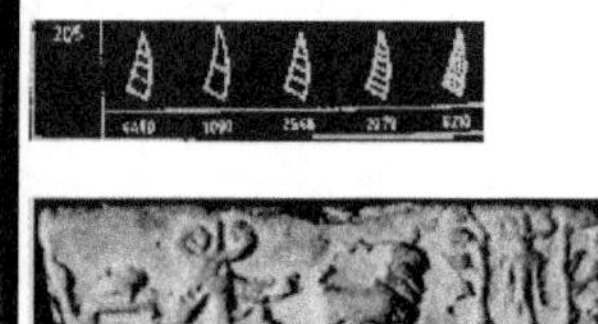

1931, Pl. CXVIII,9]

Standard device glyph

san:gaḍa, 'lathe, portable furnace'; rebus: battle; jangaḍiyo 'military guard who accompanies treasure into the treasury' (G.) Rebus: sanghāḍo (G.) cutting stone, gilding (G.); san:gatarāśū = stone cutter; san:gatarāśi = stone-cutting;

san:gsāru karan.u = to stone (S.) san:ghāḍiyo, a worker on a lathe (G.)

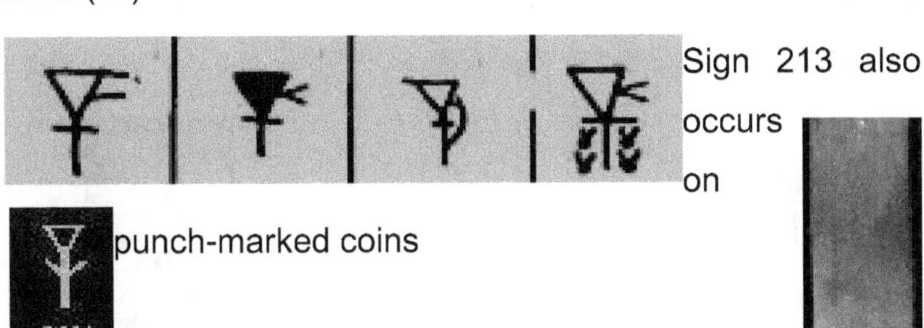

Sign 213 also occurs on punch-marked coins

There are a number of glyptic elements on this ligatured device normally shown in front of the one-horned heifer.

1. lathe in a turning motion on the top register

2. gimlet

3. smoke emanating from the bottom register portable furnace

4. dotted circles inscribed on the portable furnace.

śagaḍī (G.) = lathe san:gāḍo a lathe; sa~ghāḍ.iyo a worker on a lathe (G.lex.) sa~gaḍ part of a turner's apparatus (M.); sā~gāḍī lathe (Tu.)(CDIAL 12859). sāṅgaḍa That member of a turner's apparatus by which the piece to be turned is confined and steadied. सांगडीस धरणें To take into linkedness or close connection with, lit. fig. (Marathi) सांगाडी [sāṅgāḍī] f The machine within which a turner confines and steadies the piece he has to turn. (Marathi)

सगडी [sagaḍī] f (Commonly शेगडी) A pan of live coals or embers. (Marathi) san:ghāḍo, saghaḍī (G.) = firepan; saghaḍī, śaghaḍi = a pot for holding fire (G.)[culā sagaḍī portable hearth (G.)]

h196b tablet portable furnace carried on shoulder

Pict-123 Standard device which is normally in front of a one-

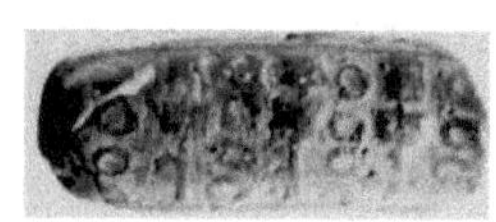

horned bull. The device is flanked by columns of dotted circles. The dotted circles are an indication of 'perforation' by the gimlet.

m0008, m0021, h228B

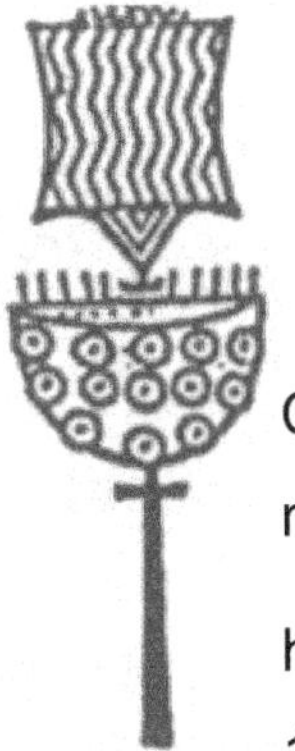  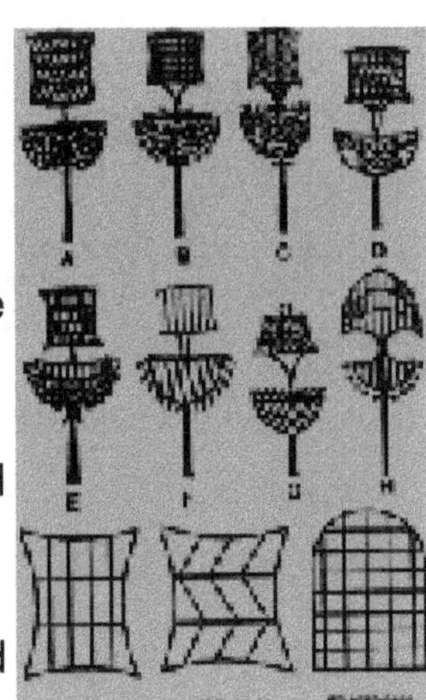

Carved Ivory Standard in the middle

har501 Harappa 1990 and 1993.

Standard device, model reconstructed after Mahadevan

m1203A •Note the gimlet precisely indicated on the standard device on m1203A, the sharp point is drilling into a disc-shaped

bead].

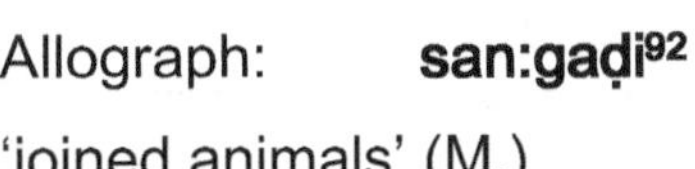

Allograph: **san:gaḍi[92]** 'joined animals' (M.)

Dwaraka śankha seal (joined animals) M1169a, m1170, m1171

m417   six   heads   from   a   core

m0298 Two bovine heads on one body + fish

K043 Three bovid heads on one body

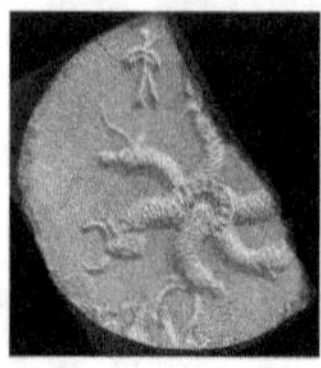  

Rebus: sanghāḍo[93] (G.) = cutting stone, gilding; san:gatarāśū = stone cutter; san:gatarāśi = stone-cutting; san:gsāru karan.u = to stone (S.), can:katam = to scrape (Ta.), san:kaḍa (Tu.), san:kaṭam = to scrape (Skt.)

m1430C, body of bison, three heads: bison, antelope, bull; a pair of goat(s), tree

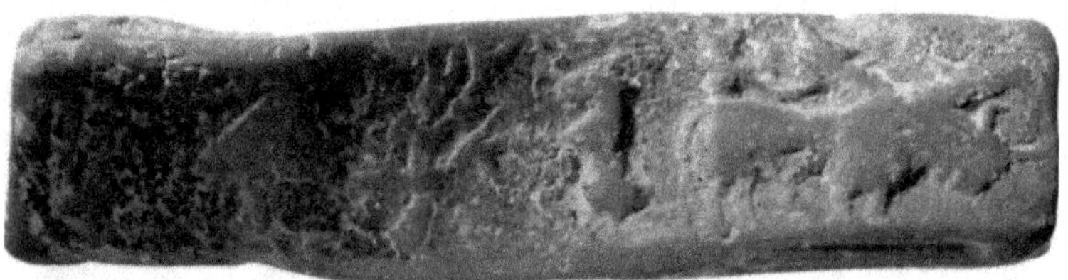

bison, bos gaurus 'sal'; rebus: sal 'workshop' (Santali)

mẽḍha 'antelope'; rebus: meḍ 'iron' (Ho.) ḍangar 'bull' ḍangar 'blacksmith'.

Structure of the Corpus of inscriptions

This references to pictorial motifs are based the corpus of Indus Seals and Inscriptions (CISI) and the citations of seals refer to this corpus (CISI, 3 vols., 1987, 1991, 2010). Script signs and texts of inscriptions are based on Mahadevan

(Mahadevan, 1977). BB Lal's work points out the essential continuity of cultural traits in India, with particular reference to the re-discovery of River Sarasvati basin which accounts for the majority of civilization archaeological sites. (Lal, 2002).

CISI vols. 1, 2 and 3 contain a corpus of 4984 inscriptions. Adding inscriptions collected and kept outside India and Pakistan and inscriptions discovered in excavations at sites such as Bhirrana, Famana, Kanmer, the total Indus inscriptions are likely to be about 5,200. About 300 inscriptions are composed of either one sign or two signs. There are about 10 inscriptions which contain only pictorial motifs (without any sign). Seppo Koskenniemi et al (1973) had observed that there were over 170 inscriptions with only one sign (in addition to the field symbol); about 30 inscriptions had only two signs. Many pictorials in inscriptions in field symbols also occur in pairs: two tigers, two bison, and two heads of the unicorn. Many signs occur in predictable pairs; 57 pair wise combinations account for a total frequency of 3154 occurrences (32% of 9798 occurrences of all pair wise combinations). Given the statistical evidence that the average length of a text is 5 signs, it is apparent that one sign or a pair of signs represents a 'substantive category' of information, i.e., a complete message. In addition to the field symbol (or, pictorial motif), the texts of the inscriptions are composed of an average of five signs. The longest inscription has 26 signs (found on two identical three-sided tablets: M-494 and M-495 of Parpola corpus). These statistics lead to the following reasonable assumptions:

 A combination of pictorials without the use of any sign constitutes the message.

One or two signs and/or a pair of signs are adequate to compose the core of the messages.

The solus sign or each sign in pair wise combinations (which constitute the core of information conveyed) is not an alphabet or a syllable, but a WORD.

As Koskenniemi et al note: "... the Indus script is in all likelihood a relatively crude morphemographic writing system. The graphemes would usually stand for the lexical morphemes... This hypothesis is based on the approximate date this writing system was created (circa 26th century B.C.), the parallel presented by the Sumerian writing system of that time (the Fara texts of the 26th century), the brevity of recurring combinations, and the number of different graphemes." [Koskenniemi and Parpola (1982)].

Another echo is found in the structural analysis of Mahadevan: "G.R. Hunter (1934, p. 126) formulated a set of criteria for segmentation of the texts and found that almost every sign of common occurrence functioned as a single word.

"The Soviet group Probst et al (1965) analyzed texts on the computer and concluded that the Indus script is essentially morphemic in character, resembling the Egyptian hieroglyphic system in this respect. I have described the logical word-division procedures developed by me [Mahadevan (1978, p.34)], which show that most of the signs of the Indus script are word-signs... no one has so far been able to establish by objective analytical procedures the existence of purely phonetic syllabic signs in the Indus script... Phonograms formed by the rebus principle can be recognized only if the underlying language is known or assumed as a working hypothesis. Since the identity of the Harappan language has not yet been established beyond doubt, I cannot be said that any phonogram has been recognized with certainty... It is however very likely that there are rebus-based phonograms in the Indus script, as otherwise, it is very difficult to account for the presence of such unlikely objects such as the fish, birds, animals and insects in what are most probably names and titles on the seal-texts. It is likely that the Indus script resembles in this respect the Egyptian scrip in which pictographic signs serve as phonetic signs based on the rebus principle (e.g. the picture of a 'goose' stands for 'son' as the two words are homonymous in the Egyptian language). It is no always possible in the present state of our knowledge to distinguish between ideograms and phonograms..." (Mahadevan, 1966, pp. 18-19).

That the corpus of glyphs points to an underlying language is also argued by RPN Rao et al. using a Markov model:[94] "Although no historical information exists about the Indus civilization (flourishedca. 2600–1900 B.C.), archaeologists have uncovered about 3,800 short samples of a script that was used throughout the civilization. The script remains undeciphered, despite a large number of attempts and claimed decipherments over the past 80 years. Here, we propose the use of probabilistic models to analyze the structure of the Indus script. The goal is to reveal, through probabilistic analysis, syntactic patterns that could point the way to eventual decipherment. We illustrate the approach using a simple Markov chain model to capture sequential dependencies between signs in the Indus script. The trained model allows new sample texts to be generated, revealing recurring patterns of signs that could potentially form functional subunits of a possible underlying language. The model also provides a quantitative way of testing whether a particular string belongs to the putative language as captured by the Markov model. Application of this test to Indus seals found in Mesopotamia and other sites in West Asia reveals that the script may have been used to express different content in these regions. Finally, we show how missing, ambiguous, or unreadable signs on damaged objects can be filled in with most likely predictions from the model. Taken together, our results indicate that the Indus script exhibits rich syntactic structure and the ability to represent diverse content. Both of which are suggestive of a linguistic writing system rather than a nonlinguistic symbol system."[95]

Kenoyer and Meadow[96] refer to decipherment of the Indus script as an 'unattainable goal' : " [(Farmer, Sproat and Witzel (2004)] They argue that the Indus script is not likely to have been linked directly to a spoken language and was probably a system of non-linguistic symbols, Wem however, contend that given the development in the system of inscriptions over time as seen at Harappa and given the extensive use of the 'signs' or 'symbols' both formally and informally and on many media (see text discussion), making the distinction between a language-based script and a not-so-tied-to-language symboling system is not a particularly interesting distinction. In any event, in the absence of multi-lingual texts, long texts, and/or a successor symboling system or script, there can be no widely accepted understanding of what the symbols or signs of the 'Indus script' actually meant to those who employed them, and thus there can be no true resolution of this issue…In our opinion, too much scholarly (and lay) emphasis has been placed on the unattainable goal of decipherment of the Indus script and not enough on treating seals, tablets, and other inscribed materials as archaeological finds that went through processes of materials selection, production, use and discard." Parpola disagrees: "There are great difficulties, it is true – above all the total lack of bi- or multilingual texts, which have provided the key to most of the successfully deciphered forgottenscripts. A full decipherment of the script is admittedly impossible with the present materials. Yet, if the Indus script is of the same logo-syllabic type as all the other writing systems that were in existence by 2400 BCE, a partial decipherment can be achieved, provided the language underlying the script belonged to a language family known from other sources, as seems to be the case – after all, the Harappan population is estimated to have been around one million. Language-based logo-syllabic type of writing was first invented in the Late Uruk period (c. 3500-3100 BCE) in southern Metopotamia, from where the idea of writing spread to Proto-Elamite western Iran (c. 3200-2900 BCE) and by 3200 BCE also to Pre-Dynastic Egypt. The

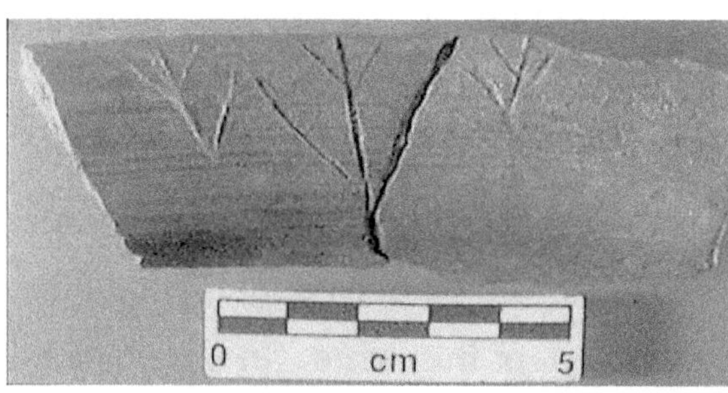

Indus Civilization (c. 2600-1900 BCE) was the fourth oldest culture of the world to have a script of its own. The HARP excavations suggest that the Indus script – distinct from the pot marks already employed during the preceding period – was created during the Early Harappan Kot-Diji phase (c. 2800-2600 BCE)[97]

The origins of Indus writing can now be traced to the Ravi Phase (c. 3300-2800 BC) at Harappa. Some inscriptions were made on the bottom of the pottery before firing. Other inscriptions such as this one were made after firing. This inscription (c. 3300 BC) appears to be three plant symbols arranged to appear almost anthropomorphic. The trident looking projections on these symbols seem to set the foundation for later symbols... (Slide 124 Harappa.com) An Early Harappan: Ravi phase inscribed potsherd (H-1522A) contains a symbol which is comparable to the later evolved sign of Indus script. This phase is dated to c. 3700 -2800 BCE. If this is evidence of an Indus script inscription, Indus script could be chronologically dated as an early writing system, coterminous with the Late Uruk period (c. 3500-3100 BCE) in southern Metopotamia. This inscription can be called a 'graphic expression using a symbol.'

Inclusion of the inscribed material from Harappa excavations between 1986-2007 is a significant advancement of understanding of the evolution of the script. As Kenoyer and Meadow note: "When both seal carving styles and boss types are considered together, there is good evidence for an evolution in seal forms over time. Whether there were parallel changes in the script needs to be investigated in detail. In the past, studies of the Indus script have lumped all of the best-preserved seal impressions together and used this combined assemblage as the basis for a study of the script. Based on the discoveries at Harappa, it is now possible for that site at least to separate out different chronological periods of seal production and to compare seal inscriptions with those found on other types of objects such as incised and molded tablets and pottery, which together greatly outnumber the seals and seal impressions recovered from the site."[98] That incised and molded tablets and pottery inscriptions outnumbered the seals is significant, indeed. They point to the use of Indus writing by a group of artisans within a guild; the incised and molded tablets were, perhaps, identical professional identity cards of the artisans of guilds.

Some remarkably exquisite photographs have been included in the CISI volume 3 Part 1(though many of the incised and molded tablets have already been published earlier by the HARP team; cf. slides on harappa.com)
This is one example of ten identical tablets with four molded sides (h2023 to h2032). From this set, some sides can be shown with clarity to enable the reading of the inscription with reasonable precision and avoiding ambiguity.

Pictures of various tablets thus show an inscription with 5 signs on one side (including an antelope with a tail ending in a rice-plant glyph); the glyph of a horned, standing person with horns and bangles on the arms on the second side; two persons wearing bangles seated on stools on the third side (with one of the two seated in a penance posture); and a person on all-fours, bent down facing the bos gaurus (bison) on the fourth side. Thanks to the excellent photographic production achieved in this volume, Parpola et al have indeed contributed to a better reading of the glyptic elements depicted on inscribed objects. Of significance are he photographs of the following seals depicted for the first time in any corpus:

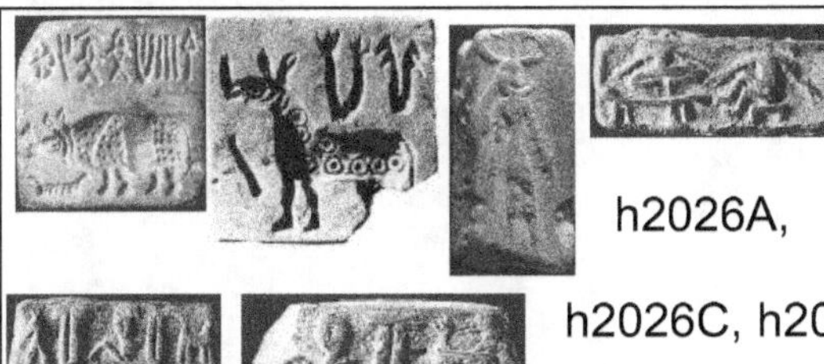

h2026A, h2031A, h2028D, h2026C, h2026D m1908A, m1906A (The rhinoceros seal m1906 is taken from photo archive of ASI, Sind series, vol. 12 91926-27), no. 542).

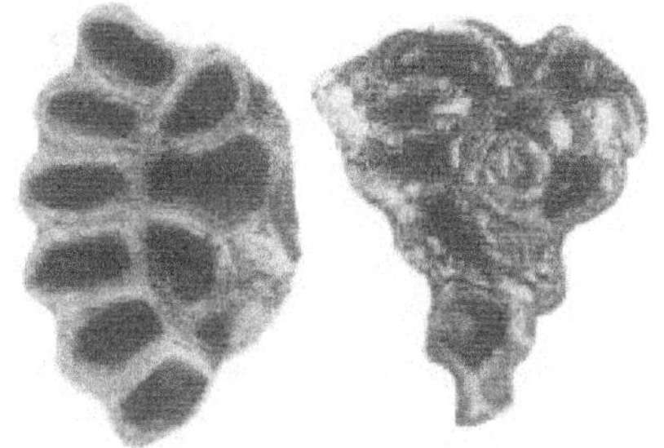

The volume also includes an essay by Ute Franke, with an extensive bibliography. She provides clear pictures of the two compartmented seals from Mohenjo-daro. "The dome-shaped head, the eye and a nostril are easily discernable. It seems that a bell is depicted below the head. Two small horns are shown en face. On the right, an ear might be visible. Judging from the physiognomy, the depiction seems to be that of a small calf...it might rather be a short-horned bull... (compartmented seals) their presence is important evidence for long distance trade interaction at a time when Margiana was emerging as a new center."[99]

To show this interaction for trade, the Mohenjodarro compartmented seal showing a bull calf is compared with other such seals:

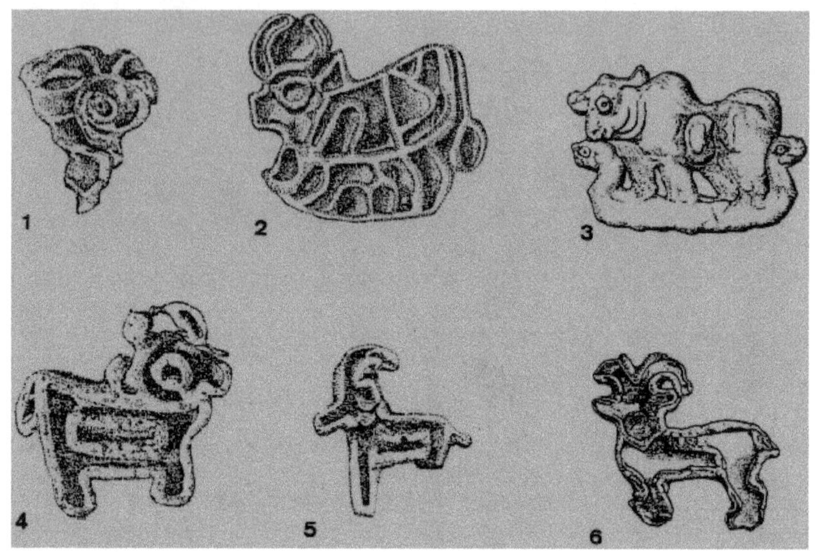

Seals and copper tablets. (1) Compartmented seal fragment from Mohenjo-daro (MIC, pl. CLVIII:3) (2) Seal from Nausharo (CISI 2, NS-1); (3) Silver seal from Bactria (Sarianidi, 1986: 292) (4) Seal from Altyn Depe (Masson, 1988, p[l. XXIX:9); (5) Seal from Altyn Depe (Masson, 1988, pl. XVII:14 (6) Seal, Kelleli (Sarianidi, 1986: 293).

Another welcome addition in this volume 3.1 of the Corpus is the depiction, in brilliant color photographs, of some earlier published (CISI 1,2) inscribed objects. Scholars engaged in Indus script studies owe a deep sense of gratitude to the authors Asko Parpola, BM Pande and Petteri Koskikallio for producing this volume with numbers ranging from m1660 to m2132 and h1020 to h2590 – an addition of 472 and 1570 inscriptions, respectively from Mohenjo-daro and Harappa to the corpus of Indus script inscriptions, including a large number of incised potsherds and incised/molded tablets from HARP excavations of 1986-2007. Hopefully, Part 2 of the volume with inscribed objects outside India and Pakistan will be brought out soon, including many new objects discovered in sites outside of Mohenjo-daro and Harappa, in sites such as Bhirrana, Farmana, Kanmer, Gola Dhoro – sites in the proximity of the Sarasvati river basin.

That Sarasvati was a more important river than the Sindhu may be noted from the following observations of John Marshall (1931, pp. 1-6): "(Mohenjo-daro) stands on what is known locally as the 'The Island'-a long, narrow strip of land between the main river bed and the Western Nara lop, its precise position being 27.19N by 68.8E, some 7 miles by road from Dokri... Twelve centuries ago, when the Arabs first came to Sind, there were two great rivers flowing through the land: to the west, the Indus: to the east, the Great Mihran, also known as the Hakra or Wahindah. Of these two rivers, the eastern one seems to have been the more important... Major Raverty, the foremost authority on the subject, concluded that at the time of the Arab invasion the main channel of the Great Mihran flowed a line roughly coincident with the existing Eastern Nara canal, which was once an important rive rbed (i.e. it passed close by the city of Alor...flowed...west of Umarkot, and so the Rann of Cutch (then an estuary of the sea) and by the Kori creek to the Arabian Sea. Cf. Raverty, The Mihran of Sind, and its tributaries, JASB, Vol. LXI, 1892, pp. 156-508). According to him, the terminal course of the Indus, which flows by Mohenjo-daro, was then a subsidiary branch of the Mihran, buts course was not the same as at prsent... the existence of two important Chalcolithic sites of Mohenjo-daro and Jhukar, the one in the near vicinity of the Indus, the other of the Western Nara loop...Griffin Vyse recalls observations that Alexander the Great had also sailed to the great lake and to the sea by this 'eastern branch of the Indus'...'the eastern or greater arm of the Mikran described by Rashid-ud-deen as branching off from above Mansura to the east, to the borders of Kutch, and known by the name of Sindh Sagara (Elliot, Vol. I, p. 49). This ancient river is also identical with the Sankra Nala which was constituted by Nadir Shah the boundary between his dominions and those of the Emperor of Delhi."

In the context of Indus script debate, the views of Samir S. Patel are apposite: "The elusive true nature of an ancient script inspires passionate debate. This article could be used to build a model of the English language. It would be imperfect--the text is short and the content specialized--but it would probably show that this collection of simple symbols encodes a spoken language, even if an alien observer was unable to decipher it. Written language has rules, which can be revealed through mathematical analysis, that make it understandable and grant it almost infinite communicative power. The mathematical modeling of natural language, known as computational linguistics, is the latest battleground in one of the most contentious scholarly, and often not-so-scholarly, debates left to us by the ancient world: the nature of the Indus script, short series of symbols that appear on a variety of small artifacts from the sophisticated and wide-ranging Indus civilization in South Asia around 4,000 years ago. We don't know what the symbols mean--in fact, we don't know whether the "script" encodes language at all or is a kind of symbol system, like heraldry or signs in an airport. Undeciphered ancient texts are archaeology at its most mysterious and romantic, but the Indus is more than a maddening intellectual puzzle. Knowing the nature of the script and understanding its signs will change our view of the earliest civilizations, but it is also a matter of modern identity--many South Asians, from rickshaw drivers to politicians, have pet theories--and a source of equal measures of academic frustration, nationalistic fervor, and raw emotion. The last decade has seen cooperation among scholars, as well as new theories and discoveries. But it has also seen accusations of racism and scientific bias, name-calling, and even threats."[100]

Resolution of language problem

The evidences presented, on historical cultural continuum in

India, lead to a reasonable inference that the language of the writing system should be a language of the people, artisans, in particular, used even today in India since language and culture are closely intertwined phenomena in a sprachbund (language union).

The identification of a particular Indian language as the Indus language has presented some problems because of the received wisdom about grouping of language families in Indo-European linguistic analyses. Some claims of decipherment have assumed the language to be Tamil, of Dravidian language family; some have assumed the language to be Sanskrit, of Indo-Aryan language family. A resolution to these problems comes from a surprising source: Manu.

Mleccha, Indus language of Indian linguistic area

A language family, mleccha (?language X), is attested in the ancient literature of India. This is the lingua franca, the spoken version of the language of the civilization of about 5000 years ago, distinct from the grammatically correct version called Sanskrit represented in the vedic texts and other ancient literature. Ancient texts of India are replete with insights into formation and evolution of languages. Some examples are: Bharata's Natya Shastra, Patanjali's Mahabhashya, Hemacandra's Deśī nāmamālā, Nighaṇṭus, Panini's Aṣṭādhyayi, Tolkappiyam–Tamil grammar. The evidence which comes from Manu, dated to ca. 500 BCE. Manu (10.45) underscores the linguistic area: ārya vācas mleccha vācas te sarve dasyuvah smṛtāh [trans. "both ārya speakers and mleccha speakers (that is, both speakers of literary dialect and colloquial or vernacular dialect) are all remembered as dasyu"]. Dasyu is a general reference to people. Dasyu is cognate with dasa, which in Khotanese language means 'man'. It is also cognate with daha, a word which occurs in Persepolis inscription of Xerxes, a possible reference to people of Dahistan, a region east of Caspian sea. Strabo wrote :"Most of the scythians, beginning from the Caspian sea, are called Dahae Scythae, and those situated more towards the east Massagetae and Sacae." (Strabo, 11.8.1). Close to Caspian Sea is the site of Altyn-tepe which was an interaction area with Meluhha and where three Indus seals with inscriptions were found, including a silver seal showing a composite animal which can be called a signature glyph of Indus writing..

The identification of mleccha as the language of the Indus script writing system is consistent with the following theses which postulate an Indian linguistic area, that is an area of ancient times when various language-speakers interacted and absorbed language features from one another and made them their own.[101]

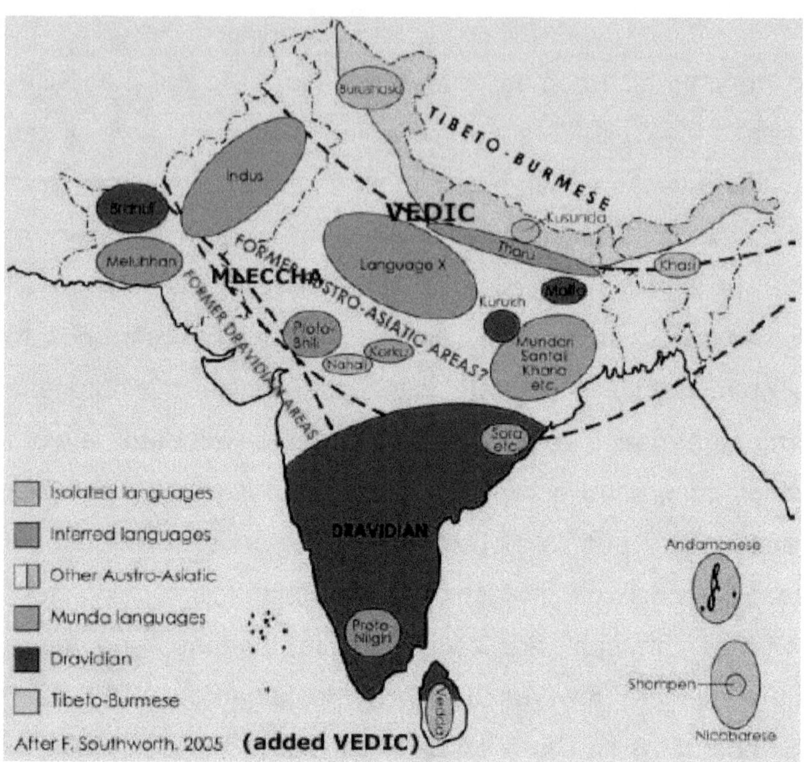

Indian linguistic area map, including mleccha and vedic (After F. Southworth, 2005)

Indus script debate can be resolved by using the following controls: 1. continuity of the underlying culture and language of the civilization; 2. consistent rebus readings of all glyphs (irrespective of their being pictorial motifs or signs) in two or more languages of Indian linguistic area; and 3. relating the homophones to repertoire of artisans attested archaeologically.

Use of these controls establishes the fact that the lapidaries, inventors of early bronze-age artifacts and techniques were also the inventors of a writing system which was necessitated by the imperative of trading surplus metal products across a vast interaction area stretching from Rakhigarhi (near Delhi) of Indus valley civilization area to Ur in Tigris-Euphrates river valley across the Persian Gulf of Mesopotamian civilization area. That the inscribed objects were used in the context of trade is also attested by the presence of seal impressions on packages and by the finds of seals with Indus writing in Mesopotamia civilization area. A by-product of this decoding of Indus script as mleccha provides a framework for decoding many pictorial motifs displayed on Mesopotamian cylinder seals, explained as a result of cultural exchanges and interaction with Meluhha (cognate: mleccha) speakers and possible acculturation of Meluhhans in the interaction area extending from Tigris-Euphrates doab to Indus-Sarasvati doab.

The decoding of Indus script glyphs as rebus representations of mleccha glosses reinforces the brilliant insights of scholars: Kuiper, Emeneau, Masica, Southworth and others, about Indian linguistic area on the Vedic River Sarasvati basin which has nurtured most of the settlements of the civilization created by the artisans from 7th millennium BCE.

Many glyphs of the writing system are clearly identifiable and unambiguous.[102] These glyphs relate to the depiction of animals and geometric patterns, for example: elephant, tiger, bos indicus (zebu), bos gaurus (buffalo), bull, heifer, types of antelopes/ram/ibex/goat, crocodile, svastika, dotted circle, trough in front of wild or domesticated animal; ligatures of animal faces/animal bodies or parts of animals; rings on neck of heifer or pannier on shoulder of heifer or horns ligatured to glyphs; buttocks/legs of a bovine ligatured to the upper body of a human being with horns sometimes decorated with twigs; leaves or petioles of leaves ligatured to mountain-summit, person seated on a leafless branch of a tree, tree-on-platform. Each such glyph is assumed to be an integral part of the message conveyed by the writing system. Thus, each glyptic element and glyph is read rebus, irrespective of classification in the corpus of inscriptions as 'pictorial motifs' or 'signs'.

Archaeological context as a control to explain why Indus script glyphs are hieroglyphs

That the hieroglyphs read rebus relate to the work of artisans -- lapidary or turner or carpenter or miner or smith -- is concordant with the archaeological evidence of early bead-making, metal working including working in iron in the civilization interaction area and evidence of seal impressions for use of Indus script inscriptions in trade contexts.

According to Mesopotamian texts, Imports into Mesopotamia from meluhha: copper, silver, gold, carnelian, ivory, uśu wood (ebony), and another wood which is translated as 'sea wood'; and shell

Trading cast beads, cast metal

Md 602, m1429 prism tablet, gharial holding fish, boat with 2 birds and cabin, text (A pair of ingots glyptically comparable to the Cretan copper ox-hide ingots, are shown inside the cabin of the boat).

Inscribed Cretan copper ox-hide ingot (After Fig.82 in: Sinclair Hood, 1971, TheMinoans: Crete in the Bronze Age, Thames and Hudson) In the Late Bronze Age, oxhide and plano-convex shaped ingots were used in the

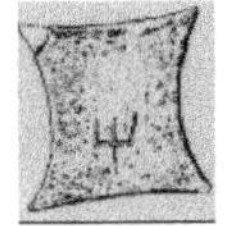 Aegean; elsewhere, only small plano-convex (bunshaped) ingots were used."Bronze tools and weapons were cast in double moulds. The cire perdue process was evidently employed for the sockets of the fine decorated spear-heads of the Late Minoan period. Copper was available in some parts of Crete, notably in the Asterousi mountains which border

the Mesara plain on the south, but it may have been imported from Cyprus as well. The standard type of ingot found throughout the East Mediterranean in the Late Bronze Age was about two or three feet long, with inward-curving sides and projections for a man to grasp as he carried it on his shoulder. Smaller bun-shaped ingots were also in use." (Sinclair Hood, opcit., p. 106).

Fragment of a man carrying an ox hide-shaped copper ingot Cypriot Late Bronze Age, ca. 1200 BCE http://www.lancette-arts-journal.ca/art20.htm

Side 1 of prism tablet:

bagalo = an Arabian merchant vessel (G.) bagala = an Arab boat of a particular description (Ka.); bagalā (M.); bagarige, bagarage = a kind of vessel (Ka.)(Ka.lex.); rebus: ban:gala = kumpaṭi = an:gāra śakaṭī = a chafing dish a portable stove a goldsmith's portable furnace (Te.lex.) cf. ban:garu ban:garamu = gold (Te.)

kuṭi 'tree' (Santali) Rebus: kuṭhi 'smelter furnace' (Santali)

dula pota 'pair pigeons' (Kashmiri.Pkt.); rebus: dul pota 'cast beads' (Santali.Pkt.) குரவம் kuravam, n. < குரா kurā 1. cf. kura- va. Date palm. See பேரீந்து. (மலை.) Rebus: khuro 'silver'; dula 'pair'; rebus: dul 'cast (metal)'. குரு kuru, n. cf. ghṛ. 1. Brilliancy, lustre, effulgence; ஒளி. குருமணித் தாலி (தொல். சொல். 303, உரை). குருமை¹ kurumai , n. < ghṛ. Lustre, brightness; நிறம். (தொல். சொல். 303.)

Side 2 of prism tablet: ayaka_ra 'ironsmith' (Pali) [fish = aya (G.); crocodile = kāru (Te.)]

Side 3 of prism tablet: Large smelted, cast metal ingots and beads

kolmo 'rice plant'; kolmo 'three' (Santali); rebus: kolme smithy (Ka.) kolami 'forge, smithy' (Te.) Thus, the first glyph on the right denotes forged ingot. The next glyph (three short numeral strokes) denotes kolmo 'three'; rebus: 'smithy' (Santali)

ayo, hako 'fish'; rebus: aya 'metal' (G.)

dula 'pair' (Kashmiri); rebus: dul 'cast (metal)'(Santali) d dhāḷako 'large ingot'; the pair of ovals with inlaid stroke = cast large ingots

med. 'body'; rebus: med. 'iron' (Mu.)

Glyptic elements on the boat: Two trees, two birds, two copper ingots (ox-hide ingots)

dul meṛeḍ cast iron (Mundari. Santali) dul to cast metal in a mould' (Santali) ḍāḷ= a branch of a tree (G.) Rebus: ḍhāḷako = a large ingot (G.) ḍhāḷakī = a metal heated and poured into a mould; a solid piece of metal; an ingot (G.)

kut.i 'tree'; rebus: kut.hi 'smelter' (Santali)

pota[103] 'pigeon'; pot 'beads' (H.G.M.)(CDIAL 8403).

Crocodile + fish: A tablet from Mohenjo-daro

ayo, hako 'fish' (Santali) Rebus: aya = iron (G.);ayah, ayas = 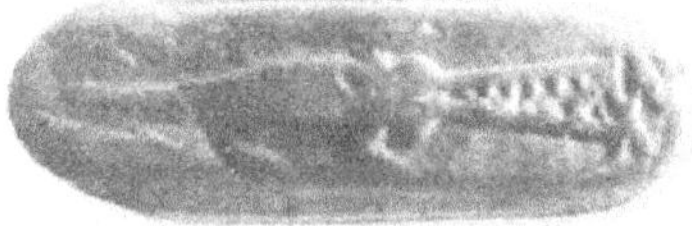 metal (Skt.) ayaskāṇḍa a quantity of iron, excellent iron (Pāṇ.gaṇ) Old Norse eir 'brass, copper', German ehern 'brassy, bronzen', Gothic aiz 'ore',

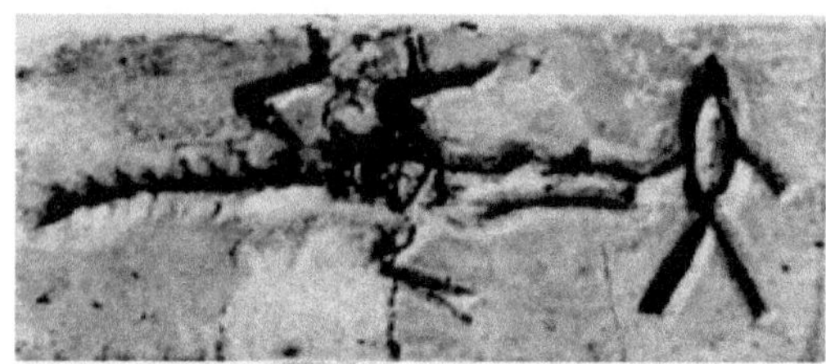

Old English ār 'brass, copper, bronze'

kāru[104] a wild crocodile or alligator (Te.) **ayakāra**[105] 'blacksmith' (Pali)

kāruvu[106] = mechanic, artisan[107], Viśvakarma, the celestial artisan (Te.)

Glyph of a crocodile and a lying-in woman: kārakuna 'scribe'

This glyph is part of one side of h180 tablet. A sequence of

signs is repeated on both sides of the tablet.

h705B,h172B

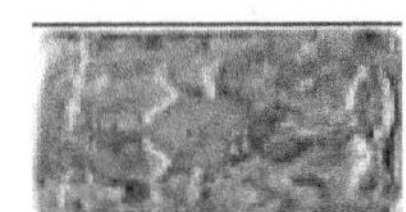

The object between the outspread legs of the woman lying upside down is comparable orthography of a crocodile holding fiish in its jaws shown on tablets h705B and h172B. The snout of the crocodile is shown in copulation with the lying-in woman.

The gloss for 'copulation' is kamḍa, khamḍa (Santali); rebus: kammaṭia coiner (Ka.); kampa ṭṭam coinage, coin, mint(Ta.) cf. kammaṭīḍu = a goldsmith, a silversmith (Te.)

The combined glyptic elements can be read: kamḍa + kāru; rebus: kammaṭa + khār 'mint + smith'.

कारकुन [108][kārakuna] *m* (P A factor, agent, or business-man.) A clerk, scribe, writer. (Marathi)

Continued use of the crocodile glyph in historical periods

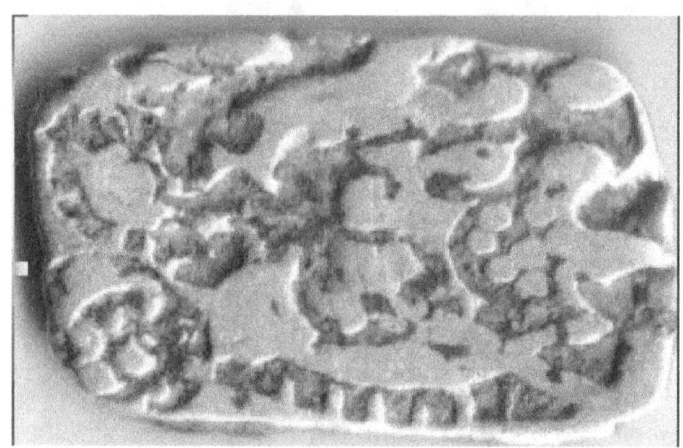

Together with humped bull, buffalo, elephant, tiger, rhino, antelope, fish, tortoise, crocodile glyph is also a punch-mark on Indian punch-marked coins from ca. 6th cent. BCE (Not illustrated). Silver punch drachm of Anuruddha, Munda and Nagadasaka period (c. 445-413 BCE). Magadha mint[109] used the crocodile-fish-in-jaw glyph, together with four other glyphs.

This glyptic element on one side of tablet h180. This shows a seated woman with disheveled hair. The standing man is armed with a sickle and discus. This hieroglyph is decoded as kuṭhāru 'armourer' (Skt.)

salae sapae = untangled, combed out, hair hanging loose (Santali.lex.) Rebus: sal workshop (Santali) The glyptic composition is decoded as kuṭhāru sal 'armourer workshop.'

koḍi 'flag' (Ta.)(DEDR 2049). koḍ 'workshop' (Kuwi)

Sign 187 is comparable to the sign used to depict a koṣhāgāra[110] 'warehouse' on Sohgaura copper plate. Rebus: kuṭhāru 'arrmourer' (Skt.)

Sign 343 sal 'splinter'; rebus: sal 'workshop' (Santali) kaṇḍa kanka 'rim of jar' (Santali); rebus: 'furnace scribe' Thus the first three glyphs (signs) from left read: koḍ kuṭhāru sal kaṇḍa kanka 'armourer workshop furnace scribe'. The Santali gloss kan-ka is instructive.It may be a dimunitive form of **kan-khār** 'copper smith' comparable to the cognate gloss: kaṉṉār 'coppersmiths, blacksmiths' (Tamil) If so, kaṇḍa kan-khār connotes: 'copper-smith furnace.'

The set of next three glyphs (signs) read rebus: ranku 'liquid measure'; rebus: ranku 'tin' (Santali) kolmo 'paddy plant' (Santali); rebus: kolami 'forge, smithy' (Telugu) kuṭi 'water-carrier' (Te.); rebus: kuṭhi 'smelter, furnace'. **ranku kolami kuṭi** 'tin forge smithy'.

Archaeological context of early iron in Ganga river basin

Map showing locations of the Early Iron Age sites in the

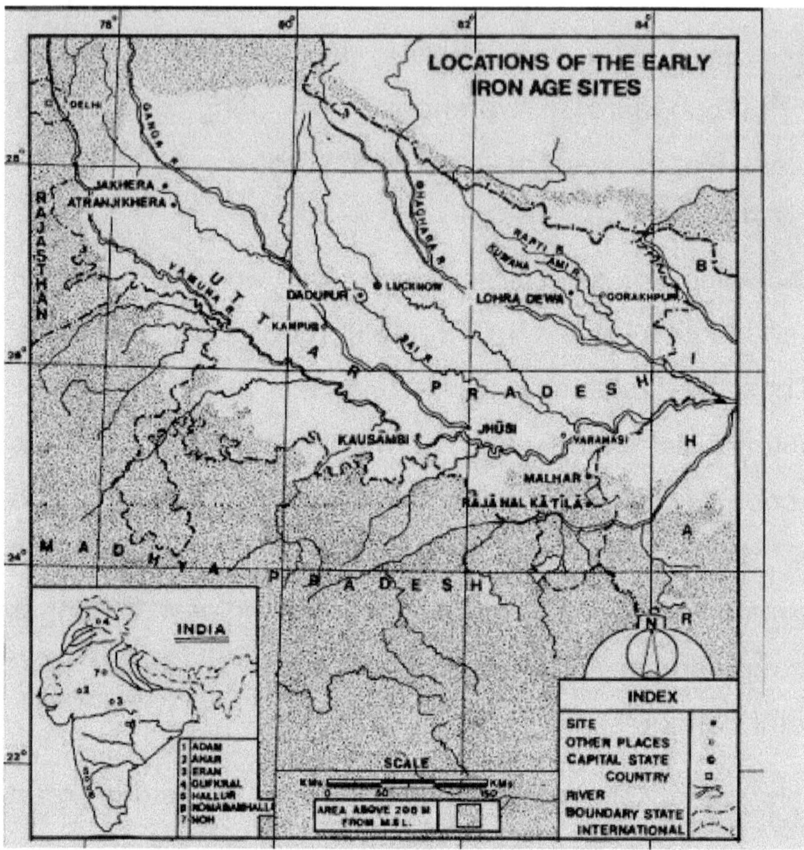

Central Ganga Plain, the Eastern Vindhyas, and different regions of India.

In 1999, Possehl and Gullapalli (1999) had evaluated the presence of iron artifacts in Indus civilization. Almost every site of the civilization has yielded many stone-beads and perforated beads of carnelian, lapis lazi, agate and other precious, semi-precious stones. Between 1996 and 2002, a number of excavations on Ganga river basin have revealed iron workings which point to the indigenous beginnings of iron. The excavated sites are Raja Nala-ka-tila (1996-98), Malhar (1998-99), Dadupur (1999-2001) and Lahuradewa or Lohradewa (2001-2002). Iron artefacts, furnaces, tuyeres and slag in layers found in these sites have been radiocarbon dated to between c. 1800 and 1000 BCE. (Tewari 2003).

Damaged circular clay furnace, comprising iron slag and tuyeres and other waste materials stuck with its body, exposed at lohsanwa mound, Period II, Malhar, Dist. Chandauli. Dates cal BCE: 1882, 1639; 2012, 1742

Meluhhan (mleccha) speakers were all over India, and also established villages close to Guabba, seaport (not far from Tigris-Euphrates): "In order to form a comprehensive view of the Meluhhan remnants (in Mesopotamia) a variety of texts could be consulted, although they display a picture of a people that have been integrated into the Sumerian and Babylonian cultures much earlier than the Ur III period. " [i.e., earlier than (2112-2004 BC)][111] It should be possible to identify mleccha (meluhha) substratum words in Sumerian/Akkadian. Such an identification may, perhaps, help resolve the 'meanings' of glyptics on Mesopotamian cylinder seals with motifs comparable to those found on Indus script inscriptions.

That the inventor and user of the writing system is a metal-smith or a lapidary or a miner or a merchant acting as an agent for the artisans, is surmised from the evidence of writing found on metal objects and on beads. Who else but a lapidary or a smith could have had the competence to inscribe on metal? Examples of Indus writing on metal objects can be cited.[112]

Daha are the people who spoke mleccha. Mleccha words have been retained in one or more of the present-day languages of the Indian linguistic area. It is not unreasonable to assume that homonymous words from one or more of the Indian linguistic area can decode the glyptics of pictorial motifs and glyptic signs and the messages of Indus inscriptions can be read as artisans' or metal-smiths' repertoire.

Consistent rebus reading of the script reinforces the

messaging imperative of artisans' work. The glyphs and related glosses themselves prove the validity of the application of rebus methof decoding. There are about 500 glyphs (signs and pictorial motifs); it is not mere coincidence that almost all the identifiable, unambiguous glyphs can be read rebus consistently in an artisan -- a lapidary or a smithy setting or trade setting. It sets the framework of the Indian sprachbund in reference to the artisans' repertoire.The composite animal glyph is one example to show that rebus method has to be applied to every glyptic element in the writing system. How does one explain a person seated on a leaf-less tree branch? The entire composition is a set of hieroglyphs. So it is with the rim of a short-necked jar. The focus of the orthography is on the rim; karṇaka, kanaka; rebus: writer. See another example of a human face ligatured to a markhor. The key is the face. This face, as a glyptic element, is the rosetta stone proving it as a hieroglyph to be read rebus. So is the water-carrier a hieroglyph (as noted by Gadd). She is kuṭi 'water-carrier' (Telugu). Rebus: kuṭhi 'smelter furnace'. This object can also be denoted by pudendum muliebre. So is the glyph showing copulation scene: kamaḍha. This gloss can also be denoted by a person seated in penance. kamaḍha 'penance' (Pkt.) Rebus: kampaṭṭam 'coiner, mint'. A svastika glyph within a square is shown next to an elephant or an endless-knot; all the three -- svastika, elephant, endless-knot-- are hieroglyphs. A Marathi gloss explains why an endless-knot is shown together with svastika: meḍhā m. 'curl, snarl, twist or tangle in cord or thread' (M.)(CDIAL 10312) Rebus: meḍ 'iron' (Ho.) This also explains the semantic context in which over 58 svastika occurrences in inscriptions can be read rebus: grapheme: svastika glyph; rebus: svastika 'zinc' (Ka.); jasth, jasti 'zinc, pelter, pewter'sg. dat. jastas जस्तस्). That svastika glyph denoted a material in historical context is explained in a magnum opus by Thomas Wilson[113]. This semantic decoding of svastika yields the reinforcement for decoding elephant and tiger glyphs, in the context of an artisans' workshop, since these animal glyphs occur on either side of the svastika glyph on an inscription.

A trough is shown in front of some domesticated animals and also wild animals like rhinoceros, tiger, elephant. The trough glyph is clearly a hieroglyph, in fact, a category classifier. The artisan is trying to depict his or her core professional competence, be it on a seal or tablet or a weapon or tool or an advertisement board as at Dholavira using hieroglyphs read rebus. Many Indus script inscriptions are professional calling cards of artisans listing their professional skill repertoire and traded resources and artifacts.

Trough in front of a rhinoceros depicted on an Indus seal

Dominant glyphs of Indus script

Pictorial motifs are dominant glyphs of the Indus script, given the frequency of occurrence and since they occupy a large segment of the limited space used by artisans to prepare the inscriptions. Trough as a glyph occurs on about one hundred inscriptions, though not identified as a distinct pictorial motif in the corpus of inscriptions. So is 'dotted circle' a glyptic element even when ligatured to the standard device or shown as an eye of a young animal.

Glyph	Frequency
One-horned heifer + standard device	1159
Shor-horned bull (in opposition)	95 +2 (in
Zebu or Bra_hman.i bull	54
Buffalo	14
Elephant	55 + 1 (horned)
Tiger (including tiger looking back)	16 + 5 (horned)
Boar (in opposition)	39 + 1 (in
Goat-antelope (flanking a tree)	36 + 1 (flanking
Ox-antelope	26
Hare (object shaped like hare)	10 +1 (object

Ligatured animal	41	
Alligator	49	
Fish	14	(objects shaped like fish); fish also a high-frequency sign
Cart frame + wheels	26	
Sprout (or, seedling stylized)	800	
Water-carrier	220	
Scorpion/rat	106	
Claws (of crab) (shaped like pincers)	130 + 90	
Arrow (spear)	227	
Rimless, wide-mouthed pot	350	
Frog	1	
Serpent	10	
Tree	34 + 1 (leaves)	
Dotted circle	67	
Svastika	23	
Endless-knot	4	
Rimmed narrow-necked jar	1395	
Frog	1	
Tree	34 + 1 (leaves)	
Double-axe	14	

Standard device   1395

Fish signs   1241

Spoked wheel (nave)   203

Leaf signs   100

Depiction in pairs of glyphs (signs)

An orthographic style of the writing system is to use glyphs
in reduplicated pairs, such as two goats, to short-horned
bulls, two tigers, to heads of heifers, two fencing persons.
Analogously, glyphs (as signs) are also reduplicated in pairs.

The following twelve glyphs (signs)' are shown re-duplicated
on inscriptions.

The reduplication connotes: dula[114] 'likeness, a pair'
(Kashmiri); rebus: dul 'cast (metal)'.e.g., dul meṛed, cast iron
(Mu.) dol = likeness, picture, form (Santali) Some glyphs
categorised as field-symbols (or, pictorial motifs) are also
reduplicated: e.g. two antelopes [meḍho (G.)[115]], two heifers
(koḍiyum[116], dāmṛa[117], damrā ' young bull (A.)(CDIAL 6184),
two bulls (ḍangar[118]); rebus: meḍ[119] 'iron'; tam(b)ra 'copper';
ḍangar[120] 'blacksmith'.

Reduplication of a glyph (pictorial motif of sign) -- such as two antelopes, two heifers, two bulls -- can be explained as process involving 'casting' by artisans(lapidaries or smiths).

The gloss **dula** is chosen as a proto-indic word decoding a 'pair, likeness' because of the occurrence of a homonym of this word is attested in some Munda glosses: Rebus: **dul** mered cast iron (Mundari. Santali) **dul** 'to cast metal in a mould' (Santali) pasra mered, pasāra mered = syn. of koṭe mered = forged iron, in contrast to **dul** mered, cast iron (Mundari.lex.) The choice of this word from among vikalpa (alternative words) is justified since the method of 'casting' applies not only to metals but also to the creation of hundreds of molded or cast tablets using burnt terracotta material.

Thus, phrases can be formed to represent 'cast' objects using this word, **dul**:

baṭhu m. 'large pot in which grain is parched (S.) Rebus: baṭa = a kind of iron (G.) bhaṭa 'furnace' (G.) baṭa = kiln (Santali); Thus, dul baṭa means: cast iron or iron kiln (for casting);   cast iron or iron furnace (for casting).

( ) 'curved, bent'; rebus: **dul kut.ila** 'cast bronze'. A variant of the curve (bracket) is to flip it vertically as in Sign 312.

Sign 312 is repeated several times on metal objects. The grapheme may be: **kuṭila** 'bent'; Rebus: **kuṭila** 'bronze (8 parts copper, 2 parts tin); reduplication may indicate a specified number of 'ingots' [dula 'likeness' (Kashmiri)Rebus: dul 'cast (metal)(Santali)]' This grapheme may explain a ligatured sign which occurs on a metal weapon.

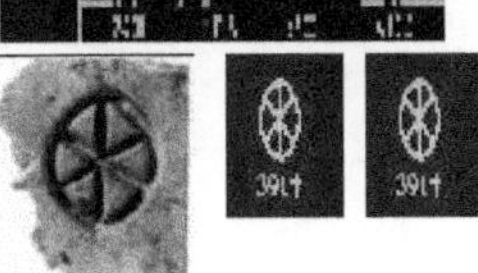

m1066 dula eraka 'pair, nave of wheel'; aara 'spokes'; dul 'cast metal'; eraka-aara 'molten cast copper, brass turner'

mēd, mēd 'body' (Kur.)(DEDR 5099) Rebus: meḍ 'iron'; mẽṛhẽt id. (Mu.Ho.) **dul** mereḍ cast iron (Mundari. Santali)

Part of text on m1429 prism tablet showing a pair of 'signs': ḍhālako; rebus: 'a large metal ingot (G.)'thus, dul ḍhālako 'cast metal ingot'.

ayo, hako 'fish'; a~s = scales of fish (Santali); rebus: aya = iron (G.); ayah, ayas = metal (Skt.). Thus, a pair of 'fish' glyphs connotes: **dul ayo** meaning: cast metal.

lo 'ficus' (Santali); Rebus: **lo** 'copper'. Thus, dul loh 'cast copper'

 **kōtur** कोतुर् A **cock** pigeon is also **nar-kōtur,** and a hen is **māda-kōtur** (W. 17). kōtar-bāz (Kashmiri) kuṭharu 'cock'; . a cock VS. xxiv , 23 MaitrS. TS. v ; a tent L. [288,3] (Skt.); kukkuṭa 'cock' (Skt.) Rebus: **kuṭhāru** 'weapons maker, armourer, writer' (G.) Thus, reduplicated glyphs may connote rebus: dul kuṭhāru 'cast weapons-maker'.

 **baṭai** = to divide, share (Santali) [Note the glyphs of nine rectangles divided.] Vikalpa: **bhaṭa**[121] = an oven, kiln, furnace (Santali)

Allograph: baṭa= quail (Santali)

Evidence for this allograph of quail glyph comes from two Failaka tablets.

Bull's head (bucranium) between two seated figures drinking from two vessels through straws.[122] Decoding the bull: ḍhangar 'bull'; ḍhangar 'blacksmith' (H.)

We find that on the top register, above the bull's head, the Yale tablet shows two squares with divisions flanking a circle while in the 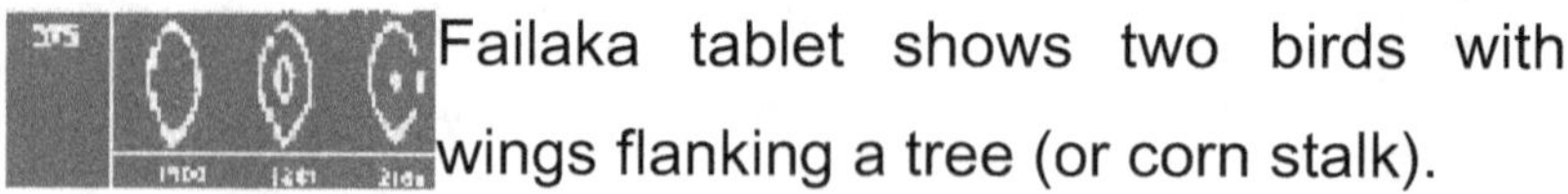 Failaka tablet shows two birds with wings flanking a tree (or corn stalk).

Decoding the circle on the Failaka tablet: koṭṭa 'seed' (Ma.); •*gōṭṭa— 'something round'. [Cf. guḍá—1. — In sense 'fruit, kernel' cert. ← Drav., cf.

Tam. koṭṭai 'nut, kernel'; A. goṭ 'a fruit, whole piece',
°ṭā 'globular, solid', guṭi 'small ball, seed, kernel'; B.
goṭā 'seed, bean, whole'; Or. goṭā 'whole, undivided',
goṭi 'small ball, cocoon', goṭāli 'small round piece of
chalk'; Bi. goṭā 'seed'; Mth. goṭa 'numerative particle'
(CDIAL 4271) Rebus: koṭe 'forging (metal)(Mu.)

Pigeon and quail/duck glyphs as an allograph

The Failaka tablet referred to showing two birds points
to a pair of pigeon glyphs as an allograph of the two
squares with divisions.

Mohenjodaro MIC, Pl. CVI,93
baṭṭai[123] quail (N.) vartaka = a duck
(Skt.)(CDIAL 11361). Rebus:
vartaka 'merchant' (Skt.)

varta = *circular object; *turning round (Skt.); vaṭu =
twist (S.)(CDIAL 11346) Vikalpa: **s**āk 'a goose' (Santali)
Rebus: **s**āk 'one who sells coral beads' (Santali)
Grapheme: Grapheme: कोंड [kōṇḍa] *m* C A circular hedge or
field-fence. 2 A circle described around a person under
adjuration. 3 The circle at marbles. 4 A circular hamlet; a
division of अमौजा or village, composed generally of the huts
of one caste. 5 Grounds under one occupancy or tenancy.
(Marathi) The duck within a circle is decoded : vartaka kōṇḍ

'duck circle'; rebus: **vartaka koḍ** 'merchant workshop'. Together with the rim-of-jar-glyph on either side, and fish glyph on line 2, part of the inscription on seal Pl. CVI,93 reads:**ayo vartaka koḍ kaṇḍa kanka** 'iron merchant workshop furnace scribe'. The last line reads: dula kolmo 'pair of paddy plants'; rebus: dul kolmo 'casting smithy'; **kaṇḍa kanka** 'casting smithy fire-altar, furnace scribe'.

Thus, the two squares with divisions may be decoded rebus: **dula baṭai** Rebus: **dul baṭa** casting furnace.

> Vikalpa: khaṇḍ 'field, division' (Skt.); Rebus: kaṇḍ 'furnace' (Skt.) Thus, reduplicated glyph connotes dul kaṇḍ 'casting furnace'. Vikalpa: **khoṇḍu**[124] 'divided into parts' (Kashmiri) A pair of such glyphs divided into parts, may thus be decoded as: **dul khoṇḍ** 'casting workshop'.

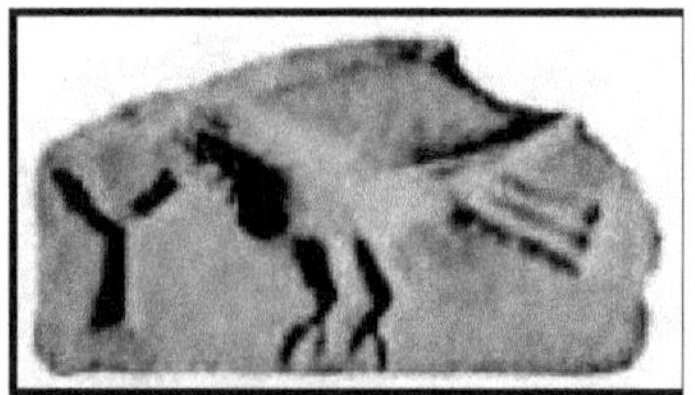

Lothal 050 cogu = food for birds (S.); coggā (L.); food for birds (P.)(CDIAL 4920). jhokā = one whose business is to feed a furnace or an oven (P.); jokha = to measure; lekha jokhaemok hoyoktama = you must give an account (Santali) jhokṇ = to cast to throw fuel into a furnace; jhokh = a flame (P.lex.) jō to put in insert (Pe.); jū id. (Mand.)(DEDR 2868). jokkānā, johkānā to kill (Go.); soka to strike at (Kui)(DEDR 2831). cokka-k-katt i-veḷḷi, cokkaveḷḷi pure silver (Ta.); cokkabeḷḷi id. (Ka.); cokkaboḷḷi id. (Te.); cokku gold; cokucā < sogsā pinchbeck, gold-like alloy of copper and zinc (U.); cokucu refinement, neatness; fineness, as of work; superior quality (Ma.)

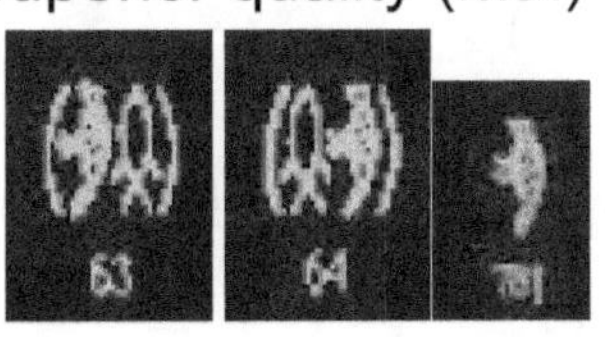

h452 Text 4124 **baṭa**[125] = a quail, or snipe (Santali) Rebus: bhaṭa 'kiln, furnace' (H.) ayo 'fish' (Mu.); Rebus: aya 'iron' (G.) Thus, the bracketed ligatured quail + fish glyph is decoded: **ayo kuṭila bhaṭa** 'iron, bronze furnace ingot'.

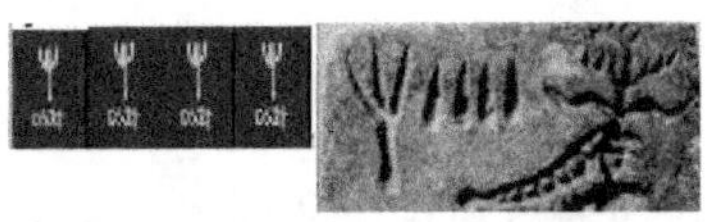

kolmo 'rice plant' (Mu.) Rebus: kolami 'furnace, smithy' (Te.) That is, **dul kolami** 'casting smithy'. Vikalpa: : gaṇḍa 'four' (Santali); hence, : gaṇḍa kolami 'Rebus: kaṇḍa 'furnace; kolami 'smithy'. Vikalpa: pon 'four' (Santali); Rebus: pon 'metal'

(Ta.); hence, dul pon kolami "casting metal smithy'.The sequence of 'four rice-plants' could be a variant of this pair of signs on K050 seal.

K050 body of a tiger, a human body with bangles on arm, a scarf (on pigtail), horns of a markhor crowned by a twig.

dhaṭu m. (also dhaṭhu) m. 'scarf' (WPah.) (CDIAL 6707) Rebus: dhatu 'minerals' (Santali)

pon 'four' (Santali) rebus: pon 'gold' (Ta.)

kōlupuli = Bengal tiger (Te.); kol = tiger (Santali) kōla = woman (Nahali) Rebus: kol 'metal' (Ta.)
kūdī, kūṭī 'bunch of twigs' (Skt.) Rebus: kuṭhi 'smelter furnace' (Santali)

Pk. ḍhaṁkhara -- m.n. ' branch without leaves or fruit ' (CDIAL 5524) Rebus: ḍhangar 'blacksmith' (H.) The seal is decoded: pon kolami 'gold furnace'; ḍhangar dhatu kol kuṭhi 'blacksmith mineral, metal smelter'.

 Allograph: Sign sequence 190-102 occurs at the end of inscriptions. Sign 190 may be a four-fold representation of Sign 162.

 puṭia 'fellies'; Rebus: puṭa 'calcining furnace'; puṭia 'copper'. Thus, dul puṭa 'cast, calcined copper'.

Or. doḷā, ḍoḷā 'pupil of eye'(CDIAL 6582); Rebus: ḍol 'the shaft of an arrow, an arrow' (Santali) Vikalpa: dul 'casting' (Santali) kolmo 'three' (Mu.) Rebus: kolami 'furnace, smithy' (Te.). Thus, the three glyphs together are read: **dol kolami** 'smithy for making arrows'. Vikalpa: Rebus: **dul kolami** 'casting smithy'.

śanku 'twelve-fingers' measure' (Skt.); Rebus: 'arrowhead' (Skt.) Vikalpa: talka 'palm of the hand (with twelve phalanges on four fingers'; Rebus: talika 'inventory, list of articles'. The paired glyph: **dul talika** to mean: 'list of cast articles'. Vikalpa: **dul śanku** 'cast arrowheads'.

An orthographic variant of denoting reduplication of signs is shown in ligatured signs 172, 173 and 174. **aḍar** 'harrow' Rebus: **aduru** 'native, unsmelted metal'. Thus, reduplication is decoded as dul aduru 'cast native metal'.

Glyphs in predictable pairs (signs) or stable pairs of signs

There are some stable sequences of signs in inscriptions, stability being measured by the frequency of occurrence of two signs within each inscription.

There are five pairs with between 65 and 87 occurrences in the inscriptions.

An orthographic variant of a pairs of signs is the creation of a ligatured sign. Sign 372 ('oval' grapheme) ligatures with sign 162, yielding sign 387

The following pair of signs terminate 87 inscriptions.

meḍ 'body'; Rebus: meḍ 'iron' (Ho.) kaṇḍ kanka 'rim of jar'; Rebus: karṇaka 'scribe'; kaṇḍ 'furnace, fire-altar'. Thus the pair is decoded: meḍ kaṇḍ kanka 'iron furnace scribe.' Vikalpa: **kánaka**[126] n. ' gold ' (Skt.) கன் **kaṉ** ,n. perh. கன்மம். 1. workmanship; வேலைப்பாடு. கன்னார் மதில்சூழ் குடந்தை (திவ். திருவாய். 5, 8, 3). 2. copper work; கன்னார் தொழில். (W.) 3. copper; செம்பு. (ஈடு, 5, 8, 3.) 4. See கன்னத்தட்டு. (நன். 217, விருத்.) There is clearly a semantic expansion of the morpheme: **kaṉ (-aka)** as a gloss denoting workmanship in general, and, in particular: copper, copper work, scribe (who had the competence to inscribe on copper/bronze). karaṇamu. [Skt.] n. A village clerk, a writer, an accountant. Sthala k* 'the registrar of a district'; karaṇīkamu 'clerkship, the office of a k* or clerk (Telugu) karaṇīka, karṇika, karaṇika 'a writer, a scribe; village clerk or accountant; a royal scribe or accountant (S.Mhr.); head native official of a district collector's office; the head assistant to the Tahsildar of a taluk; an arithmetician; karaṇika maṇḍalīka 'a chief scribe' (Kannada) Consistent with the archaeological context of all Indus script inscriptions and given the evidence that the glyph 'rim of jar' (homonym:

karṇaka 'a prominence or handle or projection on the side or sides (of a vessel)' (ŚBr. KātyŚr.) is the most frequently-occurring sign on inscriptions, an meaning 'scribe' is surmised. A meaning 'artisan workmanship' as a classifying semantic category can also be surmised for the glyptic element: 'rim of jar'. The glyptic element is used in a ligature with a glyph denoting a 'water-carrier' read as kuṭi; rebus: kuṭhi 'smelter, furnace' (Santali). This ligatured glyph is read: kuṭhi kan-ka 'furnace scribe',   i.e. the scribe accounting for and writing to create Indus script inscriptions of 'furnaced' artifacts such as terracotta bangles, beads or minerals or metal alloys.

 This pair of Sign 8 and Sign 176 terminates 8 sequences.

 Variant pair (sign sequence using 'body' glyph without horns) with 6 occurrences.

Combination of Sign 8 and Sign 1 is also orthographically  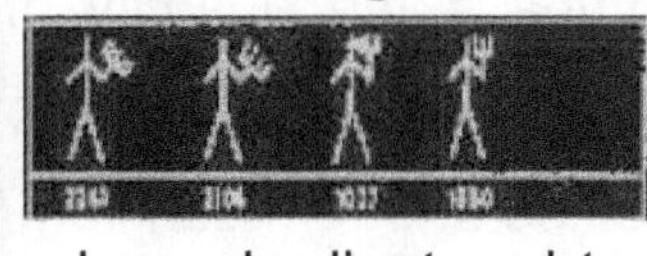 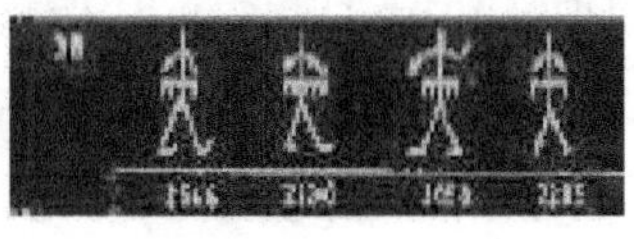 shown by ligatured to   the body or ahand:Sign 38 or Sign 19 or Sign 22.

kuṇḍī = crooked buffalo horns (L.) **khareḍo** = a currycomb (G.) Rebus: **kharādī** ' turner' (G.) Thus, meḍ kharādī 'iron turner'

- Vikalpa: **kuṇḍī** = chief of village. **kuṇḍi-a** = village headman; leader of a village (Pkt.lex.) I.e. **śreṇi jeṭṭha** chief of metal-worker guild.

• Sign 17 and variants. This is a ligature of a body (with a shoulder stick) and *ficus religiosa* leaf.

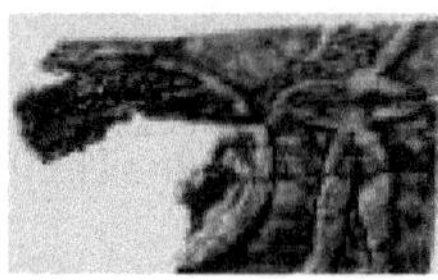 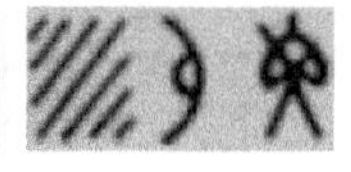 m1653 ivory plaque. Text 1905

bhaṭa 'warrior'; bhaṭa 'six' (G.) rebus: baṭa = kiln (Santali); baṭa = a kind of iron (G.) bhaṭṭhī f. 'kiln, distillery', awāṇ. bhaṭh; P. bhaṭṭh m., °ṭhī f. 'furnace', bhaṭṭhā m. 'kiln'; S. bhaṭṭhī keṇī 'distil (spirits)   dhātu 'mineral' (Pali)

loa 'ficus religiosa' (Santali) rebus: loh 'metal' (Skt.) Sign 17 is decode rebus: loh bhaṭa 'metal furnace'.

 A pair of 'currycomb' glyphs are ligatured (in-fixed) within an 'oval' glyph. The 'oval' glyph has been decoded as an ingot: **mūhā** = the quantity of iron produced at one time in a native smelting furnace of the Kolhes; iron produced by the Kolhes and formed like a four-cornered piece a little pointed at each end (Santali). The pair of 'currycombs' are read rebus: dula 'pair'; rebus; dul 'cast (metal)'; **khareḍo** = a currycomb (G.) Rebus: **kharādī** ' turner' (G.) Thus the ligatured Sign 382 is decoded as: dul **mūhā kharādī** 'cast ingot turner'.

Ayo 'fish' (Santali); Rebus: aya 'metal, iron' (G.); aḍar

'harrow' Rebus: aduru 'native, unsmelted metal'. Thus, the pair is decoded as: **ayo aduru** 'metal-unsmelted'.

ib 'two' (Kannada); Rebus: **ib** 'iron' (Santali) **aṭar** 'a splinter'; **aṭaruka** 'to burst, crack, sli off,fly open; **aṭarcca** ' splitting, a crack'; **aṭar** ttuka 'to split, tear off, open (an oyster) (Ma.); aḍaruni 'to crack' (Tu.) (DEDR 66)

ib 'two' (Kannada); Rebus: **ib** 'iron' (Santali) baṭhu m. 'large pot in which grain is parched (S.) baṭa = a kind of iron (G.) bhaṭa 'furnace' (G.) baṭa = kiln (Santali); Thus, ib baṭa means: iron kiln or iron furnace.

keṇṭa 'fish'; ayo 'fish'; Rebus: **kērē̃** 'brass or bell-metal'; ayas 'iron, metal' Thus, the pair is decoded: **ayo kērē̃** 'brass metal'.

kharedo = a currycomb (G.) Rebus: **kharādī** ' turner' (G.) chief of village; that is, **kharādī kuṇḍi-a,** 'chief of turners' guild'. Vikalpa: **kāmsako, kāmsiyo**[127] = a large sized comb (G.); Rebus: **kāsāri**[128] 'pewterer' (Bengali) Or.**kāsārī;** H. **kasārī** m. ' maker of brass pots ' + **kuṇḍī** =: **kāsāri kuṇḍi-a,** 'chief of metal-worker guild'

Sign 342: kaṇḍ kanka 'rim of jar'; Rebus: karṇaka 'scribe'; kaṇḍ 'furnace, fire-altar'. Thus the ligatured sign is decoded: kaṇḍ kanka 'furnace scribe

The pair of signs: 342 + 48 can be decoded: Yellow

brass/bell metal fire-altar scribe

The following pair terminates 184 inscriptions:

   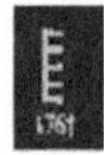 (10) (Variant sign pair, sign sequence reversed).

The following pairs of signs terminates 8 and 26 sequences, respectively:

    Sign 12: **kuṭi** 'water-carrier' (Te.); Rebus: **kuṭhi** 'smelter' (Santali) **kharedo** = a currycomb (G.) Rebus: **kharādī** ' turner' (G.) Vikalpa: **kāmsako, kāmsiyo** = a large sized comb (G.); Rebus: **kāsāri** 'pewterer' (Bengali) The ligature of 'rim of jar' glyph is denoted by the ligatured Sign 15; this ligaturing glyptic element has been decoded as 'furnace scribe'. Thus, the pair of Sign 176 together with either Sign 342 or Sign 15 can be read, respectively as: **kuṭhi kan-ka kharādī** 'smelter-furnace-scribe, turner' or **kan-ka kharādī** 'scribe, turner'.

 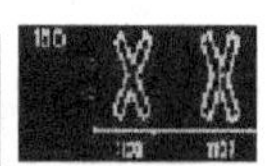 **dāṭu** 'cross over; **daṭ** 'to cross' (Ko.)(DEDR 3158) Rebus: **dhatu** 'a mineral, metal' (Santali); **dhātu** 'mineral' (Skt.) **taṭṭai** 'mechanism made of split bamboo for scaring away parrots from grain fields (Ta.);**taṭṭe** 'a thick bamboo or an areca-palm stem, split in two' (Ka.) (DEDR 3042) **toṭxin, toṭ.xn** goldsmith (To.);**taṭṭān** 'gold- or silver-smith' (Ta.); **taṭṭaravāḍu** 'gold- or silver-smith' (Te.); ***ṭhaṭṭakāra** 'brass-worker' (Skt.)(CDIAL 5493). Thus, the pair is decoded: **dhatu taṭṭara** 'worker in gold, silver,

minerals'.

The following seven pairs have between 93 and 291 occurrences in the corpus of inscriptions:

kolmo 'three' (Mu.); Rebus: kolami 'smithy' (Te.) baṭhu m. 'large pot in which grain is parched (S.) Rebus: baṭa = a kind of iron (G.) bhaṭa 'furnace' (G.) baṭa = kiln (Santali). Thus, the pair is decoded: baṭa kolmo 'smithy (iron) furnace'

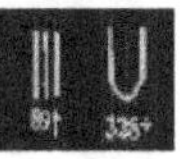

In addition to the above reading, an additional glyptic element is the 'ladle or spoon' glyph (ligatured to the 'pot' glyph). ḍabu 'an iron spoon' (Santali) Rebus: **ḍab, ḍhimba, ḍhompo** 'lump (ingot?)', clot, make a lump or clot, coagulate, fuse, melt together (Santali) The pair of signs is decoded: baṭa ḍab kolmo 'iron ingot furnace'

Sign 267 has glyptic elements 1) ingot (-shape); 2) corner Sign sequence Sign 267- Sign 99 decoded as: **kañcu mūhā aduru kundār** 'turner (of) bronze ingot, native metal.'

> **mūhā** = the quantity of iron produced at one time in a native smelting furnace of the Kolhes; iron produced by the Kolhes and formed like a four-cornered piece a little pointed at each end; **mūhā mē̃ṛhẽt** = iron smelted by the Kolhes and formed into an equilateral lump a little pointed at each end; kolhe tehen me~ṛhe~t mūhā akata = the Kolhes have to-day

produced pig iron (Santali.lex.)

Vikalpa: **kana, kanac** = corner (Santali); Rebus: **kañcu** = bronze (Te.)

G. **khuṇ f., khū̃ṇɔ** m. 'corner'.2. S. **kuṇḍa** f. 'corner'; P. **kūṭ** f. 'corner, side' (← H.). (CDIAL 3898) Tu. kōḍi corner; kōṇṭu angle, corner, crook. Nk. kōṇṭa corner (DEDR 2054b) Rebus: **kundār**[129] turner (A.)

Thus the ligatured sign 267 may be decoded as: **kañcu mūhā kundār** turner "bronze ingot turner'.

Sign 99: **aṭar**[130] 'a splinter' (Ma.) Rebus: **aduru** 'native, unsmelted metal'

Thus the pair of signs can be decoded together as: turner (of) bronze ingot, native metal'.

Mirror-reflected pairs of glyphs (signs)

Another orthographic variant is the mirror-reflected pairing:

 Both these types of variants may also connote 'likeness, pair' connoted by the word **dula** (Kashmiri) and read rebus: **dul** 'cast (metal or terracotta)

 Reduplicated (mirror-imaged) mountain ridge can be decoded:

डगर [ḍagara[131]]A slope or ascent (as of a river's bank, of a small hill). Rebus: ḍāṅgar 'blacksmith' (H.) Mirror-reflected glyph: **dul ḍāṅgar** 'pair of hill-ranges'; rebus: **dul ḍāṅgar**

'caster, metalsmith'. Grapheme: kōḍu a point, the peak or top of a hill (DEDR 2049) Rebus: koḍ 'workshop' (Kuwi) koṭe 'forge' (Santali) Kui (K.) koḍi hoe. (DEDR 2064) Pa. koṭṭēti 'hews, breaks, crushes', Pk. koṭṭēi (CDIAL 3241)

Thus, the hill glyph is read rebus: **dul ḍāṅgar koḍ** 'blacksmith cast, forge workshop.'

 Reduplicated (or, ligatured) Sign 228 (pair of smith's vices) can be decoded:

Grapheme: **sannī, sannhī** = pincers, smith's vice (P.)

Vikalpa grapheme : **caṇila** squirrel (To.) **Koḍ. aṇekoṭṭï** id. **Tu. caṇil, canil, taṇil**, (B-K. also) **aṇil** id. (DEDR 2315).

h419

Rebus: **śannī** (WPah.) may denote a small shed (?workshop): Woṭ. šen ' roof ', Bshk. šan, Phal. šān (AO xviii 251, followed by Buddruss Woṭ 126, < śar(a)na --); WPah. (Joshi) **śannī** f. ' small room in a house to keep sheep in '.(CDIAL 12326). The duplicated grapheme may thus be decoded as: **dul sannī** 'casting workshop (small shed or workshop).'

Ficus religiosa glyph

lo = nine (Santali); no = nine (B.)   on-patu = nine (Ta.)

loa = a species of fig tree, ficus glomerata, the fruit of ficus glomerata (Santali) Rebus: loh 'metal' (Skt.)

daṭhi, daṭi the petioles and mid-ribs of a compound leaf 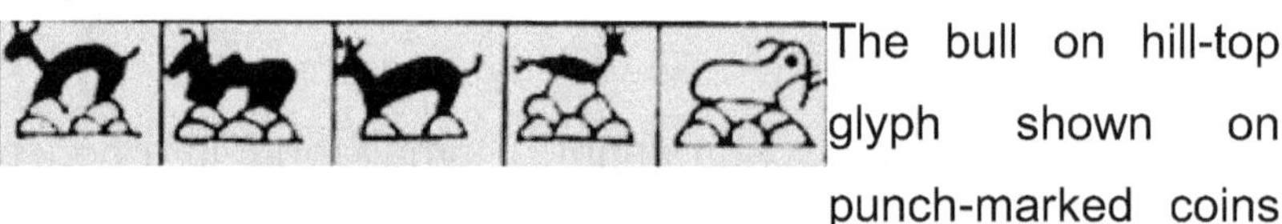 after the leaflets have been plucked off, stalks of certain plants, as Indian corn, after the grain has been taken off (Santali) Rebus: dhatu 'mineral' (Santali)

डगर [ḍagara] f A slope or ascent (as of a river's bank, of a small hill). 2 unc An eminence, a mount, a little hill डांग [ḍāṅga] m n (H Peak or summit of a hill.) (Marathi).ṭākuro = hill top (N.); ṭāngī = hill, stony country (Or.); ṭān:gara = rocky hilly land (Or.); ḍān:gā = hill, dry upland (B.); ḍā~g = mountain-ridge (H.)(CDIAL 5476). Rebus: ḍhaṅgar 'blacksmith' (H.) The set of nine ficus religiosa leaves (showing theirmid-ribs/petioles) is read rebus: loh dhatu ḍāṅgar 'copper mineral blacksmith'.

The bull on hill-top glyph shown on punch-marked coins is an allograph: ḍhaṅgar 'bull'; rebus: ḍhaṅgar[132] 'blacksmith' (H.)

Artisan, lapidary, carver, engraver, turner (e.g. lapidary drilling beads, artisan engraving Indus script inscriptions)

One-horned heifer as a glyph composed of glyptic elements

These variants of the heifer glyph which occurs on over 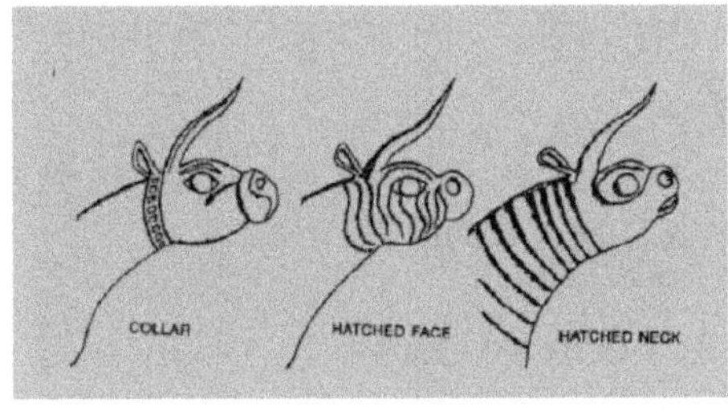1150 inscriptions of Indus script, show a glyptic elements used: 1. one horn; 2. rings on the neck of the animal; 3. heifer or young bull. One horn.

That this is not a 'mythical' animal, but is only a glypic composition with orthographic emphasis on glyptic elements, is clear from the occurrence of the glyph with two horns, with the characteristic ring on neck, a pannier on its shoulder and a standard device in front.

H006 composite bovid (imagined?) With one horn, pannier, neck rings, standard device in front.

koḍiyum 'heifer' (G.) [kōḍiya] kōḍe, kōḍiya. [Tel.] n. A bullcalf. . k* దూడA young bull. Plumpness, prime.

తరుణము. జోడుకోడియలు a pair of bullocks. kōḍe adj. Young. kōḍe-kāḍu. n. A young man.పడుచువాడు. [kārukōḍe] kāru-kōḍe. [Tel.] n. A bull in its prime. खोंड [khōṇḍa] m A young bull, a bullcalf. (Marathi) గోద [gōda] gōda. [Tel.] n. An ox. A beast. kine, cattle.(Telugu) koḍiyum (G.)

These glyptic elements have been read rebus:

1. A young bull is kōḍe, khōṇḍa

2. One horn is koḍ[133], kōṇḍa

3. Rings on neck are: koṭiyum[134] (G.)

4. A sack slung on the front shoulder of the young bull is khōṇḍā[135], khōṇḍī , kothḷo

Rebus: B. kōḍā 'to turn in a lathe'; Or. kūnda 'lathe', kūdibā, kūd 'to turn' (→ Drav. Kur. kūd 'lathe') (CDIAL 3295)

Rebus: koṭṭil 'workshop' (Ma.)(DEDR 2058). koṭe 'forged metal' (Santali) koḍ[136] 'artisan's workshop' (Kuwi)

The glyph depicting

rings on the neck of the animal can thus be decoded as phonetic determinant of the gloss denoting a heifer, kōde

M1656 pectoral: Frequency of occurrence of glyph composition: 1159 kanda = a pot of certain shape and size (Santali) Rebus: kand = altar, furnace (Santali) kanka 'rim'; khanaka 'miner' Glyph of overflowing pot: khara [Sk. kṣara] water J iii.282; kharati flows.

kshar, cl. 1. P. *kshárati* (ep. also Ā. °*te*; Ved. cl. 2. P. *kshariti*, Pāṇ. vii, 2, 34; Subj. *ksharat*; impf. *áksharat*; aor. 3. sg. *akshār* (cf. Nir. v, 3); *akshārīt*, Pāṇ. vii, 2, 2; p. *kshárat*; inf. *kshāradhyai*, RV. i, 63, 8), to flow, stream, glide, distil, trickle, RV.; AV.; ŚBr.; R. &c.; to melt away, wane, perish, Mn.; MBh. iii, 7001; to fall or slip from, be deprived of (abl.), MBh. xiii, 4716; to cause to flow, pour out, RV.; AV. vii, 18, 2; Mn. ii, 107; MBh. &c. (with *mūtram*, 'to urine,' Car. ii, 4); to give forth a stream, give forth anything richly, MBh.; Hariv. 8898 (pf. *cakshāra*); R.; Ragh.: Caus. *kshārayati*, to cause to flow (as urine), Vait.; to overflow or soil with acrid substances (cf. *kshāra*), MārkP. viii, 142; (cf. *kshārita*.)

Kshara, mf(*ā*)n. (gaṇa *jvalādi*) melting away, perishable, ŚvetUp.; MBh.; Bhag.; (*as*), m. a cloud, L.; (*am*), n. water, L.; the body, MBh. xiv, 470. **—ja**, mfn. (=*kshare-ja*, Pāṇ. vi, 3, 16) produced by distillation, W. **—pattrā**, f., N. of a small shrub, W. **—bhāva**, mfn. mutable, dissoluble. **Ksharātmaka**, mfn. of a perishable nature, perishable, MārkP. xxiii, 33. **Kshare-ja**, mfn. =°*ra-ja*, Pāṇ. vi, 3, 16.

Ksharaka, mf(*ikā*)n. pouring forth (ifc.), Devīm.

Ksharana, *am*, n. flowing, trickling, distilling, dropping (e.g. *anguli*-, perspiration of the fingers, Ragh. xix, 19), Suśr.; pouring forth, Vop.; splashing, spattering, ib.

Ksharita, mfn. dropped, liquefied, oozed, W.; flowing, trickling, W.

Ksharin, *ī*, m. 'flowing, dropping, trickling,' the rainy season, L.

(Pali) Rebus: khār[137] खद॒रf a blacksmith (Kashmiri)

kammarsāla 'pannier' (Telugu) karmāraśāla[138] = workshop of blacksmith (Skt.)

kodiyum 'heifer' (G.); koṭ 'workshop' (Kuwi) Rebus: koṭe

meṛed = forged iron, in contrast to dul meṛed, cast iron (Mundari.lex.) damṛa m. a steer (G.) ; tamb(r)a = copper (Skt.); tamba = copper (Santali) tambra = copper (Skt.) damaḍi_ (H.) damṛi, dambṛi = one eighth of a copper pice (Santali) Hence, koṭe = forge (Santali) ere = to cast, as metal; to overflow (Ka.) eṛaka = any metal infusion (Ka.Tu.) Vikalpa: Ta. vār (-v-, -nt-) to flow, trickle, overflow (DEDR 535)வார்ப்பு vārppu n. < வார்²-. 1. Pouring; ஒழுக்குகை. 2. Casting; உருக்கி வார்க்கை. வார்ப்பி னமைத்த யாப்பமை யரும்பொறி (பெருங். இலாவாண. 18, 24).

The overflowing pot is a motif which occurs on a Mesopotamian cylinder seal.

 Cylinder seal impression of Ibni-sharrum[139], a scribe of Shar-kalisharri ca. 2183–2159 BCE The inscription reads "O divine Shar-kali-sharri, Ibni-sharrum the scribe is your servant."

Allographs

M1168 2360 ka ṇḍ kanka 'rim of jar' (Santali); Pa. kōḍ (pl. kōḍul) horn (DEDR 2200) கோடு

kōṭu : *நடுநிலை நீங்குகை. கோடிறீக் கூற் றம் (நாலடி, 5). [K. kōḍu.] Tusk; யானை பன்றிகளின் தந்தம். மத்த யானையின் கோடும் (தேவா. 39, 1). 4. Horn; விலங்கின் கொம்பு. கோட்டிடை யாடினை கூத்து (திவ். இயற். திருவிருத். 21)(Tamil)

Rebus: kanda 'fire-trench' (Pe.) + koḍ 'artisan's workshop' (Kuwi) kõdā 'to turn in a lathe' (B.)

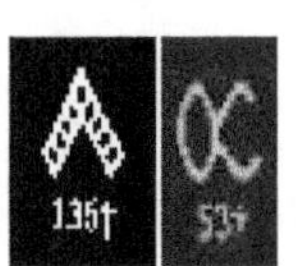 ḍato 'claws or pincers (chelae) of crabs'; ḍaṭom, ḍiṭom to seize with the claws or pincers, as crabs, scorpions; ḍaṭkop = to pinch, nip (only of crabs) (Santali) Vikalpa: ᐱ ḍāṭo, dāṭo a plug, a cork, a stopple (G.) ᐱ Graphemes: Ko. koṇḍ a bend; Tu. kōḍi corner; kōṇṭu angle, corner, crook. Nk kōṇṭa corner (DEDR 2054b) Vikalpa: khoṇḍ square (Santali) Kol. koḍval (pl. koḍvasil), (Kin.) koṛva sickle; (Pat., p.119), Nk. koṛval sickle. Pa.kũḍaŋgey elbow; koḍka billhook. Ga. (Oll) konḍke id.

Rebus: dhātu 'mineral' (Vedic); a mineral, metal (Santali) Ko. koṇḍ a bend (DEDR 2054b) Rebus: koḍ 'artisan's workshop' (Kuwi) koḍ = place where artisans work (G.) कोंडण [kōṇḍaṇa] f A fold or pen. (Marathi) B. kõḍā 'to turn in a lathe'.

Positional order and varieties of 'fish' glyphs[140]

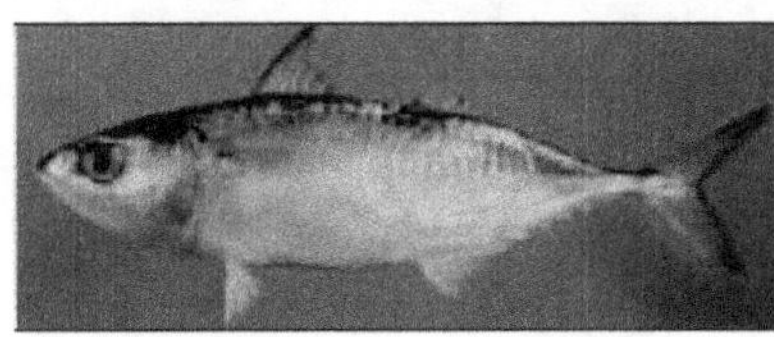 Santali 'hako' is concordant with a proto-Indic form which can be identified as **ayo**[141] in many glosses, Munda, Sora glosses in particular, of the Indian linguistic area. Rebus: **aya**[142] 'metal' (G.)

Fish hieroglyphs

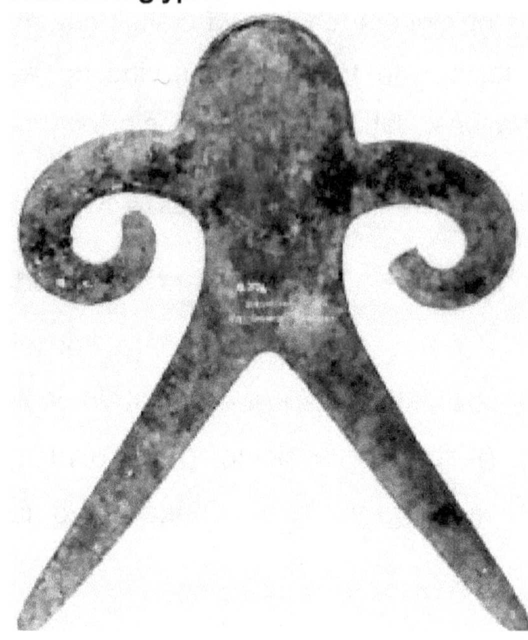

Copper anthropomorph with 'fish' glyph incised

Wkh. merg f. 'ibex' (CDIAL 9885).Rebus: med. 'iron' (Mu.)

Anthropomorph with 'fish' sign incised on the chest and with curved arms like the horns of a markhor. Sheorajpur (Kanpur Dist., UP, India). State Museum, Lucknow (O.37) Typical find of Gangetic Copper Hoards. 47.7 X 39 X 2.1 cm. C. 4 kg. Early 2nd millennium BCE.

miṇḍāl markhor (Tor.wali) meḍho a ram, a sheep (G.)(CDIAL 10120) Vikalpa: kala[143] 'ibex'; rebus: kallan[144] 'stone mason' (Ta.)

meḍ iron (Ho.) meṛed-bica = iron stone ore, in contrast to bali-bica, iron sand ore (Mu.lex.)

Allographs, graphemes of meḍ

urseal8Seal; BM 118704; U. 6020; Gadd PBA 18 (1932), pp. 9-10, pl. II, no.8; two figures carry between them a vase, and one presents a goat-like animal (not an antelope) which he holds by the neck.

Vikalpa: meḍa 'neck' (Te.) Rebus: meḍ 'iron' (Ho.)

kár, kãr[145] 'neck' (Kashmiri) Rebus: khār, khar 'blacksmith' (Kashmiri) Vikalpa: sāgh[146] m. ' throat ' (L.); ', śaṅge f. ' neck, throat '. (WPah.)(CDIAL 12264). Rebus: **sāk**[147] 'one who sells coral beads' (Santali)

melh 'goat' (Br.) Rebus: **meṛha, meḍhi** 'merchant's clerk; (G.) Thus, the seal denotes a coral beads merchant. mehto [Hem. Des. meḍhi = Skt. vaṇik-sahāya: a merchant's clerk, fr. Skt. mahita praised, great fr. mahto praise, to make great] a schoolmaster; an accountant; a clerk; a writer (G.lex.) The seal is decoded rebus: **meḍhi kãr** 'merchant blacksmith'.

The goat is depicted looking back which is a phonetic determinant of 'blacksmith': krammara 'turning neck back'; rebus: kamar 'smith' (Santali); kammāra id. (Pali)

Glyphs of two animals looking back

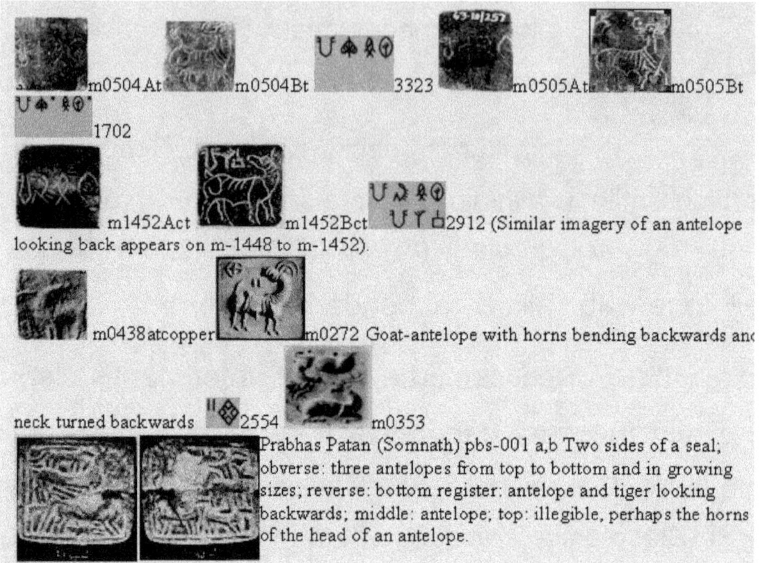

M1452 copper plate; molded tablet, harappa: antelope and tiger look back (mlekh 'goat' (Br.); rebus: milakku 'copper' (Pali); mleccha 'copper' (Skt.); kol 'tiger' (Santali); rebus: kol

'metal alloy, pañcaloha'(Ta.)

krammar-ucu, krammarincu = to turn back (Te.) *kamra = the back (Skt.); krem = the back (Kho.)(CDIAL 2776).

•Turning back is an artistic device to represent rebus: kamma_ra, 'smith, artisan': kol kammāḷa, mēḍha (milakku, 'antelope') kammāḷa semant. = alloy-smith, or copper-smith

kamar[148] blacksmiths (Santali)

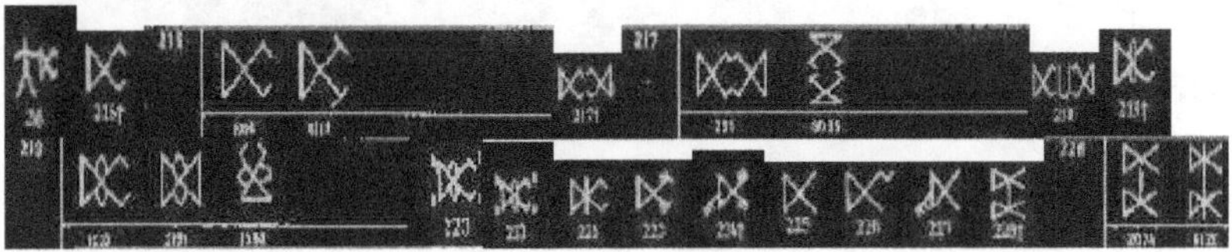

M1185, m1431A, Sibridamb01A (tiger looking back; obverse: X)

kol 'tiger'; rebus: kol 'pancaloha, working in iron' (Ta.)

krammaru. [Tel.] v. n. To turn, return, go back. (Telugu) **krəm**[149] back'(Kho.)(CDIAL 3145) Rebus: kammāra[150] [Vedic karmāra] a smith, a worker in metals, a goldsmith. (Pali)

•karmārakula 'smithy' (Pa.) Rebus: kol 'tiger'; krammara 'turn back' (Te.); rebus: kamar 'metalsmith' (Santali) The 'crossing' glyhph: dāṇṭu = to cross (Ka.); dāṭu id. (Te.) Rebus: dhatu 'mineral' (Santali) Thus, the Sibridamb seal is decoted as: **dhatu kamar** 'mineral smith'

Allographs: ḍaṭo 'claws or pincers (chelae) of crabs'; ḍaṭom to seize with the claws or pincers, as crabs, scorpions (Santali) Rebus: dhatu 'mineral'.

m0146 **aṭar** a splinter; aṭaruka to burst, crack, slit off, fly open; aṭarcca splitting, a crack; aṭarttuka to split, tear off,

open (an oyster)(Ma.); aḍaruni to crack (Tu.)(DEDR 66).
dāravum = to tear, to break (G.) dar = a fissure, a rent, a

trench; darkao = to crack,to break;
bhit darkaoena = the wall is cracked
(Santali)

The pair of signs on m0146 is decoded rebus: **adaruu dhatu** 'native metal mineral'.

X glyph: dhatu; 'splinter' glyph: **aṭar** (Ma.) Rebus: **adaru** = native metal (Ka.) aduru = gan.iyinda tegadu karagade iruva aduru = ore taken from the mine and not subjected to melting in a furnace (Ka. Siddha_nti Subrahman.ya' S'astri's new interpretation of the Amarakos'a, Bangalore, Vicaradarpana Press, 1872, p. 330)

putli[151] ' doll, pupil of eye (B.) Rebus: pot 'glass bead'

(H.) śunda 'rat'; rebus: kũdār 'turner' (B.) perhaps,

semant.
cũdār 'ivory

turner'.   kaṇḍ
kanka   'furnace
scribe'.   Thus,

inscription on seal m0146 is decoded as: adaru dhatu pot kũdār kaṇḍ kanka koḍ 'workshop native metal, mineral bead turner, furnace scribe.' A veritable list of lapidary-smith-artisan repertoire.

Obverse of steatite Dilmun stamp seal from Failaka Island (c. 2000 BCE)[152]. A human figure and a variety of animals – two antelopes one with its head looking backward; possibly a scorpion at the feet of the human figure. A dotted circle is seen above one antelope and a vase in between the antelope and the human figure.

ḍhan:ga = tall, long shanked; maran: ḍhan:gi aimai kanae = she is a big tall woman (Santali.lex.) Rebus: ḍangar 'blacksmith' (H.)

m1181A Text 2222 Pict-80: Seated horned person, bristled face (with a three-leaved pipal twig on the crown); hoofed platform

The pair of signs is decoded: dhatu adaru 'mineral, native metal'. Hoofed platform glyph: ḍangar 'bull'; ḍhangar 'blacksmith' (H.); koṇḍo 'stool'; rebus: koḍ 'workshop'. Seated person in penance: kamaḍha 'penance' (Pkt.); rebus: kampaṭṭa 'mint'. Other glyphs of horned-twig, tiger's mane on face, bangles on arms, fish-with-splinter-glyph have been decoded in the context of other inscriptions.

 Seal impression, Ur (Upenn; U.16747 मेढ [mēḍha] The polar star[153] (Marathi) Rebus: meḍ 'iron' (Ho.) kuṭi 'water-carrier'(Telugu); rebus: kuṭhi 'smelter furnace' (Santali) Thus, the seal is decoded: **meḍ kuṭhi** iron smelter furnace.

 मेंढसर [mēṇḍhasara] m A bracelet of gold thread. (Marathi)

Signs 127 to 130; Sign 161 मेंढा [mēṇḍhā] A crook or curved end (of a stick, horn &c.) and attrib. such a stick, horn, bullock. मेढा [mēḍhā] m A stake, esp. as forked. 2 A dense arrangement of stakes, a palisade, a paling. 3 fig. A supporter or backer (Marathi). Vikalpa: ḍhanga = a crook used for pulling down the branches of trees, for goats, sheep and camels (P.)

h242A The pair: endless-knot + svastika can be read as a

 set of metals: iron and pewter (zinc alloy).

मेढा [mēḍhā[154]] menḍa[155] A twist or tangle arising in thread or cord, a curl or snarl. (Marathi) (CDIAL 10312). (Marathi) Rebus: meḍ 'iron' (Ho.)

Glyph: sathiyā (H.),   sāthiyo (G.);   satthia,

sotthia (Pkt.) Rebus: svastika[156] pewter (Kannada)

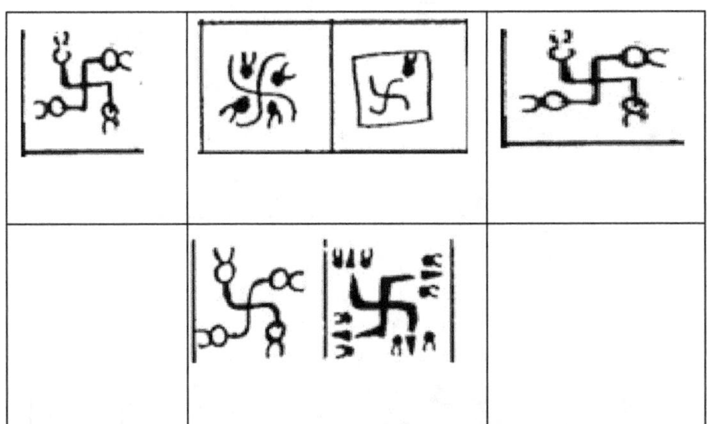

•[Pl. 28, A, Ramnagar, Lotapur, Mamdar, Singavaran: Punch-marked coins]

•[Pl. 28, B to E: svastikā symbol on punch-marked/cast copper coins]

•[Pl.28, F: Ujjayini, copper coins with svastikā symbol]

•[Pl. 28, G to J, Taxila, Ayodhya, Arjunayana, Sibis, Kuṇinda, Kuluta, yaudheya, •śātavāhana coins: Svastikā symbol]

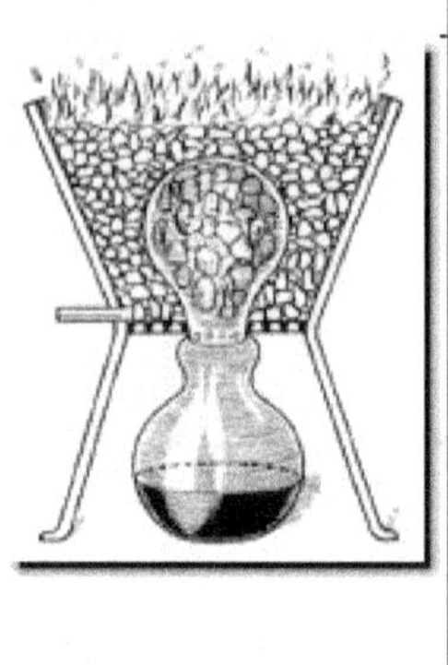

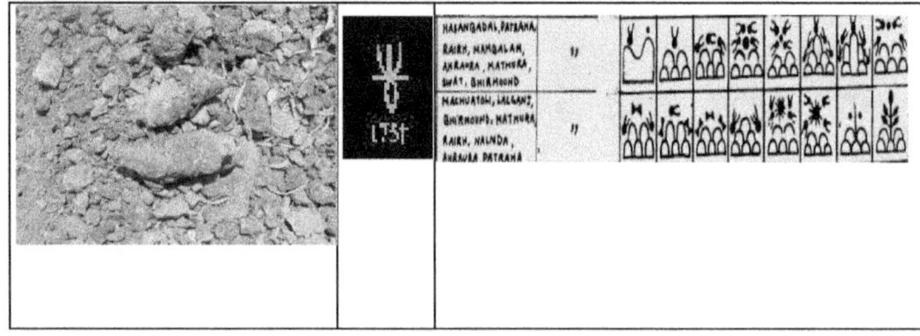

Zawar; ancient zinc retorts. Zinc distillation: tiryak patana yantram

Zinc ore (oxide)

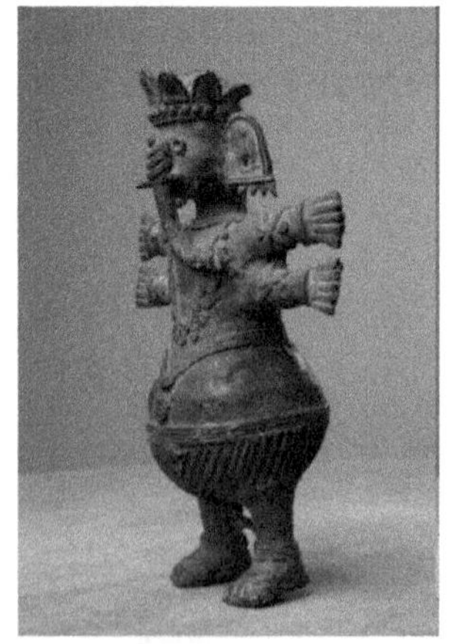

Dhokra brassware, using cire perdue technique brass = two parts copper to one part zinc.[157]

Early cementation processes roasted zinc ore (oxide) was mixed with copper fragments and charcoal (reducing agent) and the mixture was heated in a sealed crucible upto 1000 degrees C. The zinc vapour dissolved to yield a quality of brass. Examples of brass have been found in Lothal and Atranjikhera (6.28 to 16.2 % zinc) dated to c. 3rd and 2nd millennia BCE respectively. Carbon 14 dates (uncalibrated) for the Zawar mines of Rajasthan (40 kms. south of Udaipur) are PRL 932, 430+100 BCE and BM 2381, 380+ 50 BCE. Mining of lead zinc ores are found in the old workings at Rajpura-Dariba (375 BCE) and Rampura-Agucha (370 BCE) . At Prakashe, a Chalcolithic site (2nd millennium BCE) in Deccan, two copper objects each containing 25.86 and 17.75 percent zinc has been found. A vase found at Bhir mound (3rd cen. BCE), Taxila contained 34.34% zinc. A part of chariot in submerged Dwarka assayed 10.68% zinc (unknown date); many copper coins and many bronze images of historical periods contain upto 25% zinc. Silver used in many punch-marked coins was obtained from Zawar mines which yielded copper, zinc, lead and silver.

m0665, text 1139

h182 A,B Tablet in bas-relief

Identical tablet har609

Terracotta tablet in bas-relief.

Drummer and a tiger. Five svastika glyphs alternate with right- and left-handed arms.

dhol 'a drum beaten on one end by a stick and on the other by the hand' (Santali); ḍhol (Nahali); dhol (Kurku);　ḍhol (H.); dhol a drum (G.) **ḍhōla** m. ' large drum ' Rudray. 2. *__ḍhōlla__ -- . [Only OAw. definitely attests -- /--]1. Gy. pal. daul ' drum ',

Paš. ḍūl (← Par. ḍuhūl IIFL iii 3, 65),

Kho. (Lor.) dol, K. ḍōl m., kash. ḍhōl, L. P. Ku. N. A. B. ḍhol, OAw. ḍhora m., H. **ḍhol** m. -- Ext. -- kk -- : L. ḍholkī f. ' small drum ', Ku. ḍholko, H. ḍholak f. 2. Pk. ḍholla -- m., Or. ḍhola, Mth. Bhoj. Aw. lakh. Marw. G. M. ḍhol m. (CDIAL 5608) Rebus: dul 'to cast in a mould'; koṭe mereḍ 'forged iron' (Santali) cf. WPah.ktg. ḍhòllu drummer'.

Vikalpa: dual 'drum' (Gypsy)(CDIAL 5608) daul 'temple'(A.); dewal id. (H.)(CDIAL 6542).

kol 'tiger' (Santali); rebus: kol 'pañcaloha, an alloy of five metals'.

The alternating glyphs with right- and left-handed arms of the svatika point to two types of zinc ore (perhaps zinc sulphie and zinc oxide) used in the casting (alloying) to produce brass, āra kūṭa. (lit. mixed or joined copper).

bhāraṇ' to spread or bring out from a kiln ' (L.)(CDIAL 9462)

Use of svastika glyphs may relate to the practice of using 5 parts of copper to 4 parts of zinc and 1 part of tin to create an alloy called bharan: In the Punjab, the mixed alloys were generally called, bharat (5 copper, 4 zinc and 1 tin). In Bengal, an alloy called bharan or toul was created by adding some brass or zinc into pure bronze. bhārata = casting metals in moulds; bharavum = to fill in; to put in; to pour into (G.lex.) Bengali. ভরন [bharana] n an inferior metal obtained from an alloy of coper, zinc and tin (Bengali). The Bengali gloss toul is phonetically homonymous with dhol 'drum'.

Early numerals of the Indian linguistic area included:**mit eka** one; **bar, barea, don** two; **pea, pe, peaṭa, pene** three; **pon, ponea, car** four; **mÕṛẽ** five; **turui** six; **eae, sat** seven; **iral** eight; **are, lo** nine; **gel** ten.

Allograph: Serpent's tail: moṇḍ the tail of a serpent (Santali)

mÕṛẽ[158] five; hence, the early phonetics of the five repeated glyphs of svastika is decoded as: **mÕṛẽ jasti(ka)** 'five svastika'; rebus: polished zinc ore. Zinc ore was used in the casting process of brass to get a polished shine of golden color of the alloy. **munde**[159] a jar-like brass vessel (Ka.); **monta** cruse, goglet (Ma.)(DEDR 4965) Cruse is a small jar for holding water.

Md. moḍenī[160] ' massages, mixes '. Kal.rumb. moṇḍ -- ' to thresh ', urt. maṇḍ -- ' to soften ' (CDIAL 9890) Kui mrānḍa[161] (mrānḍi-) to plaster, smear; n. plastering. Te. m(r)ēgu, mrēvu to smear; ? (K.) mēdu id., daub, mix together (CDIAL 5082).

svastika 'zinc' (Ka.); jasth, jasti 'zinc, pelter, pewter'sg. dat. jastas जस्तस्).(Kashmiri)

It is possible that zinc oxide and zinc sulphide were used in the alloying process.

Spelter (referring indiscriminately to zinc and bismuth), likely from the similar colored lead-tin alloy, pewter or Indian tin.

Spelter, while sometimes merely a synonym for zinc, is often used to identify a zinc alloy. In this sense it might be an alloy of equal parts copper and zinc used for hard soldering and brazing http://www.encyclo.co.uk/nol.php

The word *pewter* is probably a variation of the word *spelter*, a colloquial name for zinc (Skeat, Walter William (1893), *An etymological dictionary of the English language* (2nd ed.), Clarendon Press.) Zinc ingots formed by smelting might also be termed spelter http://www.encyclo.co.uk/nol.php

Text of inscription

kaṇḍ kanka glyph decodes as a copper furnace scribe.

The glyph of drum is an allograph of the two long-linear-strokes, denoting two, a pair. Dula 'a pair' (Kashmiri); rebus:

180

dul 'to cast metal in a mould' (Santali)

bangaḍī 'a bracelet of glass, gold or other material, a bangle 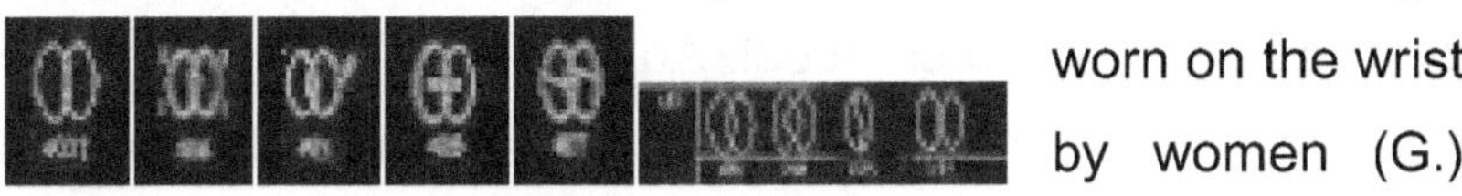 worn on the wrist by women (G.) Rebus: bangala 'a goldsmith's portable furnace' (Te.)[162]

A source of zinc is Zinc Carbonate (ZnCO3) called zinc spar or Smithsonite, for which the term calamine is also used.Oxide occurs in nature as the mineral zincite. Oxide of zinc is called tutty. This is the reason why zinc-lead compound is called tutu-nag or tutenag or tutanego (derived from the Persian tutiya, meaning smoke).

The ore of Zawar mines (Rajasthan) is sphalarite, ZnS, Zinc sulphide.

Brass is an alloy of copper with zinc.

Tutty collects in furnaces where copper or brass is smelted, while zinc sublimes. Calamine brass is an alloy of copper with zinc, produced by heating fragments of copper with charcoal and a zinc ore, calamine or smithsonite, in a closed crucible to rred heat (about 1300 degrees C or 2400 degrees F). The ore is reduced to zinc vapour that diffuses into the copper. This method of brass manufactured is attested from 1st millennium BCE. The earliest brass, called calamine brass, dated to Neolithic times; it was probably made by reduction of mixtures of zinc ores and copper ores. (Encyclopaedic Britannica). Calamine (zinc ore containing blende (ZnS), zinc carbonate (SnCO) and zinc oxide (ZnO) have been used to make brass ever since ancient times. This was done using the cementation process called the 'calamine process'. "In this process, finely ground calamine is mixed with ground charcoal. An organic binder (urine, rice water, resin, tallow, salt etc.) is added and the preparation is usually agglomerated in pellets. In ancient times, this mix was then made to react with puree divided copper for very long periods, between 8 and 24 hours. This resulted in a brass that typically contained less than 30% zinc."[163]

Glyph of shawl, a gaudy dress for an idol; rebus: potti 'priest'

The glyphs decorating the shawl are trefoils, that is, three hollow circles. Read rebus, the shawl is potti. potti[164], pottika n. Same as. Doll's clothes, a gaudy dress for an idol or for a little girl. (Telugu) S. potī f. ' shawl ' Pk. potta -- , °taga -- , °tia -- n. ' cotton cloth ', pottī -- , °tiā -- , °tullayā -- , puttī -- f. ' piece of cloth, man's dhotī, woman's sārī ', **pottia** -- ' wearing clothes ' (CDIAL 8400) pōtramu ' a cloth' (Telugu) போத்து² pōttu , n. < பொத்து. 1. Hole, hollow (Tamil) **buḍhi** mala 'a bead with wide hole' (Santali) **peaṭa** 'three' (Santali) trika, a group of three (Skt.) The occurrence of a three-fold depiction on a trefoil may thus be a phonetic determinant, a suffix to potṛ as in potṛka

Rebus reading of the hieroglyph: potti[165] 'temple-priest' (Ma.)

Sacredness connoted by the temple-priest explains the

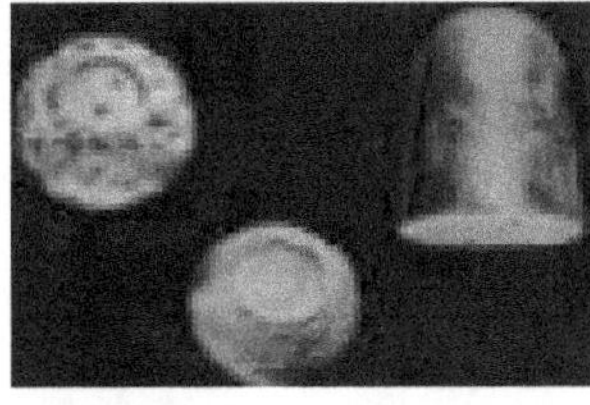

occurrence of the trefoil glyph on the base for holding a śivalinga. Two bases decorated with trefoil and a lingam. Smoothed, polished pedestal of dark red stone. National Museum of Pakistan, Karachi. After Mackay 1938: 1,411; II, pl. 107:35; cf. Parpola, 1994, p. 218.

pheṭār a heifer (Santali) Heifer with trefoil inlays, Uruk (W.16017) c. 3000 BCE; shell mass with inlays of lapis lazuli, 5.3 cm long. Vorderasiatisches Museum, Berlin; cf. Parpola, 1994, p. 213.

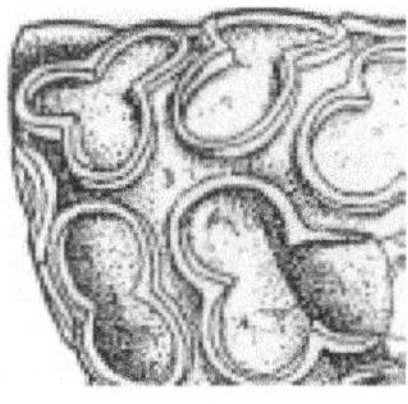

Trefoil decorated bull; traces of red pigment remain inside the trefoils. Steatite statue fragment. Mohenjodaro (Sd 767). After Ardeleanu-Jansen, 1989: 196, fig. 1; cf. Parpola, 1994, p. 213. **pōtu** 'male of animals' (Telugu) A phonetic determinative of the trefoil motif.

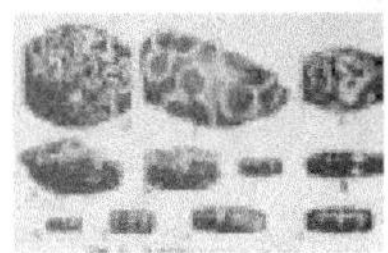

Trefoils painted on steatite beads. Harappa (After Vats. Pl. CXXXIII, Fig. 2)

Fish and ligatured fish glyphs:

In the corpus of epigraphs, fish signs frequency is 1241 and there are 14 objects shaped like fish, all of which were found at Harappa.

381 Fish

279 Fish (+ four gills)

216 Fish (+ inverted 'V' ligatured)

188 Fish (+ oblique cross-line)

29 Fish (+ circumgraph of 4 short strokes)

26 Fish-shaped objects

ayo, hako 'fish'; ās = scales of fish (Santali); rebus: aya = iron (G.); ayah, ayas = metal (Skt.)

kaṇḍa kanka; fire-altar-scribe; vikalpa: rebus: kaṇḍa khanaka 'fire-altar (of) miner'

Kalibangan 37, 34

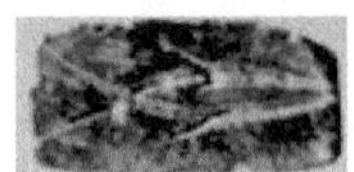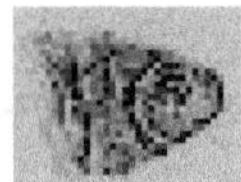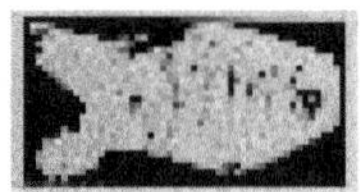

h350B, 330, h329 tablets

The gold pendant is made from a hollow cylinder with soldered ends and perforated point. Museum No. MM 1374.50.271; Marshall 1931: 521, pl. CLI, B3. [After Fig. 4.17a, b in: JM Kenoyer, 1998, p. 196].

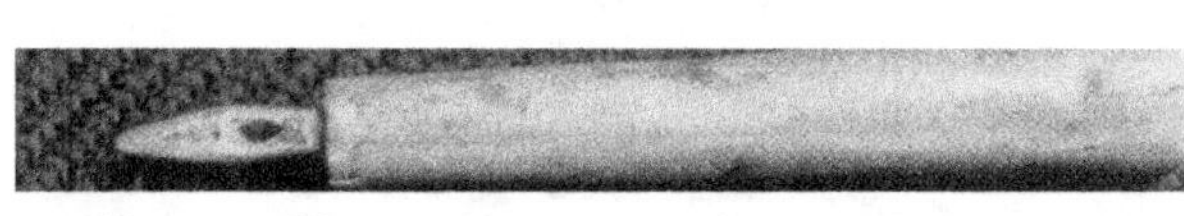

kana, kanac = corner

 (Santali); kañcu = bronze (Te.) sal 'splinter'; sal 'workshop' (Santali) dāṭu 'cross' (Te.); dhātu = mineral (Skt.); ?ea 'seven'; rebus: ?eh-ku 'steel'; **kolli**[166] 'fish'; rebus: **kol**[167] 'working in iron'; vikalpa: ayo, hako 'fish' (Santali); rebus: ayas 'metal'

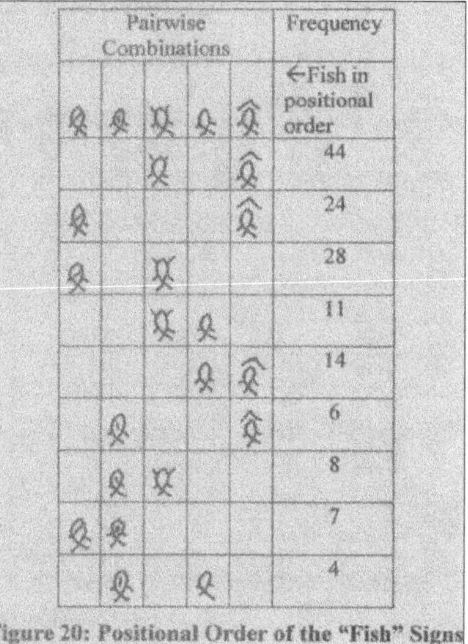

Figure 20: Positional Order of the "Fish" Signs

(Skt.)

Sign 70 A short stroke within the body of the fish) affixed to the basic 'fish' pictograph.

sal stake, spike, splinter, thorn, difficulty (H.); sal 'workshop' (Santali) *

badhoṛ 'a species of fish with many bones' (Santali) Rebus: badhoria 'expert in working in wood'(Santali) Vikalpa: Glyph: kolli 'fish' (Ma) Rebus: kole.l 'smithy, temple'

(Ko.) kol 'working in iron, blacksmith (Ta.)(DEDR 2133)

h095

Allograph: boṭor 'hare'
(Santali); Rebus: badhoṛ 'expert in working in wood'(Santali)
[Glyph of hare shown on coper tablets in front of a bush.]
balle a thicket, bush (Tu.); vallai extensive thicket (Ta.); balle
thick bush, thick jungle (Ka.); vallara, vallura arbour, bower,
thicket (Skt.); vallara id. (Pkt.)(DEDR 5289). Rebus: bali 'iron
sand sore'(Mu.)

kenṭa[168] 'fish'; Rebus: kēṛe~ brass or bell-metal 

 Vikalpa: ḍhāḷiyum = adj. sloping, inclining; rebus: ḍhāḷako = a large metal ingot (G.)

Glyph of fish ligatured to circumgraph of four short strokes.
gaṇḍa set of four (Santali) kaṇḍa 'fire-altar' cf. ayaskāṇḍa a
quantity of iron, excellent iron (Pāṇ.gaṇ)

 Glyph of fish ligatured to ᐱ The
ligature may be interpreted as a graphic
element to denote 'angle'. **koṇḍa**[169]
bend (Ko.); Rebus: **kõdā**[170] 'to turn in a lathe'(B.) कोंद
kōnda[171] 'engraver, lapidary setting or infixing gems'

(Marathi)Thus, the ligatured glyph of 'fish' can be read as:
ayo + **kõdā** = an 'iron turner workshop'.

m1086a: Sign 65-Sign 60 The sign sequence on m1086a is decoded as: ḍhangar pattar ayas kōnda,ayas kāṇḍa ' merchant, lapidary, smith, **ayas kāra** iron-worker (with) metal turner workshop, (producing) excellent quantity of iron'. Decoding the bull + trough: ḍhangar 'blacksmith, lapidary merchant'. patthara[172] 'stone'; pattar 'trough'; rebus pattar, vartaka 'merchant'. [khārun]), the trough into which the blacksmith allows melted iron to flow after smelting (Kashmiri) Rebuss: ayas kāra 'iron-worker' (Skt.) Thus, the Seal 1086 is of a merchant-guild, lapidary, smith with a turner workshop (producing) excellent quantity of iron.

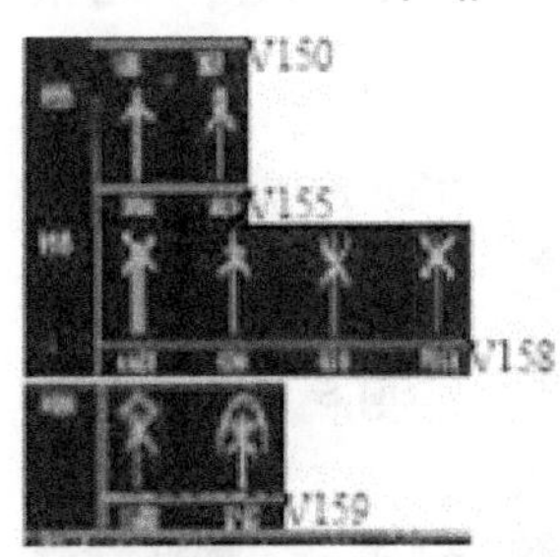

ārā[173] ' awl ' (Pkt.) (CDIAL 1313). Rebus: āra 'brass' as in ārakūṭa (Skt.)

Groups of animals in a glyptic composition

M0304 composition: yogi, human figure, elephant, tiger, rhinoceros, water buffalo. 2 ibex below platform. Analysis by Huntington: Headdress: water-buffalo horns, fan-shaped in center; Face is human, profile faces, bovine

187

ears; Tiger's mane(?) Torso enveloped in garment with ties around the waist. Restored view (after Huntington).

A person is seated in penance, on a stool with legs of hayricks. kama ḍha 'penance' (Pkt.) Rebus: kampaṭṭam 'mint' (Ta.) Kur. kaṇḍō a stool. Malt. kando stool, seat. (DEDR 1179) Rebus: kaṇḍ = a furnace, altar (Santali.lex.)

A pair of hayricks, a pair of antelopes: kundavum = manger, a hayrick (G.) Rebus: **kundār** turner (A.); **kũdār, kũdāri** (B.); **kundāru** (Or.); **kundau** to turn on a lathe, to carve, to chase; **kundau dhiri** = a hewn stone; **kundau murhut** = a graven image (Santali) **kunda** a turner's lathe (Skt.)(CDIAL 3295) kal aṛ Nilgiri ibex (Ko.);

kalai stag, buck, male black monkey (Ta.); kalan:kompu stag's horn (Ta.)(DEDR 1312) Rebus: kallan mason (Ma.); kalla glass beads (Ma.); kalu stone (Kond.a); xal id., boulder

(Br.)(DEDR 1298). kala stag, buck (Ma.) Rebus: kallan 'stone-bead-maker'. Vikalpa: mlekh 'antelope'(Br.); milakkhu 'copper' (Pali) Glyph: krammara 'look back' (Te.); kamar

'smith' (Santali) dula 'pair' (Kashmiri); dul 'cast ' (Santali)

Glyph: clump between the two horns: kuṇḍa[174] n. ' clump ' e.g. darbha-- kuṇḍa-- Pāṇ.(CDIAL 3236). kundār turner (A.)(CDIAL 3295).

kuṇḍī = crooked buffalo horns (L.) rebus: kuṇḍī = chief of village. kuṇḍi-a = village headman; leader of a village (Pkt.lex.) I.e. śreṇi jet.t.ha chief of metal-worker guild. cūḍa, 'head-dress'. Rebus: cuḷḷai = potter's kiln, furnace (Ta.); cūḷai furnace, kiln, funeral pile (Ta.); cuḷḷa potter's furnace; cūḷa brick kiln (Ma.); culḷī fireplace (Skt.); culḷī, ulḷī id. (Pkt.)(CDIAL 4879; DEDR 2709). sulgao, salgao to light a fire; sen:gel, sokol fire (Santali.lex.) hollu, holu = fireplace (Kuwi); sod.u fireplace, stones set up as a fireplace (Mand.); ule furnace (Tu.)(DEDR 2857).

kūtī = bunch of twigs (Skt.) Rebus: kuṭhi = furnace (Santali)

kamarasāla = waist-zone, waist-band, belt (Te.) karmāraśāla

= workshop of blacksmith (Skt.) kamar 'blacksmith' (Santali)

baḍhia = a castrated boar, a hog (Santali) baḍhi 'a caste who work both in iron and wood' (Santali)

sal 'bos gaurus'; rebus: sal 'workshop' (Santali)

ibha 'elephant' (Skt.); rebus: ib 'iron' (Santali) karibha

'elephant' (Skt.); rebus: karb 'iron' (Ka.)

kol 'tiger' (Kon.Santali); kola kukur 'white tiger' (A.); dāṭu 'leap' (Te.); rebus: kol 'pan~caloha' (Ta.); dhātu 'mineral' (Skt.)

sekeseke, sekseke covered, as the arms with ornaments; **sekra** those who work in brass and bell metal; sekra sakom a kind of armlet of bell metal (Santali) cūḍā 'bracelets', a number of other phonetic detrminatives are used in the orthography of the horned, seated person: [note the mane on the face.] **bāhula** n. armour for the arms (Skt.) **Rebus:** బంగల bangala. [Tel.] n. An oven. కుంపటి⁹. (Telugu)

There are two glyptic elements denoted on the face.

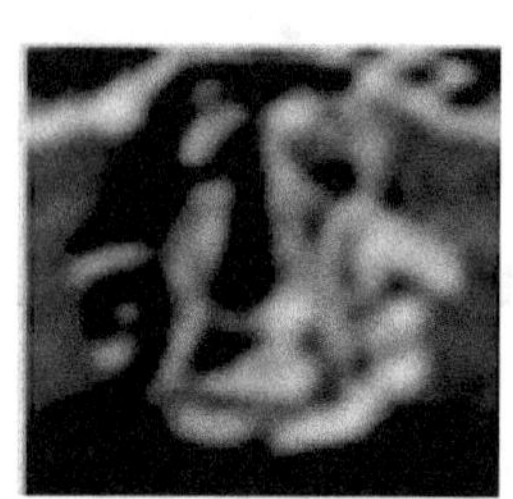

Shoggy hair; tiger's mane. sodo bodo, sodro bodro adj. adv. rough, hairy, shoggy, hirsute, uneven; sodo [Persian. sodā, dealing] trade; traffic; merchandise; marketing; a bargain; the purchase or sale of goods; buying and selling; mercantile dealings (G.lex.) sodagor = a merchant, trader; sodāgor (P.B.) (Santali.lex.) The face is depicted with bristles of hair, representing a tiger's mane. cūḍā, cūlā, cūliyā tiger's mane (Pkt.)(CDIAL 4883)

Text 2420 on m0304

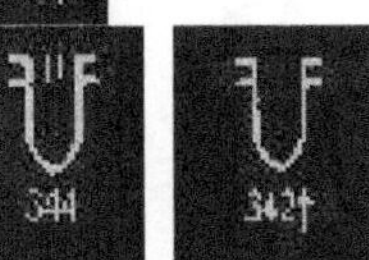

ayo, hako 'fish'; **a~s** = scales of fish (Santali); rebus: aya = iron (G.); **ayah, ayas** = metal (Skt.)

sal stake, spike, splinter, thorn, difficulty (H.); **sal** 'workshop' (Santali)

kaṇḍ kanka 'rim of short-necked jar' (Santali); Rebus: karṇaka copper fire-altar scribe

ḍato 'claws or pincers (chelae) of crabs'; ḍaṭom, ḍiṭom to seize with the claws or pincers, as crabs, scorpions;  ḍaṭkop = to pinch, nip (only of crabs) (Santali) Rebus: dhatu 'mineral' (Santali) Vikalpa: erā 'claws'; Rebus: era 'copper'.

mēd 'body' (Kur.)(DEDR 5099); meḍ 'iron' (Ho.)

sannī, sannhī = pincers, smith's vice (P.) **śannī**[175] f. ' small room in a house to keep sheep in ' (WPah.) Bshk. šan, Phal.šān 'roof' (Bshk.)(CDIAL 12326). seṇi (f.) [Class. Sk. **śreṇi** in meaning "guild"; Vedic= row] 1. a guild Vin iv.226; J i.267, 314; iv.43; Dāvs ii.124; their number was eighteen J vi.22, 427; VbhA 466. ° -- **pamukha** the head of a guild J ii.12 (text seni --). -- 2. a division of an army J vi.583; ratha -- ° J vi.81, 49; seṇimokkha the chief of an army J vi.371 (cp. senā and seniya). (Pali)

Pict-49 Uncertain animal with dotted circles on its body. m1908

This seal has sign 347, 342 sequence, which is a terminal pair with 110 occurrences. An additional glyph shown in front of the animal is: a sloped stroke.

Glyptic element (or sign) on Seal m1908. ḍhāḷ = a slope; the inclination of a plane (G.) Rebus: : **ḍhāḷako** = a large metal ingot (G.) The three signs can be read: **ḍhāḷako dul kolmo baṭa kaṇḍ kanka** 'ingot casting smithy (iron) furnace scribe'.

The seal has other glyptic elements: 1. Tusk of a rhinoceros 2. Young spotted animal (?deer or antelope) 3. Dotted circles for the animal's eye and inscribed all over the body.

Antelope: miṇḍāl 'markhor' (Tōrwāḷī) meḍho a ram, a sheep (G.)(CDIAL 10120); rebus: mẽṛhẽt, meḍ 'iron' (Mu.Ho.)
The indication is that the pasra 'forge' also deals with meḍ 'iron'.

The ligatured animal can be read as a set of hieroglyphs:

piserā[176] 'small deer' ; rebus: **pasra** 'smithy'; **kãg** 'boar's tusk'; rebus: **kãgar** 'portable brazier'; **kandi**[177] 'hole, opening' (Ka.); kan[178] 'eye' (Ka.); rebus: **kandi** (pl. -l) [179] necklace, beads (Pa.) Thus, the entire ligatured animal is decoded rebus: **meḍ pasra kãgar kandil** 'iron smithy, forge, portable furnace, beads'.

Phonetic determinant of **kãgar** 'portable brazier' is the

set of glyphs showing 'full of holes': Glyph: khan:ghar, ghan:ghar, ghan:ghar gon:ghor 'full of holes' (Santali) Rebus: kan:gar 'portable furnace' (K.) Vikalpa: putli[180] ' doll, pupil of eye (B.); pottal[181] 'hole' (Ta.); póta[182] 'young of animal or plant' (Skt.); pōtalaka 'young animal' (Kashmiri)

Phonetic determinant of **kandi** 'beads' and **kaṇḍ** 'furnace' is the tusk glyph, which is read **khaṇḍ[183]** 'ivory'; rebus: **kaṇḍ[184]** = altar, furnace (Santali) Vikalpa: Glyph: pāso 'die' (orthography: dotted circle). Rebus: pāśo = a silver ingot; pāśātāṇiyo = one who draws silver into a wire (G.) **pāslo** = a nugget of gold or silver having the form of a die (G.)

Together with the sequence of signs (glyphs), which read, the seal belongs to a lapidary-scribe working with casting smithy and bead-making furnace: **ḍhāḷako dul kolmo baṭa kaṇḍ kanka** 'ingot casting smithy (iron) furnace scribe'.

> **khãg, khãg[185]** m. ' rhinoceros horn, boar's tusk (H.); rebus: **kãgar[186]** portable brazier (Kashmiri)

> **pasata** 'spotted deer' (Pali); **piserā** 'small deer' (H.) rebus: **pasra** 'smithy, blacksmith's forge' (Santali)

piserā = a small deer brown above and black below (H.)(CDIAL 8365). **pr̥ṣatá[187]** ' spotted ' m., ' spotted deer ' VS. 2. **pr̥ṣita** -- ' *spotted ' (n. ' rain ' Gobh.). [pr̥ṣat -- ' spotted ' AV., m. ' spotted antelope ' R. -- √pr̥ṣ] 1. Pa. pasata -- miga -- m. ' spotted deer '; Pk. pasaya -- m. ' a kind of deer

2. Pk. pusia -- m. ' id. '. (CDIAL 8364). Rebus: **pasra**[188] = a smithy (Santali) blacksmith's forge (Sad.) P. **pahārā**[189] m. 'goldsmith's workshop' (CDIAL 8835).

Grapheme: pasu = animal; ato posu = domestic animal;  bir pasu = wild animal (Santali); paśu = animal (Skt. Ta.) Rebus: pasra 'smithy, forge'.

Grapheme: pasaramu, pasalamu = an animal, a beast, a brute, quadruped (Te.)

 Sign 347 is a ligature of a wide-mouthed, rimless pot and a pair of 'sprout[190], paddy-plant' glyphs. kolom'sprout'; **kolom** = cutting, graft; to graft, engraft, prune; **kolma horo** = a variety of the paddy plant (Desi)(Santali.) **kolmo** 'rice plant' (Mu.) Rebus: **kolami** 'furnace,smithy' (Te.) Since a pair of 'sprout.rice-plant' glyphs are used, the pair connotes : **dula** 'pair'; Rebus: **dul** 'cast (metal)(Santali) This pair is ligatured to: baṭhu m. 'large pot in which grain is parched (S.) Rebus: baṭa = a kind of iron (G.) bhaṭa 'furnace' (G.) baṭa = kiln (Santali). +

Sign 342: **kaṇḍ kanka** 'rim of jar'; Rebus: karṇaka 'scribe'; kaṇḍ 'furnace, fire-altar'. Thus the ligatured sign is decoded: kaṇḍ karṇaka 'furnace scribe

Thus, the pair os signs 347 + 342 is decoded: **dul kolmo baṭa kaṇḍ kanka** 'casting smithy (iron) furnace scribe'.

Reduplicated glyphs (pictorial motifs)

Comparable to the reduplication of signs or mirror-reflected pairs of glyphs (signs) is the reduplication of pictorial motifs of animals   which can also be read in the same method demonstrated for reduplicated pairs of signs.

Rahman-dheri01 Urseal11; UPenn; a scorpion and an elipse [an eye (?)][191]

Decoding a pair: dula दुल ꠰ युग्मम् m. a pair, a couple, esp. of two similar things (Rām. 966) (Kashmiri); dol 'likeness, picture, form' (Santali) Rebus: dul 'to cast metal in a mould' (Santali) dul meṛeḍ cast iron (Mundari. Santali)

Kur. mūxā frog. Malt. múqe id. Cf. Skt. mūkaka- id. (DEDR 5023). **mūh**[192] 'metal ingot' (Santali)Side 1: **dul bica mūhe** 'stone ore ingot'. A pair of ibexes. dula kal 'pair of ibexes'; rebus: **dul kalla**[193] 'cast glass (stone) beads'. 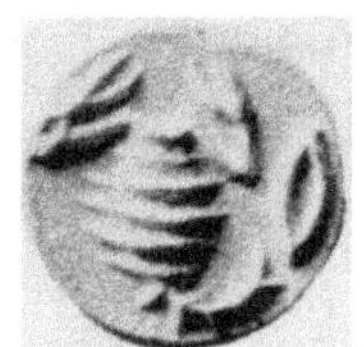

Oval glyph on second line of the inscription of Urseal 15. Ur seal 15 is decoded: **bica mūh** 'scorpion, ingot'; rebus: **bica mūh** 'stone ore ingot'

Cylinder-seal impression from Ur showing a squatting

female.[194] bichā[195]'scorpion' (A.); rebus: bica[196] 'stones containing ore' (Mu.) 'meṟed-bica = iron stone ore, in contrast to bali-bica, iron sand ore (Mu.lex.) kuṭh[197]i = the pubes (lower down than pan.d.e) (Santali) Rebus: kuṭhi 'smelting furnace' (Santali) Thus, the glyptic composition is decoded: **dula bica kuṭhi** 'casting, iron stone ore smelter.Examples of depiction of glyphs in pairs

h180, k065, m0296, m0306, m0308, m0477, m0480, m0492, m1367, m1431, m1534, Gadd18, h95-2524, h2000-4483

?Pleiades clustered in the context of other Indus script glyphs

Text 4251 h097 Pict-95: Seven robed figures (with stylized

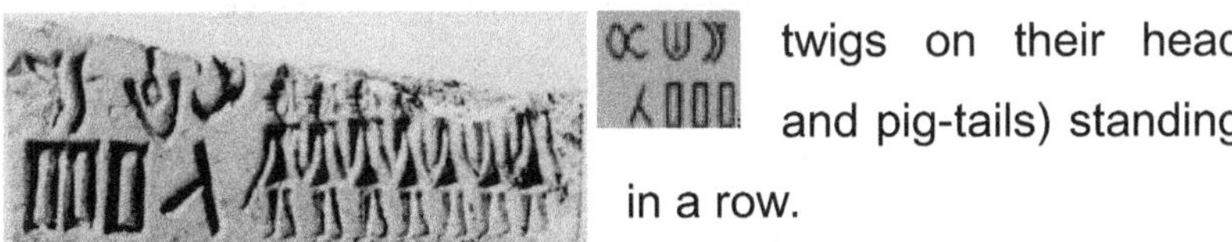 twigs on their head and pig-tails) standing in a row.

A group of six or seven women wearing twigs may not represent Pleiades, bagaḷā[198]). The groups of such glyphs occur on four inscribed objects of Indus writing. (See four pictorial compositions on: m1186A, h097, m0442At m0442Bt shown below).

- bhaṭa 'six'; rebus: bhaṭa 'furnace'

- eae 'seven' (Santali); rebus: eh-ku 'steel' (Ta.)

adaru 'twig'; rebus: aduru 'native, unsmelted metal'. kola 'woman'; rebus: kol 'working in iron' (Ta.) Thus the group of women (six or seven) may connote: pl. kole.l rebus: 'smithy, temple' (Ko.)(DEDR 2133). Six women with twigs: adaru kol bhaṭa 'native metal, iron furnace'; seven women with twigs: adaru kol eh-ku 'native metal, iron, steel'.

A group of six or seven persons constitute unique glyphs. Each of the six or seven glyphs is ligatured with a twig on the head and a scarf as a hair-dress. The other glyphs associated with the Pleiades, in the four pictorial compositions are:

- Human face ligatured to a ram with neck-bands
- Kneeling adorant with horns and scarf as pigtail
- Standing person (horns, twig as head-dress, scarf as pigtail) within a pot ligatured with leaves
- Temple (smithy?) glyph (third line of signs)
- Dotted fish, rim of jar, body (person)
- Pincers, claws (ligatured to ingots) ḍhālako Sign 274; rebus: 'a large metal ingot (G.)'
- Spoon in a rimless pot (Second sign on line 1, text 4251)

()The first sign from right on line 1 of Inscribed text 4251 and connotes 'cast bronze'; it is a glyptic formed of a pair of brackets (): kuṭila 'bent'; rebus: **kuṭila, katthīl** = bronze (8 parts copper and 2 parts tin) [cf. āra-kūṭa, 'brass' (Skt.) (CDIAL 3230) **kuṭi**[199]— in cmpd. 'curve' 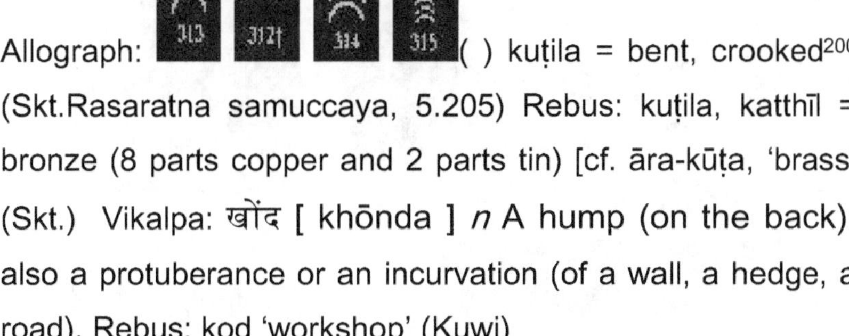 (Skt.)(CDIAL 3231). Thus, **dul kuṭila** 'cast bronze'.

Allograph: ( ) kuṭila = bent, crooked[200] (Skt.Rasaratna samuccaya, 5.205) Rebus: kuṭila, katthīl = bronze (8 parts copper and 2 parts tin) [cf. āra-kūṭa, 'brass' (Skt.) Vikalpa: खोंद [khōnda] n A hump (on the back): also a protuberance or an incurvation (of a wall, a hedge, a road). Rebus: koḍ 'workshop' (Kuwi)

Allograph

kuṭi— in cmpd. 'curve', kuṭika— 'bent' MBh. (CDIAL 3231); rebus: kuṭhi 'smelter' (Santali) [Shape of oval is consistent with the traditiojn of Koles to form equilateral lumps pointed at each end of ingots: mũh metal ingot (Santali) mũhā = the quantity of iron produced at one time in a native smelting furnace of the Kolhes; iron produced by the Kolhes and formed like a four-cornered piece a little pointed at each end; mũhā me~r.he~t = iron smelted by the Kolhes and formed into an equilateral lump a little pointed at each end; kolhe tehen me~r.he~tko mūhā akata = the Kolhes have to-day produced pig iron (Santali.lex.) kaula mengro 'blacksmith' (Gypsy) paired: dul 'likeness'; dul 'cast (metal)']

M1179, m1180 Human-faced markhor with long wavy horns, with neck-bands and a short tail.

mũhe 'face' (Santali) mũh opening or

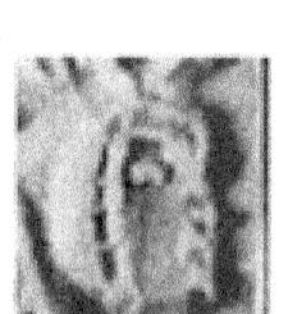

hole (in a stove for stoking (Bi.); ingot (Santali)

mũh metal ingot (Santali) mũhā = the quantity of iron produced at one time in a native smelting furnace of the

Kolhes; iron produced by the Kolhes and formed like a four-cornered piece a little pointed at each end; **mūhā mẽṛhẽt** = iron smelted by the Kolhes and formed into an equilateral lump a little pointed at each of four ends; **kolhe tehen mẽṛhẽt ko mūhā akata** = the Kolhes have to-day produced pig iron (Santali.lex.) kaula mengro 'blacksmith' (Gypsy) mleccha-mukha (Skt.) = milakkhu 'copper' (Pali) The Sanskrit loss mleccha-mukha should literally mean: copper-ingot absorbing the Santali gloss, mu~h, as a suffix.

The sign on the left may indicate an ingot **mu~h** made into an equilateral lump a little pointed at each of four ends as described in the Santali gloss.

Two signs from the left on m1180 are decoded rebus. kana, kanac = corner (Santali); Rebus: kañcu = bronze (Te.)

 Allograph: kã_s artificial canal for irrigation (G.)(CDIAL 2909). Rebus: kamsa, kañcu 'bronze' (Telugu)

sal 'splinter'; Rebus: sal 'workshop' (Santali)

xolā = tail (Kur.); qoli = id. (Malt.)(DEDR 2135).

kole.l 'smithy, temple' (Ko.) [The glyph on line 3 of inscription on seal, m1186A; this glyph is also ligatured in another context, with a rimless pot, bhaTa, 'furnace, kiln'. Hence, the decoding as smithy is internally consistent.]

 **dato** 'claws or pincers (chelae) of crabs'; **datom, ditom** to seize with the claws or pincers, as crabs, scorpions; datkop = to pinch, nip (only of crabs) (Santali) Rebus: dhatu 'mineral' (Santali) Vikalpa: kamatha crab (Skt.) Rebus: **kammata** = portable furnace (Te.) **kampattam** coiner, mint (Ta.)

sannī, sannhī = pincers, smith's vice (P.) Rebus: **sāna 'grindstone' (Te.)**

 A horned person (with a three-leaved pipal branch on the crown with two stars on either side), wearing bangles and armlets. Two stars adorn the curved buffalo horns of the seated person **with a scarf on pigtail**. kūdī, kūṭī bunch of twigs (Skt.lex.)

mēdha The polar star. (Marathi) Rebus: meḍ 'iron' (Ho.)

dabe, dabea 'large horns, with a sweeping upward curve, applied to buffaloes' (Santali) Rebus: **dab, dhimba, dhompo** 'lump (ingot?)', clot, make a lump or clot, coagulate, fuse, melt together (Santali)

kūdī (also written as kūṭī in manuscripts) occurs in the Atharvaveda (AV 5.19.12) and Kauśika Sūtra (Bloomsfield's ed.n, xliv. cf. Bloomsfield, American Journal of Philology, 11, 355; 12,416; Roth, Festgruss an Bohtlingk, 98) denotes it as a twig. This is identified as that of Badarī, the jujube tied to the body of the dead to efface their traces. (See Vedic Index, I, p. 177).

Rebus: **kuṭhi** 'smelting furnace' (Santali) koṭe 'forged (metal) (Santali)

- Vikalpa: aḍaru twig; aḍiri small and thin branch of a tree; aḍari small branches (Ka.); aḍaru twig (Tu.)(DEDR 67). aḍar = splinter (Santali); rebus: **aduru** = native metal (Ka.)

Slide 142. Moulded tablets from Trench 11 Harappa

(Kenoyer); m1186; m488C adorant with 'scarf'; markhor in front, with rings (or neck-bands) on neck.

miṇḍāl 'markhor' (Tōrwālī) meḍho a ram, a sheep (G.)(CDIAL 10120); rebus: mẽṛhet, meḍ 'iron' (Mu.Ho.) m1186A, Text 2430 Composition: horned person with a pigtail standing between the branches of a pipal on a creeper; a low pedestal with offerings (? Bowl with two ladles?);a horned person kneeling in adoration;a ram with short tail and curling horns; a row of seven robed figures,

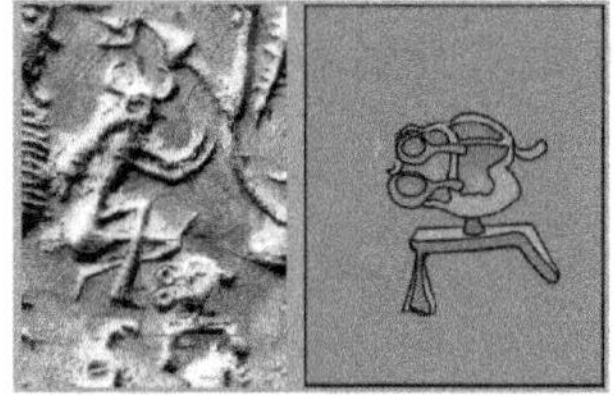

with twigs on their pigtails. bārṇe, bāraṇe = an offering of food to a demon; a meal after fasting, a breakfast (Tu.) barada, barda, birada = a vow (G.lex.) Rebus: baran, bharat (5 copper, 4 zinc and 1 tin)(P.B.)

mergo = rimless vessels (Santali) Rebus: meḍ 'iron' (Ho.)

ḍabu 'an iron spoon' (Santali) Rebus: **ḍab, ḍhimba, ḍhompo** 'lump (ingot?)', clot, make a lump or clot, coagulate, fuse, melt together (Santali)

m0478A

S. **baṭhu** m. 'large pot in which grain is parched, Rebus; **bhaṭṭhā** m. 'kiln' (P.) **baṭa**[201] = a kind of iron (G.) Vikalpa: mergo = rimless vessels (Santali) Rebus: meḍ iron (Ho.)

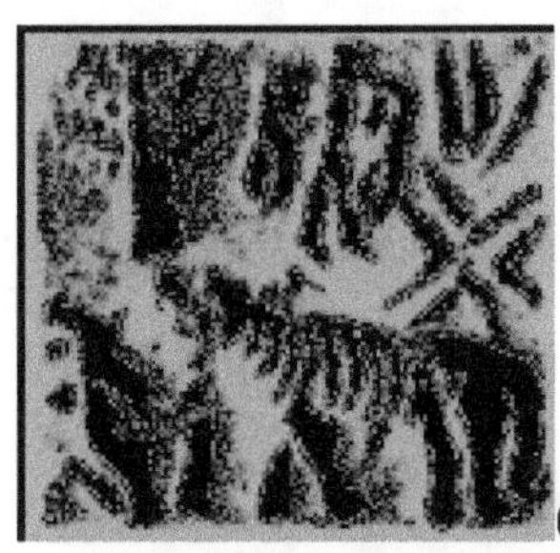
Chanhudaro6118

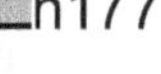h177

h238A
h242A 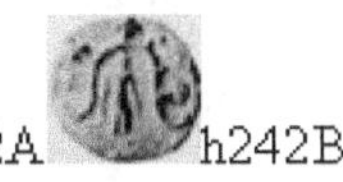h242B Pict-84

Konḍa dolu a creeper plant, shrub, plant of shoot height. Pe. dol plant; stem, trunk. Manḍ. dul plant; sapling. Kui. (Mah. p. 96) kūḍi-ḍoḍu rice plant; (p. 102) ḍoḍu tree. Kuwi (Mah.) kūli-dolu rice plant; (Isr.) dulomi plant. (DEDR 3517) Vikalpa: kolo 'a large jungle climber, dioscorea doemonum (Santali) Rebus: dul 'cast (metal)(Santali) Vikalpa: koṭi[202] creeper(DEDR 2050); rebus; koḍ 'workshop' (Kuwi)

Grapheme: **karadamu** present to a superior (Te.) karetum = an annual offering and present to a godess or to an evil spirit (G.) karavrtti (Skt.) Rebus; **kharādī**[203] 'turner' (G.) Decoding glyph (Sign 45): **kharādī bhaṭṭhā** 'turner kiln'

Vikalpa: **saman:** = to offer an offering, to place in front of; front, to front or face (Santali) Rebus: samr.obica, stones containing gold (Mundari.lex.) cf. soma (ṛgveda) **samanom** = an obsolete name for gold (Santali).

ḍhaṁkhara[204]-- m.n. ' branch without leaves or fruit (Pkt.) 'Rebus: **ḍangar** 'blacksmith' (H.)

gaṇḍa 'four' (Santali); rebus: **kaṇḍ** 'furnace, fire-altar'

midh 'one' (Savara) meḍ 'body'; rebus: meḍ 'iron' (Ho.) A pair of long linear strokes: dula 'pair'; rebus: dul 'cast (metal)(Santali) The ligaturing element of a pair of long linear strokes circumscribe the 'body' glyph (as a phonetic determinant). The ligatured glyph can be decoded as: **dul meḍ** 'cast iron' (Mu.)

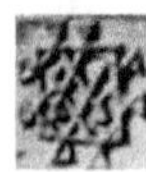

kharedo = a currycomb (G.) Rebus: **kharādī** ' turner' (G.)

medhā m. 'curl, snarl, twist or tangle in cord or thread' (M.)(CDIAL 10312) Rebus: **meḍ** 'iron' (Ho.)

Decoding the **text** of inscription on m0478A and the **glyph** showing a tangled thread shown 

on the tablet: **kharādī ,gaṇḍa bhaṭṭhā ,dul meḍ , meḍ** 'turner, fire-altar, kiln, cast iron, iron

 **dhaṭu** m. (also dhaṭhu) m. 'scarf' (WPah.)(CDIAL 6707) Pa. **dhātu** 'mineral' Decoding glyph (Sign 46): **dhātu kharādī bhaṭṭhā** 'mineral turner kiln'

bhāraṇ = to bring out from a kiln (G.) bāraṇiyo = one whose profession it is to sift ashes or dust in a goldsmith's workshop (G.lex.) baran, bharat (5 copper, 4 zinc and 1 tin)(P.B.)

In the Punjab, the mixed alloys were generally called, bharat (5 copper, 4 zinc and 1 tin). In Bengal, an alloy called bharan or toul was created by adding some brass or zinc into pure bronze. bhārata = casting metals in moulds; bharavum = to fill in; to put in; to pour into (G.lex.) Bengali. ভরন [bharana] n an inferior metal obtained from an alloy of coper, zinc and tin (Bengali).

bharatiyo = a caster of metals; a brazier; Bhāratar, bhāratal, bhāratal = moulded; an article made in a mould; Bhārata = casting metals in moulds; bharavum = to fill in; to put in; to pour into (G.lex.) bhart = a mixed metal of copper and lead; bhart-īyā = a barzier, worker in metal; bhat., bhrāṣṭra = oven, furnace (Skt.) bhārata = a factitious metal compounded of copper, pewter, tin (M.)

bharaḍo a devotee of S'iva; a man of the bharaḍā caste in the brāmaṇa-s (G.) barar = name of a caste of jat- around

Bhaṭiṇḍa; bararaṇḍā melā = a special fair held in spring
(P.lex.) bharāḍ = a religious service or entertainment
performed by a bharāḍī; consisting of singing the praises of
some idol or god with playing on the d.aur (drum) and
dancing; an order of aṭharā akhād.e = 18 gosāyi_ group;
bharād. and bhāratī are two of the 18 orders of gosāyi_
(M.lex.)

 bharaḍo[205] = cross-beam in the roof of a house
(G.lex.)

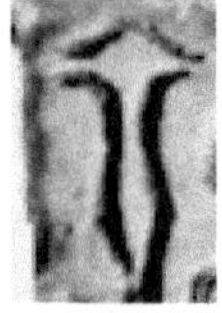 ḍaren, aḍaren cover, lid (Santali); Rebus: **koṇḍa**
bend (Ko.); Rebus: **kõdā** 'to turn in a lathe'(B.)
Vikalpa: aduru 'native metal' (Ka.) The ligatured
jar can be read rebus: kaṇḍ karṇaka kõdā 'furnace scribe,
turner'.

m0478B tablet

kōla = woman (Nahali)

Rebus: kol[206] 'furnace, forge' (Kuwi)
erg a = act of clearing jungle (Kui) [Note image showing two
men carrying uprooted trees]. This glyptic composition
depicting the act of clearing jungle may be a phonetic

determinant for the person seated on the tree branch and the glyph of a woman pushing them apart:

ḍāl = a branch of a tree (G.) ḍhālako = a large ingot (G.) ḍhālakī = a metal heated and poured into a mould; a solid piece of metal; an ingot (G.)

eraka, hero = a messenger; a spy (G.lex.) heraka = spy (Skt.); er to look at or for (Pkt.); er uk- to play 'peeping tom' (Ko.) Rebus: eraka 'copper' (Ka.) Thus, the glyphs of tree-branch and a spy are read rebus: **eraka ḍhālako** 'copper ingot'.

- era female, applied to women only, and generally as a mark of respect, wife; hopon era a daughter; era hopon a man's family; manjhi era the village chief's wife; gosae era a female Santal deity; buḍhi era an old woman; era uru wife and children; nabi era a prophetess; diku era a Hindu woman (Santali)

- gaṇḍra[207] = tree trunk (Kuwi); kaṇḍa = bough (Pali); rebus: kaṇḍ 'fire-altar' (Santali)

Kur. kaṇḍō a stool. Malt. kaṇḍo stool, seat. (DEDR 1179) Rebus: kaṇḍ = a furnace, altar (Santali.lex.)

er-agu = a bow, an obeisance; er-aguha = bowing, coming down (Ka.lex.) er-agisu = to bow, to be bent; tomake obeisance to; to crouch; to come down; to alight (Ka.lex.) cf. arghas = respectful reception of a guest (by the offering of rice,   du_rva   grass,   flowers   or   often   only   of water)(S'Br.14)(Skt.lex.) erugu = to bow, to salute or make obeisance (Te.)

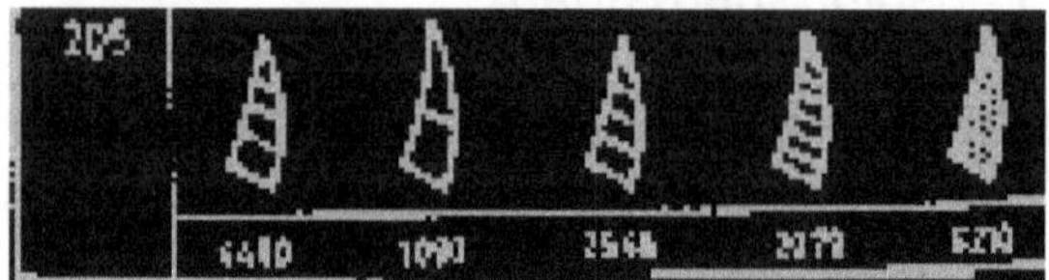

erka = ekke (Tbh. of arka) aka (Tbh. of arka) copper (metal); crystal (Ka.lex.) eraka, er-aka = any metal infusion (Ka.Tu.) eruvai 'copper' (Ta.); ere dark red (Ka.)(DEDR 446). er-r-a = red; (arka-) agasāle, agasāli, agasālavāḍu = a goldsmith (Te.lex.)

WPah. dhaṭu m. (also dhaṭhu) m. 'scarf' (CDIAL 6707) Pa. **dhātu** 'mineral' Vikalpa: **panǰãr** 'ladder, stairs'(Bshk.) (CDIAL 7760); **pasra** 'smithy' (Santali)
kulullu 'fish-man'; apkallu 'sage'

- **kuṇḍī** = crooked buffalo horns (L.)
- **kuṇḍī** = chief of village. **kuṇḍi-a** = village headman; leader of a village (Pkt.lex.) I.e. s'ren.i jet.t.ha chief of metal-worker guild.

  - **kolli** = a fish (Ma.); koleji id. (Tu.)(DEDR 2139). kōlā flying fish, exocaetus, garfish, belone (Ta.) kōlān, **kōli** needle-fish (Ma.)(DEDR 2241). Cf. **kulullu**, 'fish-man; **kuliltu**, 'fish-woman'; fish-garbed figure: **apkallu**, 'sage' (in fish-guise); Apkallu is shown in two ligatures: one with wings and one with fish (Contextual glyphs relate to tree and water). Lishtar notes: "The apkallu were also known as the priests of

Enki...Enki's organized world...in which wealth can be brought to the Land as a whole. " (Lishtar, Understanding Enki and the world order). http://www.gatewaystobabylon.com/essays/essa yenkiworld.html

- Ayo 'fish' (Mu.)

Rebus: ayaskāṇḍa a quantity of iron, excellent iron (Pāṇ.gaṇ) ayas 'metal' (Skt.) **ayir** = iron dust, any ore (Ma.) aduru = gan.iyinda tegadu karagade iruva aduru = ore taken from the mine and not subjected to melting in a furnace (Ka. Siddha_nti Subrahman.ya' S'astri's new interpretation of the Amarakos'a, Bangalore, Vicaradarpana Press, 1872, p. 330)

- ḍhagarām pl. the buttocks; the hips (G.lex.) Rebus: **ḍhā~gar., dhā~gar** blacksmith; digger of wells (H.)

ḍaulā 'upper arm' (IL 4982) Rebus: dāula 'a gold or silver washer' (P.) Vikalpa: **eṛaka** 'upraised arm' (Ta.); rebus: **eraka** = copper (Ka.)

meṛgo = rimless vessels (Santali) Rebus: **meḍ** iron (Ho.)

sekeseke covered, as the arms with ornaments

(Santali; Rebus: sekra 'those who work in brass and bell metal'; sekra sakom a kind of armlet of bell metal (Santali)

Vikalpa: **bāhula**[208] n. armour for the arms (Skt.)(CDIAL 9233). **Rebus:** బంగల bangala. [Tel.] n. An oven. కుంపటి[9].

M0488, Text 2801

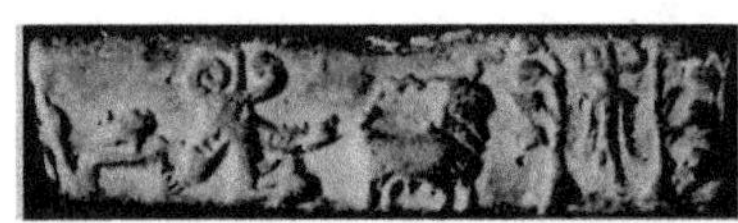

 Vikalpa: **kamaṛkom** = fig leaf (Santali.lex.) **kamarmaṛā** (Has.), **kamaṛkom** (Nag.); the petiole or stalk of a leaf (Mundari.lex.)

kampaṭṭam[209] coinage, coin (Ta.)(DEDR 1236) kampaṭṭa-muḷai die, coining stamp (Ta.)

bhaṭa 'six' (G.)

lo 'iron' (Assamese, Bengali); **loa** 'iron' (Gypsy) Glyph: lo = nine (Santali); no = nine (B.) on-patu = nine (Ta.)

mēd 'body' (Kur.)(DEDR 5099)

Rebus: mẽṛhẽt, meḍ 'iron' (Mu.Ho.)

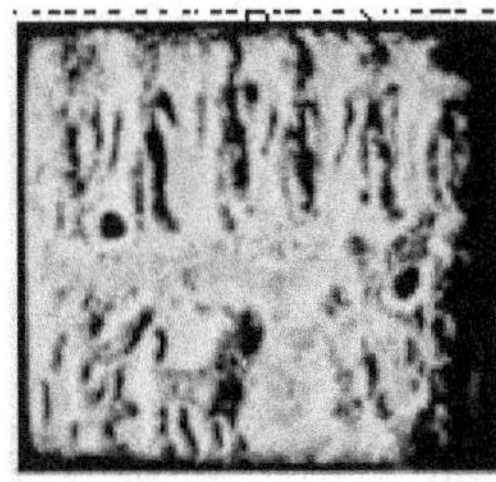  

Mohenjo-daro, excavation number HR 4161, now in the National Museum of India, New Delhi. A seal from Mohenjo-daro, excavation number DK 6847 (m1186A), now in the National Museum of Pakistan, Karachi. Copyrighted photo by the Department of Archaeology and Museums, Government of Pakistan.

Bos indicus and fish glyphs of Indus script:artisan-guild. Resolving Indus script debate.

The late George F. Dales noted, "There is no doubt that the Harappans were literate, or had at least a literate social class. There are abundant examples of their script to verify this but as yet not a single word can be read. We know virtually nothing of the structure of the language nor do we even know to which linguistic family it belongs." (Dales, 1967: 34) After surveying over 100 claims of decipherment, Gregory L. Possehl concluded that the writing system remains undeciphered. (Possehl, 1966). The glyphs of bos indicus and fish are decoded and read rebus as mleccha words denoting an artisan guild, in the context of recent discoveries of early iron-working in the civilization interaction area and many types of stone-beads made by lapidaries.

The continuity of the civilization is the keynote which is affirmed by the postulation of an Indian linguistic area by a number of linguists (Kuiper 1948, 1967; Emeneau 1956; Masica 1971; Southworth 2005). Przyludski had, 80 years ago, noted non-aryan loans in Indo-Aryan (Przyludski 1929). The language of the writing system is hypothesized to be a proto-version of the Indian linguistic area or sprachbund (Indian language union). Thus, one or more of present-day languages of India are likely to retain the glosses of the Indian language union. Glosses which are common to two or more of the language families (Indo-Aryan, Dravidian, Mundarica, Tibeto-Burman) are likely to relate to the Indian language union.

Ca. 3rd millennium BCE, the pictorial motifs used on inscriptions and script signs (most of which are also pictographic) are treated as logographs and read rebus, using these glosses. The sound-value and substantive meaning value of the homonymous glosses relate to one semantic category: metallurgy. New finds of inscriptions from recently excavated sites such as Kanmer (Kharakwal et al, 2007) are also found together with metallurgical artefacts.

Consistent with the date of the earliest iron in India which is pushed back, by recent discoveries, into the early 2nd millennium BCE and the arguments of archaeologists about the underlying language of the script, the decoding of the seals showing the bos indicus points to the possibility that the inventors of early metallurgy were also inventors of the Indus writing system.

There are over 50 epigraphs of the civilization showing bos taurus indicus which is decoded as a hieroglyph denoting in mleccha a metal-smithy-guild (community, khu~t.) This reference to a community through a glyph is indicative of the early guild working in the civilization. This is a surmise that the early semantics of the word khu~t. may have related to such a group formation of metalsmiths and artisans.

Long-linear-stroke as hieroglyph

1254		2155	
2504		2581	
		2557	
		0238	
		1004	
		2612	
		1620	
		2066	
		3074	
		2157	
		4116	
		3148	
		0135	
		5064	
		2039	
		3628	
		2343	
		2587	

Parpola suggests that the sign appears to be redundant since many texts occur with comparable sign sequences but without such a sign. The sign may be a determinative, just as a

'man' glyph may be semantic determinative of a function or title. (Parpola, 1994, p. 80). Just as a 'body' glyph is read rebus to indicate meḍ 'body, rebus:

iron'(Ho.), an alternative is to read the long-linear-stroke glyph also rebus as a determinative of an artisan's workshop: goṭ = one (Santali); goṭi = silver (G.) koḍa 'one'(Santali); koḍ 'workshop' (G.)

The long linear stroke on m0318 decoded rebus : koḍa, koṛa = in arithmetic one[210]; 4 koṛa or koḍa = 1 gaṇḍa = 4 (Santali) Rebus: koḍ, 'artisan's workshop' (Kuwi.)

Archaeological context of material resources and artisans' Indus writing system

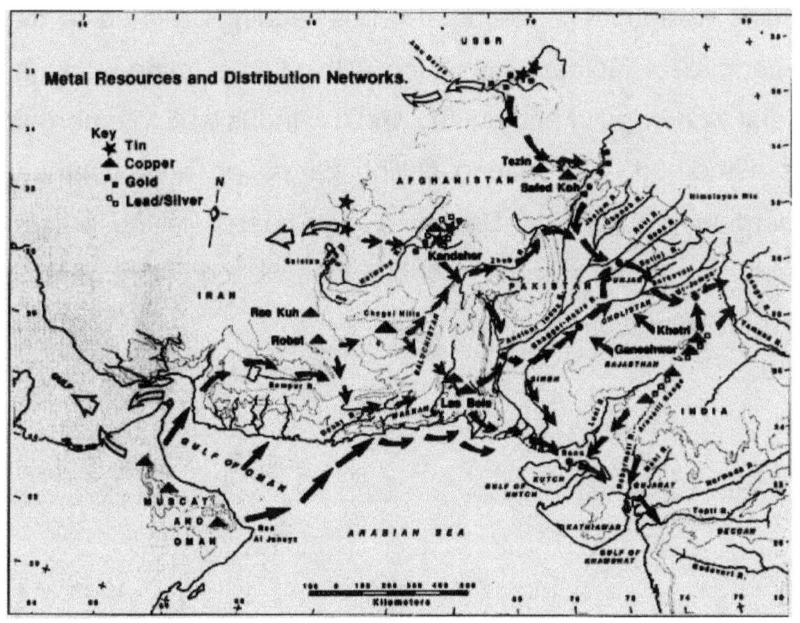

Map of Metal Resources and Distribution Networks (After Fig. 5.20f, Kenoyer, 1998)

When sound values related to the glyphs of the Indus writing system were evidenced from the glosses of the linguistic area, a surprising semantic cluster emerges with sets of homophones matching the pictorials of Indus writing. While the glosses directly relatable to the emphatically, unambiguously identifiable glyphs were tabulated, the corresponding homophones produced a semantic cluster related to the work of artisans -- lapidary work (working with precious stones), metallurgical work, (working with minerals, metals, alloys, smithy, smelters, furnace types and forge).

The rebus method automatically justified itself as a valid method and helped decode majority of the unambiguously identified glyphs (both pictorial motifs and signs) of the writing system. The decoded rebus readings related to the repertoire of lapidaries working with stones, mine-workers, metal worker guild and smithy and the Indus writing emerged as a method of preparing calling cards (or, advertisement board in the case of Dholavira sign-board) of the artisan guilds/sea-faring merchantsof Meluhha working with material resources and distribution networks.

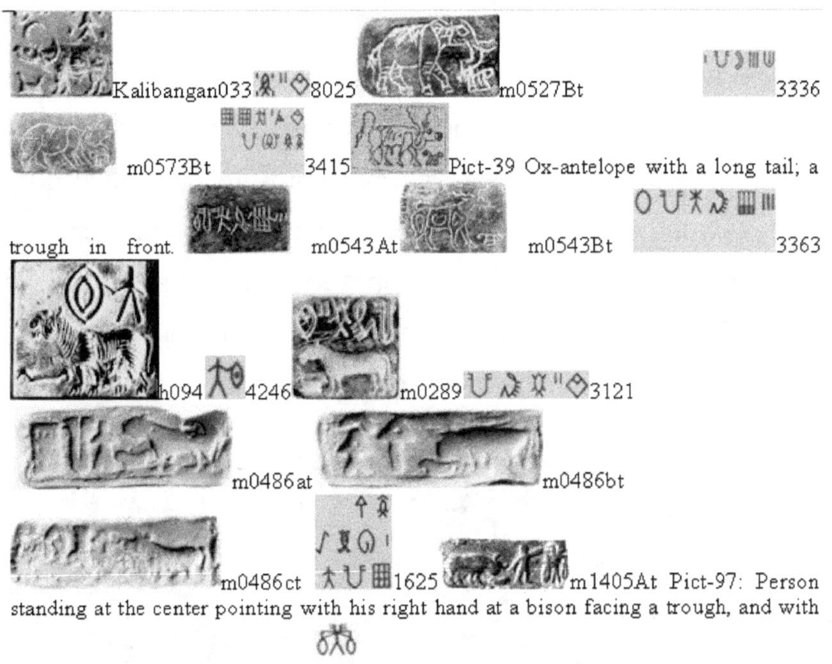

Kalibangan033 8025   m0527Bt   3336

m0573Bt   3415   Pict-39 Ox-antelope with a long tail; a

trough in front.   m0543At   m0543Bt   3363

h094 4246   m0289 3121

m0486at   m0486bt

m0486ct   1625   m1405At Pict-97: Person standing at the center pointing with his right hand at a bison facing a trough, and with

his left hand pointing to the sign

That a guild was in vogue is inferred from the glyph of a trough shown in front of not only domesticated animals but also wild animals and the homophone for the trough (paatra[211]) indicates a guild, pattar, guild of goldsmiths and lapidaries[212] working with precious stones: OMarw. pātharī ' precious stone ' (CDIAL 8857)

Pinnowmap of Austro-AsiaticLanguage speakers correlates with bronze age sites[213]

The areal map of Austric (Austro-Asiatic languages) showing regions marked by Pinnow correlates with the bronze age settlements in Bharatam or what came to be known during the British colonial regime as 'Greater India'. The bronze age sites extend from Mehrgarh-Harappa (Meluhha) on the west to Kayatha-Navdatoli (Nahali) close to River Narmada to Koldihwa- Khairdih-Chirand on Ganga river basin to

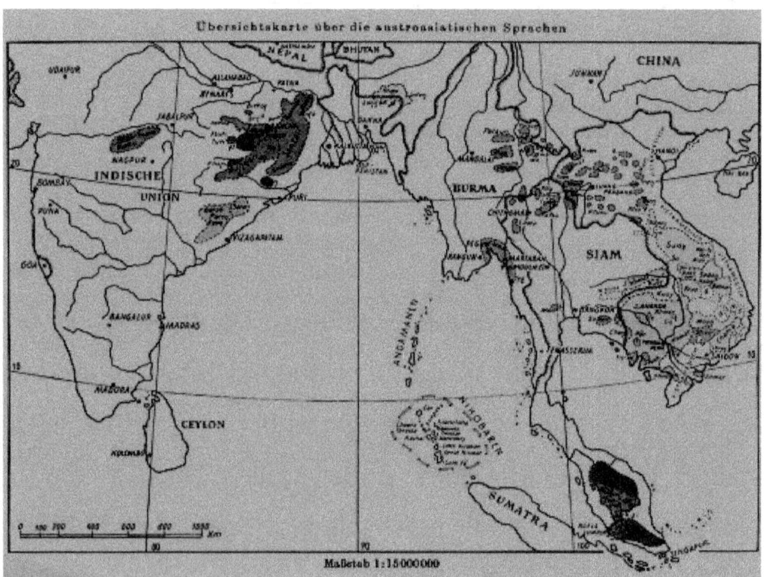

Mahisadal – Pandu Rajar Dhibi in Jharia mines close to Mundari area and into the east extending into Burma, Indonesia, Malaysia, Laos, Cambodia, Vietnam, Nicobar islands. A settlement of Inamgaon is shown on the banks of River Godavari.

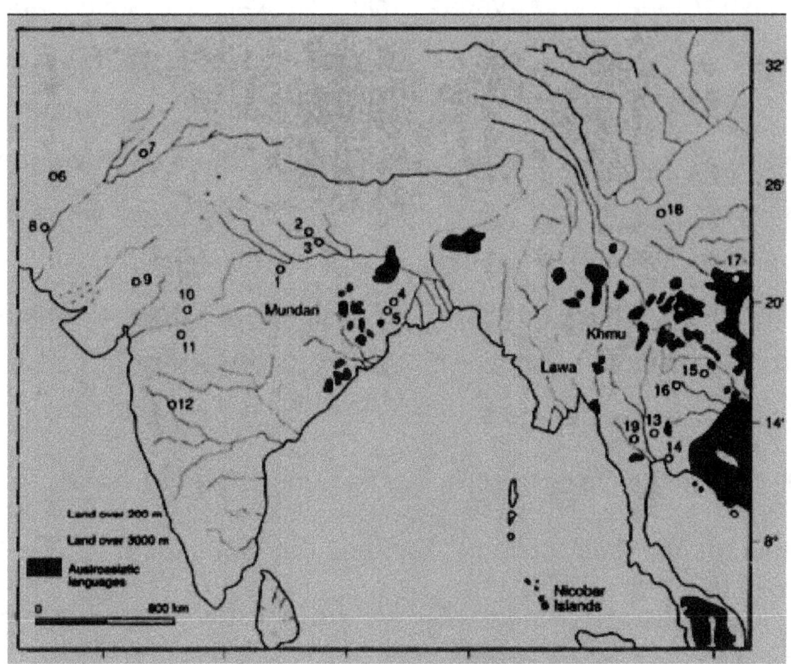

Bronze Age sites of eastern India and neighbouring areas: 1. Koldihwa; 2.Khairdih; 3. Chirand; 4. Mahisadal; 5. Pandu Rajar Dhibi; 6.Mehrgarh; 7. Harappa;8. Mohenjo-daro; 9.Ahar; 10. Kayatha; 11.Navdatoli; 12.Inamgaon; 13. Non PaWai; 14. Nong Nor;15. Ban Na Di andBan Chiang; 16. NonNok Tha; 17. Thanh Den; 18. Shizhaishan; 19. Ban Don Ta Phet [After Fig. 8.1 in: Charles Higham, 1996, The Bronze Age of Southeast Asia, Cambridge University Press].

Evidence related to proto-Indian or proto-Indic language

The proto-Indic language is attested in ancient Indian texts. For example, Manusmṛti refers to two languages, both of dasyu (daha): ārya vācas, mleccha vācas. [mukhabāhū rupajjānām yā loke jātayo bahih mlecchavācas'cāryav ācas te sarve dasyuvah smṛt āh Trans. 'All those people in this world who are excluded from those born from the mouth, the arms, the thighs and the feet (of Brahma) are called Dasyus, whether they speak the language of the mleccha-s or that of the ārya-s.' (Manu 10.45)] This distinction between lingua franca and literary version of the language, is elaborated by Patañjali as a reference to

1) grammatically correct literary language and

2) ungrammatical, colloquial speech (perhap, deshi).

Ancient text of Panini also refers to two languages in Shiksha: Sanskrit and Prākṛt. Prof Avinash Sathaye provides a textual reference on the earliest occurrence of the word, 'Sanskrit' :

triṣaṣṭiścatuh ṣaṣṭirvā varṇāh ṣambhumate matāh |

prākṛite samskṛte cāpi svayam proktā svayambhuvā || (pāṇini's śikṣā)

This demonstrates that pāṇiniknew both samskṛta and prākṛita as established languages. (Personal communication, 27 June 2010 with Prof. Shrinivas Tilak.)

Trans. There are considered to be 63 or 64 varṇā-s in the school (mata) of shambhu. In Prakrit and Sanskrit by swayambhu (manu, Brahma), himself, these varṇā-s were stated.

Chapter 17 of Bharatamuni's Nāṭyaśāstram is a beautiful disvourse about Sanskrit and Prakrit and the usage of lingua franca by actors/narrators in dramatic performances. Besides, Raja Shekhara, Kalidasa, Shudraka have also used the word Sanskrit for the literary language. (Personal communication from Prof. TP Verma, 7 May 2010). Nāṭyaśāstra XVII.29-30): dvividhā jātibhāṣāca prayoge samudāhṛtā mlecchaśabdopacārā ca bhāratam varṣam aśritā 'The jātibhāṣā (common language), prescribed for use (on the stage) has various forms. It contains words of mleccha origin and is spoken in Bhāratavarṣa only...' Vātstyāyana refers to mlecchita vikalpa (cipher writing of mleccha) Vātstyāyana's Kamasutra lists three arts related to language:

- deśa bhāṣā jñānam (knowledge of dialects)

- mlecchita vikalpa (cryptography used by mleccha) [cf. mleccha-mukha 'copper' (Skt.); the suffix –mukha is a reflex of mũh 'ingot' (Mu.)

- akṣara muṣṭika kathanam (messaging through wrist-finger gestures)

Thus, semantically, mlecchita vikalpa as a writing system relates to cryptography (perhaps, hieroglyphic writing) and to the work of artisans (smiths). It is not a mere coincidence that early writing attested during historical periods was on metal punch-marked coins, copper plates, two-feet long copper bolt used on an Aśokan pillar at Rampurva, and even on the Delhi iron pillar clearly pointing to the smiths as those artisans who had the competence to use a writing system. "Here then these signs occur upon an object which must have been made by craftsmen working for Asoka or one of his predessors." (F.R. Allchin, 1959, Upon the contextual significance of certain groups of ancient signs, School of Oriental and African Studies, London.)

Mahabhārata also attests to mleccha used in a conversation with Vidura. Śatapatha Brāhmaṇa refers to mleccha as language (with pronunciation variants) and also provides an example of such mleccha pronunciation by asuras. A Pali text, Uttarādhyayana Sutra 10.16 notes: ladhdhaṇa vimānusattaṇṇam āriattam puṇrāvi dullaham bahave dasyū milakkhuyā; trans. 'though one be born as a man, it is rare chance to be an ārya, for many are the dasyu and milakkhu'. Milakkhu and dasyu constitute the majority, they are the many. Dasyu are milakkhu (mleccha speakers). Dasyu are also ārya vācas (Manu 10.45), that is, speakers of Sanskrit. Both ārya vācas and mleccha vācas are dasyu, people. Such people are referred to in Rgveda by Viśvāmitra as 'Bhāratam janam.' Mahābhārata alludes to 'thousands of mlecchas', a numerical superiority equaled by their valour and courage in battle which enhances the invincibility of Pandava (MBh. 7.69.30; 95.36).

That Pali uses the term 'milakkhu' is significant (cf.

Uttarādhyayana Sutra 10.16) and reinforces the concordance between 'mleccha' and 'milakkhu' (a pronunciation variant) and links the language with 'meluhha' as a reference to a language in Mesopotamian texts and in the cylinder seal of Shu-ilishu.[214]This seal shows a seafaring Meluhha merchant who needed a translator to translate meluhha speech into Akkadian. The translator's name was Shu-ilishu as recorded in cuneiform script on the seal. This evidence rules out Akkadian as the Indus or Meluhha language and justifies the search for the proto-Indian speech from the region of the Sarasvati river basin which accounts for 80% (about 2000) archaeological sites of the civilization, including sites which have yielded inscribed objects such as Lothal, Dwaraka, Kanmer, Dholavira, Surkotada, Kalibangan, Farmana, Bhirrana, Kunal, Banawali, Chandigarh, Rupar, Rakhigarhi. The language-speakers in this basin are likely to have retained cultural memories of Indus language which can be gleaned from the semantic clusters of glosses of the ancient versions of their current lingua franca available in comparative lexicons and nighaṇṭu-s.

Evidence from Valmiki Rāmāyaṇa

Slokas 5.30.16 to 21 in the 29th sarga of Sundara Kandam, provide an episode of Hanuman introspecting on the language in which he should speak to Sita. This evidence refers to two dialects: Sanskrit and mānuṣam vākyam (lit. jāti bhāṣā). In this narrative mānuṣam vākyam (spoken dialect) is distinguished from Sanskrit of a Brahmin (or, grammatically correct and well-prouncedd Sanskrit used in yajña-s).

1. "antaramtvaha māsādya rākṣasīnam iha sthitah"

2. "śanairāśvāsaiṣyāmi santāpa bahulām imām"

(Staying here itself and getting hold of an opportunity even in the midst of the female-demons (when they are in attentive), I shall slowly console Sita who is very much in distress.)
3. "aham hi atitanuścaiva vānara śca viśeṣata"

4. "vācam ca udāhariṣyāmi mānuṣīm iha samskṛtām" (However, I am very small in stature, particularly as a monkey and can speak now Sanskrit, the human language too.)
5. "yadi vācam pradāsyami dwijātiriva samskṛtām"
6. "rāvaṇam manyamānā mām sītā bhītā bhavi ṣyati"

7. vānarasya viśeṣena kathamsyādabibhāṣaṇam (If I use Sanskrit language like a brahmin, Sita will get frightened, thinking that Rāva ṇ a has come disguised as a monkey. Especially, how can a monkey speak it?)
8. "avaśyameva vaktavyam mānuṣam vākyam arthavat"

9. "mayā śāntvayitum śakyā"

10. "nānyathā iyam aninditā"
(Certainly, meaningful words of a human being are to be spoken by me. Otherwise, the virtuous Sita cannot be

consoled.)

11. "sā iyam ālokya me rūpam jānakī bhāṣitam tathā ||

rakṣobhih trāsitaa pūrvam bhuūah trūsam gamiṣyati |"

(Looking at my figure and the language, Seetha who was already frightened previously by the demons, will get frightened again.)[215]

Evidence from Śatapatha Brāhmaṇa for mleccha vācas

An extraordinary narrative account from Śatapatha Brāhmaṇa is cited in full to provide the context of the yagna in which vaak (speech personified as woman) is referred to, emphasising the importance of grammatical speech in yagna performance and this grammatical, intelligible speech is distinguished from mlecccha, unintelligible speech. The example of the usage of phrase 'he 'lavo is explained by Sayana as a pronunciation variant of: 'he 'rayo. i.e. 'ho, the spiteful (enemies)!' This grammatically correct phrase, the Asuras were unable to pronounce correctly, notes Sayana. The ŚB text and translation are cited in full because of the early evidence provided of the mleccha speech (exemplifying what is referred to Indian language studies as 'ralayo rabhedhah'; the transformed use of 'la' where the syllable 'ra' was intended. This is the clearest evidence of a proto-Indian language which had dialectical variants in the usage by asuras and devas (i.e. those who do not perform yagna and those who perform yagna using vaak, speech.) This is comparable to mleccha vācas and ārya vācas

227

differentiation by Manu. The text of ŚB 3.2.1.22-28 and translation are as follows:

yoṣā vā iyaṃ vāgyadenaṃ na yuvitehaiva mā tiṣṭhantamabhyehīti brūhi tām tu na āgatām pratiprabrūtāditi sā hainaṃ tadeva tiṣṭhantamabhyeyāya tasmādu strī pumāṃsaṃ saṃskṛte tiṣṭhantamabhyaiti tāṃ haibhya āgatām pratiprovāceyaṃ vā āgāditi tāṃ devāḥ |

asurebhyo 'ntarāyaṃstāṃ svīkṛtyāgnāveva parigṛhya sarvahutamajuhavurāhutirhi devānāṃ sa yāmevāmūmanuṣṭubhājuhavustadevaināṃ taddevāḥ svyakurvata te 'surā āttavacaso he 'lavo he 'lava iti vadantaḥ parābabhūvuḥ atraitāmapi vācamūduḥ |

upajijñāsyāṃ sa mlecastasmānna brāhmaṇo mlecedasuryā haiṣā vā natevaiṣa dviṣatāṃ sapatnānāmādatte vācaṃ te 'syāttavacasaḥ parābhavanti ya evametadveda o 'yaṃ yajño vācamabhidadhyau |

mithunyenayā syāmiti tāṃ saṃbabhūva indro ha vā īkṣāṃ cakre |

mahadvā ito 'bhvaṃ janiṣyate yajñasya ca mithunādvācaśca yanmā tannābhibhavediti sa indra eva garbho bhūtvaitanmithunam praviveśa sa ha saṃvatsare jāyamāna īkṣāṃ cakre |

mahāvīryā vā iyaṃ yoniryā māmadīdharata yadvai meto mahadevābhvaṃ nānuprajāyeta yanmā tannābhibhavediti tāṃ pratiparāmṛśyaveṣṭyācinat |

tām yajñasya śīrṣanpratyadadhādyajño hi kṛṣṇaḥ sa yaḥ sa yajñastatkṛṣṇājinaṃ yo sā yoniḥ sā kṛṣṇaviṣāṇātha yadenāmindra āveṣṭyācinattasmādāveṣṭiteva sa yathaivāta indro 'jāyata garbho bhūtvaitasmānmithunādevamevaiṣo 'to jāyate garbho bhūtvaitasmānmithunāt tāṃ vā uttānāmiva badhnāti |

Translation: 22.The gods reflected, 'That Vaak being a woman, we must take care lest she should allure him. – Say to her, "Come hither to make me where I stand!" and report to us her having come.' She then went up to where he was standing. Hence a woman goes to a man who stays in a well-trimmed (house). He reported to them her having come, saying, 'She has indeed come.' 23. The gods then cut her off from the Asuras; and having gained possession of her and enveloped her completely in fire, they offered her up as a holocaust, it being an offering of the gods. (78) And in that they offered her with an anushtubh verse, thereby they made her their own; and the Asuras being deprived of speech, were undone, crying, 'He 'lavah! He 'lavah!' (79) 24. Such was the unintelligible speech which they then uttered, -- and he (who speaks thus) is a Mlekkha (barbarian). Hence let no Brahman speak barbarous language, since such is the speech of the Asuras. Thus alone he deprives his spiteful enemies of speech; and whosoever knows this, his enemies, being deprived of speech, are undone. 25. That Yajna (sacrifice) lusted after Vaak (speech [80]), thinking, 'May I pair with her!' He united with her. 26. Indra then thought within himself, 'Surely a great monster will spring from this union of Yagna and Vaak: [I must take care] lest it should get the better of me.' Indra himself then became an embryo and entered into that union. 27. Now when he was born after a year's time, he thought within himself, 'Verily of great vigour is this womb which has contained me: [I must take care] that no great monster shall be born from it after me, lest it should get the better of me!' 28. Having seized and pressed it tightly, he tore it off and put it on the head of Yagna (sacrifice [81]); for the black (antelope) is the sacrifice: the black deer skin is the same as that sacrifice, and the black deer's horn is the same as that womb. And because it was by pressing it tightly together that Indra tore out (the womb), therefore it (the horn) is bound tightly (to the end of the garment); and as Indra, having become an embryo, sprang from that union, so is he (the sacrifice), after becoming an embryo, born from that union (of the skin and the horn). (ŚB 3.2.1.23-25). (fn 78) According to Sayana, 'he 'lavo' stands for 'he 'rayo' (i.e. ho, the spiteful (enemies)!' which the Asuras were unable to pronounce correctly. The Kaanva text, however, reads te hātavāko 'su hailo haila ity etām ha vācam vadantah parābabhūvuh (? i.e. he p. 32 ilaa, 'ho, speech'.) A third version of this passage seems to be referred to in the Mahā bhāṣya (Kielh.), p.2. (p.38). (fn 79) Compare the corresponding legend about Yagna and Dakṣiṇā (priests' fee), (Taitt. S. VI.1.3.6. (p.38) (fn 79) 'Yagnasya sīrṣan'; one would expect 'kṛṣṇa(sāra)sya sīrṣan.' The Taitt.S. reads 'tām mṛgeṣu ny adadhāt.' (p.38) (fn81) In the Kanva text 'atah (therewith)' refers to the head of the sacrifice, -- sa yak khirasta upasprisaty ato vā enām etad agre pravisan pravisaty ato vā agre gāyamāno gāyate tasmāk khirasta upasprisati. (p.39)(cf. śatapatha Brāhmaṇa vol. 2 of 5, tr. By Julius Eggeling, 1885, in SBE Part 12; fn 78-81).

Mesopotamian texts refer to a language called meluhha (which required an Akkadian translator); this meluhha is cognate with mleccha. Seafaring meluhhan merchants and artisans created metal artifacts and lapidary artificats of terracotta and ivory and used the script in trade transactions. Glosses of the proto-Indic or Indus language are used to read rebus the Indus script inscriptions. The glyphs of the script include both pictorial motifs and signs and both categories of glyphs are read rebus. As a first step in delineating the Indus language, an Indian lexicon has been compiled to semantically cluster about 8000 glosses from ancient Indian languages as a proto-Indic substrate dictionary.[216]

"The word meluh.h.a is of special interest. It occurs as a verb in a different form (mlecha-) in Vedic only in ŚB 3.2.1, an eastern text of N. Bihar where it indicates 'to speak in barbarian fashion'. But it has a form closer to Meluh.h.a in Middle Indian (MIA): Pali, the church language of S. Buddhism which originated as a western N. Indian dialect (roughly, between Mathura, Gujarat and the Vindhya) has milakkha, milakkhu. Other forms, closer to ŚB mleccha are found in MIA *mliccha > Sindhi milis, Panjabi milech, malech, Kashmiri bri.c.hun 'weep, lament' (< *mrech-, with the common r/l interchange of IA), W. Pahari mel+c.h 'dirty'. It seems that, just as in other cases mentioned above, the original local form *m(e)luh. (i.e. m(e)lukh in IA pronunciation, cf. E. Iranian bAxdhl 'Bactria' > AV *bahli-ka, balhi-ka) was preserved only in the South (Gujarat? >Pali), while the North (Panjab, Kashmir, even ŚB and Bengal) has *mlecch. The sound shift from-h.h.-/-kh- > -cch- is unexplained; it may have been modeled on similar correspondences in MIA   (Skt. akṣi 'eye' _ MIA akkhi, acchi; ks. etra '_eld' _ MIA khetta, chetta, etc.) The meaning of Mleccha must have evolved from 'self-designation' > 'name of foreigners', cf. those of the Franks > Arab farinjl 'foreigner.' Its introduction into Vedic must have begun in Meluh.h.a, in Baluchistan-Sindh, and have been transmitted for a long time in a non-literary level of IA as a nickname, before surfacing in E. North India in Middle/Late Vedic as Mleccha. (Pali milāca is influenced by a `tribal' name, Piśā ca, as is Sindhi milindu, milidu by Pulinda; the word has been further `abbreviated' by avoiding the difficult cluster ml- : Prākṛt mecha, miccha, Kashmiri m ĩ c(h), Bengali mech (a Tib.-Burm tribe) and perhaps Pashai mece if not < *mēcca `defective' (Turner, CDIAL 10389. | Parpola 1994: 174 has attempted a Dravidian explanation. He understands Meluh.h. a (var. Melah.h.a) as Drav. *Mēlakam [mēlaxam] `high country' (= Baluchistan) (=Ta-milakam) and points to Neo-Assyr. baluh.h.u `galbanum', sinda `wood from Sindh'. He traces mlech, milakkha back to *mleks. , which is seen as agreeing, with central Drav. metathesis with *mlēxa = mēlaxa-m. Kuiper 1991:24 indicates not infrequent elision of (Dravid.) -a- when taken over into Skt. | Shafer 1954 has a Tib-Burm. etymology *mltse; Southworth 1990: 223 reconstructs PDrav. 2 *muzi/mizi `say, speak, utter', DEDR 4989, tamil `Tamil' < `own speech'.)"[217]

Note: Coining a term, "Para-Munda", denoting a hypothetical language related but not ancestral to modern Munda languages, thee author goes on to identify it as "Harappan", the language of the Harappan civilization. The author later recounts this and posits that Harappan were illiterate and takes the glyphs of the script to be symbols without any basis in any underlying language.[218]

ṛgveda (ṛca 3.53.12) uses the term, 'bhāratam janam', which can be interpreted as 'bhārata folk'. The ṛṣi of the sūkta is viśvāmitra gāthina. India was called Bhāratavarṣa after the king Bhārata. (Vāyu 33, 51-2; Bd. 2,14,60-2; lin:ga 1,47,20,24; Viṣṇu 2,1,28,32).

ya ime rodasī ubhe aham indram atuṣṭavam

viśvāmitrasya rakṣati brahmedam bhāratam janam

3.053.12 I have made Indra glorified by these two, heaven and earth, and this prayer of viśvāmitra protects the people of Bhārata. [Made Indra glorified: indram atuṣṭavam -- the verb is the third preterite of the casual, I have caused to be praised; it may mean: I praise Indra, abiding between heaven and earth, i.e. in the firmament].

The evidenceis remarkable that almost every single glyph or glyptic element of the Indus script can be read rebus using the repertoire of artisans (lapidaries working with precious stones and terracotta, mine-workers, metal-smiths working with a variety of minerals, furnaces and other tools) who created the inscribed objects and used many of them to authenticate their trade transactions. Many of the inscribed objects are seen to be calling cards of the professional artisans, listing their professional skills and repertoire.

The identification of glosses from the present-day languages of India on Sarasvati river basin is justified by the continuation of culture evidenced by many artifacts evidencing civilization continuum from the Vedic Sarasvati River basin, since language and culture are intertwined, continuing legacies:

Smiths'/Artisans' repertoire

Huntington notes[219]: "There is a continuity of composite creatures demonstrable in Indic culture since Kot Diji ca. 4000 BCE"

Mriga (pair of deer or antelope) in Buddha sculptures compare with Harappan period prototype of a pair of ibexes on the platform below a seated yogin[220]

Continued use of śankha (turbinella pyrum) bangles which tradition began 6500 BCE at Nausharo;

Continued wearing of sindhur at the parting of the hair by married ladies as evidenced by two terracotta toys painted black on the hair, painted golden on the jewelry and painted red to show sindhur at the parting of the hair;

Finds of shivalinga in situ in a worshipful state in Harappa (a metaphor of Mt. Kailas summit where Maheśvara is in tapas, according to Hindu tradition);

Terracotta toys of Harappa and Mohenjodaro showing Namaste postures and yogasana postures;

Three-ring ear-cleaning device

Legacy of architectural forms

Legacy of puṣkariṇi in front of mandirams; as in front of Mohenjodaro stupa

Legacy of metallurgy and the writing system on punch-marked coins

Legacy of continued use of cire perdue technique for making utsava bera (bronze murti)

Legacy of the writing system on Rampurva copper bolt

Legacy of the writing system on Sohgaura copper plate

Legacy of glyphs continuing on aṣṭamangalahāra, Śrīvatsa glyph metaphor; Śrīvatsa and śrīsuktam, jaina āyāgapaṭṭa-s, Bharhut ligatures; Gautama the Buddha refers to eṣa dhammo sanantano; Mahavira refers to 'ariya' dhamma (arya meaning 'right conduct, respectful')

Legacy: Engraved celt tool of Sembiyan-kandiyur with Sarasvati hieroglyphs: calling-card of an artisan

Legacy of acharya wearing uttariyam

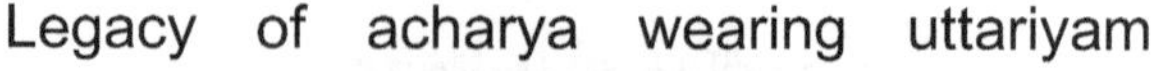

(shawl) leaving right-shoulder bare

Form of addressing a person respectfully as: arya, ayya (Ravana is also referred to as arya in the Great Epic Rāmāyaṇa)

Plate X [c] Lingam in situ in Trench Ai (MS Vats, 1940, Excavations at Harappa, Vol. II, Calcutta) Lingam, grey

sandstone in situ, Harappa, Trench Ai, Mound F, Pl. X (c) (After Vats). "In an earthenware jar, No. 12414, recovered from Mound F, Trench IV, Square I... in this jar, six lingams were found along with some tiny pieces of shell, a unicorn seal, an oblong grey sandstone block with polished surface, five stone pestles, a stone palette, and a block of chalcedony..." (Vats, MS, 1940, Excavations at Harappa,

Delhi, p. 370).

Continued use of cire perdue technique of bronze-casting. Bronze murti: cire perdue technique used today in Swamimalai to make bronze utsavabera (idols carried in procession). Eraka Subrahmanya is the presiding divinity in Swamimalai. Eraka! Copper.Devices on punch-marked coins comparable to Sarasvati hieroglyphs.

Continued use of some glyphs of Indus script by artisans (smiths) during historical periods

Rampurva bull capital, 3rd cent. BCE

Rampurva bull capital on the Ashokan pillar.

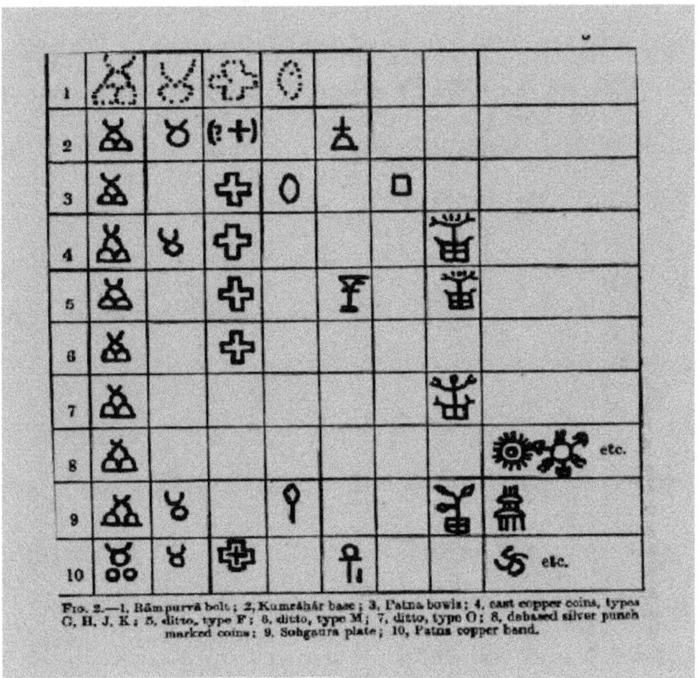

FIG. 2.—1, Rāmpurvā bolt; 2, Kumrāhār base; 3, Patna bowls; 4, cast copper coins, types G, H, J, K; 5, ditto, type F; 6, ditto, type M; 7, ditto, type O; 8, debased silver punch marked coins; 9, Sohgaura plate; 10, Patna copper band.

Rampurva pillar edict text:

- Thus saith king Priyadarsi, Beloved of the Gods. Twelve years after my coronation, records relating to Dharma were caused to be written by me for the first time for the welfare and happiness of the people, so that, without violation thereof, they might attain the growth of Dharma in various respects.

- Thinking: "Only in this way the welfare and happiness of the people may be secured." I scrutinize as to how I may bring happiness to the people, no matter whether they are my relatives or residents of the neighborhood of my capital or of distant localities. And I act accordingly. In the same manner, I scrutinize in respect of all classes of people. Moreover, all the religious sects have been honored by me with various kinds of honors. But what I consider my principal duty is meeting the people of different sects personally.

- This record relating to Dharma has been caused to be written by me twenty-six years after my coronation.

Rampurva bull capital is a depiction of bos indicus comparable to the glyph on an Indus seal m1103.

A remarkable example is a 24 inch long and 12 inch dia. copper bolt with an inscription of four glyhphs, used to bolt in the bull capital on an Ashokan pillar at Rampurva. See item 1 of the list of four glyphs used on this copper bolt. Similar use of Indus script glyphs occurs on nine other metal objects, pointing to the continued use of Indian hieroglyphs by metalsmiths of India.

A solid copper bolt (24 1/2" in length and a circumference of 14" at the center and 12" at the ends), was found in the Rampurva Asoka Pillar near Nepal border.

The glyphs of the Indus script comparable to these inscribed metal objects are:

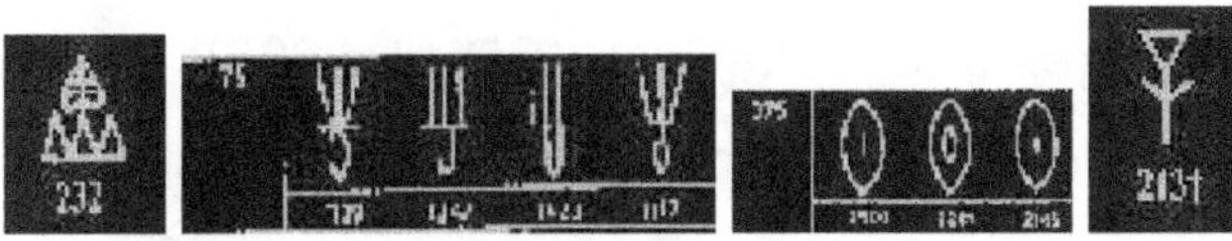

h188, h196, h291, h630, h631

The + glyph may connote: M. अग्निकुंड [agnikuṇḍa] n (S) A hole in  the ground, or an enclosed space on the surface, or a metal square-mouthed vessel, for receiving and preserving consecrated fire.

Sohgaura copper plate inscription (Item 9 of the table)

Sohgaura copper plate (Pre-Mauryan) Date? Pre-Mauryan, that is first millennium BCE

The line 1 of the inscription using Indus script glyphs details the repertoire of facilities provided to itinerant

merchants/artisan guild caravans in the two koṣṭh āgāra
(sheds/workshops/storerooms/ warehouses).

Hieroglyph 1 (from left): glyph: tree, rebus: smelting furnace

kuṭhi kuṭa, kuṭi, kuṭha a tree (Kaus'.); kuḍa tree (Pkt.); kuṟā tree; kaṟek tree, oak (Pas;.)(CDIAL 3228). kuṭha, kuṭa (Ka.), kudal (Go.) kudar. (Go.) kuṭhāra, kuṭha, kuṭaka = a tree (Skt.lex.) kuṭ, kurun: = stump of a tree (Bond.a); khuṭ = id. (Or.) kuṭa, kuṭha = a tree (Ka.lex.) guṇḍra = a stump; khuṇṭut = a stump of a tree left in the ground (Santali.lex.) kuṭamu = a tree (Te.lex.) कुঁদ² [kuňda²] n a stock or butt (of a gun); a stump or trunk (of a tree); a log (of wood); a lump (of sugar etc.). (Bengali) Rebus: kũdār[221] 'turner' (B.)

kuṭi, 'smelting furnace' (Mundari.lex.).kuṭhi, kuṭi (Or.; Sad. kothi) (1) the smelting furnace of the blacksmith; kuṭire bica duljaḍko talkena, they were feeding the furnace with ore; (2) the name of ēkuṭi has been given to the fire which, in lac factories, warms the water bath for softening the lac so that it can be spread into sheets; to make a smelting furnace; kut.hi-o of a smelting furnace, to be made; the smelting furnace of the blacksmith is made of mud, cone-shaped, 2' 6" dia. At the base and 1' 6" at the top. The hole in the center, into which the mixture of charcoal and iron ore is poured, is about 6" to 7" in dia. At the base it has two holes, a smaller one into which the nozzle of the bellow is inserted, as seen in fig. 1, and a larger one on the opposite side through which the molten iron flows out into a cavity (Mundari.lex.)

Hieroglyph 3 glyph: spear rebus: furnace

śūla = spear (Skt.)

cuḷḷai = potter's kiln, furnace (Ta.); cūḷai furnace, kiln, funeral pile (Ta.); cuḷḷa potter's furnace; cūḷa brick kiln (Ma.); cullī fireplace (Skt.); cullī, ullī id. (Pkt.)(CDIAL 4879; DEDR 2709). sulgao, salgao to light a fire; sen:gel, sokol fire (Santali.lex.) hollu, holu = fireplace (Kuwi); soḍu fireplace, stones set up as a fireplace (Mand.); ule furnace (Tu.)(DEDR 2857).

Hieroglyph 4 glyph: peak mounted by a rimless pot rebus: furnace

kūṭa = peak (Telugu)

baṭa = rimless pot (Kannada)

kūṭam = workshop (Tamil); baṭa = furnace (Santali) bhrāṣṭra = furnace (Skt.)

Hieroglyph 5 glyph: tree (as shown on hieroglyph 1) with a rim of a jar and a quail ligatured on the branches of tree

kuṭi = tree; rebus: kuṭi = smelting furnace.

kaṇḍ kanka = rim of jar (Santali); kaṇḍ = fire-altar (Santali); kan = copper (Tamil) baṭa = quail (Santali)

bata = furnace (Santali) bhrāṣṭra = furnace (Skt.)

Hieroglyph 2 and hieroglph 6: koṣṭhāgāra[222], a pair of storehouses

Thus the line 1 is a hieroglyphic representation of facilities provided to artisan guilds, itinerant metalsmiths at the tri-junction of three highways.

Śrīvatsa on āyāgapaṭṭa-s of Manoharpura.

Śrīvatsa symbol variants found at Kankalitila, Mathura,late1st cent.BCE: Jaina āyāgapaṭṭa-s; in these five specimen, a fish is shown in the middle apparently tied to two strings (or, molluscs) on either side; apparently, this ligatured pictorial formed the basis for the evolution of the Śrīvatsa symbol almost looking like a stylized trident. (After

Pl. 30 C in: Savita Sharma, 1990,
Early Indian Symbols, Numismatic Evidence, Delhi, Agam

Kala Prakashan; cf. Shah, U.P., 1975, Aspects of Jain Art and Architecture, p. 77).

The hieroglyph composition of fish tied to a pair of molluscs can be read rebus: ayira 'fish'; dhama 'tie'; hangi 'snail'; pair 'dul'; Rebus: arya, ayira 'noble'; dhama 'global ethic': ayira dhama; ayira sangha 'community'; dol 'picture,form'. Thus, the composition connotes the message: ariya dhamma, ariya sangha. When the scribe had to depict a grapheme which sounded close to the word, 'dhamma', the artisan chose the

form of a tied up up – tied to a fish, ayir; rebus: ayira, arya.

This dhamma composition using a hieroglyph finds its expression onn the Sanchi stupa.

An idential symbol is depicted at sāñci stūpa (Smith, VA, Jaina Stupa, p. 15, Pl. VII, L. Buhler, Epigraphica Indica II, pp. 200, 313; Agrawala, VS, Guide to Lucknow Museum, p. 4). See many variants presented and discussed in a monograph[223].

The use of 'fish' glyphs (ayir 'fish') can be explained as rebus representations of the nobility associated in Jaina tradition with the word ayira (metath. Arya) 'noble person'.

Pali: **Ayira (& Ayyira)** (n. -- adj.) [Vedic ārya, Metathesis for ariya as diaeretic form of ārya, of which the contracted (assimilation) form is ayya. See also ariya][224]

The glyphs on the aṣṭamangala hāara also appear with some variations in Jaina āyāgapaṭṭa-s. See for example: Manoharpura. āyāgapaṭṭa-. Kusana 50 to 299 CE. Red Sandstone. National Museum, New Delhi. (Scan no. 0053014)

Weapons worn on the Mangalasūtra -- or protective necklaces -- parallels the tradition of aṣṭamangala (eight symbols of welfare) . Chanda Yakṣi (c. 200 BCE, Indian Museum, Calcutta) ear-ring a seven-string necklace; the drawing shows lower three pearl strings consisting of flat stones or cylindrical beads; the upper row has symbols including:

pipal leaf, elephant goad, śrivatsa (which is the middle glyph)

[Cunningham, Bharhut, pl. L.7]]
[After Figs. 232 and Pl. XI in:

Dr.Mohini Verma, 989, Dress and Ornaments in Ancient India: The Maurya and S'un:ga Periods, Varanasi, Indological Book House, p. 24.] A figure on a mithuna plaque from Ahicchatra isinterpreted: 'There are three additional

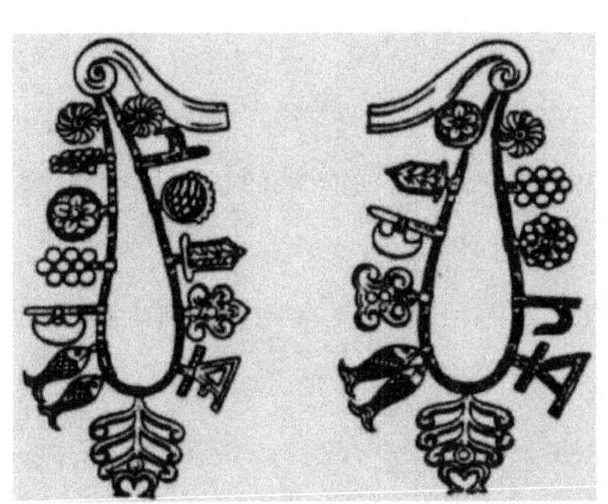

symbols woven in her long necklace, namely a dagger on the left, a puppet (śrivatsa in the center) and on the right, a vajra with a pointed angle prongs.' These symbols also occur on a terracotta of Mathura. [VS Agrawa, a Terracotta figurines ofAhichchatra, Dist. Bareilly, UP, Ancient India, No. 4, pl. XXXII, 2; VS Agrawala, Mathura Terracottas, JUPHS, Vol. IX, fig.6,0,2,3).

Necklaces with a number of pendants aṣṭamaṅgalaka hāra depicted on a pillar of a gateway (toraṇa) at the stūpa of Sanchi, Central India, 1st century BCE. [After VS Agrawala, 1969,The deeds of Harsha (being a cultural study of Bāṇa's Harṣacarita, ed. By PK Agrawala, Varanasi: fig. 62] The hāra or necklace shows a pair of fish signs together with a number of motifs indicating weapons (cakra, paraśu, aṅkuś a), including a device that parallels the standard device normally shown in many inscribed objects of Sarasvati civilization in front of the one-horned bull. (cf. Marshall, J. and Foucher, The Monuments of Sanchi, 3 vols., Callcutta,

1936, repr.1982, pl. 27).

The first necklace has eleven and the second one has thirteen pendants (cf. V.S. Agrawala, 1977, Bhāratīya Kalā, Varanasi, p. 169); he notes the eleven pendants as: sun, śukra, padmasara, aṅkuśa, vaijayanti, paṅkaja, mīna-mithuna, śrīvatsa, paraśu, darpaṇa and kamala. "The axe (paraśu) and aṅkuśa pendants are common at sites of north India and some of their finest specimens from Kausambi are in the collection of Dr.MC Dikshit of Nagpur." (Dhavalikar, M.K., 1965, Sanchi: A cultural Study, Poona, p. 44;loc.cit. Dr.Mohini Verma, 1989, Dress and Ornaments in Ancient India: The Mauryaand śuṅga Periods, Varanasi, Indological Book House, p. 125).• Note that one of the pendants looks like the 'device' normally found in front of the onehornedbull, the saṅgaḍa, portable brazier and lathe (also meaning. rebus, battle).• On the second hāra, clock-wise, after iṇaikkayal or mīnayugala (twin fish), and axe, thependant looks like a tree or a bunch of coral? [tukir = coral, pavaṟam; vaicayanti =tukir-koṭi, i.e. creeper containing coral; thus a sign interpreted as a maṅgala sign, i.e. vaijayanti may be connoted by this Tamil phrase: tukir- koṭi, i.e. a bunch of corals on a creeper. In Skt., vaijayanti can be interpreted as an attribute of victory].

[Pl. 33, Nandipāda-Triratna at: Bhimbetka, Sanchi, Sarnath and Mathura] śrivatsa symbol [with its

BHIMBETKA	ROCK SHELTER PAINTING						
SĀÑCHI (C. 2nd. 1st cent. B.C.)	EASTERN + NOTHERN GATE WAY						
SARNATH MATHURA (C. 1st cent A.D.)	STONE UMBRELLA						
MATHURA	JAINA – ĀYĀGAPAṬAS						

hundreds of stylized variants, depicted on Pl. 29 to 32] occurs in Bogazkoi (Central Anatolia) dated ca. 6th to 14th cent. BCE on inscriptions.

The link with ayir 'iron' is explicit in the use of ayir in reference to a marriage badge of a woman, asin: aṣṭamaṅgalaka hāra

makara may be seen from a Bharhut panel (ca. 100 BCE).

Glyph components are: snout of a crocodile, elephant trunk,  head and forequarters of an elephant, body of a snake, curved-in mollusc, and fins and tail of a fish. (Indian Museum, Calcutta)[225]

Khandagiri caves (2nd cent. BCE). In the religious cults, ashtamangalass are eight glyphs which stand for good luck, auspiciousness, prosperity or are marks of enlightenment. In Jaina tradition, they  become standardized only from about the 4th cent. CE. A. Cave 3 (Ananta  gumpha), certain jaina motifs are depicted; nandipada, it is the same as triratna of Bauddha. B. Cave 3 (Ananta gumpha); a tree under a canopy enclosed within a railing. (Yuvraj Kerishan, 1996, The Buddha image: its origin and development, Bharatiya Vidya Bhavan, p. 24).

Continuum legacy of Indus script glyphs on punch-marked   **coins**

The association of auspiciousness with the glyphs shown on

sculptures of Khandagiri caves, is comparable to the association of smithy with a temple in two glosses of Indian linguistic area:

Ko. kole·l smithy, temple in Kota

village. To. kwala·l Kota smithy. (DEDR 2133).

This extraordinary and cultural phenomenon of equating a smithy with a temple, perhaps unique to the Indian linguistic area, may explain the sacredness associated with glyphs used on thousands of punch-marked coins which came from mints of all parts of India, treating the glyphs as hieroglyphs.

Most of the symbols employed on ancient coins are traceable to Indus script glyphswhich are composed of pictorial motifs and unambiguous glyptic signs. That these glyphs on punch-marked coins which came out of the mints demonstrates the continuing legacy of the writing system of artisans who created Indus script.

Cast bronze coin.Mauryan empire. 3rd cent. BCE

British Museum: Silver k ār ṣ āpa ṇa of the Mauryan empire[226].

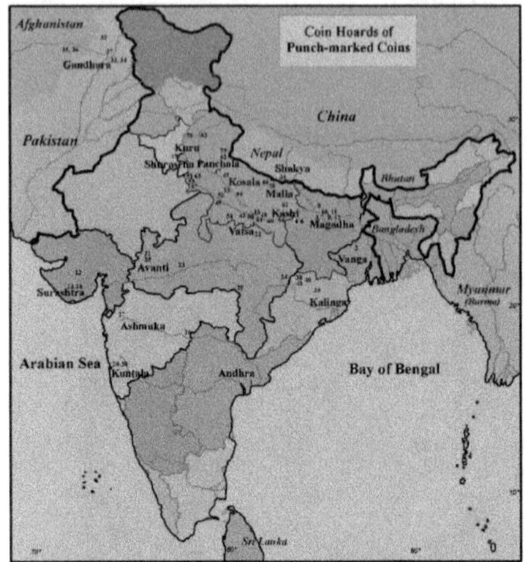

Map of coin hoards of punch-marked coins after D. Rajgor[227].

CL Fabri and Thapliyal found similariity between Indus script glyphs and the glyphs on punch-marked coins. (Fabri, CL, 1935, JRAS, pp. 307-318 and

The following comparison charts pair punch-mark glyphs with Indus Valley glyphs and their sign reference numbers.

PUNCH	INDUS VALLEY
	288
	296
	301
	(Plate CXIV, 51)
	120
	48
	49
	73
	77
	80
	99
	217
	200

PUNCH	INDUS VALLEY
	364
	355
	97
	251
	183
	192
	322
	Plate CXIV, part
	53
	178

PUNCH	INDUS VALLEY
	331
	341
	370
	369
	389
	379
	277
	371
	324
	378
	157
	254
	139

Comparison of Punch and Indus Valley Writing

PUNCHMARK	INDUS SIGNS
Theobald 55.	159, 317, 217.

Thapliyal, KK in: Studies in Ancient Indian Seals found that many Indian seals from the 3rd cent. BCE to 7th centt. CE portrayed animals, with an inscription above the animal (just as in the case of the Indus seals).

W. Theobald, 1890, Notes on some of the symbols found on the punch-marked coins of Hindustan, and on their relationship to the archaic symbolism of other races and distant lands, Journal of the Asiatic Society of Bengal, Bombay Branch (JASB), Part 1. History , Literature etc., Nos. III & IV, 1890, pp. 181 to 268; W. Theobald, 1901, A revision of the symbols on the 'Karshapana' Coinage,described in Vol. LIX,JASB, 1890, Part I, No. 3, and Descriptions of many additional symbols, *Journal of the Asiatic Society of Bengal, Bombay Branch (JASB)*, No. 2, 1901 (Read December, 1899).

Plates VIII to XI of Theobald, 1890 listing symbols on punch-marked coins:

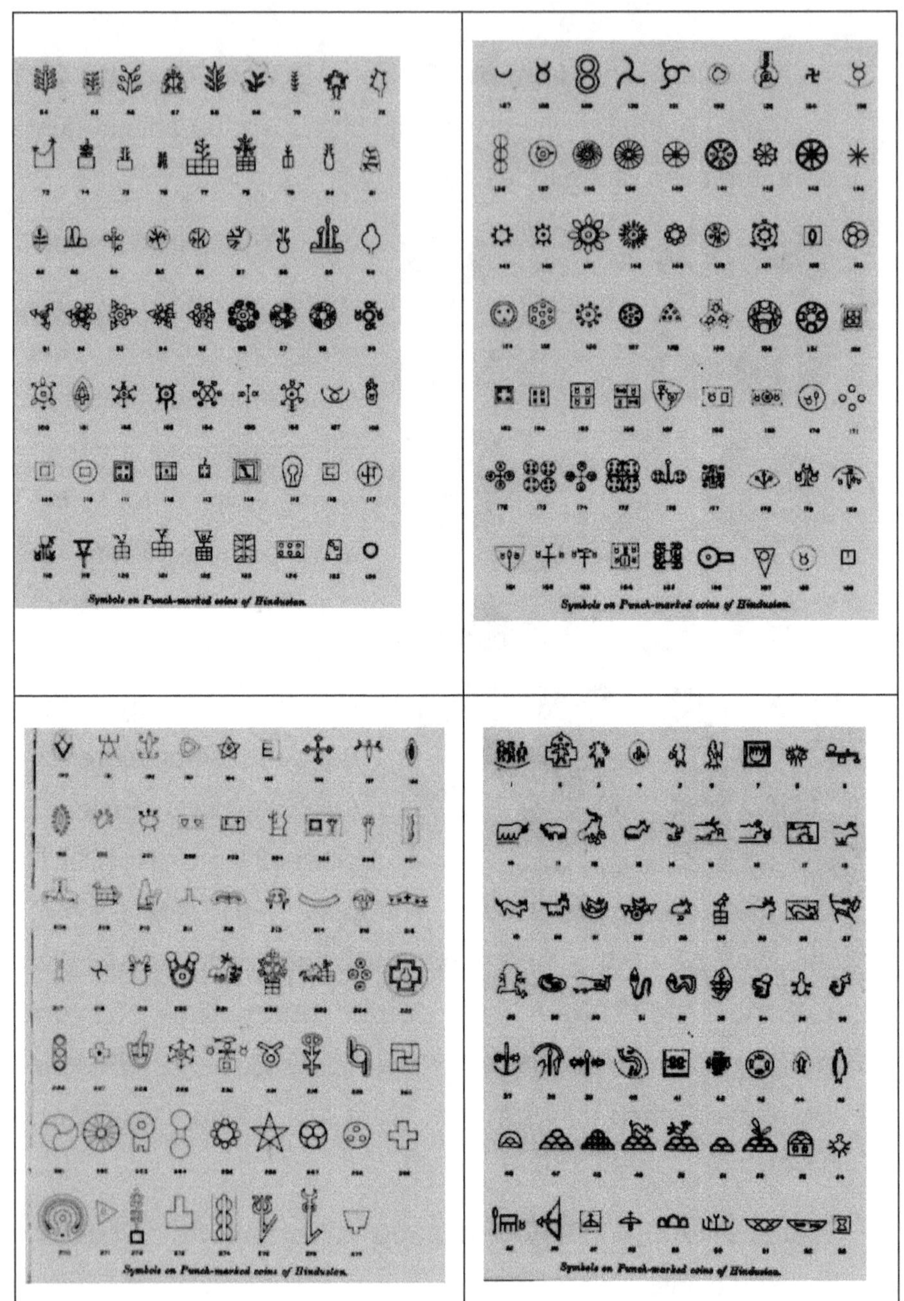
Symbols on Punch-marked coins of Hindustan.
Symbols on Punch-marked coins of Hindustan.
Symbols on Punch-marked coins of Hindustan.
Symbols on Punch-marked coins of Hindustan.

Glyph 30 shown by Theobald compares with the glyph on a Harappa tablet.

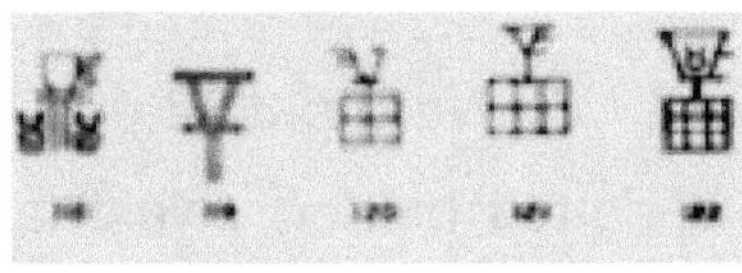

Theobald identifies glyphs 118 to 122 on punch-marked which are similar to the standard devic of Indus script. (After Fig. 7.32, Kenoyer, 1998).

Theobald identifies glyph 136 on punch-marked coins which is similar to the one shown

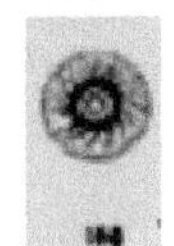

on m1406 (Mohenjodaro tablet).

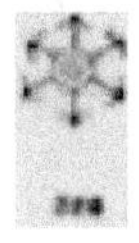

Theobald identifies glyph 138 which is similar to the glyph on an Indus script inscription on m0428 seal.

Theobald identifies glyph 209 which is similar to the glyph on Harappa seal h243.

Taxila coin. Anonymous. Period of Agathokles, ca. 185 to 170 BCE. AV quarter stater (2.34 gms). Humped bull standing left. Taxila symbol before fish-like symbol with pellet and crescents. Bopeerachchi –SNG ANS – MIG 163 (Pushkalavati); BMC India pl. 11.

Yotamira, silver drachm. C. 2nd cent. CE. Weight: 3.72 gms. Dia. 16 mm. diademed bust right, dotted border, swastika right, brahmi legend around (at Bh)Yotamirasa Bagarevaputasa Parataraja (Of Yotamira, son of Bagareva, Parata king).

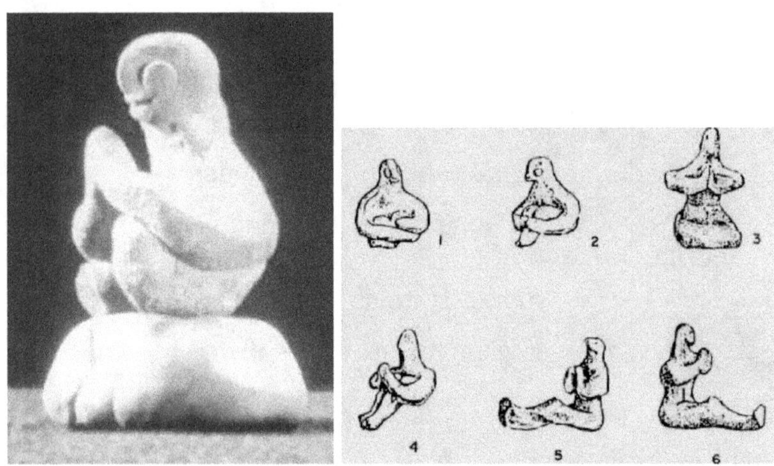

Terracotta toys show yogic asanas: 1-4, from Harappa; 5-6, from Mohenjo-daro.

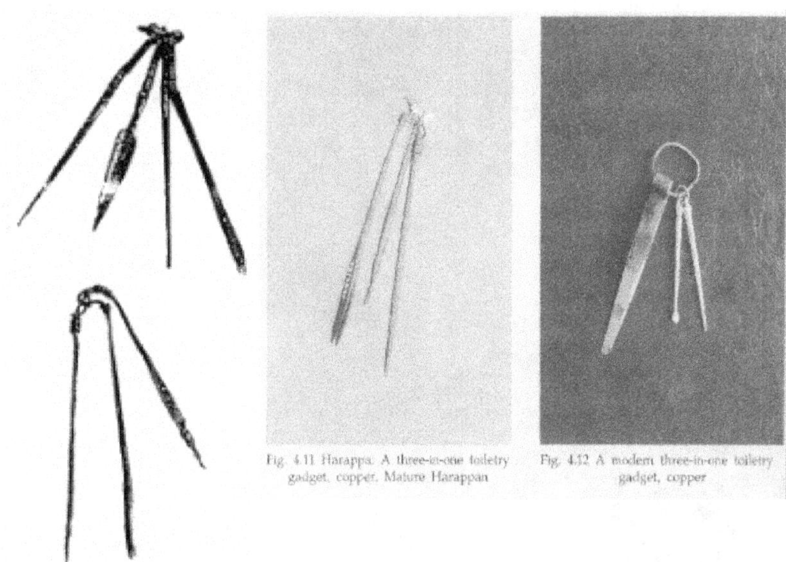

Toilet gadgets: Ur and Harappa After Woolley 1934, Vats 1941

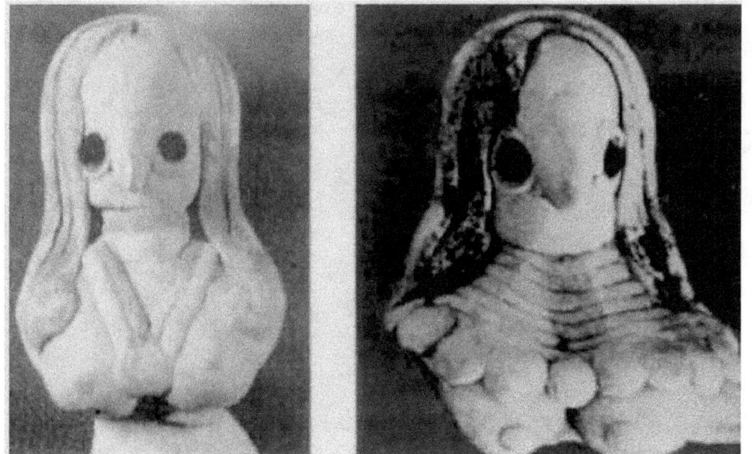

Nausharo: female figurines. Wearing sindhur at the parting of the hair. Hair painted black, ornaments golden and sindhur red. Period 1B, 2800 – 2600 BCE. 11.6 x 30.9 cm.[After Fig. 2.19, Kenoyer, 1998].

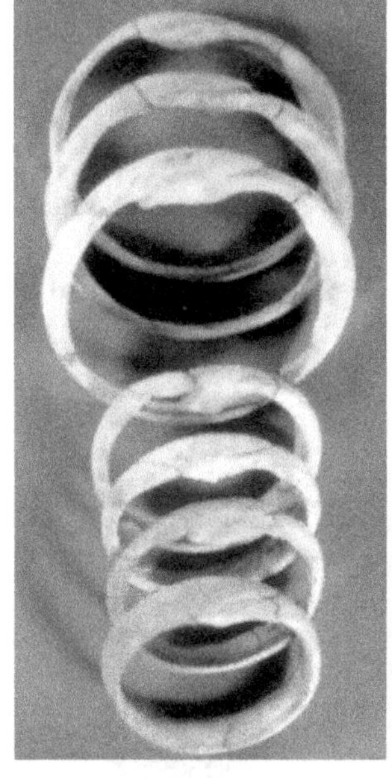

S'ankha artifacts: Wide bangle made from a single conch shell and carved with a chevron motif, Harappa; marine shell, Turbinella pyrum (After Fig. 7.44, Kenoyer, 1998) National Museum, Karachi. 54.3554. HM 13828. Seal, Bet Dwaraka 20 x 18 mm of conch shell. Seven shell bangles from burial of an elderly woman, Harappa; worn on the left arm; three on the upper arm and four on the forearm; 6.3 X 5.7 cm to 8x9 cm marine shell, Turbinella pyrum (After Fig. 7.43, Kenoyer, 1998) Harappa museum. H87-635 to 637;

676 to 679. Modern lady from Kutch, wearing shell-bangles.

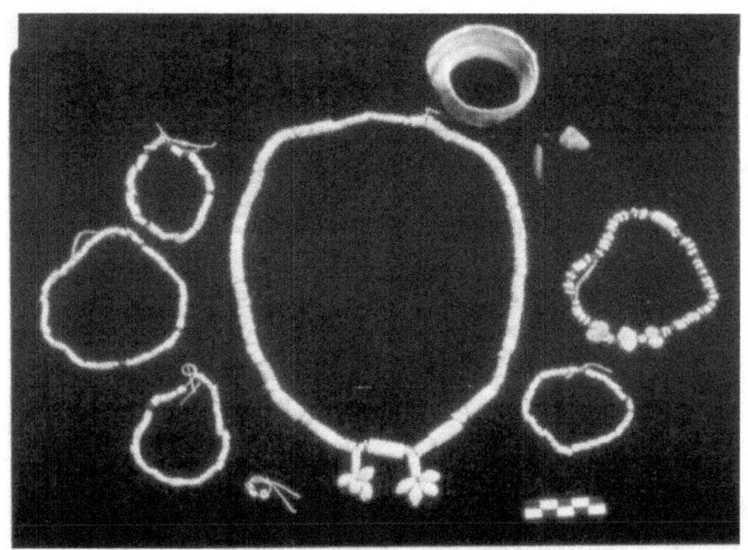

6500 BCE. Date of the woman's burial with ornaments including a wide bangle of shankha. Mehergarh. Burial ornaments made of shell and stone disc beads, and turbinella pyrum (sacred conch, s'an:kha) bangle, Tomb MR3T.21, Mehrgarh, Period 1A, ca. 6500 BCE. The nearest source for this shell is Makran coast near Karachi, 500 km. South. [After Fig. 2.10 in Kenoyer, 1998]. S'ankha wide bangle and other ornaments, c. 6500 BCE (burial of a woman at Nausharo)

S'ankha, *turbinella pyrum* a signature tune of Hindu civilization and traditions of Jaina and Bauddham; a species which occurs only in Indian Ocean coastline. śankha kṛśāna (a phrase used in Rigveda, Atharvaveda) – śankha bowman, śankha cutter (who uses a bow like sword or saw to cut the śankha). A continuing, 8500 year-old industry. At Tiruchendur (kīrakkarai, Gulf of Mannar), WB Handicrafts Dev. Corpn. has an office; annual turnover of śankha obtained: Rs. 50 crores.[228]

Ligature, a technique used by scribes/artisans of the civilization

  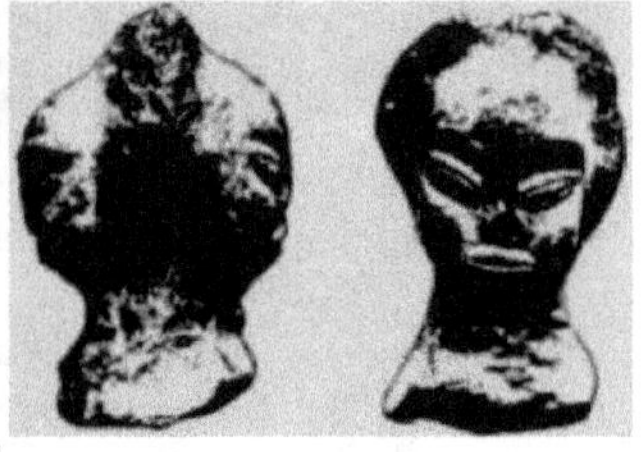

Ligatured sculpture: three-faced: tiger, bovine, elephant, Nausharo NS 92.02.70.04 6.76 cm (h); three-headed: elephant, buffalo, bottom jaw of a feline. NS 91.02.32.01.LXXXII. Dept. of Archaeology, Karachi. EBK 7712

There are about 500 glyphs or glyptic elements of Indus script; it is significant that almost all the unambiguously identifiable glyphs can be read rebus consistently in a smithy setting. The composite animal glyph is one example to show that rebus method has to be applied to every glyptic element in the writing system. How does one explain a person seated on a leaf-less tree branch? The entire composition is a set of hieroglyphs. So it is with the rim of a short-necked jar. The focus of the orthography is on the rim; karṇaka, kanaka; rebus: writer. See another example of a face ligatured to a markhor. The key is the face. This face is the rosetta stone proving it as a hieroglyph to be read rebus. So is the water-carrier a hieroglyph (as noted by Gadd). She is kuṭi 'water-carrier' (Telugu). Rebus: kuṭhi 'smelter furnace'. This object can also be denoted by pudendum muliebre. So is the glyph showing copulation scene: kamaḍha. This gloss can also be denoted by a person seated in penance. kamaḍha 'penance' (Pkt.) Rebus: kampaṭṭam 'coiner, mint'.

Indian linguistic area or Indian sprachbund

The glyphs of Indus script have been read rebus using homonymous glosses of the linguistic area or Indian sprachbund using over 1000 glosses of this substrate dictionary. This means that most of the glosses in one or more of present-day Indian languages will be assumed to retain the memories of the Indus language. Homonyms of the set of such glosses define the underlying language of Indus script depicted on about 4000 inscribed objects of the corpus of Indus inscriptions.

Many rearchers have reached a consensus that ancient India constituted a linguistic area (cf.Southworth, FC 2005; Emeneau, MB 1980; Masica, CP 1993; Kuiper, FBJ

1967, Indo-Iranian Journal 10: 81-102), that is, an area wherein specific language-speakers absorbed features from other languages and made the features their own. To delineate such a linguistic area and the glosses that might have been used in that area, the glosses are chosen from all Indian languages. Indian language glosses are compared because there is evidence for <u>cultural continuum of the civilization</u> which produced the objects inscribed with Indus script. (cf. <u>Sarasvati – Vedic River and Hindu Civilization by S. Kalyanaraman (2008)</u>.The glosses are semantically-phonetically clustered together in an <u>Indian lexicon</u> **which is a veritable substrate dictionary of the linguistic area. The assumption is that one or more languages of this lexicon could hold the legacy of the words used by the authors of the civilization who also invented the writing system. Ancient texts from India confirm this linguistic area.

Akkadian is ruled out as a possible underlying language because a cuneiform cylinder seal showing a seafaring Meluhhan merchant (carrying an antelope) required an interpreter, Shu-ilishu, confirming that the Meluhhan's language was not Akkadian; and 3) there is substantial agreement among scholars pointing to the Indian civilization area as Meluhha mentioned in Mesopotamian texts of 3rd-2nd millennium BCE. That meluhha and mleccha are cognate and that mleccha is attested as a mleccha vaacas (mleccha speech) distinguished from arya vaacas (arya speech) indicates that the linguistic area had a colloquial, ungrammatical mleccha speech and a grammatically correct arya speech. The substrate glosses of the Indian lexicon are thus reasonably assumed to be the glosses of mleccha vaacas, the speech of the artisans who produced the artifacts and the inscribed objects with the writing system. This assumption is further reinforced by the fact that about 80% of archaeological sites of the civilization are found on the banks of Vedic River Sarasvati leading some scholars to rename the Indus Valley civilization as Sarasvati-Sindhu civilization.

In this context, the following monumental work by Sylvan Levi, Jules Bloch and Jean Przyluski published in the 1920's continues to be relevant, even today, despite some advances in studies related to formation of Indian languages and the archaeological perspectives of and evidences from the civilization.

Przyluski notes the principal forms of the words signifying 'man' and 'woman' in the Munda languages:

Man: hor, hōrol, harr, ho~ro~r, haṛa, hoṛ, koro

Woman: kū ṛī, ērā, koṛi, kol

Comparing 'son' and 'daughter' in Santali:

Son = kora hapan; daughter = kuri hapan

"...a root kur, kor is differentiated in the Munda languages for signifying: man, woman, girl and boy. That in some cases this root has taken a relatively abstract sense is proved by Santali koḍa, koṛa, which signify 'one' as in the expression 'koḍa ke koḍa' 'each single one'. Thus one can easily understand that the same root has served the purpose of designating the individual not as an indivisible unity but as a numerical whole…Thus we can explain the analogy between the root kur, kor 'man' the number 20 in Munda kūṛī kūṛī , koḍī and the number 10 in Austro-Asiatic family ko, se-kūr, skall, gal." (ibid., pp. 28-30)

Homonym: कोल [kōla] *n* An income, or goods and chattels, or produce of fields &c. seized and sequestered (in payment of a debt). *v* धरून ठेव, सोड. 2 *f* The hole dug at the game of विटीदांडू, at marbles &c. कोलणें [kōlaṇēṃ] *v c* To strike the विटी in the hole कोली with the bat or दांडू. (In the game of विटीदांडू) 2 To cast off from one's self upon another (a work). Ex. पैका मागावयास लागलों म्हणजे बाप लेंकावर कोल- तो लेंक बापावर कोलतो. 3 To cast aside, reject, disallow, flout, scout. कोलून मारणें To kick up the heels of; to trip up: also to turn over (from one side to the other). किरकोळी [kirakōḷī] *f* (किरकोळ) A heap of miscellaneous articles.

An old Munda word, kol means 'man'. S. K. Chatterjee called the Munda family of languages as Kol, as the word, according to him, is (in the Sanskrit-Prākṛt form Kolia) an early Aryan modification of an old Munda word meaning 'man'.[229] Przyluski accepts this explanation.[230]

Skanda Purana refers to kol as a mleccha community.

(Hindu *śabdasagara*)

kolhe, 'the koles, an aboriginal tribe of iron smelters speaking a language akin to that of Santals' (Santali) kōla m. name of a degraded tribe Hariv. Pk. kōla -- m.; B. kol name of a Muṇḍā tribe (CDIAL 3532). কোল্ [kōla¹] an aboriginal tribe of India; a member of this tribe. (Bengali) That an early form of Indian linguistic area, kol means 'man' gets substantiated by a Nahali and Assamese glosses: kola 'woman'. See also: WPah. khaś.kuṛi, cur. kuĭṛ, cam. kŏḷā ' boy ', Sant. Muṇḍari koṛa ' boy ', kuṛi ' girl ', Ho koa, kui, Kūrkū kōn, kōnjē).[231]

Mleccha and Bharatiya languages

•Mleccha was substratum language of bharatiyo (casters of metal) many of whom lived in dvīpa (land between two rivers –Sindhu and Sarasvati -- or islands on Gulf of Kutch, Gulf of Khambat, Makran coast and along the Persian Gulf region of Meluhha)

Mleccha were bharatiya (Indians) of Indian linguistic area

According to Matsya Purāṇa (10.7), King Veṇa was the ancestor of the mleccha; according to Mahābhārata (MB. 12.59, 101-3), King Veṇa was a progenitor of the Niṣāda dwelling in the Vindhya mountains. Nirukta 3.8 includes Niṣāda among the five peoples mentioned in the ṛgveda 10.53.4, citing Aupamanyava; the five peoples are: brāhmaṇa, kṣatriya, vaiśya, śūdra and Niṣāda. Niṣāda gotra is mentioned in the gaṇapātha of Pāṇini (Aṣṭādhyāyī 4.1.100). It should be noted that Pāṇini associated yavana with the Kāmboja (Pāṇini, Gaṇapātha, 178 on 2.1.72).

Mullaippāṭṭu (59-66) (composed by kāvirippūmpāṭṭinattuppon vāṇiganār mahanārṇ.app ūḍanār) are part of Pattuppāṭṭu , ten Tamil verses of Sangam literature; these refer to a chief of Tamil warriors whose battle-field tent was built by Yavana and guarded by mleccha who speak only through gestures. (JV Chelliah, 1946, Pattuppāṭṭu; ten Tamil idylls, translated into English verse, South India Saiva Siddhanta Works Publishing Society, p. 91).

Mahābhārata notes that the Pāṇḍava army was protected by mleccha, among other people (Kāmboja , śaka, Khasa, Salwa, Matsya, Kuru, Mleccha, Pulinda, Draviḍa, Andhra and Kāñci) (MBh. V.158.20). Sūta laments the misfortune of the Kaurava-s: 'When the Nārāyaṇa-s have been killed, as also the Gopāla-s, those troops that were invincible in battle, and many thousands of mleccha-s, what can it be but Destiny?' (MBh. IX.2.36: Nārāyaṇā hatāyatra Gopālā yuddhadurmahāh mlecchāśca bahusāhasrāh kim anyad bhāgadheyatah?)

Nahali, Meluhhan, Language 'X'

On the banks of River Narmada are found speakers of Nahali, the so-called language isolate with words from Indo-Aryan, Dravidian and Munda – which together constitute the indic language substratum of a linguistic area, ca. 3300 BCE on the banks of Rivers Sarasvati and Sindhu – a region referred to as Meluhha in Mesopotamian cuneiform records; hence the language of the inscribed objects can rightly be called Meluhhan or Mleccha, a language which Vidura and Yudhiṣṭhira knew (as stated in the Great Epic, Mahābhārata).

Elsewhere in the Great Epic we read how Sahadeva, the youngest of the Pāṇḍava brothers, continued his march of conquest till he reached several islands in the sea (no doubt with the help of ships) and subjugated the Mleccha inhabitants thereof. Brahmāṇḍa 2.74.11, Brahma 13.152, Harivaṁśa 1841, Matsya 48.9, Vāyu 99.11, cf. also Viṣṇu 4.17.5, Bhāgavata 9.23.15, see Kirfel 1927: 522: pracetasah putraśatam rājānah sarva eva te // mleccharāṣṭrādhipāh sarve udīcīm diśam āśritāh which means, of course, not that these '100' kings conquered the 'northern countries' way beyond the Hindukuṣ or Himalayas, but that all these 100 kings, sons of pracetās (a descendant of a 'druhyu'), kings of mleccha kingdoms, are 'adjacent' (āśrita) to the 'northern direction,' -- which since the Vedas and Pāṇini has signified Greater gandhāra.Kirfel, W. Das Purāṇa Pañcalakṣaṇa. Bonn : K. Schroeder 1927. This can be construed as a reference to a migration of the sons of Pracetas towards the northern direction to become kings of the mleccha states. The son of Yayati's third son, Druhyu, was Babhru, whose son and grandsons were Setu, Arabdha, Gandhara, Dharma, Dhṛta, Durmada and Praceta. It is notable that

Pracetas is related to Dharma and Dhṛta, who are the principal characters of the Great Epic, the Mahābhārata. It should be noted that a group of people frequently mentioned in the Great Epic are the mleccha, an apparent designation of a group within the country, Bhārata. This is substantiated by the fact that Bhagadatta, the king of Pragjyotis.a is referred to as mleccha and he is also said to have ruled over two yavana kings (2.13).

Melakkha, island-dwellers, lapidaries

According to the great epic, Mlecchas lived on islands: "sa sarvān mleccha nṛpatin sāgara dvīpa vāsinah, aram āhāryàm àsa ratnāni vividhāni ca, andana aguru vastrāṇi maṇi muktam anuttamam, kāñcanam rajatam vajram vidrumam ca mahādhanam: (Bhima) arranged for all the mleccha kings, who dwell on the ocean islands, to bring varieties of gems, sandalwood, aloe, garments, and incomparable jewels and pearls, gold, silver, diamonds, and extremely valuable coral... great wealth." (MBh. 2.27.25-27). The reference to gems, perls and corals evokes the semiprecious and precious stones, such as carnelian and agate, of Gujarat traded with Mesopotamian civilization. According to Sumerian records from the Agade Period (Sargon, 2373-2247 BC), Sumerian merchants traded with people from (at least) three named foreign places: Dilmun (now identified as the island of Bahrain in the Persian Gulf); Magan (a port on the coastline between the head of the Persian Gulf and the mouth of the Sindhu river); and

Meluhha. Mentions of trade with Meluhha become frequent in Ur III period (2168-2062 BC) and Larsa dynasty (2062-1770 BCE). To the end of the Sarasvati Civilization period, the trade declines dramatically attesting to Meluhha being the Sarasvati Civilization. By Ur III Period, Meluhhan workers residing in Sumeria had Sumerian names, leading to a comment: '...three hundred years after the earliest textually documented contact between Meluhha and Mesopotamia, the references to a distinctly foreign commercial people have been replaced by an ethnic component of Ur III society' This is an economic presence of Meluhhan traders maintaining their own village for a considerable span of time. Parpola, Simo, Asko Parpola, and Robert H. Brunswig, Jr., 1977, "TheMeluhha Village - Evidence of Acculturation of Harappan Traders in Late Third Millenium Mesopotamia?", Journal of the Economic and Social History of the Orient, Volume 20, Part II.)

The epic also refers to the pāṇḍava Sahadeva's conquest of several islands in the sea with mleccha inhabitants.

A reference also to the salty marshes of Rann of Kutch in Gujarat (and also, perhaps, the Makran coast, south of Karachi), may also be surmised, where settlements and fortifications such as Amri Nal, Allahdino, Dholavira (Kotda) and Sur-kota-da have been excavated – both in the Sarasvati River Basin as the River traversed the rann. Kathāsaritsāgara (tr. CH Tawney, 1880, Calcutta; rep. New

Delhi, 1991), I, p. 151 associates mleccha with Sind. Mleccha kings paid tributes of sandalwood, aloe, cloth, gems, pearls, blankets, gold, silver and valuable corals.

Nakula conquered western parts of Bhāratavarṣa teeming with mleccha (MBh.V.49.26: yah pratīcīm diśam cakre vaśe mlecchagaṇāyutām sa tatra nakulo yoddhā citrayodhī vyavasthitah). Bṛhatsamhitā XIV.21 refers to lawless mleccha who inhabited the west: nirmaryādā mlecchā ye paścimadiksthit āsteca. A Buddhist chronicle, āryaManjuśrī Mūlakalpa [ed. Ganapati Śāstri, II, p. 274] associates pratyanta (contiguous)with mlecchadeśa in western Bhāratavarṣa: pacimām diśīm āsṛtya rājāno mriyate tadā ye 'pi pratyantavāsinyo mlecchataskaraj īvinah. (trans. 'Then (under a certain astrological combination) the kings who go to the west die; also inhabitants of pratyanta live like the mlecchas and taskara.')

Where the black-antelope roams, along the sea-coast: mleccha areas Blackbuck[232] (Antelope cervicapra)

This metaphor defines the region fit for yajna. This metaphor also explains the movements of mleccha, such as kamboja-yavana, pārada-pallava along the Indian Ocean Rim as sea-faring merchants from Meluhha. This parallels the hindu-bauddha continuum exemplified by the

Mathura lion capital with śrivatsa and Angkor Wat (Nagara vātika) as the largest Viṣṇu mandiram in the world, together with celebration of Bauddham in many parts of central, eastern and southeastern Asian continent. Mleccha were at no stage described in any text as people belonging to one ethnic, religious or linguistic group. This self-imposed restriction evidenced by all writers of the early Indian cultural tradition – Veda, Bauddha, Jaina alike – is of fundamental significance in understanding that mleccha constituted the core of the people on the banks of River Sarasvati and were the principal architects, artisans, workers, and people, in general, of the Sarasvati Civilization throughout its stages of evolution through modes of production – pastoral, agricultural, industrial – and interactions with neighbours, trading in surplus food products and artefacts generated and sharing cultural attributes/characteristics.

Various terms are used to describe mleccha social groups and communities: pratyantadeś'a (Arthaśāstra VII.10.16), paccantimā janapada (Vinaya Piṭaka V.13.12, vol. I, p. 197), aṭavi, aṭavika (DC Sircar, Selected Inscriptions, vol. I, 'Thirteenth Rock Edict Shābhāzgaṛhī, text line 7, p.37; 'Khoh Copper Plate Inscription of Saimkshobha', text line 8; Arthaśāstra VII.10.16; VII.4.43: mlecchaṭavi who were considered a thread to the state; ArthaśāstraIX.2.18-20 mentions aṭavibala, troops from forests as one of six types of troops at the disposal of a ruler). Some mleccha lived in border areas and forests, e.g. pratyanta nṛpatibhir (frontier kings: JF Fleet, CII, vol. II, 'Allahabad Posthumous Pillar Inscription of Samudragupta, text line 22, p. 116) cf. Arthaśāstra– a 4th century BCE text -- I.12.21; VII.14.27; XIV.1.2; mleccha jāti are: bheda,kirāta, śabara, pulinda: Amarakośa II.10.20, a fifth century CE text).

In many Persian inscriptions Yauna, Gandhāra and Saka occur together. [For e.g., DC Sircar, Selected Inscriptions, no.2 'Persepolis Inscription on Dārayavahuṣ (Darius c. 522-486 BCE),' lines 12-13, 18, p.7; no. 5, 'Perseplis Inscription of Khshayārshā (Xerxes c. 486-465)', lines 23, 25-6, p. 12]. Thus, yavana may be a reference to people settled in the northwest Bhāratavarṣa (India).

There are references to Mleccha (that is, śaka, Yavana, Kamboja, Pahlava) in Bāla Kāṇḍa of the Valmiki Rāmāyaṇa (1.54.21-23; 1.55.2-3). taih asit samvrita bhūmih śakaih-Yavana miśritaih || 1.54-21 || taih taih Yavana-Kamboja barbarah ca akulii kritaah || 1-54-23 || tasya humkaarato jātah Kamboja ravi sannibhah | udhasah tu atha sanjatah Pahlavah śastra panayah || 1-55-2|| yoni deśāt ca Yavanah śakri deśāt śakah tathā | roma kupeṣ u Mlecchah ca Haritah sa Kiratakah || 1-55-3 ||.Kāmboja Yavanān caiva śakān pattaṇāni ca | Anvīkṣya Varadān caiva Himavantam vicinvatha || 12 || — (Rāmāyaṇa 4.43.12)

The Yavanas here refer to the Bactrian Yavanas (in western Oxus country), and the Sakas here refer to the Sakas of Sogdiana/Jaxartes and beyond. The Vardas are same Paradas (Hindu Polity, 1978, p 124, Dr K. P. Jayswal;

Goegraphical Data in Early Purana, 1972, p 165, 55 fn, Dr M. R.Singh). The Paradas were located on river Sailoda in Sinkiang (MBH II.51.12; II.52.13; VI.87.7 etc) and probably as far as upper reaches of river Oxus and Jaxartes (Op cit, p 159-60, Dr M. R.Singh).

Vanaparva of Mahābhārata notes: "......Mlechha (barbaric) kings of the śaka-s, Yavanas, Kambojas, Bahlikas etc shall rule the earth (i.e India) un-rightously in Kaliyuga..." (viparīte tadā loke purvarūpān kṣayasya tat || 34 || bahavo mechchha r\ājānah pṛthivyām manujādhipa | mithyanuśāsinah pāpa mṛ savadaparāṇah || 35 || āndrah śakah Pulindaśca Yavanaśca narādhipāh | Kamboja Bahlikah śudrastathābhīra narottama || 36|| MBH 3/188/34-36). Anushasanaparava of Mahābhārata affirms that Mathura, was under the joint military control of the Yavanas and the Kambojas (12/102/5). tathā Yavana Kambojā Mathurām abhitaś ca ye ete niyuddhakuśalā dākshiinātyāsicarminah. Mahābhārata speaks of the Yavanas, Kambojas, Darunas etc as the fierce mleccha from Uttarapatha : uttaraścāpare mlechchha jana bharatasattama. || 63 || Yavanashcha sa Kamboja Daruna mlechchha jatayah. | — (MBH 6.11.63-64) They are referred to as papakritah (sinful): uttara pathajanmanah kirtayishyami tanapi. | Yauna Kamboja Gandharah Kirata barbaraih saha. || 43 || ete pāpakṛtāstatra caranti pṛrthivīmimām. | śvakakabalagridhraṇān sadharmaṇo narādhipa. || 44 || — (MBH 12/207/43-44)[233]

Yavana are descendants of Turvaśu, one of the four sons of Yayāti. The sons were to rule over people such as Yavana, Bhoja and Yādava (MBh. 1.80.23-4; Matsya Purāṇa 34.29-30). ṛgveda notes that Yadu and Turvaśa are dāsa (RV 10.62.10). Yavana, descendants of Turvaśu are noted as meat-eaters, sinful and hence, anārya.[234] These people were brought over the sea safely by Indra (RV 6.20.12). In the Mahābhārata, sons of Anu are noted as mleccha.

sanema te vasā navya indra pra pūrava stavanta enā yajnaih

sapta yat purah śarma śāradīr dadruiśa dhan dāsīh purukutsāya śikṣan

tvam vrdha indraprvyarja bhūr varivasyann uśane kāvyāya

parā navavāstvam anudeyam mahe pitre dadātha svam napātam

tvam dhunir indra dhunimtrṇor āpah sīrā na sravantīh

pra yat samudram ati śūra parśi pāraya turvaśam yadum svasti

RV 6.020.10 (Favoured) by your proection, Indra, we solicit new (wealth); by this adoration men glorify you at sacrifices, for that you have shattered with your bolt the seven cities of śarat, killing the opponents (of sacred rites), killing the opponents (of sacred rites), and giving (their spoils) to Purukutsa. [Men: puravah = manuṣyah; śarat = name of an asura].

RV 6.020.11 Desirous of opulence, you, Indra, have been an ancient benefactor of Us'anas, the son of Kavi; having slain Navava_stva, you have given back his own grandson, who was (fit) to be restored o the grandfather.

RV 6.020.12 You, Indra, who make (your enemies) tremble, have caused the waters, detained by Dhuni, to flow like rushing rivers; so, hero, when, having crossed the ocean, you have reached the shore, you have brought over in safety Turvas'a and Yadu. [samudram atiprapars.i = samudram atikramya pratirṇo bhavasi = when you are crossed, having traversed the ocean, you have brought across Turvaśa and Yadu, both standing on the future shore, samudrapāretiṣṭhantau apārayah].

Nandana, another commentator of Mānava Dharma śāstra. X.45, defines āryavāc as samskṛtavāc . Thus, according to Medhātithi, neither habitation nor mleccha speech is the ground for regarding groups as Dasyus, but it is because of their particular names Barbara etc., that they are so regarded. Yavana, descendants of Turvaśu are noted as meat-eaters, sinful and hence, anārya.[235] These people were brought over the sea safely by Indra, as noted by this ṛca. This ṛca also notes that Yadu and Turvaśa (dāsa); and that Turvaśu is a son of Yayāti. The sons of Yayāti were to rule over people such as Yavana, Bhoja and Yādava. Turvaśu and Yadu crossed the oceans to come into Bhāratavarṣa. In this ṛca., 'samudra' can be interpreted only as an ocean. The ocean crossed by Indra, may be not too far from Sindhu. Sindhu is a 'natural ocean frontier' in ṛgveda. Given the activities of the Meluhha along the Makran Coast (300 km. south of Mehergarh, in the neighbourhood of Karachi), Gulf of Kutch and Gulf of Khambat, (evidence? turbinella pyrum--śankha − bangle found in a woman's grave in Mehergarh, dated to c. 6500 BCE, yes 7th millennium BCE; the type of shell found nowhere else in the world excepting the coastline of Sindhu sāgara upto to the Gulf of Mannar).

The ocean referred to may be the ocean in the Gulf of Kutch was situated witha number of dvīpas. In places north of Lamgham district, i.e. north bank of river Kabul, near Peshawar were regions known as Mi-li-ku, the frontier of the mleccha lands.[236] Harivamśa 85.18-19 locates the mleccha in the Himalayan region and mleccha are listed with yavana, śaka, darada, pārada, tuṣāra, khaśa and pahlava in north and north-west Bhāratavarṣa: sa viv ṛddho yad ā rāj ā yavan ānām mah ābalāh tata enam nṛpā mlecch āh sams'rity ānuyayaus tad ā śakās tuṣār ā daradāh pāradās tan:gaṇāh khasśāh pahlavāh śataśaścānye mlecch ā haimavat ās tathā. Matsya Pur ān.a 144.51-58 provides a simialr list. Pracetā had a hundred sons all of whom ruled in mleccha regions in the north.[237] Bhīṣma Parvan of Mahābhārata notes That mleccha jāti people lived in Yavana, Kāmboa, Dāruṇā regions and are listed together with several other peoples of the northern and north-western parts of Bhāratavars.a (MBh. VI.10.63-66: uttarāścāpare mlecchā janā bharatasattama yavanāśca śaka, kāmbojā dārun.ā mlecchajātayah). In the Rām āyan.a IV.42.10, Sugrīva is asked to search for Sītā in the northern lands of mleccha, pulinda, sūrasena, praṣalā, bhārata, kuru, madraka, kamboja and yavana before proceeding to Himavat: tatra mlecchān pulindāmśūrasen āmś tathaiva ca prasthalān bharatāmścaiva kurūmssca saha madraih. Mlecchas came from the valley adjoining the Himalaya.[238]

When Sagara, son of Bāhu, was prevented from destroying śaka, Yavana, Kāmboa, Pārada and Pāhlava after he recovered his kingdom, Vasiṣṭha, the family priest of Sagara, absolved these people of their duties but Sagara commande the Yavana to shave the upper half of their heads, the Pārada to wear long hair and Pahlava to let their beards grow. Sagara also absolved them of their duty offer yajna to agni and to study the Veda.[239] This is how these Yavana, Pārada and Pahlava also became mleccha.[240] The implication is that prior to Sagara's command, these kṣatriya communities did respect Vasiṣṭha as their priest, studied the Veda and performed yajna.[241] śaka who were designated as kings of mleccha jāti by Bhaṭṭa Utpala (10th century) in his commentary on Bṛhatsamhitā, were defeated by Candragupta II. That the mleccha were also adored as ṛṣi is clear from the vere of Bṛhatsamhitā 2.15: mlecch ā hi yavan ās te ṣu samyak śāstram kadam sthitam ṛṣivat te 'pi pūjyante kim punar daivavid dvijāh (The yavana are mleccha, among them this science is duly established;

therefore, even they (although mleccha) are honoured as ṛṣi; how much more (praise is due to an) astrologer who is a brāhmaṇa'). Bṛhatsamhitā 14.21 confirms that the yavana, śaka and pahlava lived on the west. Similarly, Konow notes that Sai-wang (Saka King) mentioned in Chinese accounts should be interpreted as Saka Murun.d.a and the territory he occupied as Kāpiśa.[242] śaka migrated to Bhāratavarṣa through Arachosia via the Bolan Pass into the lower Sindhu, a region called Indo_Scythia by Greek geographers and called śaka-dvīpa in Bharatiya texts.[243] Another view expressed by Thomas is that the migration was through Sindh and the valley of the Sindhu River.[244] Kalhaṇa notes that Jalauka, a son of As'oka took possession of Kāśmīra, advanced as far as Kanauj, after crushing a horse of mleccha.[245] Greek invasions occurred later, during the reign of Puṣyamitra śunga (c. 185-150 BCE). The regions inhabited by the 'milakkha' could be the Vindhyan region. The term, 'mleccha ' of which 'milakkha " is a variant, could as well have denoted the indigenous people of Bhāratavarṣa who had lived on the Sarasvati River basin and who moved towards other parts of Bhāratavarṣa after the gradual desiccation of the river, over a millennium, between c. 2500 and 1500 BCE. Medhātithi, commenting on the verse of Manu, defines a language as mleccha : asad avidyam ān\ārthās ādhu śabdatayā vāk mleccha ucyate yathā śabarāṇām kirātānām anyeyām va antyānām: Medhātithi on Mānava Dharmaśāstra X.45 – 'Language is called mleccha because it consists of words that have no meaning or have the wrong meaning or are wrong in form. To this class belong the languages of such low-born tribes as the śabara-s, Kirāta and so forth...'... He further proceeds to explain that āryavāc is refined speech and the language of the inhabitants of āryāvarta, but only of those who belong to the four varṇa-s. The others are called Dasyus.: ibid. – āryavāca āryāvartam vāsinas te cāturvarṇy ādanyajātīyatvena prasiddhas tadā dasyava ucyante ' Arya (refined) language is the language of the inhabitants of āryāvarta. Those persons being other than the four varṇa-s are called Dasyus.'

In Dhammapada's commentary on Petuvathu, Dwaraka is associated with Kamboja as its Capital or its important city.[246] See evidence below:

"Yasa asthaya gachham Kambojam dhanharika/ ayam kamdado yakkho iyam yakham nayamasai// iyam yakkham gahetvan sadhuken pasham ya/ yanam aaropyatvaan khippam gaccham Davarkān iti // [Buddhist Text Khudak Nikaya (P.T.S)]

Mleccha who came to the Rājasūya also included those from forest and frontier areas (MBh. III. 48.19:sāgarān ūpagāmścaiva ye ca paṭṭaṇavāsinah simhal ān barbarān mlecchān ye ca jān:galavāsinah). Bhīmasena proceeded east towards Lohitya (Brahmaputra) and had conquered several mleccha people who bestowed on him wealth of various kinds (MBh. II.27.23-24: suhmānāmādhipam caiva ye ca sāgaravāsinah sarvān mlecchagaṇāmścaiva vijigye bharatarṣabhah evam bahu vidhān deśān vijitya pavanātmajah vasu tebhya upādya lauhityam agad balī.[247]

Celebrations at the Kalinga capital of Duryodhana were attended by preceptors and mleccha kings from the south and east of Bhārata (MBh. XII.4.8: ete cānye ca bahavo dakṣinām diśam āśritah mlecchā āryāśca rāj ānah prācyodicyāśca bhārata).

Bhāgadatta, the great warrior of Prāgjyotiṣa accompanied by mleccha people inhabiting marshy regions of the sea- coast (sāgarānūpavāsibhih), attends the Rājasūya of Yudhiṣṭhira (MBh. II.31.9-10: prāgjyotiṣaśca nṛpatir bhagadatto mahāyaśāh saha sarvais tathā mlecchaih sāgarānūpavāsibhih). This is perhaps a reference ot the marshy coastline of Bengal. Amarakośa II, Bhūmivarga – 6: pratyanto mlecchade śah syāt; Sarvānanda in his commentary, ṭīkāsarvasva, elaborates that mleccha deśa denotes regions without proper conduct such as Kāmarūpa: bhāratavarṣasyāntadeśah śiṣṭācārā rahitah kāmarūpādih mlecchadeśāh[248] ; he also cites Manu that where four

varṇa-s are not established that region is mlecchade śa. A contemporary of Harṣavardhana was Bhāskaravarman of Kāmarūpa; this king was supplanted by another dynasty founded by śālastambha who was known as a mleccha overlord.[249]

Meluhha, Mleccha areas: Sarasvati River Basin and Coastal Regions of Gujarat, Baluchistan

Meluhha referred to in Sumerian and old Akkadian texts refers to an area in Sarasvati Civilization; Asko and Simo Parpola add: '...probably, including NW India with Gujarat as well as eastern Baluchistan'.[250]

Imports fromMeluhha into Mesopotamia included the following commodities which were found in north-western and western Bhāratavarṣa: copper, silver, gold, carnelian, ivory, uśu wood (ebony), and another wood which is translated as 'sea wood' – perhaps mangrove wood on the coasts of Sind ad Baluchistan.[251] The Ur texts specifically refer to 'seafaring country of Meluhha" and hence, Leemans' thesis that Meluhha was the west coast (modern state of Gujarat) of Bhārata.[252] The Lothal dockyard had fallen into disuse by c. 1800 BCE, a date when the trade between Mesopotamia and Meluhha also ended.[253] In Leemans' view, Gujarat was the last bulwark of the (Indus or Sarasvati) Civilization. Records refer to Meluhhan ships docking at Sumer. There were Meluhhans in various Sumerian cities; there was also a Meluhhan town or district at one city. The Sumerian records indicate a large volume of trade; according to a Sumerian tablet, one shipment from Meluhha contained 5,900 kg of copper (13,000 lbs, or 6 1/2 tons)! The bulk of this trade was done through Dilmun, not directly with Meluhha. In our view, the formative stages of the Civilization also had their locus in the coastal areas – in particular, the Gulf of Khambat, Gulf of Kutch and Makran coast, as evidenced by the wide shell-bangle, dated to c. 6500 BCE, made of turbinella pyrum or śankha, found in Mehergarh, 300 miles north of the Makran coast.

Evidence exists for trade in shells found uniquely in the region, in particular, a shell called xancus pyrum: See: Xancus Pyrum and trade routes emanating from the subcontinent. "Silvio Durante's study (1979) of marine shells from India and their appearance in the archaeological record in such distant sites as Tepe Yahya and Shahr-i Sokhta in Iran, as well as in the Indus Valley, sheds light on the ancient trading routes of certain types of shells which are specifically and exclusively found along the Indian coastline proper. Following Phil Kohl's arguments, where shells were traded, so culture, technology, religion, etc. must have followed.[254] "Durante primarily discusses the marine shell Xancus pyrum and the fact that it was traded whole and intact, then worked or reworked at its destination site, perhaps then moving on to other locations. The importance of this specific shell is that 'Xancus Pyrum has a very limited geographic distribution and thus has almost the same significance in the field of shells as that of lapis lazuli in the context of mineral resources as regards the determination of the possible routes along which a locally unavailable raw material is transported from a well-defined place of origin to the place where it is processed and, as also in the case of

Xancus Pyrum, consumed' (Durante 1979:340). Durante also interestingly points out that as the shells were traded as a raw resource for later working, the trade phenomena of 'increasingly high degrees of product finishing in order to add a surplus value to the goods' (Durante 1979:340) does not exist. Perhaps, as these shells crossed so many cultural hands, they were left un-worked in order for the final owner or consumer to work the raw material into a style and usage specific to their region. Durante offers four possible trade routes from their gathering zone along the west and northwest Indian coast to destinations west: sea route direct to the Iranian coastal area; sea route to Sutkagen-dor and Sotka-koh on the Makran coast, then overland westwards; overland through the Indus plain and then through the Makran interior to Sistan; overland through the Indus Valley and then through the Gomal Valley to Sistan. "Thus we now have hard evidence for trade and cultural exchange, plus traceable routes for objects emanating from the farthest south eastern reaches of the Harappan cultural sphere to destinations far west of the Indus. There can be no doubt that the Harappans were part of multiple trading networks involving their immediately peripheral neighbors and others far beyond... "To facilitate the obtainment of the sought after goods, sites were located in such far flung locations as Sutkagen-dor in Makran as a source for ocean materials such as shell and for the site's proximity to Persian Gulf trade routes; Bala Kot in eastern Makran, which, like

Sutkagen-dor, was a source for ocean materials and access to Persian Gulf trade routes; Lothal in Gujarat, India, which is usually considered the 'gateway to the east;' Shortugai in Badakhshan, Afghanistan, for its proximity to the lapis mines..."[255]

Like Nahali (Nahari > Nagari) on banks of River Tapati, mleccha is a language-composite of Indo-Aryan, Dravidian and Munda linguistic area circa 5000 years Before Present on Sarasvati-Indus River Basins; all proto-versions of present-day languages of Bharat are a dialectical continuum from this linguistic area (Further researches and identification of isoglosses called for).

It is possible to derive the underlying language of Indus script of the Indus civilization using the insights provided by areal linguistics pointing to an Indian sprachbund. Based on the reality of this underlying sprachbund, a substrate dictionary has been compiled with over 8000 semantic clusters. These clusters include about 4000 etyma with cognates in Indo-Aryan (CDIAL), Dravidian (DEDR) and Munda (Santali, Mundarica) language groups. That about 4000 of the 5200 dravidian etyma in Dravidian Etymological Dictionary (DEDR) get so clustered also substantiates the Indian sprachbund.

Indian Lexicon (Kalyanaraman, 1992) [256] lists cognate lexemes of 25+ ancient languages of Bharat; including about 4,000 of the 5,200 etyma of Dravidian Etymological Dictionary and hundreds of Munda lexemes. The 8000 semantic clusters of this lexicon are a veritable substrate lexicon of the Indus language or proto-Indic.

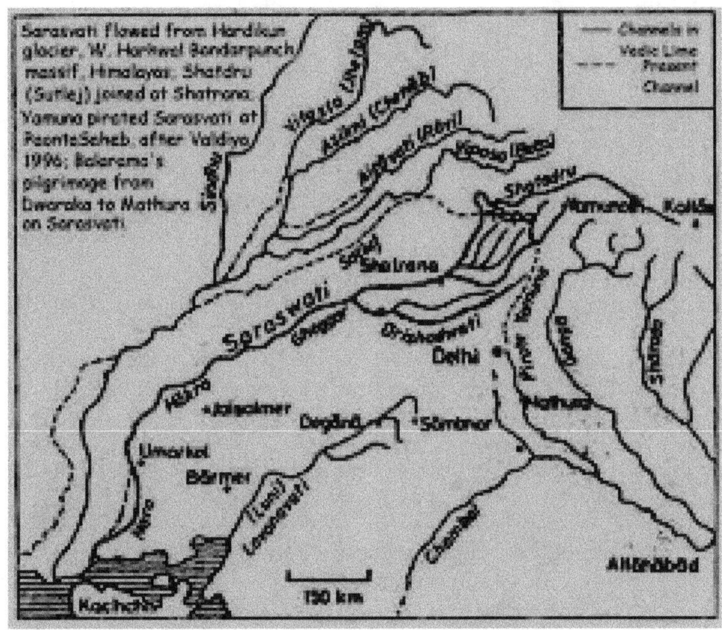

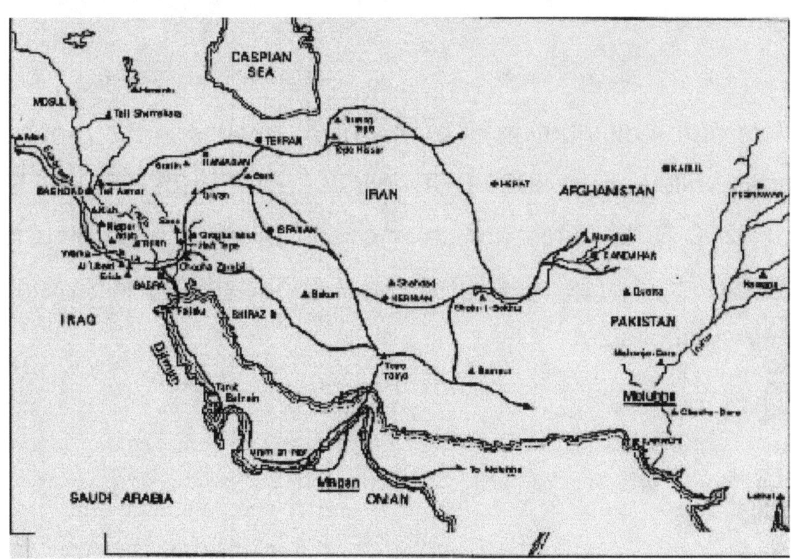

Location of Meluha. Interaction areas.[257]

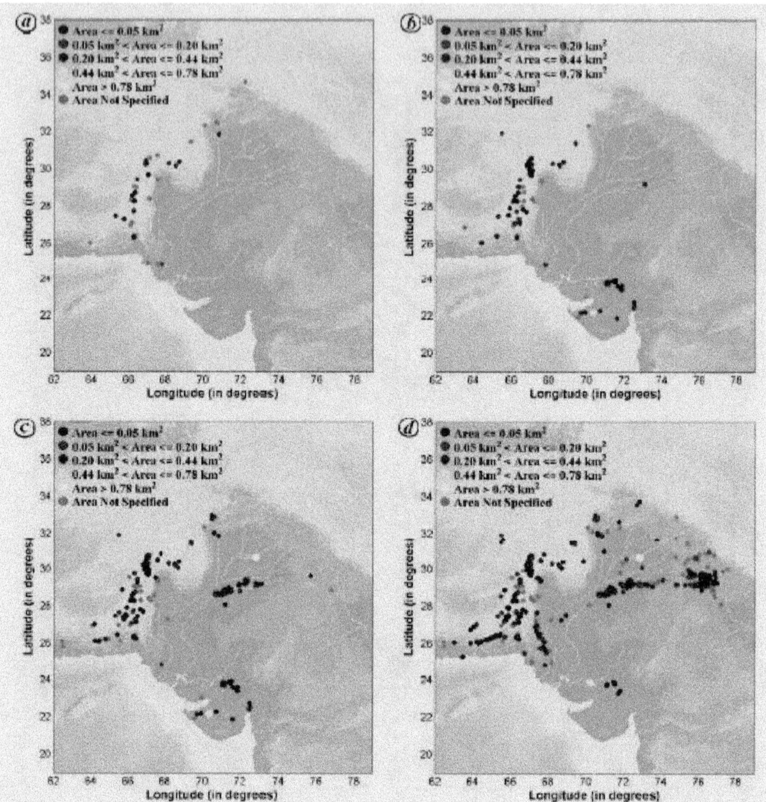

Plots of the distribution of archaeological sites in the greater Indus valley at (a) 5000 BCE; (b) 4000 BCE; (c) 3700 BCE; (d) 3200 BCE. Sites are color coded by area according to the legend. Large area sites are emphasized by increasing their symbol size.

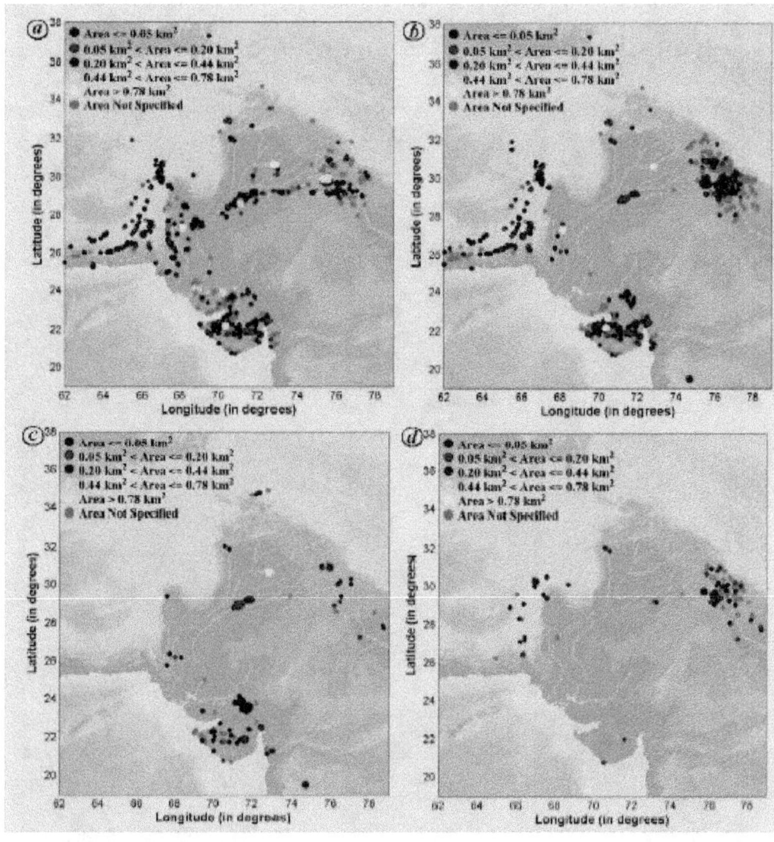

Plots of the distribution of archaeological sites in the greater Indus valley at (a) 2500 BCE; (b) 1900 BCE; (c) 1500 BCE; (d) 1000 BCE. Sites are color coded by area according to the legend. Large area sites are emphasized by increasing their symbol size.[258]

Sarasvarti river basin and Gujarat have about 2000 (80%) of archaeological sites of the civilization.

285

The principal interaction areas were within Meluhha and in the regions identified as Turan towards the Caspian Sea,

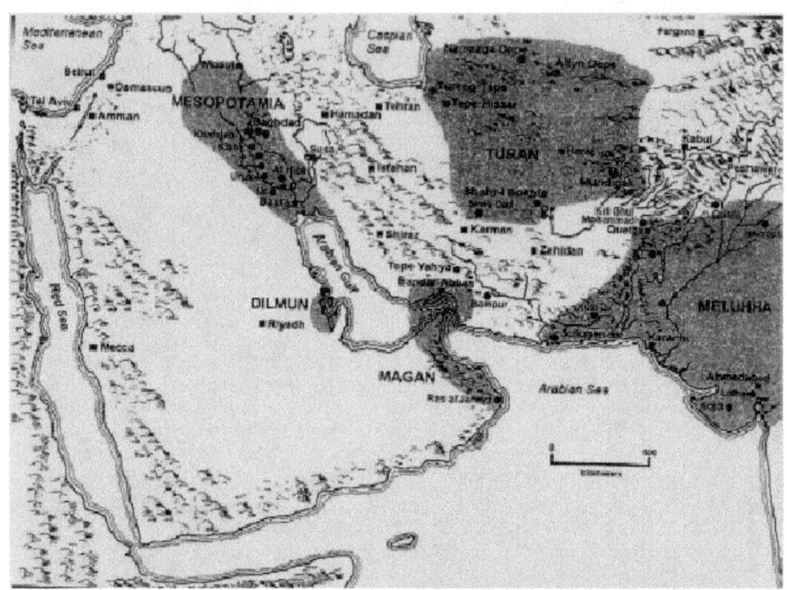

Magan, Dilmun and Mesopotamian cultural zones across the Persian Gulf and the Tigris-Euphrates doab.

Western Asia showing Mesopotamia, Turan, Dilmun, Meluhha.[259]

Over 45 sites where objects with epigraphs have been discovered

Tanana mleccha

A Jaina text, Avasyaka Churani notes that ivory trade was managed by tanana mleccha, who also traveled from Uttaravaha to Dakshinapatha.[260] Guttila Jataka (ca.4th cent.) makes reference to itinerant ivory workers/traders journeying from Varanasi to Ujjain.[261] The word, tanana in tanana mleccha may be related to: (i) tah'nai, 'engraver' mleccha; or (ii) tana, 'of (mleccha) lineage'. 1. See Kuwi. tah'nai 'to engrave' in DEDR and Bsh. then, thon, 'small axe' in CDIAL: DEDR 3146 *Go.* (Tr.) tarcana , (Mu.) tarc- to scrape; (Ma.) tarsk- id., plane; (D.) task-, (Mu.) tarsk-/tarisk- to level, scrape (*Voc.*1670).

Sea-faring merchants/artisans of Meluhha

Akkadian. Cylinder seal Impression. Inscription records that it belongs to 'S'u-ilis'u, Meluhha interpreter', i.e., translator of the Meluhhan language (EME.BAL.ME.LUH.HA.KI) The Meluhhan being introduced carries an goat on his arm. Musee du Louvre. Ao 22 310, Collection De Clercq 3rd millennium BCE. The Meluhhan is accompanied by a lady carrying a kamaṇḍalu.

Since he needed an interpreter, it is inferred that Meluhhan did not speak Akkadian.

Antelope carried by the Meluhhan is a hieroglyph: mlekh 'goat' (Br.); mreka (Te.); mēṭam (Ta.); meṣam (Skt.) Thus, the goat conveys the message that the carrier is a Meluhha speaker. A phonetic determinant.mrreka, mlekh 'goat'; Rebus: melukkha Br. mēl̲h 'goat'. Te. mreka (DEDR 5087) **meluh.h.a !**

"While Prof. Thomson maintained that a Munda influence has probably been at play in fixing the principle regulating the inflexion of nouns in Indo-Aryan vernaculars, such influence appeared to be unimportant to Prof. Sten Konow… Prof. Przyluski in his papers, translated here, have tried to explain a certain number of words of the Sanskrit vocabulary as fairly ancient loans from the Austro-Asiatic family of languages. He has in this opened up a new line of enquiry. Prof. Jules Bloch in his article on Sanskrit and Dravidian, also translated in this volume, has criticised the position of those who stand exclusively for Dravidian influence and has proved that the question of the Mnn<j& substratum in Indo-

Aryan cannot be overlooked...In 1923, Prof. Levi, in a fundamental article on Pre-Aryen et PrJ-Draviditn dans VInde tried to show that some geographical names of ancient India like Kosala-Tosala, Anga-Vanga, Kalinga-Trilinga, Utkala-Mekala and Pulinda-Kulinda, ethnic names which go by pairs, can be explained by the morphological system of the Austro-Asiatic languages. Names like Accha-Vaccha, Takkola-Kakkola belong to the same category. He concluded his long study with the following observation, " We must know whether the legends, the religion and the philosophical thought of India do not owe anything to this past. India has been too exclusively examined from the Indo-European standpoint. It ought to be remembered that India is a great maritime country... the movement which carried the Indian colonization towards the Far East... was far from inaugurating a new route...Adventurers, traffickers and missionaries profited by the technical progress of navigation and followed under better conditions of comfort and efficiency, the way traced from time immemorial, by the mariners of another race, whom Aryan or Aryanised India despised as savages." In 1926, Przyluski tried to explain the name of an ancient people of the Punjab, the Udumbara, in a similar way and affiliate it to the Austro-Asiatic group. (cf. Journal Asiatique, 1926, 1, pp. 1-25, Un ancicn peuple du Pendjables Udumbaras : only a portion of this article containing linguistic discussions has been translated in the Appendix of this book.) In another article, the same scholar discussed some names of Indian towns in the geography of Ptolemy and tried to explain them by Austro-Asiatic forms...Dr. J. H. Hutton, in an interesting lecture on the Stone Age Cult of Assam delivered in the Indian Museum at Calcutta in 1928, while dealing with some prehistoric monoliths of Dimapur, near Manipur, says that " the method of erection of these monoliths is very important, as it throws some light on the erection of prehistoric monoliths in other parts of the world. Assam and Madagascar are the only remaining parts of the world where the practice of erecting rough stones still continues....The origin of this stone cult is uncertain, but it appears that it is to be mainly imputed to the Mon-Khmer intrusion from the east In his opinion the erection of these monoliths takes the form of the lingam and yoni. He thinks that the Tantrik form of worship, so prevalent in Assam, is probably due to " the incorporation into Hinduism of a fertility cult which preceded it as .the religion of the country. The dolmens possibly suggest distribution from South India, but if so, the probable course was across the Bay of Bengal and then back again westward from further Asia. Possibly the origin was from Indonesia whence apparently the use of supari (areca nut) spread to India as well as the Pacific." (From the Introduction by PC Bagchi and SK Chatterjee, 1 May 1929).

On 'Sanskrit and Dravidian', comments by Jules Bloch: "There is, therefore, nothing to justify the assertion that Indo-Aryan cerebrals are of indigenous origin. The local pronunciation has rendered the development of this class possible ; and in this sense the action of the substratum is undeniable. But it is necessary at once to insist upon the fact that the Munda languages have dentals and cerebrals just like Dravidian, and nothing, therefore, stands in the way of attributing theoretically the origin of the Sanskrit pronunciation to the action of a substratum of either Munda or some other language connected with it, if not of a fourth linguistic family still unknown…A curious fact that might be noted here is the continuous character of the Sanskrit sentences, which has given rise to the rules of sandhi, because Tamil and Canarese admit a rigorous sandhi in writing, But the same languages in their spoken form ignore it; Gondi and Kurukh also ignore it. In so far as these literary languages admit this tandhi, it is certainly due to the influence of Sanskrit ; and even in Sanskrit it is probable that the use of the rules in question has very much surpassed in extension the real use ; Aśoka ignores them absolutely. There is, therefore, no clear phonetic proof of the action of Dravidian on Indo-European, at any rate, in ancient times…The facts of a substratum result from the unconscious blending of two systems existing amongst the same people ; the loan results from a willing effort to add elements taken from outside to the mass of the vocabulary. The loan proves the contact of the two languages and not the substitution of the one by the other. On the other hand it is often difficult to recognise in what sense the borrowing is made between two given languages and to make sure that it has not been made by each of the two languages from a third one, known or unknown... Perhaps the principal interest for ourselves in the study of ancient loans (and it would be necessary to try both ways since Dravidian has borrowed much from Aryan) would be to form an idea of prehistoric Dravidian ; because even those Dravidian languages which have a past are only attested in a definite way, for the first time, a few centuries after the Christian Era. Moreover the complications we have met with, suggest that Dravidian like Sanskrit may have taken loans of vocabulary from Munda, which must be at least as ancient as Dravidian in India." (pp. 40-59).

Kuiper[262] notes: " ...a very considerable amount (say some 40%) of the New Indo-Aryan vocabulary is borrowed from Munda, either via Sanskrit (and Prākṛt), or via Prākṛt alone, or directly from Munda; wide-branched and seemingly native, word-families of South Dravidian are of Proto-Munda origin; in Vedic and later Sanskrit, the words adopted have often been Aryanized, resp. Sanskritized. "In view of the intensive interrelations between Dravidian, Munda and Aryan dating from pre-Vedic times even individual etymological questions will often have to be approached from a Pan-Indic point of view if their study is to be fruitful. It is hoped that this work may be helpful to arrive at this all-embracing view of the Indian languages, which is the final goal of these studies."

Emeneau[263] notes: "In fact, promising as it has seemed to assume Dravidian membership for the Harappa language, it is not the only possibility. Professor W. Norman Brown has pointed out (The United States and India and Pakistan, 131-132, Cambridge, Harvard University Press, 1953) that Northwest India, i.e. the Indus Valley and adjoining parts of India, has during most of its history had Near Eastern elements in its political and cultural make-up at least as prominently as it had true Indian elements of the Gangetic and Southern types. The passage is so important that it is quoted in full: 'More ominous yet was another consideration. Partition now would reproduce an ancient, recurring, and sinister incompatibility between Northwest and the rest of the subcontinent, which, but for a few brief periods of uneasy cohabitation, had kept them politically apart or hostile and had rendered the subcontinent defensively weak. When an intrusive people came through the passes and established itself there, it was at first spiritually closer to the relatives it had left behind than to any group already in India. Not until it had been separated from those relatives for a fairly long period and had succeeded in pushing eastward would I loosen the external ties. In period after period this seems to have been true. In the third millennium B.C. the Harappa culture in the Indus Valley was partly similar to contemporary western Asian civilizations and partly to later historic Indian culture of the Ganges Valley. In the latter part of the next millennium the earliest Aryans, living in the Punjab and composing the hymns of the Rig Veda, were apparently more like their linguistic and religious kinsmen, the Iranians, than like their eastern Indian contemporaries. In the middle of the next millennium the Persian Achaemenians for two centuries held the Northwest as satrapies. After Alexander had invaded India (327/6-325 B.C.) and Hellenism had arise, the Northwest too was Hellenized, and once more was partly Indian and partly western. And after Islam entered India, the Northwest again was associated with Persia, Bokhara, Central Asia, rather than with India, and considered itself Islamic first and Indian second. The periods during which the Punjab has been culturally assimilated to the rest of northern India are ew if any at all. Periods of political assimilation are almost as few; perhaps a part of the fourth and third centuries B.C. under the Mauryas; possibly a brief period under the Indo-Greek king menander in the second century B.C.; another brief period under the Muslim kingdom of Delhi in the last quarter of the twelfth century A.D.; a long one under the great Mughals in the sixteenth and seventeenth centuries A.D.; a century under the British, 1849-1947.' "Though this refers to cultural and political factors, it is a warning that we must not leap to linguistic conclusions hastily. The early, but probably centuries-long condition in which Sanskrit, a close ally of languages of Iran, was restricted to the northwest (though it was not the only language there) and the rest of India was not Sanskritic in speech, may well have been mirrored earlier by a period when some other language invader from the Near East-a relative of Sumerian or of Elamitic or what not-was spoken and written in the Indus Valley-perhaps that of invaders and conquerors-while the indigenous population spoke another language-perhaps one of the Dravidian stock, or perhaps one of the Munda stock, which is now represented only by a handful of languages in the backwoods of Central India. "On leaving this highly speculative question, we can move on to an examination of the Sanskrit records, and we find in them linguistic evidence of contacts between the Sanskrit-speaking invaders and the other linguistic groups within India...the early days of Indo-European scholarship were without benefit of the spectacular archaeological discoveries that were later to be made in the Mediterranean area, Mesopotamia and the Indus Valley... This assumption (that IE languages were urbanized bearers of a high civilization) led in the long run to another block-the methodological tendency of the end of the nineteenth and the beginning of the twentieth century to attempt to find Indo-European etymologies for the greatest possible portion of the vocabularies of the Indo-European languages, even though the object could only be achieved by flights of phonological and semantic fancy... very few scholars attempted to identify borrowings from Dravidian into Sanskrit...The Sanskrit etymological dictionary of Uhlenbrck (1898-1899) and the Indo-European etymological dictionary of Walde and Pokorny (1930-1932) completely ignore the work of Gundert (1869), Kittel (1872, 1894), and Caldwell (1856,1875)... It is clear that not all of Burrow's suggested borrowings will stand the test even of his own principles...'India' and 'Indian' will be used in what follows for the subcontinent, ignoring the political division into the Republic of India and Pakistan, and, when necessary, including Ceylong also... the northern boundary of Dravidian is and has been for a long time retreating south before the expansion of Indo-Aryan... We know in fact from the study of the non-Indo-European element in the Sanskrit lexicon that at the time of the earliest Sanskrit records, the R.gveda, when Sanskrit speakers were localized no further east than the Panjab, there were already a few Dravidian words current in Sanskrit. This involves a localization of Dravidian speech in this area no lather than three millennia ago. It also of course means much bilingualism and gradual abandonment of Dravidian speech in favor of IndoAryan over a long period and a great area-a process for which we have only the most meagre of evidence in detail. Similar relationships must have existed between Indo-Aryan and Munda and between Dravidian and Munda, but it is still almost impossible to be sure of either of these in detail... The Dravidian languages all have many Indo-Aryan items, borrowed at all periods from Sanskrit, Middle Indo-Aryan and Modern Indo-Aryan. The Munda languages likewise have much Indo-Aryan material, chiefly, so far as we know now, borrowed rom Modern Indo-Aryan, thogh this of course inlcudes items that are Sanskrit in form, since Modern Indo-Aryan borrows from Sanskrit very considerably. That Indo-Aryan has borrowed from Dravidian has also become clear. T. Burrow, The Sanskrit Language, 379-88 (1955), gives a sampling and a statement of the chronology involved. It is noteworthy that this influence was spent by the end of the pre-Christian era, a precious indication for the linguistic history of North India: Dravidian speech must have practically ceased to exist in the Ganges valley by this period... Most of the languages of India, of no matter which major family, have a set of retroflex, cerebral, or domal consonants in contrast with dentals. The retroflexes include stops and nasal certainly, also in some languages sibilants, lateral, tremulant, and even others. Indo-Aryan, Dravidian, Munda and even the far northern Burushaski, form a practically solid bloc characterized by this phonological feature... Even our earliest Sanskrit records already show phonemes of this class, which are, on the whole, unknown elsewhere in the Indo-European field, and which are certainly not Proto-Indo-European. In Sanskrit many of the occurrences of retroflexes are conditioned; others are explained historically as reflexes of certain Indo-European consonants and consonant clusters. But, in fact, in Dravidian it is a matter of the utmost certainty that retroflexes in contrast with dentals are Proto-Dravidian in origin, not the result of conditioning circumstances... it is clear already that echo-words are a pan-Indic trait and that Indo-Aryan probably received it from non-Indo-Aryan (for it is not Indo-European)... The use of classifiers can be added to those other linguistic traits previously discussed, which establish

India as one linguistic area ('an area which includes languages belonging to more than one family but showing traits in common which are found not to belong to the other members of (at least) one of the families') for historical study. The evidence is at least as clear-cut as in any part of the world... Some of the features presented here are, it seems to me, as 'profound' as we could wish to find... Certainly the end result of the borrowings is that the languages of the two families, Indo-Aryan and Dravidian, seem in many respects more akin to one another than Indo-Aryan does to the other Indo-European languages. (We must not, however, neglect Bloch's final remark and his reasons therefor: *'Ainsi donc, si profondes qu'aient ete les influences locales, elles n'ont pas conduit l'aryen de l;inde... a se differencier fortement des autres langues indo-europeennes.*)"[264]

The profundity of these observations by Emeneau and Bloch will be tested through clusters of lexemes of an Indian Lexicon, which relate to the archaeological finds of the civilization. These clusters of lexemes will be presented in a separate website together with the corpus of inscriptions of the civilization as aids to the process of deciphering the pictorials and signs on the inscriptions.

Tamil and all other Dravidian languages have been influenced by Sanskrit language and literature. Swaminatha Iyer[265] posits a genetic relationship between Tamil and

Sanskrit. He cites GU Pope to aver that several Indo-European languages are linguistically farther away from Sanskrit than Dravidian. He cites examples of Tamil and Sanskrit forms of some glosses: hair: mayir, s'mas'ru; mouth: vāya, vā c; ear: s śevi, śrava; hear: kēḷ keṇ (Tulu), karṇa; walk: śel, car; mother: āyi, yāy (Paiśāci). Evaluating this work, Edwin Bryant and Laurie Patton[266] note: "It is still more simple and sound to assume that the words which need a date of contact of the fourth millennium BCE on linguistic grounds as loan words in Dravidian might be words originally inherited in Dravidian from the Proto-speech which was the common ancestor of both Dravidian and Indo-Aryan...It will be simpler to explain the situation if both Indo-Aryan and Dravidian are traced to a common language family. In vocables they show significant agreement. In phonology and morphology the linguistic structures agree significantly. It requires a thorough comparative study of the two language families to conduct a fuller study. "

The influence of Vedic culture is profoundly evidenced in early sangam texts.[267]

Proto-Munda continuity and Language X

- Sources of OIA agricultural vocabulary based on Masica (1979)

-

  - Percentage

- IE/IIr   40%

- Drav   13%

- Munda   11%

- Other   2%

- Unknown   34%

- Total   100%

- Hence, a Language X is postulated; Language 'X' to explain a large number of agriculture-related words with no IE cognates: Colin Masica, 1991, Indo-Aryan Languages, Cambridge Univ. Press

- Since there is cultural continuity in India from the days of Sarasvati civilization, it is possible to reconstruct Language X by identifying isoglosses in the linguistic area.

Contributions of the following language/archaeology scholars[268] have followed upon these insights of Sylvan Levi, Jules Bloch and Jean Przyluski published over 90 years ago: Emeneatu, MB, Kuiper, FBJ, Masica, CP, Southworth F.

Resemblances between two or more languages (whether typological or in vocabulary) can be due to genetic relation (descent from a common ancestor language), or due to borrowing at some time in the past between languages that were not necessarily genetically related. When little or no direct documentation of ancestor languages is available, determining whether a similarity is genetic or areal can be difficult.

Hermeneutics and mleccha

Hermeneutics is the science of discovering new meanings and interpretations in 'all those situations in which we encounter meanings that are not immediately understandable but require interpretive effort' (Gadamer 1976: xii). Gadamer, Hans-Georg. 1976, Philosophical Hermeneutics, ed. and trans. by David E. Linge, Berkeley: University of California Press. Such an interpretive effort has led to the decoding of Sarasvati hieroglyphs as the repertoire of miners and metalsmiths of the civilization in a linguistic area. The ancient words read rebus can be traced in many Bharatiya languages as borrowings from proto-mleccha (Language X + proto-Munda) resulting in the Indian sprachbund.

A sprachbund (also known as a linguistic area, convergence area or diffusion area), is a group of languages that have become similar in some features because of geographical proximity.[269]

Note: This area can be called speakers of 'mleccha, meluhha' or mleccha vācas according to Manusmṛti (lingua franca of the artisans). Manusmṛti distinguishes two spoken language-groups: mleccha vācas and arya vaacas (that is, spoken dialect distinguished from grammatically correct glosses).

"A Sprachbund...in German, plural "Sprachbünde" IPA, from the German word for "language union", also known as a linguistic area, convergence area, or diffusion area, is a group of languages that have become similar in some way because of geographical proximity and language contact. They may be genetically unrelated, or only distantly related. Where genetic affiliations are unclear, the sprachbund characteristics might give a false appearance of relatedness...In a classic 1956 paper titled "India as a Linguistic Area", Murray Emeneau[270] laid the groundwork for the general acceptance of the concept of a Sprachbund. In the paper, Emeneau observed that the subcontinent's Dravidian and Indo-Aryan languages shared a number of features that were not inherited from a common source, but were areal features, the result of diffusion during sustained contact." _Common features of a group of languages in a Sprachbund are called 'areal features'. In linguistics, an areal feature is any typological feature shared by languages within the same geographical area. An example refers to retroflex consonants in the Burushaski[271], Nuristani[272], Dravidian, Munda[273] and Indo-Aryan language families of the Indian subcontinent.

Notes on Indian linguistic area: pre-aryan,pre-Munda and pre-dravidian in India

It will be a hasty claim to make that Old Tamil or Proto-Munda or Santali or Prakṛt or Pali or any other specific language of the Indian linguistic area, by itself (to the exclusion of other languages in contact), explains the language of the Indus civilization. In this context, the work by Sylvan Levi, Jules Bloch and Jean Przyluski published in the 1920's (cited elsewhere) continues to be relevant, even today, despite some advances in studies related to formation of Indian languages and the archaeological perspectives of and evidences from the civilization.

Some glyphs of the script are yet to be decoded[274]. If the glyphs are unambiguously identified and read in archaeological context and the context of other glyphs of the inscription itself, it will be possible to decipher them. For this purpose, some graphemes[275] (which have homonyms and can be read rebus) are provided from the Indian Lexicon of the Indian linguistic area.

Indus Script Cipher, together with the substrates of the *Indian Lexicon*, provide the framework for further studies in evolution of general semantics, identification of isogloss bundles and history of changes in languages in the Indian linguistic area which continues to be a cultural continuum for over eight millennia, from the days the Indus civilization produced an artifact of a wide *turbinella pyrum* bangle dated to c. 6500 BCE from a woman's burial in Nausharo.

Further researches

I am grateful to TRN Rao for encouraging me in this decryption effort, providing leads on Information Theory and adding his comment on the *Indus Script Cipher* (private communication).

In addition to studies in the evolution of and historical contacts among Indian languages, further researches are also needed in an archaeological context. Karl Menninger[276] cites a remarkable instance. In the Indian tradition, finger signals were used to settle the price for a trade transaction. Finger gestures were a numeric cipher!

Further work on the nature of the contacts between Indian artisans and their trade associates, say, in Meluhhan settlements in the Persian Gulf region, may unravel the the nature of long-distance contacts. Could it be that the Indus language and writing were Indus Artisans' cryptographic messaging system for specifications of artifacts made in and exported from Meluhha?

Hieroglyph Sign List
(After Mahadevan)

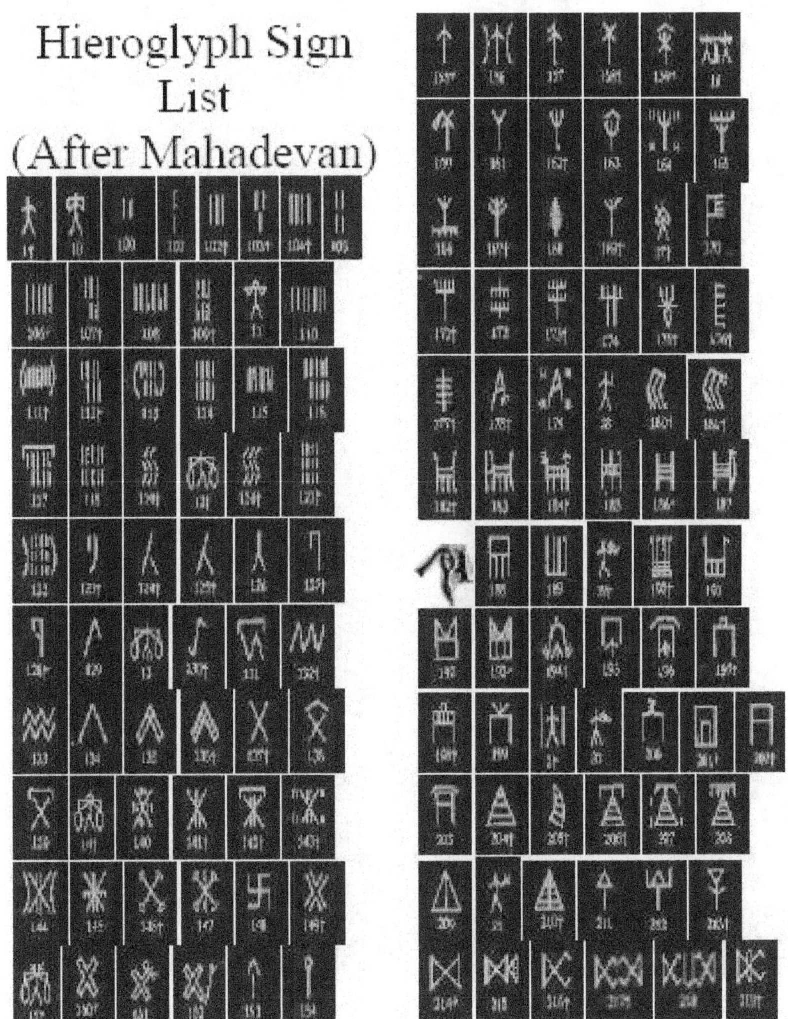

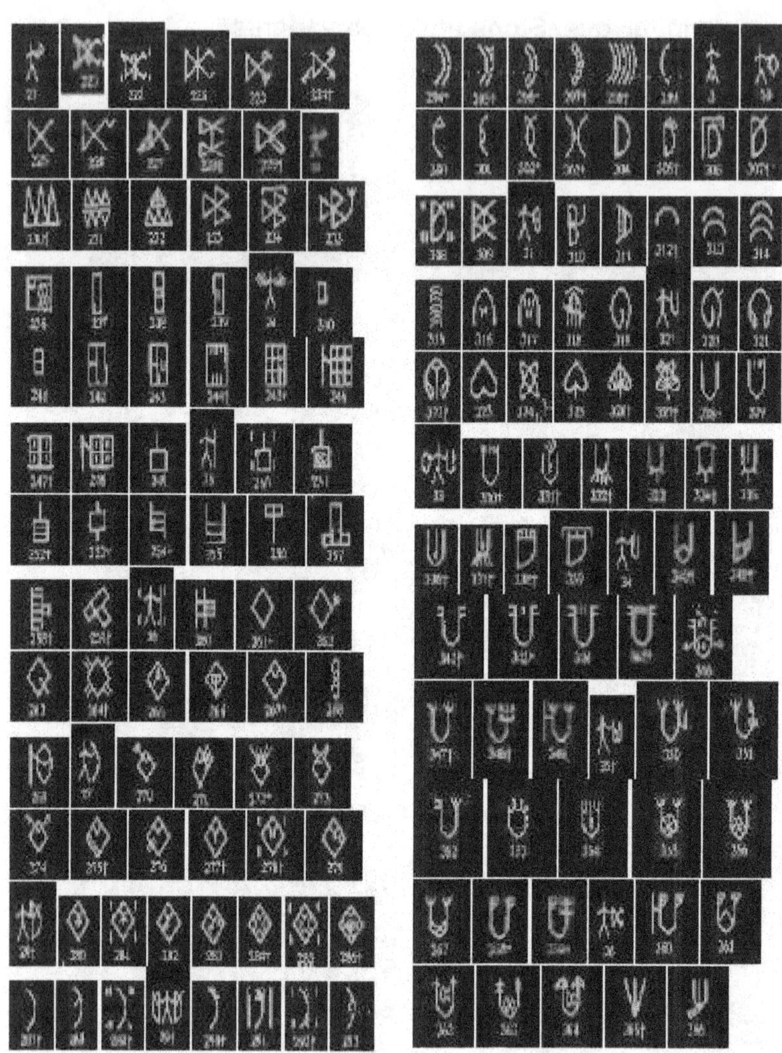

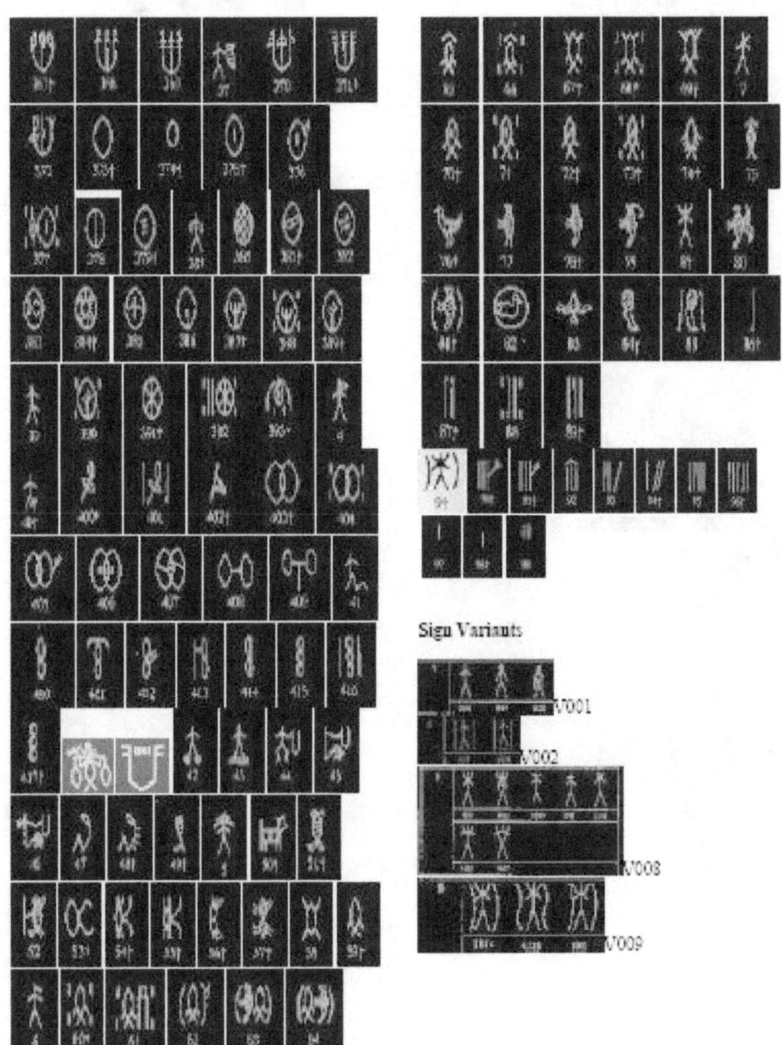

Sign Variants
V001
V002
V008
V009

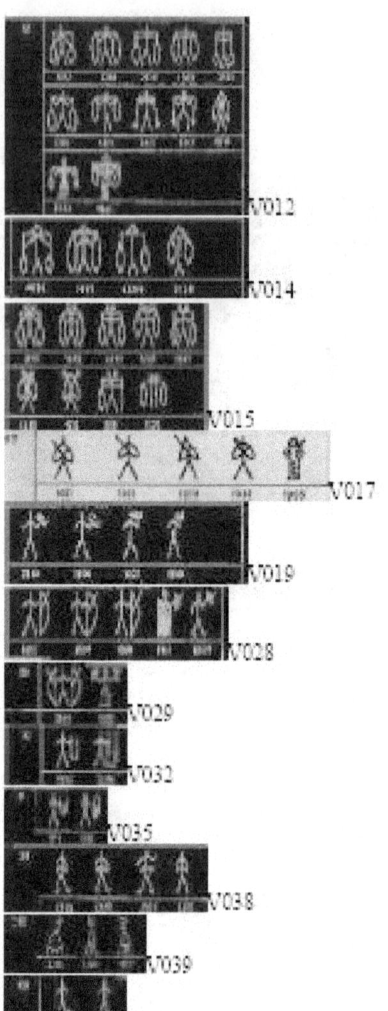

V012
V014
V015
V017
V019
V028
V029
V032
V035
V038
V039
V040
V048

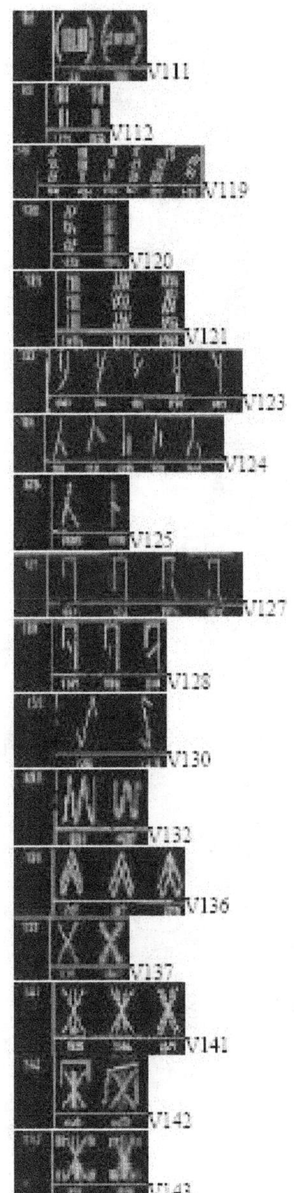

V111
V112
V119
V120
V121
V123
V124
V125
V127
V128
V130
V132
V136
V137
V141
V142
V143

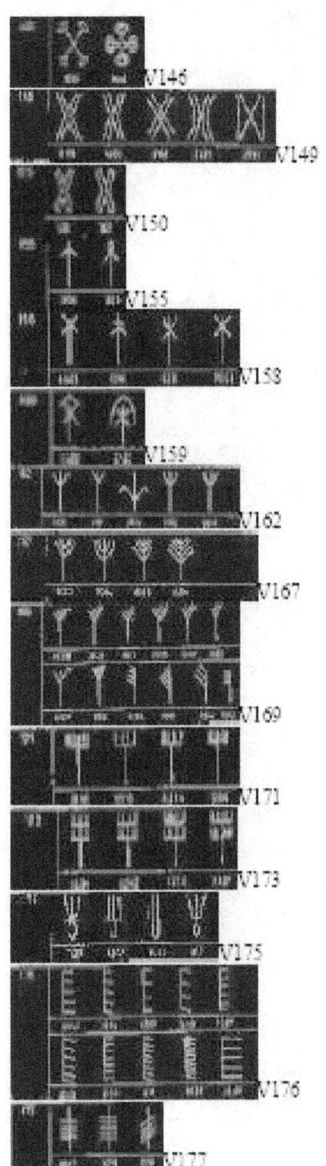

V146
V149
V150
V155
V158
V159
V162
V167
V169
V171
V173
V175
V176
V177

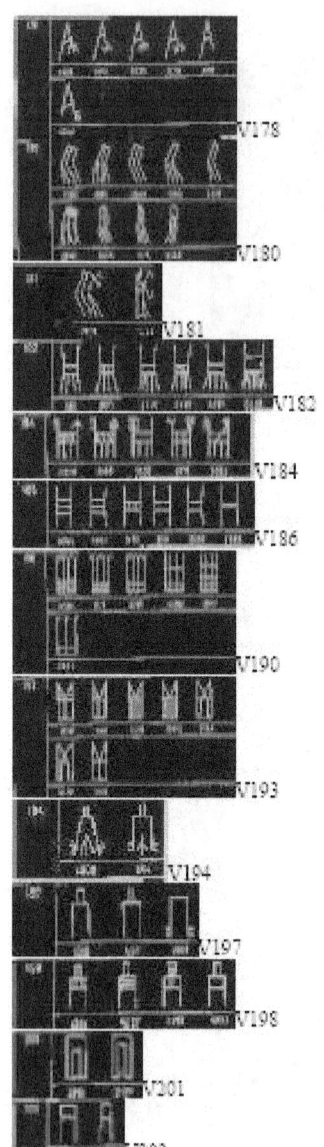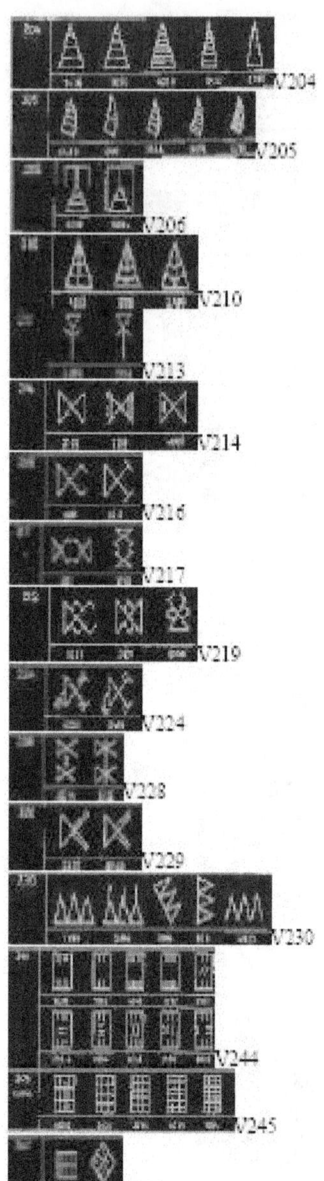

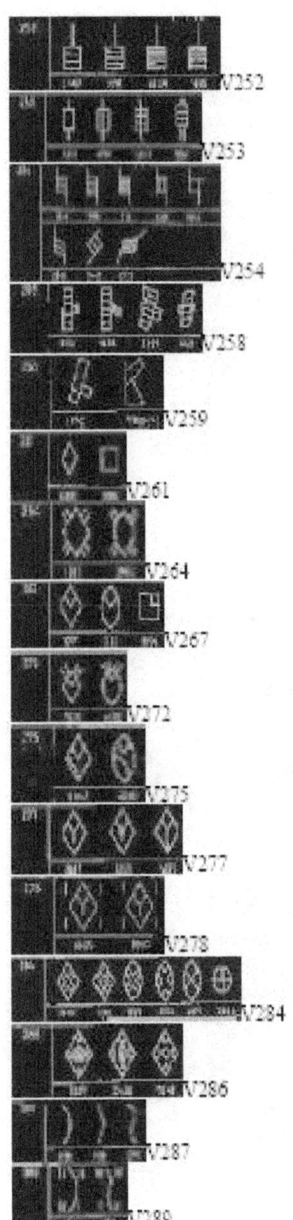
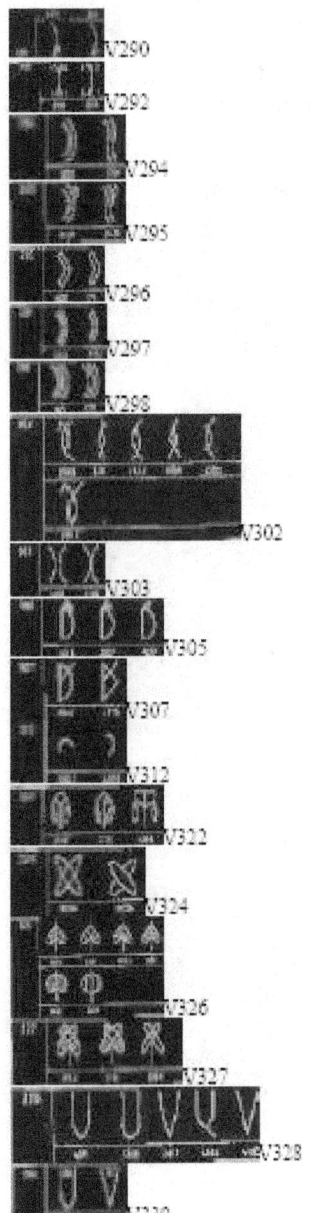

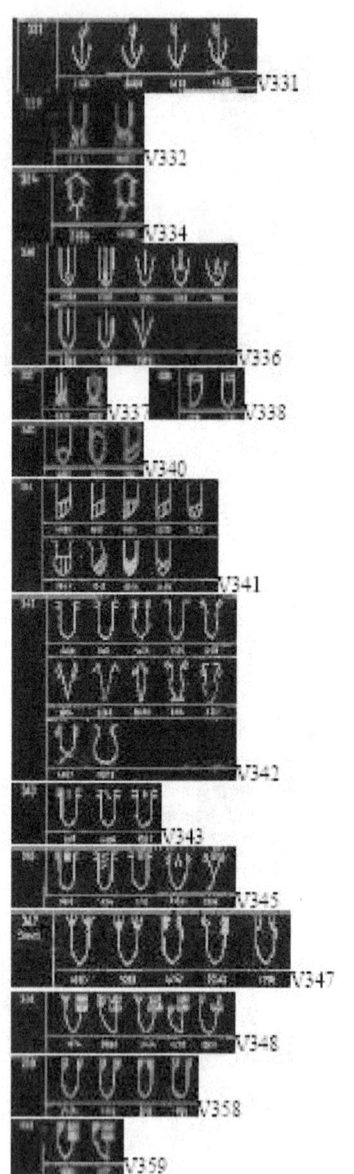
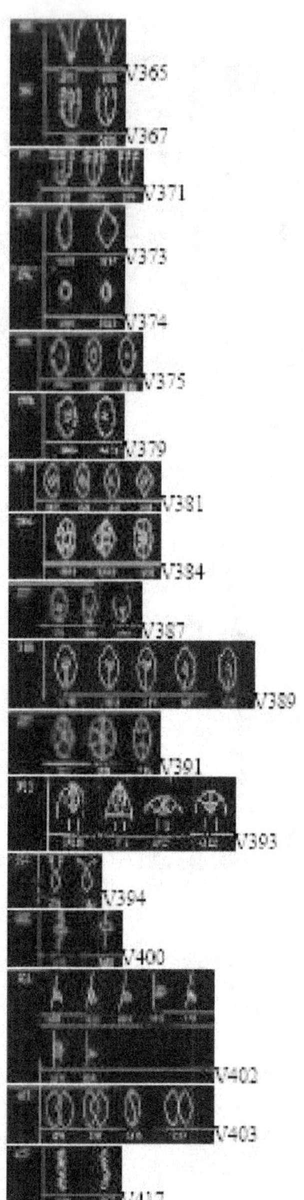

List of languages and abbreviations

Indo-Aryan semantic clusters

A. Assamese

al. Alashai dialect of Pashai

amg. Ardhamāgadhī Prakrit

Ap. Apabhraṁśa

Ar. Arabic

Ār. Aryan, i.e. Indo-iranian

ar. Areti dialect of Pashai

Aram. Aramaic

Arm. Armenian

arm. Armenian dialect of Gypsy

as. Asiatic dialects of Gypsy

Aś. Aśokan, i.e. the language of the Inscriptions of Aśoka

Ash. Ashkun (Aṣkū — Kaf.)

Austro-as. Austro-asiatic

Av. Avestan (Iranian)

Aw. Awadhī

awāṇ. Awāṇkārī dialect of Lahndā

B. Bengali (Baṅglā)

Bal. Balūčī (Iranian)

bāṅg. Bāṅgarū dialect of Western Hindī

Bashg. Bashgalī (Kaf.)

bh. Bairāṭ Bhābrū Minor Rock Edict of Aśoka

bhad. Bhadrawāhī dialect of West Pahāṛī

bhal. Bhalesī dialect of West Pahāṛī

bhaṭ. Bhaṭĕālī sub-dialect of Ḍogrī dialect of Panjābī

bhiḍ. Bhiḍlāī sub-dialect of Bhadrawāhī dialect of West
Pahāṛī

Bhoj. Bhojpurī

BHSk. Buddhist Hybrid Sanskrit

Bi. Bihārī

bir. Birir dialect of Kalasha

boh. Bohemian dialect of European Gypsy

Brah. Brāhūī (Dravidian)

Brj. Brajbhāṣā

bro. Brokpā dialect of Shina

Bshk. Bashkarīk (Dard.)

bul. Bulgarian dialect of European Gypsy

Bur. Burushaski

cam. Cameālī dialect of West Pahāṛī

Chil. Chilīs (Dard.)

chil. Chilasi dialect of Shina or of Pashai

cur. Curāhī dialect of West Pahāṛī

Ḍ. Ḍumāki

dar. Darrai-i Nūr dialect of Pashai

Dard. Dardic

dh. Dhauli Rock Inscription of Aśoka

Dhp. Gāndhārī or Northwest Prakrit (as recorded in the
Dharmapada ed. J. Brough, Oxford 1962)

Dm. Dameli (Damɛ̃ḍī′ — Kaf.-Dard.)

ḍoḍ. Ḍoḍī (Sirājī of Ḍoḍā), a dialect of Kashmiri in Jammu

ḍog. Ḍogrī dialect of Panjābī

dr. Drās dialect of Shina

Drav. Dravidian

Eng. English

eng. English dialect of European Gypsy

eur. European (Gypsy)

Fr. French

G. Gujarātī

Ga. Gadba (Dravidian)

Garh. Gaṛhwālī

Gau. Gauro (Dard.)

gav. Gavīmaṭh Inscription of Aśoka

Gaw. Gawar-Bati (Dard.)

germ. German dialect of European Gypsy

ghis. Ghisāḍī dialect of wandering blacksmiths in Gujarat

gil. Gilgitī dialect of Shina

gir. Girnār Rock Inscription of Aśoka

Gk. Greek

Gmb. Gambīrī (Kaf.)

gng. Gaṅgoī dialect of Kumaunī

Goth. Gothic

gr. Greek dialect of European Gypsy

gul. Gulbahārī dialect of Pashai

gur. Gurēsī dialect of Shina

Gy. Gypsy or Romani

H. Hindī

hal. Ḍalabī dialect of Marāṭhī

haz. Hazara Hindkī dialect of Lahndā

h.rudh. High Rudhārī sub-dialect of Khaśālī dialect of West Pahārī

hung. Hungarian dialect of European Gypsy

IA. Indo-aryan

IE. Indo-european

Ind. Indo-aryan of India proper excluding Kafiri and Dardic

Indo-ir. Indo-iranian or Aryan

Ir. Iranian

ish. Ishpi dialect of Pashai

Ishk. Ishkāshmī (Iranian)

isk. Iskeni dialect of Pashai

it. Italian dialect of European Gypsy

jau. Jaugaḍa Rock Inscription of Aśoka

jaun. Jaunsārī dialect of West Pahārī

jij. Jijelut dialect of Shina

jmag. Jaina Māgadhī Prakrit

jmh. Jaina Mahārāṣṭrī Prakrit

[page xiv]

jt. Jāṭū sub-dialect of Bāṅgarū dialect of Western Hindī

jub. North Jubbal dialect of West Pahārī

K. Kashmiri (Kāśmīrī)

kach. Kāchṛī dialect of Lahndā

Kaf. Kafiri

Kal. Kalasha (Kaláṣa — Dard.)

kāl. Kālsī Rock Inscription of Aśoka

Kamd. See Kmd.

Kan. Kanarese (Kannaḍa — Dravidian)

Kand. Kandia (Dard.)

kar. Karači (Transcaucasian) dialect of Asiatic Gypsy

kash. or kiś. Kashṭawāṛī dialect of Kashmiri

Kaṭ. Kaṭārqalā (Dard.)

kāṭh. Kāṭhiyāvāḍi dialect of Gujarātī

kb. Kauśāmbī Pillar Edict of Aśoka

kc. Kocī dialect of West Pahāṛī

kcch. Kacchī dialect of Sindhī

kch. Kachur-i Sala dialect of Pashai

kgr. or kng. Kāṅgrā sub-dialect of Ḍogrī dialect of Panjābī

Kharl. MIA. forms occurring in Corpus Inscriptionum Indicarum Vol. II Pt. 1

khas. Khasa dialect of Kumaunī

khaś. Khaśālī dialect of West Pahāṛī

khet. Khetrānī dialect of Lahndā

Kho. Khowār (Dard.)

Khot. Khotanese (Iranian)

kiś. See kash.

kiūth. Kiūthalī dialect of West Pahāṛī

Kmd. or Kamd. Kāmdeshi (Kaf.), Kāmdesh dialect of Kati

knḍ. Kaṇḍak dialect of Pashai

kng. See kgr.

Ko. Koṅkaṇī

Koh. Kohistānī (Dard.)

koh. Kohistānī dialect of Shina

Kol. Kōlāmī (Dravidian)

kōl. Kōlā dialect of Shina

kq. Kauśāmbī (Queen's Edict) Inscription of Aśoka

Kt. Kati or Katei (Kaf.)

Ku. Kumaunī

Kur. Kuruk̲h̲ (Dravidian)

kuṛ. Kuṛaṅgali dialect of Pashai

Kurd. Kurdish (Iranian)

kurd. Kurdari dialect of Pashai

ky. Kanyawālī dialect of Maiyā

L. Lahndā

la. Lāṛī dialect of Sindhī

lagh. Laghmani dialect of Pashai

lakh. Lakhīmpurī dialect of Awadhī

Lat. Latin

lauṛ. Lauṛowānī dialect of Pashai

Lith. Lithuanian

l.rudh. Low Rudhārī sub-dialect of Khaśālī dialect of West Pahāṛī

ludh. Ludhiānī dialect of Panjābī

M. Marāṭhī

mag. Magahī dialect of Bihārī

Mai. Maiyā (Dard.)

Mal. Malayāḷam (Dravidian)

Māl. or Malw. Mālwāī

mald. See Md.

Malw. See Māl.

man. Mānsehrā Rock Inscription of Aśoka

marm. Marmatī sub-dialect of Khaśālī dialect of West Pahāṛī

Marw. Mārwāṛī

Md. or mald. Maldivian dialect of Sinhalese

mg. Māgadhī Prakrit

mh. Mahārāṣṭrī Prakrit

MIA. Middle Indo-aryan

mi. Delhi Mīrat Pillar Edict of Aśoka

mid.rudh. Middle Rudhārī sub-dialect of Khaśālī dialect of
West Pahāṛī

Mj. Munjī (Iranian)

Mth. Maithilī

mth. Mathiā (Lauṛiyā-Nandangaṛh) Inscription of Aśoka

Mu. Muṇḍā

mult. Multānī dialect of Lahndā

N. Nepāli

New. Newārī

ng. Nāgārjunī Cave Inscription of Aśoka

NIA. New (modern) Indo-aryan

NiDoc. Language of `Kharoṣṭhī Inscriptions discovered by Sir
Aurel Stein in Chinese Turkestan' edited by A. M. Boyer, E.
J. Rapson, and E. Senart

nig. Niglīvā Inscription of Aśoka

nij. Nijelami (Neẓəlā´m) dialect of Pashai

Niṅg. Niṅgalāmī (Dard.)

nir. Nirlāmī dialect of Pashai

Nk. Naiki (Dravidian)

norw. Norwegian dialect of European Gypsy

OHG. Old High German

OPruss. Old Prussian

Or. Oṛiyā

Orm. Ōrmuṛī′ (Iranian)

OSlav. Old Slavonic

Oss. Ossetic (Iranian)

P. Panjābī (Pañjābī)

Pa. Pali

pach. See pch.

pāḍ. Pāḍarī sub-dialect of Bhadrawāhī dialect of West Pahāṛī

Pah. Pahāṛī

Pahl. Pahlavi (Iranian)

paiś. Paiśācī Prakrit

pal. Palestinian dialect of Asiatic Gypsy of the Nawar

pales. Palesī dialect of Shina

paṅ. Paṅgwāḷī dialect of West Pahāṛī

Par. Parachi (Parāčī — Iranian)

Parth. Parthian (Iranian)

Paš. Pashai (Pašaī — Dard.)

paṭ. Paṭṭanī dialect of Gujarātī

pch. or pach. Pachaghani dialect of Pashai

Pers. Persian (Iranian)

pers. Persian dialect of Asiatic Gypsy

Phal. Phalūṛa (Dard.)

Pk. Prakrit

pog. Pŏgulī dialect of Kashmiri

pol. Polish dialect of European Gypsy

poṭh. Poṭhwārī dialect of Lahndā

pow. Pōwādhī dialect of Panjābī

Pr. Prasun (Kaf.)

Prj. Parji (Dravidian)

Psht. Pashto (Iranian)

pun. Punchī dialect of Lahndā

punl. Puniali dialect of Shina

rām. Rāmbanī dialect of Kashmiri in Jammu

rdh. Radhia (Lauṛiyā Ararāj) Pillar Edict of Aśoka

Rj. Rājasthānī

roḍ. Roḍiyā dialect of Sinhalese

roh. Rohruī dialect of West Pahāṛī

rp. Rāmpurvā Rock Edict of Aśoka

ru. Rūpnāth Inscription of Aśoka

rudh. Rudhārī sub-dialect of Khaśālī dialect of West Pahāṛī

[page xv]

rum. Rumanian dialect of European Gypsy

rumb. Rumbūr dialect of Kalasha

rus. Russian dialect of European Gypsy

Russ. Russian

S. Sindhī

ś. Śaurasenī Prakrit

sah. Sahasrām Inscription of Aśoka

Sang. Sanglechi (Saṅlēčī — Iranian)

Sant. Santālī (Muṇḍā)

Sar. Sarīkolī (Iranian)

SEeur. South-east European dialects of Gypsy

śeu. Śeuṭī sub-dialect of Khaśālī dialect of West Pahāṛī

Sh. Shina (Ṣiṇā — Dard.)

shah. Shāhbāzgaṛhī Rock Inscription of Aśoka

sham. Shamakaṭ dialect of Pashai

she. Shewa dialect of Pashai

Shgh. Shughnī (Iranian)

Shum. Shumashti (Šumāštī — Dard.)

shut. Shutuli dialect of Pashai

Si. Sinhalese

Sik. Sikalgārī (Mixed Gypsy Language: LSI xi 167)

sir. Sirājī dialect of West Pahāṛī

sirm. Sirmaurī dialect of West Pahāṛī

Sk. Sanskrit

sn. Sārnāth Inscription of Aśoka

snj. Sanjan dialect of Pashai

sod. Sŏdōcī dialect of West Pahāṛī

Sogd. Sogdian (Iranian)

sop. Bombay-Sopārā Inscription of Aśoka

sp. Spanish dialect of European Gypsy

srk. Sirāikī dialect of Sindhī

suk. Suketī dialect of West Pahāṛī

Sv. Savi (Dard.)

Tam. Tamil (Dravidian)

Tel. Telugu (Dravidian)

Tib. Tibetan

Tir. Tirāhī (Dard.)

Toch. Tocharian

top. Delhi-Tōprā Pillar Edict of Aśoka

Tor. Tōrwālī (Dard.)

Tu. Tuḷu (Dravidian)

Turk. Turkish

urt. Urtsun dialect of Kalasha

uzb. Uzbini dialect of Pashai

vrāc. Vrācaḍa Apabhraṁśa

waz. Waziri dialect of Pashto

weg. Wegali dialect of Pashai

wel. Welsh dialect of European Gypsy

Werch. Werchikwār or Wershikwār (Yasin dialect of Burushaski)

Wg. Waigalī or Wai-alā (Kaf.)

Wkh. Wakhi (Iranian)

Woṭ. Woṭapūrī (language of Woṭapūr and Kaṭārqalā — Dard.)

WPah. West Pahāṛī

Yazgh. Yazghulami (Iranian)

Yghn. Yaghnobi (Iranian)

Yid. Yidgha (Iranian)

Dravidian semantic clusters

ĀlKu. = Ālu Kuṟumba

Bel. = Belari

Br. = Brahui

Dr. = Dravidian

Ga. = Gadba

Go. = Gondi

Ir. = Iruḷa

Ka. = Kannaḍa

Ko. = Kota

Koḍ. = Koḍagu (Coorg)

ol. = Kolami

Kor. = Koraga

Kur. = Kuṟux (Kurukẖ)

Kurub. = Beṭṭa Kuruba

Ma. = Malayalam

Malt. = Malto

Maṇḍ. = Maṇḍa

NIA = New Indo-Aryan

Nk. = Naikṛi

Nk. (Ch.) = Naiki of Chanda

OTa. = Old Tamil

Pa. = Parji

PālKu. = Pālu Kuṟumba

PDr. = proto-Dravidian

Pe. = Pengo

Ta. = Tamil

Te. = Telugu

To. = Toda

Tu. = Tulu

Munda semantic clusters

Ga. Gatai

Go. Gorum

Gu. Gutob

Ho

Ju. Juang

Kh. Kharia

Kher. Kherwarian

Kol. Kolami

Kw. Korwa

Mu. Mundari

Nahali

Sa. Santali

Sora

References

CISI = Corpus of Indus Seals and Inscriptions.

1987 Vol. 1: Collections in India, edited by Jagat Pati Joshi and Asko Parpola

1991 Vol. 2: Collections in Pakistan, edited by Sayid Ghulam, Mustafa Shah and Asko Parpola

2010 Vol. 3: New material, untraced objects, and collections outside India and Pakistan. Edited by Asko Parpola, B.M. Pande and Petteri Koskikallio. Part 1: Mohenjo-daro and Harappa, in collaboration with Richard H. Meadow and Jonathan Mark Kenoyer. (Annales Academiae Scientiarum

Fennicae, B. 239-241.) Helsinki: Suomalainen Tiedeakatemia.

http://www.scribd.com/doc/2232464/epigraphica (ebook)

DEDR Dravidian Etymological Dictionary

CDIAL Comparative Dictionary of Indo-Aryan Languages

Boas, Franz. 1917. Introduction. International Journal of American Linguistics. (Reprinted: Boas, Franz. 1940. Race, language, and culture, 199-210. New York: The Free Press.)

1920. The classification of American languages. American Anthropologist 22.367-76. (Reprinted: Boas, Franz. 1940. Race, language, and culture, 211-8. New York: The Free Press.

1929. The classification of American Indian languages. Language 5.1-7

Campbell, 1997,.American Indian languages: the historical linguistics of Native America. Oxford: Oxford University Press, 62-6

Campbell, Lyle, 2006 Areal linguistics: a closer scrutiny. In: Linguistic Areas: Convergence in Historical and Typological

Perspective, ed.by Yaron Matras April McMahon, and Nigel Vincent, 1-31.Houndmills, Basingstoke, Hampshire: Palgrave Macmillan

Campbell, Lyle, 2006, Areal linguistics. In: Keith Brown (ed.), 2006, Encylopaedia of Languages and Linguistics, 2nd edn., Oxford, Elsevier, pp. 454-460

Campbell, Lyle, and Marianne Mithun. 1979. North American Indian historical linguistics in current perspective. The Languages of Native America: an Historical and Comparative Assessment, ed. by L. Campbell and Marianne Mithun, 3-69. Austin: University of Texas Press

Dales, George F., Jr. 1967, South Asia's earliest writing – still undeciphered, Expedition 9 (2): 30-37

Darnell, Regna and Joel Sherzer. 1971. Areal linguistic studies in North America: a historical perspective. International Journal of American Linguistics 37.20-8

Durante, Silvio, 1979,"Marine Shells from Balakot, Shahr-i Sokhta and Tepe Yahya: Their Significance for Trade Technology in Ancient Indo-Iran." In South Asian Archaeology 1977, Naples.

Emeneau, MB, 1956, India as a linguistic area, Language 32, 1956, 3-16.

Farmer, Steve, Richard Sproat, and Michael Witzel, 2004, The collapse of the Indusscript thesis: The myth of a literate Harappan Civilization. Electronic Journal of Vedic Studies 11 (2): 19–57

Gould, S.J., 2003, I have landed. Splashes and reflections in natural history, London.

Hunter, G.R., 1934, Script of Harappa and Mohenjodaro and its connection with other Scripts/G.R. Hunter.-London, p. 126

Jakobson, Roman, 1949 (1936), Sur la théorie des affinities phonologiques entre les langues. Actes du quatrieme congresinternational de linguists (tenu a Copenhague du 27 août 1 Septembre, 1936), 48-58. (Reprinted, 1949, as an appendix to: Principes de phonologie, by N. S. Troubetzkoy, 351-65. Paris: Klincksieck.)

1944. Franz Boas' approach to language. International Journal of American Linguistics 10.188-95

Kalyanaraman, S., 1992, Indian Lexicon, an etymological dictionary of south Asian languages. http://www.scribd.com/doc/2232617/lexicon (ebook)

Kalyanaraman, S., 2008, Sarasvati–Vedic river and Hindu civilization, Chennai, Sarasvati Research and Education Trust (ISBN 978-81-901126-1-1) http://www.scribd.com/doc/7734436/Sarasvati-Book (ebook)

Kharakwal, J.S., Y.S. Rawat and Toshiki Osada, 2007, Kanmer: A Harappan site in Kachchh, Gujarat, India. PP. 21-137 in: Toshiki Osada (Ed.), Linguistics, archaeology and the human past. (Occasional papers 2.) Kyoto: Indus Project. Research Institute for Humanity and Nature.

Koskenniemi, Seppo, Asko Parpola and Simo Parpola, 1973, Materials for the study of the Indus script, I. A concordance to the Indus inscriptions, Annales Academiae Scientiaram Fennicae, Ser. B, Tom. 185. xxviii, 528, 55 pp. + errata sheet. Helsinki: [Academia Scientiarum Fennica]

Koskenniemi and Parpola, 1982, A Concordance to the Texts in the Indus Script. Helsinki: [University of Helsinki]. 201pp. Department of Asian and African Studies, University of Helsinki. Research Reports, No. 3., pp. 10-11.

Kuiper, FBJ, 1948, Proto-Munda words in Sanskrit, Amsterdam, 1948

1967, The genesis of a linguistic area, IIJ 10, 1967, 81-102

Lal, B.B., 2002, The Sarasvati flows on: The continuity of Indian culture. New Delhi: Aryan Books International.

Mahadevan, Iravatham, 1966, "Towards a grammar of the Indus texts: 'intelligible to the eye, if not to the ears', Tamil Civilization, Vol. 4, Nos. 3 and 4, Tanjore, 1966.

Mahadevan, Iravatham, 1977, The Indus script: texts, concordance and tables. (Memoirs of the Archaeological Survey of India, 77) New Delhi: Archaeological Survey of India.

Mahadevan, Iravatham, 1978), "Recent advances in the study of the Indus script", Puratattva, Vol. 9.)

Marshall, J. 1931. Mohenjodaro and the Indus Civilization. Vol. I, II text, Vol. III plates. London: A. Probsthain

Masica, CP, 1971, Defining a Linguistic area. South Asia. Chicago: The University of Chicago Press.

Parpola, Asko, 1994, Deciphering the Indus Script, Cambridge University Press, Cambridge, U.K.

Possehl, Gregory L., 1996, The Indus Age: The Writing System, Philadelphia: University of Pennsylvania Press.

Possehl, Gregory and Gullapalli, Praveena,1999, 'The Early Iron Age in South Asia'; in Vincent C. Piggott (ed.).The Archaeometallurgy of the Asian Old World; University

Museum Monograph, MASCA Research Papers in Science and Archaeology, Volume 16; Pgs. 153-175; The University Museum, University of Pennsylvania; Philadelphia.

M. A. Probst, Alekseev, G. V., A. M. Kondratov, Y. V. Knorozov, I. K. Fedorova, and B. Y. Volchok, 1965, Preliminary report on the investigation of the Proto-Indian Texts. Academy of Sciences U.S.S.R., Soviet Institute of Scientific and Technical Information, Institute of Ethnography, Moscow

 Przyludski, J., 1929, Further notes on non-aryan loans in Indo-Aryan in: Bagchi, P. C. (ed.), Pre-Aryan and Pre-Dravidian in Sanskrit. Calcutta : University of Calcutta: 145-149

Rajagopal, Sukumar, Priya Raju, and Sridhar Narayanan, 2009, Illiterate Indus?, Journal of Tamil Studies, December 2009 issue (#76), pp. 69-88, International Institute of Tamil Studies.

Southworth, F., 2005, Linguistic archaeology of South Asia, London, Routledge-Curzon.

Tewari, Rakesh, 2003, The origins of Iron-working in India: New evidence from the Central Ganga Plain and the Eastern Vindhyas, Antiquity, London
http://www.antiquity.ac.uk/projgall/tewari298/tewari.pdf

Trubetzkoy 1939, Gedanken über das

Indogermanenproblem Acta Linguistica 1.81-9

Vats, M.S., 1940, Excavations at Harappa, Being an Account

of Archaeological Excavations at Harappa carried out

between the Years 1920-1921 and 1933-34, Delhi,

Archaeological Survey of India

Vidale, Massimo, 2007, The collapse melts down: A reply to

Farmer, Sproat & Witzel. East and West 57 (1-4): 333-366.

http://www.docstoc.com/docs/8916249/Indus-script-

decoded-language----Massimo-Vidale/

End notes

---

[1] Kerckhoffs published two articles in 1883 in *le Journal des Sciences Militaires* ("Journal of Military Science") entitled *La Cryptographie Militaire* ("Military Cryptography") which enunciated a principle that security of a cryptosystem must depend only on the key, and not on the secrecy of any other part of the system. Without the key, the algorithm for encryption would have no result.

[2] http://en.wikipedia.org/wiki/File:IndusValleySeals_swastikas.JPG

[3]   Wilson, Thomas (Curator, Department of Prehistoric Anthropology, U.S. National Museum) 1896,The Swastika: The Earliest Known Symbol, and Its Migrations; with Observations on the Migration of Certain Industries in Prehistoric Times. In Annual report of the Board of Regents of the Smithsonian Institution. Washington DC http://fax.libs.uga.edu/J84xSl3x1/

[4]   http://www.ancientscripts.com/sumerian.html

[5]   Schott, Siegfrfied, 1951, Hieroglyphen: Untterzuchungen zum Ursprung der Schrift (Akademie der Wissenschaften und der Literattur [in Mainz], Abhandhungen der Geistes und sozialwissenschaftlichen Klasse. Jahrrgang 1950. Nr. 24.) Mainz: Verlag der Akademie der Wissenschaften und der Literatur : 1747, Textab. 5

[6]   Parpola, Asko, 2008, Is the Indus script indeed not a writing system?' in: Varalaaru.com, 2008, Airāvati, p.127.

http://www.harappa.com/script/indus-writing.pdf   (Source of image: http://upload.wikimedia.org/wikipedia/commons/0/0b/NarmerPalette_ROM -gamma.jpg

[7] Originally fromTarkhan, now on display at theMetropolitan Museum of Art, New York City. http://upload.wikimedia.org/wikipedia/commons/thumb/5/54/MudJarSealin g-EstateOfNarmer_MetropolitanMuseum.png/118px-MudJarSealing- EstateOfNarmer_MetropolitanMuseum.png

[8] After Finders Petrie,1953, Ceremonial Slate Palettes, B.S.A.E.66, K26.

[9] Slide 200   http://www.harappa.com/indus3/200.html   See different types of beads of colored stones. Slide 199. All beads found in the deposits of a room in Trench 54.Slide 198.

[10] pottar, பொத்தல் pottal, n. < id. [Ka.poṭṭare, Ma. pottu, Tu.potre.] 1. Hole, orifice; துவாரம் N. poro ' small hole ' (or < 2); G. poṟū n. ' thin scaly crust ' (semant. cf. *pōppa --); M. poḷ, ḷē n. ' honeycomb ' (or < 3: semant. cf. *pōka --)2. S. poru m. ' cavity ', poro m. ' hollow ' (or < 3); P. por f. ' hollow bamboo ' (or < *pōra -- 2);.(CDIAL 8398) potti 'A kind of gem; இரத்தினவகை. மாணிக்கம் எழுபதும் பொத்தி நாற்பத்தொன்பதும் (S. I. I. iii, 143) பொடியல் poṭiyal, n. prob. பொடி²-. Punching pin (Tamil).Rebus: pot[10] 'glass bead' (H.); putti 'small bead' (B.)(CDIAL 8403).

[11] Ta. pōttu male of animals (cattle, tiger, deer), some birds (peafowl, heron, etc.), some aquatic animals (crocodile, etc.). Ma. pōttu male buffalo. Ka.pōta, hōta, hōtu, hōntu he

goat. Koḍ. (Cole) pōtu goat. Te. pōtu male buffalo, male of an animal or bird. Kol. po·t cock. Nk. phōt id. Pa. pōt male of birds.Go. (S. Ko.) pōt, (Ma.) pōtal male of animals (Voc. 2441). Konḍa pōt id. Kui (K.) pōtu id. Kuwi (F.) pōtū male of some animals and birds; (S.) pōtu male of some animals, of trees; (Su.) pōtu male of animals; (Isr.) pōtu male of an animal, young male animal. (DEDR 4586)

12   Glyph: M. ḍagar f. ' little hill, slope '.S. ṭakuru m. ' mountain ' N. ṭākuro, ri ' hill top '. P. ṭekrā m., rī f. ' rock, hill '; H. ṭekar, krā m. ' heap, hillock '; G. ṭekrɔ m., rī f. ' mountain, hillock '.6. K. ṭēg m. ' hillock, mound '.7. G. ṭūk ' peak '.8. M. ṭūg n. ' mound, lump '. -- Ext. -- r -- : Or. ṭuṅguri ' hillock '; M. ṭūgar n. ' bump, mound ' (see *uṭṭungara --); -- -- l -- : M. ṭūgaḷ, gūḷ n.9. K. ḍaki f. ' hill, rising ground '. -- Ext. -- r -- : K. ḍakürü f. ' hill on a road '.10. Ext. -- r -- : Pk. ḍaggara -- m. ' upper terrace of a house '; 11. Ku. ḍāg, ḍāk ' stony land '; B. ḍāṅ ' heap ', ḍāṅgā ' hill, dry upland '; H. ḍāg f. ' mountain -- ridge '; M. ḍāg m.n., ḍāgaṇ, gāṇ, ḍāgāṇ n. ' hill -- tract '. -- Ext. -- r -- : N. ḍaṅgur ' heap '.12. M. ḍūg m. ' hill, pile ', gā m. ' eminence ', gī f. ' heap '. -- Ext. -- r -- : Pk. ḍuṁgara -- m. ' mountain '; Ku. ḍūgar, ḍūgrī; N. ḍuṅgar ' heap '; Or. ḍuṅguri ' hillock ', H. ḍūgar m., G. ḍūgar m., ḍūgrī f. 13. S.ḍūgaru m. ' hill ', H. M. ḍõgar m. 14. Pa. tuṅga -- ' high '; Pk. tuṁga -- ' high ', tuṁgīya -- m. ' mountain '; K. tŏng, tŏṇgu m. ' peak ', P. tuṅg f.; A. tuṅg ' importance '; Si. tuṅgu ' lofty, mountain '. -- Cf. uttuṅga -- ' lofty ' MBh. 15. K. thŏṇgu m. ' peak '. 16. H.

dãg f. ' hill, precipice ', dãgī ' belonging to hill country '. Addenda: *takka -- 3. 12. *duṅga -- : S.kcch. ḍūṅghar m. ' hillock '. (CDIAL 5423). unc An eminence, a mount, a little hill (Marathi). ṭākuro = hill top (N.); ṭāṅgī = hill, stony country (Or.); ṭān:gara = rocky hilly land (Or.); ḍān:gā = hill, dry upland (B.); ḍā~g = mountain-ridge (H.)(CDIAL 5476). Marathi. डांग [ḍāṅga] m n (H Peak or summit of a hill.)

[13] C.J. Gadd, Seals of Ancient Indian Style Found at Ur', in: G.L. Possehl, ed., 1979, *Ancient Cities of the Indus*, Delhi, Vikas Publishing House, p. 119.

[14]   BB Lal, 1966-1969, Some observations on Indus script) http://www.docstoc.com/docs/45231738/bblalindusscript2

[15]   http://www.harappa.com/script/parpola6.html

[16]   Sukumar Rajagopal, Priya Raju, and Sridhar Narayanan, 2009,   Illiterate Indus?", Journal of Tamil Studies, December 2009 issue (#76), pp. 69-88, International Institute of Tamil Studies provides a point-by-point rejoinder to the Farmer, Sproat and Witzel paper (2004) "no script", illiterate Harappan thesis. http://www.sastwingees.org/wordpress/wp-content/uploads/2010/05/Response_to_FSW2_Paper_v3.1-Final.pdf

[17]   Massimo (2007) "The collapse melts down: a reply to Farmer, Sproat and Witzel", East and West, vol. 57, no. 1-4, pp. 333–366.

1. [18]   The points raised in the preprint referred to below,

are addressed in an updated rebuttal by Rao et al:

http://www.cs.washington.edu/homes/rao/IndusResponse.html

and in the article in IEEE Computer:

http://www.cs.washington.edu/homes/rao/ieeeIndus.pdf

Preprint reference: Richard Sproat, "Ancient symbols, computational linguistics, and the reviewing practices of general science journals," Computational Linguistics (2010, in press).

http://www.cslu.ogi.edu/~sproatr/newindex/lastwords.pdf

[19]   http://www.harappa.com/script/maha8.html

[20]

http://www.palanitemples.com/english/murugain_hinduscript.htm

[21]   http://www.thehindu.com/opinion/op-ed/article481104.ece

[22]   http://www.harappa.com/arrow/4.html

[23]   Ko. kaṇṭ-po·t flesh of hind thigh of animal; kaṇṭ-ka·l calf of leg. Ka. kaṇḍa flesh, meat. Koḍ. kaṇḍa piece or lump of meat. Te. kaṇḍa id., flesh.Nk. khaṇḍe piece, piece of flesh. Ga. (S.3) kaṇḍa muscle (< Te.). Go. (Tr.) khāṇḍum (pl. khāṇḍk), (Ch.) khāṇḍ, khāṇḍum, (Ph.) khāṇḍk flesh; (SR.)khāṇḍum id., mutton (Voc. 1001). Konḍa kaṇḍa meat, flesh, muscle. Kuwi (Isr.) kaṇḍa piece. / Probably < Skt. khaṇḍa- (Turner, CDIAL, no. 3792) with development of meaning: piece > piece of flesh > flesh. (DEDR 1175) khaṇḍá ' broken, crippled ' VarBr̥S., ' having gaps or chasms ' Suśr., m.n. ' fragment ' R., ḍaka -- 1 ' having no nails ' lex., ḍikā -- f. Pān. [Cf. ' defective ' words listed s.v. baṇḍá -- . --

√khaṇḍ] Pa. khaṇḍa -- ' broken (usu. of teeth) ', m.n. ' piece ', ḍikā -- f. ' broken bit, stick '; Pk. khaṁḍa -- m.n., ḍiā -- f. ' piece '; Gy. SEeur. xạïi ' a little ', gr. xandí, xanrík ' a little ', xarno ' humble, low ', rum. boh. xarno ' short ', it. xarnišeró ' judge, magistrate ' (< ' small -- headed, stupid ') (CDIAL 3792)

Pe. pota calf of leg. Maṇḍ. pata id. Kui pota id. ? (DEDR 4513) Pa. pot upper part of back; pottel back; adv. behind. Ga. (Oll.) poṭ, poṭṭel, (S.3) poṭṭu back. (DEDR 4514) Ko. po·t flesh, meat. To. pot id., muscle. ? (DEDR 4588) पोटरी [pōṭarī] f (पोट Bulge or protuberance.) The calf of the leg: also, sometimes, the fleshy portion of the fore arm. 2 Usually पोटरा q. v. supra. 3 See पोटडीor पोटळी. पोटळी [pōṭaḷī] f (H) sometimes पोटळा m Medicaments tied up in a corner of a cloth, to be dabbed on the eye &c. 2 Any little thing, or a small quantity of anything (as a gem, a marble, or some flour, grain &c.) put up in the corner of a cloth and tied (Marathi)

24   Pk. pottī -- f. ' glass '; S. pūti f. ' glass bead ', P. pot f.; N. pote ' long straight bar of jewelry '; B. pot ' glass bead ', puti, pũti ' small bead '; Or. puti ' necklace of small glass beads '; H. pot m. ' glass bead ', G. M. pot f.; -- Bi. pot ' jeweller's polishing stone '(CDIAL 8403)

25   kaseruka [etym. connected with Sk. kaseru backbone?] (Pali) కశేరుకము [kaśērukamu] kaśērukamu. [Skt.] n. The backbone. (Telugu) कशेरु [kaśēru] n the

backbone, the spine, the ver tebral column. কশরেুক a. vertebrate. ☐ n. vertebral bone, the backbone. কশরেুকা n. the vertebral bone, the back bone; a vertebra. (Bengali)

26   L. awāṇ. kasērā ' metal worker ', P. kaserā m. ' worker in pewter ' (both ← E with -- s --); N. kasero ' maker of brass pots '; Bi. H. kaserā m. ' worker in pewter '. (CDIAL 2988) கசம்[1] kacam , n. cf. ayas. (அக. நி.) 1. Iron; இரும்பு. 2. Mineral fossil; தாதுப்பொருள் (Tamil) N. kasār ' maker of brass pots '; A. kãhār ' worker in bell -- metal '; B. kāsāri ' pewterer, brazier, coppersmith ', Or. kāsārī; H. kasārī m. ' maker of brass pots '; G.kãsārɔ, kas m. ' coppersmith '; M. kāsār, kās m. ' worker in white metal ', kāsārḍā m. ' contemptuous term for the same '. (CDIAL 2989)

27   Sign 48: (Grapheme) riṛ 'ridge formed by the backbone' (Santali) rīḍhaka -- m. ' backbone ' lex.WPah.bhal. rĩ`ṛ f. ' backbone, high mountain '; Aw.lakh. rīrh ' backbone ', H. rĩṛh f. (CDIAL 10749a). riṛ 'ridge formed by the backbone' (Santali) rīḍhaka -- m. ' backbone ' lex.WPah.bhal. rĩ`ṛ f. ' backbone, high mountain '; Aw.lakh. rīrh ' backbone ', H. rĩṛh f. (CDIAL 10749a).Rebus (homonym): rīti 'yellow or pale brass , bell-metal' (Skt.) rīti2 f. ' yellow brass, bell metal ' Kathās., rītika - - n. ' calx of brass ', kā -- f. ' brass ' lex. 2. rīrī -- , rirī -- f. ' yellow brass ' lex. [Ac. to AO xviii 248 Dard. forms < *raktikā -- 2] 1. Dm. rit ' copper ', Gaw. rīt (→ Sv. rīda NoPhal 49);

Bshk. rīd ' brass ', Tor. žit f. 2. Pk. rīrī -- f. ' brass '; Sh. rīl m. ' brass, bronze, copper '.(CDIAL 10752). இரீதி irīti, n. < rīti. Brass; பித்தளை. (W.) *இரதி, irati , n. cf. rīti. Brass; பித்தளை. (பிங்.) Vikalpa: Pk.kaṁḍa -- m. ' backbone; L.kaṇḍ f., kaṇḍā m. ' backbone ', awāṇ. kaṇḍ, ḍī ' back '; H. kāṭā m. ' spine ', *karaṇḍa -- backbone (Skt.) Pa. piṭṭhi -- kaṇṭaka -- m. ' bone of the spine ';S. kaṇḍo m. ' back ', P. kaṇḍ f. ' back, pubes '; WPah. bhal. kaṇṭ f. ' syphilis '; N. kaṇḍo ' buttock, rump, anus ', kaṇḍeulo ' small of the back '; B. kāṭ ' clitoris '; Or. kaṇṭi ' handle of a plough '; G. kāṭɔ m., M. kāṭā m.; Si. äṭa -- kaṭuva ' bone ',piṭa -- k ' backbone '.Pk. karaṁḍa -- m.n. ' bone shaped like a bamboo ', karaṁḍuya -- n. ' backbone '. (CDIAL 2670) Rebus: Rebus: kampaṭṭam 'coiner, mint' (Ta.)

Glyph Sign 47: Vikalpa: riṛ 'ridge formed by the backbone' (Santali) rīḍhaka -- m. ' backbone ' lex. WPah.bhal. rīˋṛ f. ' backbone, high mountain '; Aw.lakh. rīrh ' backbone ', H. rīṛh f. (CDIAL 10749a). [roṇḍi] roṇḍi. [Tel.] n. The haunch, the side between the ribs and loins. (Telugu) Rebus: rīti 'yellow or pale brass , bell-metal' (Skt.) rīti2 f. ' yellow brass, bell metal ' Kathās., rītika -- n. ' calx of brass ', kā -- f. ' brass ' lex. 2. rīrī -- , rirī -- f. ' yellow brass ' lex. [Ac. to AO xviii 248 Dard. forms < *raktikā -- 2] 1. Dm. rit' copper ', Gaw. rīt (→ Sv. rīda NoPhal 49); Bshk. rīd ' brass ', Tor. žit f. 2. Pk. rīrī -- f. ' brass '; Sh. rīl m. ' brass, bronze, copper '.(CDIAL 10752). இரீதி irīti, n. < rīti. Brass; பித்தளை. (W.) *இரதி, irati , n. cf. rīti. Brass; பித்தளை. (பிங்.)

Vikalpa: bharaḍo 'spine'; Rebus: bharan 'to spread or bring out from a kiln' (P.) baran, bharat (5 copper, 4 zinc and 1 tin)(P.B.) baraḍo = spine; backbone; the back; baraḍo thābaḍavo = lit. to strike on the backbone or back; hence, to encourage; baraḍo bhāre thato = lit. to have a painful backbone, i.e. to do something which will call for a severe beating (G.lex.) baraḍ, baraḍu = barren, childless; baraṇṭu = leanness (Tu.lex.) maṇuk.o a single vertebra of the back (G.)

28 caṇila squirrel (To.); Vikalpa: sega 'a species of squirrel' (Santali)

29 cf. bangaru, bangaramu ' gold' (Te.) बांगडी [bāṅgaḍī] f A bracelet of glass (sometimes of metal or wood) worn by females. (Marathi). bhagaṇa 'a bangle (IA 19)(IEG) bangan 'bangle' (cf. K ālibangan, 'black bangle', name of a site on River Sarasvati basin) Vikalpa: kācā 'glass' (Santali); rebus: kācār 'maker of glass bangles' (M.)

30 http://www.harappa.com/goladhoro/shellworkshopgoladhoro.html

31 शङ्ख: m. (sg. dat. shēkas शेँकस्), the conch-shell (used in worship as a trumpet) (Śiv. 1847) shĕnkh शंख् । शंख: m. (sg. dat. shĕnkhas शंखस्), id. (Śiv. 386, 79, 736; Rām. 77, 224; K. 59, 491-3, 495, 19, 131) (Kashmiri) शंख [śaṅkha] m (S) The conch-shell. Used in pouring water over an idol, in offering libations &c., and as a horn to blow at sacrifices and in battles. शंख is the name for all univalve sea-shells of the general appearance of the conch, as शिंप is the general name for bivalves. One of the nine nidhi or treasures of

Kuber. (Marathi)

³² cf. bangaru, bangaramu ' gold' (Te.) बांगडी [bāṅgaḍī] f A bracelet of glass (sometimes of metal or wood) worn by females. (Marathi). bhagaṇa 'a bangle (IA 19)(IEG) bangan 'bangle' (cf. K ālibangan, 'black bangle', name of a site on River Sarasvati basin) Vikalpa: kācā 'glass' (Santali); rebus: kācār 'maker of glass bangles' (M.)

³³ Vikalpa: bangala śannī = small bangle workshop with portable gold furnace. Vikalpa: kācār śannī 'small workshop of maker of bangles'. Vikalpa: sēkhā' bhagaṇa 'conch bracelet'. sēkhā' conch bracelet ' (B.); sāk 'conch, bracelet' (A.) (CDIAL 12263).

³⁴ *hāṇḍa ' pot ', haṇḍikā -- f. ' earthen pot ' Subh. [Cf. hāḍikā -- f. ' id. ' Kathārṇ. and *haḍappha -- . -- Connexion, if any, with bhāṇḍa -- 1 not clear. -- LM 427 compares Hsüan -- Tsang's utakia -- hanch'a (= *udakahāṇḍa), but this may be < *udaka -- bhāṇḍa --]S. haṇḍī f. ' pot ' (← Center?), L. hāṇḍī f. ' cooking pot '; P. hāḍā m. ' large cooking pot '; hāḍī f. ' smaller do. '; WPah.bhal. hāṇḍi f. ' receptacle for oil in an oilmill ', khaś. heṇḍū ' kettle ', rudh. haṇḍū, marm. huṇḍū; Ku. hāno, hāḍo m. ' large earthen pot, head, brains ', hānī, hāḍī ' small pot '; N. hāṛi ' earthen cooking pot ' (whence hāṛe ' mumps ' believed to be cured by rubbing on pot -- black), A. hāri; B. hāṛā, °ri ' cooking pot ', hāṛal ' hole, pit ' (semant. cf. kuṇḍá -- 1); Or. haṇḍā,°ḍi ' pot ', haṇḍalā ' big brass pot '; Bi. hāṛā ' cavity in a sugar -- mill ', (Patna) haṇḍā, hāṛhā '

342

large copper vessel for boiling rice in '; Bhoj. hãṛī, hãṛiyā ' earthen pot '; Aw.lakh. hãṛī ' vessel '; H. hãḍ, hãḍā m. ' large cooking pot of earth or metal ', hãḍī, hãṛī, hãḍiyā, hãṛiyā f. ' earthen cooking pot '; G. hãḍɔ m. ' large pot ', hãḍī, hãḍlī f., hãḍlũ, hãllũ n. ' pot '; M. haṇḍā m. ' open -- mouthed metal vessel ', hãḍī, haṇḍī f. ' small pot of earth or metal ', haṇḍẽ n. ' general term for pot '; -- ext. -- kk -- : Ku. hankiyā ' potter, mumps ' (see N. above). *hāṇḍavāha -- .Addenda: *hāṇḍa -- :WPah.kc. haṇḍko m. ' pot ', A. also hāri ' pot ' AFD 225, 234. (CDIAL 14050)

³⁵ kaṇḍ is pot; kan-ka in Sanskrit is karṇaka 'ear or rim of jar'. kaṇḍ also means 'fire-altar'.

kárṇa— m. 'ear, handle of a vessel' RV., 'end, tip (?)' RV. ii 34, 3. [Cf. *kāra—6] Pa. kaṇṇa— m. 'ear, angle, tip'; Pk. kaṇṇa—, aḍaya- m. 'ear', Gy. as. pal. eur. kan m., Ash. (Trumpp) karna NTS ii 261, Niṅg. kõmacr;, Woṭ. kanƏ, Tir. kana; Paš. kan, kan(ḍ)— 'orifice of ear' IIFL iii 3, 93; Shum. kõmacr;ṛ 'ear', Woṭ. kan m., Kal. (LSI) kuṟõmacr;, rumb. kuṟũ, urt. kṟã (< *kaṇ), Bshk. kan, Tor. k *l ṇ, Kand. kōṇi, Mai. kaṇa, ky. kān, Phal. kāṇ, Sh. gil. koṇ pl. koṇí m. (→ Ḍ kon pl. k *l ṇa), koh. kuṇ, pales. kuāṇƏ, K. kan m., kash. pog. ḍoḍ. kann, S. kanu m., L. kann m., awāṇ. khet. kan, P. WPah. bhad. bhal. cam. kann m., Ku. gng. N. kān; A. kāṇ 'ear, rim of vessel, edge of river'; B. kān 'ear', Or. kāna, Mth. Bhoj. Aw. lakh. H. kān m., OMarw. kāna m., G. M. kān m., Ko. kānu m., Si. kaṇa, kana. — As adverb and postposition (ápi kárṇē 'from behind' RV., karṇē 'aside' Kālid.): Pa. kaṇṇē 'at one's ear, in a whisper'; Wg. ken 'to' NTS ii 279; Tir. kõ; 'on' AO xii 181 with (?); Paš. kan 'to'; K. kȧni with abl. 'at, near, through', kani with abl. or dat. 'on', kun with dat. 'toward'; S. kani 'near', kanā 'from'; L. kan 'toward', kannū 'from', kanne 'with', khet. kan, P. ḍog. kanē 'with, near'; WPah. bhal. k *l ṇ, ṇi, k e ṇ, ṇi with obl. 'with, near', kiṇ, ṇiā, k *l ṇiā, k e ṇ with obl. 'from'; Ku. kan 'to, for'; N. kana 'for, to, with'; H. kane, ni, kan with ke 'near'; OMarw. kanai 'near', kanā sā 'from near', kāñī 'towards'; G. kan e 'beside'. Addenda: kárṇa—: S.kcch. kann m. 'ear', WPah.kṭg. (kc.) kān, poet. kanṛu m. 'ear', kṭg. kanni f. 'pounding—hole in barn floor'; J. kā'n m. 'ear', Garh. kān; Md. kan— in kan—fat 'ear' (CDIAL 2830)

kárṇaka m. ' projection on the side of a vessel, handle ' ŚBr. [kárṇa --]Pa. kaṇṇaka -- ' having ears or corners '; Wg. kanə ' ear -- ring ' NTS xvii 266; S. kano m. ' rim, border '; P. kannā m. ' obtuse angle of a kite ' (→ H.kannā m. ' edge, rim, handle '); N. kānu ' end of a rope for supporting a burden '; B. kāṇā ' brim of a cup ', G. kānɔ m.; M. kānā m. ' touch -- hole of a gun (CDIAL 2831)

करण [karaṇa] m (Popular form of कर्ण S amongst artisans.) The hypotenuse of a triangle, or diagonal of a quadrangular figure (Marathi)

கர்ணம்² karṇam, n. < karaṇa. 1. Village accountantship; கிராமக்கணக்குவேலை. 2. Village accountant; கிராமக்கணக்கன்.

காரணவன் kāraṇavaṉ

, n. < id. 1. Accountant; கணக்கன். சுந்தரபாண்டியநல்லூர்க் காரணவரோம் (S. I. I. v, 105). 2. Head of a family; குடும்பத்தலைவன். Nāñ.

காரணிக்கன் kāraṇikkaṉ, n. < id. Accountant; *கணக்கன்.* (Insc.)

காரணிக்கஜோதி kāraṇikka-jōṭi, n. < id. +. Quit-rent paid by the accountant; *கணக் கன் செலுத்தும் வரி.* (I.M.P. Tj. 1302.)(Tamil)

காரணிகன் kāraṇikaṉ, n. < id. Judge; arbitrator, umpire; *நியாயமத்தியஸ்தன். நமக்கோர் காரணிகனைத் தரல்வேண்டும் (இறை. 1, உரை).*

kāraṇika m. ' teacher ' MBh., ' judge ' Pañcat. [kāraṇa]Pa. usu -- kāraṇika -- m. ' arrow -- maker '; Pk. kāraṇiya -- m. ' teacher of Nyāya '; S. kāriṇī m. ' guardian, heir '; N. kārani ' abettor in crime '; M.kārṇī m. ' prime minister, supercargo of a ship ', kul -- karṇī m. ' village accountant '. (CDIAL 3058). karṇadhāra m. ' helmsman ' Suśr. Pa. kaṇṇadhāra -- m. ' helmsman '; Pk. kaṇṇahāra -- m. ' helmsman, sailor '; H. kanahār m. ' helmsman, fisherman '. (CDIAL 2836).

karanikamu. Clerkship: the office of a Karanam or clerk. (Telugu)

कारकुनी [kārakunī] f (कारकून) The office or business of

Kárkún. 2 Remuneration to a Kárkún for service rendered. 3 The profits or fees (of Kárkúns) on services done, articles bought &c. 4 Any extra cess laid to pay Kárkún-service. 5 fig. Economizing; careful and thrifty management. कारकुनी [kārakunī] a (कारकून) Relating to Kárkún--mode of writing &c. कारकुन [kārakuna] m (P A factor, agent, or business-man.) A clerk, scribe, writer. सवा हात लेखणीचा का0 A term of ironical commendation for a clerk.देशकुळकरण [dēśakuḷakaraṇa] n The office of देशकुळकरणी.

देशकुळकरणी [dēśakuḷakaraṇī] m An hereditary officer of a Mahál. He frames the general account from the accounts of the several Khots and Kulkarṇís of the villages within the Mahál; the district-accountant.गांवकुळकरणी [gāṃvakuḷakaraṇī] m The hereditary village-accountant: in contrad. from देशकुळकरणी District accountant. नाडकरणी [nāḍakaraṇī] m An hereditary district-accountant. नारकरणी [nārakaraṇī] m An hereditary district accountant. (Marathi)

Vikalpa: khanaka m. one who digs , digger , excavator MBh. iii , 640 R. ; a miner L. ; a house-breaker , thief L. ; a rat L. ; N. of a friend of Vidura MBh. i , 5798 f. ; (%{I}) f. a female digger or excavator Pāṇ. 3-1 , 145 Pat. ; iv , 1 , 41 Ka1s3.

36   *ஆலை³ ālai, n. < šālā. 1. Apartment, hall; சாலை. ஆலைசேர் வேள்வி (தேவா. 844. 7). 2. Elephant stable or stall; யானைக்கூடம். களிறு சேர்ந் தல்கிய வழுங்க லாலை (புறநா. 220, 3).ஆலைக்குழி ālai-k-kuḻi, n. < ஆலை¹ +.

Receptacle for the juice underneath a sugar-cane press; கரும்பாலையிற் சாறேற்கும் அடிக்கலம்.* ஆலைத்தொட்டி ālai-t-toṭṭi, n. < id. +. Cauldron for boiling sugar-cane juice; கருப்பஞ் சாறு காய்ச்சும் சால். ஆலைபாய்-தல் ālai-pāy-, v. intr. < id. +. 1. To work a sugar-cane mill; ஆலையாட்டுதல். ஆலைபாயோதை (சேதுபு. நாட்டு. 93). 2. To move, toss, as a ship; அலைவுறுதல். (R.) 3. To be undecided, vacillating; மனஞ் சுழலுதல். நெஞ்ச மாலைபாய்ந் துள்ள மழிகின்றேன் (அருட்பா,) Vikalpa: sal 'splinter'; rebus: workshop (sal) '

37 ālai 'workshop' (Ta.) * ஆலை³ ālai, n. < šālā. 1. Apartment, hall; சாலை. ஆலைசேர் வேள்வி (தேவா. 844. 7). 2. Elephant stable or stall; யானைக்கூடம். களிறு சேர்ந் தல்கிய வழுங்க லாலை (புறநா. 220, 3). ஆலைக்குழி ālai-k-kuḻi, n. < ஆலை¹ +. Receptacle for the juice underneath a sugar-cane press; கரும்பாலையிற் சாறேற்கும் அடிக்கலம்.* ஆலைத்தொட்டி ālai-t-toṭṭi, n. < id. +. Cauldron for boiling sugar-cane juice; கருப்பஞ் சாறு காய்ச்சும் சால். ஆலைபாய்-தல் ālai-pāy-, v. intr. < id. +. 1. To work a sugar-cane mill; ஆலையாட்டுதல். ஆலைபாயோதை (சேதுபு. நாட்டு. 93

38 Vikalpa (alternative): ḍangra 'bull'; rebus: d.hangar 'blacksmith'.

39 குடி¹-த்தல் kuṭi-, 11 v. tr. cf. kuḍ. [K. kuḍi, M. kuṭi.] 1. [T. kuḍucu.] To drink, as from a cup, from the breast; பருகுதல். கடலைவற்றக் குடித்திடுகின்ற செவ்வேற் கூற்றம் (கந்தபு. தாரக. 183). 3232 kuṭī— f. 'hut' MBh., ṭikā— f. Divyāv., ṭīkā— f. Hariv. [Some cmpds. have ṭa(ka)—: ← Drav. EWA i 222

with lit.: cf.KŌṬA—3] Pa. kuṭī—, ṭikā— f. 'single—roomed hut';
Pk.kuḍī— f., ḍaya— n. 'hut'; Gy. pal. kúri 'house, tent, room',
as. kuri, guri 'tent' JGLS New Ser. ii 329; Sh. kúi 'village,
country'; WPah.jaun. kūṛo house'; Ku. kuṛī, ṛo 'house,
building', ghar—kuṛī house and land', gng. kuṛ 'house'; N.
kur'nest or hiding place of fish', kuri 'burrow, hole for small
animals', kaṭ—kuro 'small shed for storing wood'; B.
kuṛiyā'small thatched hut'; Or. kuṛī, ṛiā 'hut'; H. kuṛī f.
'fireplace'; M. kuḍī f. 'hut'; Si. kiḷiya 'hut, small house'.
WPah.kṭg. krvṛ f. 'granary (for corn after threshing)'; Garh.
kuru 'house'; — B. phonet. kũṛ (CDIAL 3232) kuṭumba— n.
'household' ChUp. 2. kuṭumbaka— m. Daś. 1. Pa.
kuṭumba—, ṭimba— n. 'family, riches'; Pk.kuḍuṁba—,
ḍaṁba— n. 'family', S. kuṛmu m., Ku. gng.kūm; H. kuṛum—
codī f. 'incest'. 2. P. kunbā m. 'kindred, caste, tribe'; WPah.
jaun. kuṇbā 'family'; A. kurmā, f. āni 'a connexion by marriage'; H. kuṛmā, kumbā, kunbā m. 'family, caste, tribe'.
(CDIAL 3233) குடி&sup4; kuṭi, n. cf. kuṭi. [M. kuṭi.] 1. Ryot;
குடியானவன். கூடு கெழீஇய குடிவயினான் (பொருந. 182).
2. Tenants; குடியிருப்போர். 3. Subjects, citizens;
ஆட்சிக்குட்பட்ட பிரசைகள். மன்னவன் கோனோக்கி வாழுங்
குடி (குறள், 542). 4. Family; குடும்பம். ஒருகுடிப்பிறந்த
பல்லோருள்ளும் (புறநா. 183). 5. Lineage, descent;
கோத்திரம். (பிங்.) 6. Caste, race; குலம். (பிங்.) 7. House,
home, mansion; வீடு. சிறுகுடி கலக்கி (கந்தபு. ஆற்று. 12). 8.
Town, village; ஊர். குன்றகச்சிறுகுடிக் கிளை யுடன் மகிழ்ந்து
(திருமுரு. 196). 9. [T. K. kuṭi.] Abode, residence; வாழ்விடம்.

அடியாருள்ளத் தன்பு மீதூரக் குடியாக்கொண்ட (திருவாச. 2, 8). Ta. kuṭi (-pp-, -tt-) to drink, inhale; n. drinking, beverage,drunkenness; kuṭiyaṉ drunkard. Ma. kuṭi drinking, water drunk after meals, soaking; kuṭikka to drink, swallow; kuṭippikka to give to drink, soak; kuṭiyan drunkard. Ko. kuṛy- (kuṛc-) to drink (only in: uc kuṛy- to drink urine, i.e. to be humbled). To. kuḍt- (only 2nd stem) to drink (in song; < Badaga or Ta.). Ka. kuḍi to drink, inhale; n. drinking; kuḍisu to cause to drink; kuḍika, kuḍaka drinker, drunkard; kuḍita, kuḍata drinking, a draught; kuḍu, kuḍiyuvike drinking. Koḍ. kuḍi- (kuḍip-, kuḍic-) to drink. Tu. kuḍcuni to drink excessively, swallow liquor; kuḍcel, kuḍicel; drunkenness; kuḍcele, kuḍicele drunkard. Te. kuḍucu to eat, suck, drink, enjoy, suffer;kuḍupu to feed, suckle, cause to eat, enjoy, or suffer; n. eating, food, enjoying, suffering; kuḍupari one who eats, enjoys, or suffers; kuḍi right, right-hand;kuḍiti the washings of rice, split pulse, etc., used as a drink for cattle. Cf. 1658 Ko. guṛakn. / Cf. Skt. kuṭī- intoxicating liquor. (DEDR 1654) Ta. kuṭi house, abode, home, family, lineage, town, tenants; kuṭikai hut made of leaves, temple; kuṭical hut; kuṭicai, kuṭiñai small hut, cottage;kuṭimai family, lineage, allegiance (as of subjects to their sovereign), servitude; kuṭiy-āḷ tenant; kuṭiyilār tenants; kuṭil hut, shed, abode; kuṭaṅkar hut, cottage; kaṭumpu relations. Ma. kuṭi house, hut, family, wife, tribe; kuṭima the body of landholders, tenantry; kuṭiyan slaves (e.g. in Coorg); kuṭiyāninhabitant, subject, tenant; kuṭiññil hut, thatch; kuṭil hut, outhouse near palace for menials. Ko. kuṛjl shed, bathroom of Kota house; kuṛm family; kuḍl front room of house; kuṛl hut; guṛy temple. To. kwïṣ shed for small calves; kuṣ room (in dairy or house); kuḍṣ outer room of dairy, in: kuḍṣ waṣ fireplace in outer room of lowest grade of dairies (cf. 2857), kuḍṣ moṇy bell(s) in outer section of ti· dairy, used on non-sacred buffaloes (cf. 4672); kuṛy Hindu temple; ? kwïḍy a family of children. Ka. kuḍiya, kuḍu śūdra, farmer; guḍi house, temple; guḍil, guḍalu, guḍisalu, guḍasalu, guḍasala, etc. hut with a thatched roof. Koḍ. kuḍi family of servants living in one hut; kuḍië man of toddy-tapper caste. Tu. guḍi small pagoda or shrine; guḍisal;, guḍisil;, guḍsil;, guḍicil; hut, shed. Te. koṭika hamlet; guḍi temple; guḍise hut, cottage, hovel. Kol. (SR) guḍī temple. Pa. guḍi temple, village resthouse. Ga. (Oll.) guḍi temple. Go. (Ko.) kuṛma hut, outhouse; (Ma.) kurma menstruation; (Grigson) kurma lon menstruation hut (Voc. 782, 800); (SR.) guḍi, (Mu.) guḍḍi, (S. Ko.) guṛi temple; guḍḍī (Ph.) temple, (Tr.) tomb (Voc. 1113). Kui guḍi central room of house, living room. / Cf. Skt. kūˇṭa-, kuṭi-, kūˇṭī- (whence Ga. (P.) kuṛe hut; Kui kūṛi hut made of boughs, etc.; Kur. kuṛyā small shed or outhouse; Malt. kuṛya hut in the fields; Br. kuḍ(ḍ)ī hut, small house, wife), kuṭīkā-, kuṭīra-, kuṭuṅgaka-, kuṭīcaka-, koṭa- hut; kuṭumba- household (whence Ta. Ma. kuṭumpam id.; Ko. kuṛmb [? also kuṛm above]; To. kwïḍb, kwïḍbïl [-ïl fromwïkïl, s.v. 925 Ta. okkal]; Ka., Koḍ., Tu. kuṭumba; Tu. kuḍuma; Te. kuṭumbamu; ? Kui kumbu house [balance word of iḍu, see s.v. 494 Ta. il]). See Turner, CDIAL, no. 3232, kuṭī-, no. 3493, kōṭa-, no. 3233, kuṭumba-, for most of the Skt. forms; Burrow, BSOAS 11.137. (DEDR 1655)

40   khũṭro = entire bull; khũṭ= bra_hman.i bull (G.) khuṇṭiyo = an uncastrated bull (Kathiawad. G.lex.) khũ_taḍum a bullock (used in Jhālwāḍ)(G.) kuṇṭai = bull (Ta.lex.) cf. khũ_dhi hump on the back; khuĩ_dhũ hump-backed (G.)(CDIAL 3902).

41   kūṭa a house, dwelling (Skt.lex.) khũṭ = a community, sect, society, division, clique, schism, stock; khũṭren peṛa kanako = they belong to the same stock (Santali)

        khũṭ Nag. khũṭ, kũṭ Has. (Or. khũṭ) either of the two branches of the village family.

42   Pk. pottī -- f. ' glass '; S. pūti f. ' glass bead ', P. pot f.; N. pote ' long straight bar of jewelry '; B. pot ' glass bead ', puti, pũti ' small bead '; Or. puti ' necklace of small glass beads '; H. pot m. ' glass bead ', G. M. pot f.; -- Bi. pot ' jeweller's polishing stone '(CDIAL 8403)

43 Vikalpa: ḍhagarām pl. the buttocks; the hips (G.lex.) Rebus: ḍhā~gar, ḍhā~gar blacksmith; digger of wells (H.)

44 *mṛndati: WPah.kṭg. maṇḍnõ ' to rub, smear, thrash, crush ' (Him.I 172 if not < márdati with rd > ṇḍ), J. minṇu ' to rub, pinch '; -- (X mánthati) WPah.kṭg. mánḍhnõ ' to rub oneself '. Gy. wel. mōr -- ' to rub, polish, grind '; Dm. maṇ -- ' to rub ';

Paš.laur. kur. muṇḍ -- , dar. muṇ -- , weg. mur -- , gul. muṇḍal -- tr. ' to break ' (IIFL iii 3, 123 < múṇṭati), laur. maṇḍ -- ' to rub, smear ', kur. māṇ -- ' to thresh, smear ', chil. mēṇ -- ' to crush ', ar. māṛ -- ' to rub '; Gaw. mīṇḍemím ' I crush, thresh, grind, wash (clothes) '; Phal. māṇḍ -- ' to knead '; K. manḍun ' to rub, trample, wash (woollen cloth by kneading it with the feet) '; S. manaṇu ' to shampoo, make clothes ready for steaming '; WPah. (Joshi) minṇu ' to rub '; Ku. minaṇo ' to beat, rub '; Mth. mīṛab ' to knead, grind, shampoo '; H. mī̃rnā, mī̃d° ' to rub with the hands, clean '; M. mādṇẽ ' to smear vessels '; Si. maṅḍinavā, maḍin°, maḍan° ' to rub, press, clean rice from the husk ', (inscr.) mäṅḍä absol. ' to crush ', maḍavanavā ' to prepare a field for planting by buffaloes treading it ' (pret. maṇḍā < *maṅḍvā). -- X mánthati (L. mandhaṇ, P.maddhṇā: cf. H. mā̃dhnā in 1) or poss. < mr̥ddhá -- : L.awān. middhaṇ, pp. middhā ' to crush '; P. middhṇā, pp. middhā ' to stir up, mix, knead (mortar), rumple, tumble (clothes, paper, &c.), spoil by treading on (crops) '. -- X mr̥śáti q.v. Addenda: márdati. 1. A. māriba also ' to knead (dough) ' AFD 331 (CDIAL 9890)

45Ta. kol working in iron, blacksmith; kollaṉ blacksmith. Ma. kollan blacksmith, artificer.Ko. kole·l smithy, temple in Kota village. To. kwala·l Kota smithy. Ka. kolime, kolume, kulame, kulime, kulume, kulme fire-pit, furnace; (Bell.; U.P.U.) konimi blacksmith; (Gowda) kola id. Koḍ. Kollë blacksmith. Te. kolimi furnace. Go. (SR.) kollusānā to mend implements;

(Ph.) kolstānā, kulsānā to forge; (Tr.) kōlstānā to repair (of ploughshares); (SR.) kolmi smithy (Voc. 948). Kuwi F.) kolhali to forge.(DEDR 2133). [kolimi] kolimi. n. A pit. A fire pit or furnace. mudga kolimi a smelting forge (Telugu) கொல்லுலை kol-l-ulai, n. < id. +. Black-smith's forge; கொல்லனுலை. கொல்லுலைக் கூடத் தினால் (குமர. பிர. நீதிநெறி. 14) உலை³ ulai, n. < உலை²-. [K. ole, M. ula.] 1. Smith's forge or furnace; கொல்லனுலை. கொல்ல னுலையூதுந் தீயேபோல் (நாலடி, 298). 2. Fireplace for cooking, oven; நெருப்புள்ள அடுப் பு. (W.) 3. Pot of water set over the fire for boiling rice; சோறு சமைத்தற்காகக் கொதிக்க வைக்கும் நீர். உலைப்பெய் தடுவதுபோலுந் துயர் (நாலடி, 114). 4. Flurry, excitement, agitation; மன நடுக்கம். உலைதருமலின மொன்ற தொழித்திடுஞ் சுத்த மொன்றே (ஞானவா. வைரா. 26) (Tamil). ulai < culī f. ' fireplace ' Mn. [← Drav. EWA i 396 with lit.] Pa. culī -- f., Pk. culī -- , (Deśīn.) ulī -- f., Ḍ. čila f., K. čöl f., S. culhi f., ho m., L. cullh, pl. hī̃ f., cullhā m., P. culh m., cullhī f., hā m., Ku. N. culi, lo, B. culī, culā, cullā, Or. culī, culā, Bi. Mth. cūlh, hī, hā, Mth., Bhoj. cūlhi, H. cūlhī f., hā m., G. cūl, culī, culṛī f., cūlɔ m., M. ċūl f., ċulā, llā, lvā m.*culliyasi -- , *culīkarttāra -- , *culīdhāna -- , *culīdhāra -- ; *āculī -- ; *ēkkaculī -- .Addenda: culī -- : WPah.kṭg. (kc.) ċūl (obl. -- i) f. ' fireplace, oven ', J. culi f., Brj. cūlho m. (CDIAL 4879) kolime, kolume, kulame, kulime, kulume, kulme fire-pit, furnace (Ka.); kolimi furnace (Te.); pit (Te.); kolame a very deep pit (Tu.); kulume kanda_ya a tax on blacksmiths (Ka.)

46*dumbha ' tail '. [Only Kal. attests an aspirate: poss. all NIA. forms, and cert. those of Dard. with l -- , are ← Ir., Av. duma -- , Pahl. dumbak, Pers. dum(b), Psht.ləm EVP 36. But, besides Kal., some derivatives, e.g. s.v. *dumbhaśa -- , suggest possibility of orig. IA. form]Gy. eur.Dumo m. ' back, shoulder '; Wg. dumä´r, tumtä´ ' tail ', Kt. dəmŕéi, Pr. lümū̠, dəmū´ (← Kt. Rep1 47), Paš.gul. dum(b), nir. dumā´ (← Pers. IIFL iii 3, 55), ar. līm, Shum. līmə, Gaw. limoṭá, Kal. dh*lmŕéi, Kho. rūm, K. dumba m.; L. dumb m. ' ear of millet '; P. dumb, dumm m. ' tail ', N. dum, Or. duma, Mth. dom, H. dumb, dum f., G. dum f.; M. dumālā m. ' hind part '. (CDIAL 6419) Rebus: ḍōmba m. ' man of low caste living by singing and music ' Kathās., ḍōma -- m. lex., ḍōmbinī -- f. [Connected with Mu. words for ' drum ' PMWS 87, EWA i 464 with lit.] Pk. ḍoṁba -- , ḍuṁba -- , ḍoṁbilaya -- m.; Gy. eur. rom m. ' man, husband ', romni f. ' woman, wife ', SEeur. ṛom ' aGypsy ', pal. dōm ' a Nuri Gypsy ', arm. as. (Boša) lom ' a Gypsy ', pers. damini ' woman '; D. ḍōm (pl. ma) ' a Ḍom '; Paš. ḍōmb ' barber '; Kho. (Lor.) ḍom ' musician, bandsman '; Sh. ḍom ' a Ḍom ', K. ḍūmb, ḍūm m., ḍūmbiñ f.; S. ḍūmu m., ḍūmṛī f. ' caste of wandering musicians ', L. ḍūm m., ḍūmṇī f., (Ju.) ḍom m., ḍomṇī, ḍomṛī f., mult. ḍōm m.,ḍōmṇī f., awāṇ. naṭ -- ḍūm ' menials '; P. ḍūm, ḍomrā m., ḍūmṇī f. ' strolling musician ', ḍūmṇā m. ' a caste of basket -- maker '; WPah. ḍum ' a very low -- caste blackskinned fellow '; Ku.

ḍūm m., ḍūmaṇ f. ' an aboriginal hill tribe '; N. ḍum ' a low caste '; A. ḍom m. ' fisherman ', ḍumini f.; B. ḍom, ḍam m. ' a Ḍom ', ḍumni f. (OB. ḍombī); Or. ḍoma m., aṇī f., ḍuma, aṇī, ḍamba, ḍama, aṇī ' a low caste who weave baskets and sound drums '; Bhoj. ḍōm ' a low caste of musicians H.ḍomb, ḍom, ḍomṛā, ḍumār m., ḍomnī f., OMarw. ḍūma m., ḍūmaṛī f., M. ḍõb, ḍom m. -- Deriv. Gy. wel. romanō adj. (f. nī) ' Gypsy ' romanō rai m. ' Gypsy gentleman ', nī čib f. ' Gypsy language '.*ḍōmbakuṭaka -- , *ḍōmbadhāna -- .Addenda: ḍōmba -- : Gy.eur. rom m., romni f. esp. ' Gypsy man or woman '; WPah.kṭg. ḍōm m. ' member of a low caste of musicians ', ḍv̄m m.; Garh. ḍom ' an untouchable '. (CDIAL 5570).

47   Vikalpa: goti 'woman'; rebus; goṭ 'cow-pen'; rebus: ko ḍ 'place where artisans work' (Kuwi)

48   It was molded and carved from a mix of bitumen, ground calcite, and quartz. The Elamites used bitumen, a naturally occurring mineral pitch, or asphalt, for vessels, sculpture, glue, caulking, and waterproofing.

http://www.oznet.net/iran/elamspin.htm

49   मेढा [mēḍhā] menḍa A twist or tangle arising in thread or cord, a curl or snarl. (Marathi) (CDIAL 10312). [dial., cp. Prk. mĕṇṭha & miṇṭha: Pischel, Prk. Gr. § 293. The Dhtm (156) gives a root menḍ (meḍ) in meaning of "koṭilla," i. e. crookedness. (Pali) Vikalpa: dhompo = knot on a string

(Santali) ḍhompo = ingot (Santali) Vikalpa: cūḍa 'diadem, hairdress' (Skt.) Rebus: cūḷa 'furnace' (H.)

[50] http://www.laputanlogic.com/articles/2004/01/24-0001.html

[51] खट्·ঁয়াড় [khōm̐yāḍ] n a cattle-shed, a cowshed, a cowhouse; a sheepfold; a pound for stray cattle, a pinfold. **খট্·ঁয়াড়ে আটকানে·ा, খট্·ঁয়াড়ে পে·ায়া** v. to put into or enclose in a cattleshed; to pound, to impound; to pinfold. (Bengali) कोंडण [kōṇḍaṇa] f A fold or pen. कोंडवाड [kōṇḍavāḍa] n f C (कोंडणें & वाडा) A pen or fold for cattle. कोंडी [kōṇḍī] f (कोंडणें) A confined place gen.; a lockup house, a pen, fold, pound; a receiving apartment or court for Bráhmans gathering for दक्षिणा; a prison at the play ofआत्यापात्या; a dammed up part of a stream &c. &c. गोठी [gōṭhī] f C (Dim. of गोठा) A pen or fold for calves. गोठा [gōṭhā] m (गोष्ठ S) A cow-pen. गोंदरड [gōndaraḍa] f R Litter; esp. the litter of a cow-pen. गोडगस्ता [gōḍagastā] m A village-officer in some districts. He is the informant of the Paíl respecting villageoccurrences. गोठण [gōṭhaṇa] f (गोष्ठ or गोस्थानS) A shady spot near a village whither the pasturing herds resort at noon and rest. Pr. गोठणीच्या गायी माभळभट दान घेई. गो0 घालून बसणें To sit loosely and irregularly--people in an assembly. (Marathi) Ta. koṭṭakai shed with sloping roofs, cow-stall; marriage pandal; koṭṭam cattle-shed; koṭṭil cow-stall, shed, hut; (STD) koṭambe feeding place for cattle. Ma. koṭṭil cowhouse, shed, workshop, house. Ka. koṭṭage, koṭige, koṭṭige stall or outhouse (esp. for cattle), barn, room. Koḍ. koṭṭï shed. Tu. koṭṭa hut or dwelling of Koragars; koṭya shed, stall.

Te.koṭṭāmu stable for cattle or horses; koṭṭāyi thatched shed. Kol. (Kin.) koṛka, (SR.) korkā cowshed; (Pat., p. 59) konṭoḍi henhouse. Nk. khoṭa cowshed. Nk. (Ch.) koṛka id.Go. (Y.) koṭa, (Ko.) koṭam (pl. koṭak) id. (Voc. 880); (SR.) koṭka shed; (W. G. Mu. Ma.) koṛka, (Ph.) korka, kurka cowshed (Voc. 886); (Mu.) koṭorla, koṭorli shed for goats (Voc. 884). Malt. koṭa hamlet. / Influenced by Skt. goṣṭha-. (DEDR 2058) gōṣṭhá m. ' cow -- house ' RV., ' meeting place ' MBh. 2. *gōstha -- . [gṓ -- , stha --] 1. Pa. gottha -- n. ' cowpen ', NiDoc. gotha, Pk. gottha -- , guṭ n.; Ash. gōṣṭ -- klōm ' ceiling '; Tir. guṣṭ ' house ', Woṭ. goṭ; Kal. rumb. ghōṣṭ ' cattle shed '; Mai. goṭ ' house ', Phal. ghōṣṭ, Sh. goṭ m.; K. guṭh, dat. ṭhas m. ' place in a village where the cattle collect '; S. gothu m. ' village, town '; WPah. bhal. gōṭh n. ' standing ground for cattle in meadow or forest '; Ku. goṭh ' cattle shed ', gng. ' lower storey of house '; N. goṭh ' cowshed '; B. goṭh ' pasture land, herd, flock '; Or. goṭha ' herd, flock ', (Ambalpur) guṭha ' cattle pen '; Bhoj. goṭh ' cowpen '; G. goṭhɔ m. ' cattle yard '; M. goṭhā m. ' cowpen ' ṭhī ' pen for calves ', Ko. goṭ. -- Ext. -- la -- in Si. goṭaluva ' hut, cottage '? <-> Sv. guš ' house ' is unexpl. -- Sh. goṣ ' house ' (unless a lw. with loss of -- ṭ and subsequent treatment of -- ṣ > -- ẓ<-> in obl. like an orig. -- ṣ --) prob. < ghōṣa -- . 2. Chil. goṭʻ house '; P. kgr. gohth f. ' place where sheep are penned for the night in the high ranges '. gōṣṭhī -- , gauṣṭha -- ; *gōṣṭhapāla -- ; *saṁbandhigōṣṭha Addenda: gōṣṭhá -- . 1. Sv. guš (goš

Buddruss) with regular š < šṭh ZDMG 116, 414; S.kcch. goṭh m. ' village '; Garh. goṭh ' cowshed ', Brj. goṭh f. (CDIAL 4336).

52   S.kānu m. reed ', nī f. ' topmost joint of the reed Sara, reed pen, stalk, straw, porcupine's quill '; L. kānā m. ' stalk of the reed Sara ', nī f. ' pen, small spear '; P. kānnā m. ' the reed Saccharum munja, reed in a weaver's warp Or. kānḍa, kāṛ ' stalk, arrow '; Bi. kāṛā ' stem of muñja grass (used for thatching) '; Mth. kāṛ ' stack of stalks of large millet '; Bhoj. kanḍā ' reeds '; H. kanḍā m. ' reed, bush ' (← EP.?); G.kāḍ m. ' joint, bough, arrow (CDIAL 3023). kānḍīra ' armed with arrows ' Pāṇ., m. ' archer ' lex. [kānḍa--]H. kanīrā m. ' a caste (usu. of arrow -- makers) (CDIAL 3026) L. kanērā m. ' mat -- maker ' H. kãḍerā m. ' a caste of bow -- and arrow -- makers '. (CDIAL 3024). Ta. katuppu herd of cattle. Ka. kadupu herd, flock; kadale, kadaḷi a mass, multitude. Te. kadupu id. / ? Cf. Skt. kadamba(ka)- multitude, troop. (DEDR 1198) kolom ka ṭhi 'a reed pen' (Santali)

53   कोठी The grain and provisions (as of an army); the commissariatsupplies. Ex. लशकराची कोठी चालली-उतरली- आली-लुटली. कोठ्या [kōṭhyā] कोठा [kōṭhā] m (कोष्ट S) A large granary, store-room, warehouse, water-reservoir &c. 2 The stomach. 3 The chamber of a gun, of water-pipes &c. 4 A bird's nest. 5 A cattle-shed. 6 The chamber or cell of a hunḍí in which is set down in figures the amount. कोठारें [kōṭhārēṃ] n A storehouse gen (Marathi)

54   गोटा [gōṭā] m A roundish stone or pebble. 2 A marble (of stone, lac, wood &c.) 2 A marble. 3 A large lifting stone. Used in trials of strength among the Athletæ. 4 A stone in temples described at length underउचला 5 fig. A term for a round, fleshy, well-filled body. 6 A lump of silver: as obtained by melting down lace or fringe. गोटुळा or गोटोळा [gōṭuḷā or gōṭōḷā] a (गोटा) Spherical or spheroidal, pebble-form. (Marathi)

55

http://wings.buffalo.edu/english/faculty/christian/syllabi/375/hhjw1/hhjw1.htm

56   After Moorey, PRS, 1999, Ancient mesopotamian materials and industries: the archaeological evidence, Eisenbrauns.

57   After Pottier, M.H., 1984, Materiel funeraire e la Bactriane meridionale de l'Age du Bronze, Paris, Editions Recherche sur les Civilisations: plate 20.150

58   D.T. Potts, South and Central Asian elements at Tell Abraq (Emirate of Umm al-Qaiwain, United Arab Emirates), c. 2200 BC—AD 400, in Asko Parpola and Petteri Koskikallio, South Asian Archaeology 1993: , pp. 615-666

59takaram tin, white lead, metal sheet, coated with tin (Ta.); tin, tinned iron plate (Ma.); tagarm tin (Ko.); tagara, tamara, tavara id. (Ka.) tamaru, tamara, tavara id. (Ta.): tagaramu, tamaramu, tavaramu id. (Te.); ṭagromi tin metal, alloy (Kuwi); tamara id. (Skt.)(DEDR 3001). trapu tin (AV.); tipu (Pali); tau, taua lead (Pkt.); t ū_ tin (P.); ṭau zinc, pewter (Or.); tarūaum lead (OG.); tarvu~ (G.); tumba lead (Si.)(CDIAL 5992).

[60]http://www.docstoc.com/docs/19269229/Altyndepeandmeluhha (Excavation 9 and 7) found in the shrine and in the 'elite quarter'. V.M. Masson, Seals of a Proto-Indian Type from Altyn-depe, pp. 149-162; V.M. Masson, Urban Centers of Early Class Society, pp. 135-148; I.N. Khlopin, The Early bronze age cemetery in Parkhai II: The first two seasons of excavations, 1977-78, pp. 3-34 in: Philip L. Kohl (ed.), 1981, The Bronze Age Civilization in Central Asia, Armonk, NY, ME Sharpe, Inc. "The discovery in Altyn-Depe of a proto-Indian seal with two signs deserves special mention. V.M. Masson pointed out, that what the seal depicted was a pictogram and not just a representation of animals. In his opinion this means that some of the ancient residents of Altyn-Depe were able to read this text."(G. Bongard- Levin, 1989, Archaeological Finds in Central Asia throw light on Ancient India, Jagdish Vibhakar and Usha Gard (Eds.), Glimpses of Ancient India through Soviet Eyes, Delhi, Sundeep Prakashan).

[61]   kandi (pl. –l) beads, necklace (Pa.); kanti (pl. –l) bead, (pl.) necklace; kandiṭ 'bead' (Ga.)(DEDR 1215).

[62]   Ta. kōṭaram monkey. Ir. kōḍa (small) monkey; kūḍag monkey. Ko. korṇ small monkey. To. kwrṇ monkey. Ka. kōḍaga monkey, ape. Koḍ. koḍë monkey. Tu. koḍañji, koḍañja, koḍaṅ baboon (DEDR 2196) Konḍa (BB) kōnza red-faced monkey. Kui kōnja black-faced monkey. Kuwi (F.)

360

kōnja monkey (small); (S.) konja ape; konzu monkey; (P.)
kōnja black-faced monkey. (DEDR 2194)

63   khōli f. ' quiver ' lex. P. khol f. ' sheath, case '; Ku.
khol ' covering '; N. khol ' sheath ', Or. khoḷi ' quiver ', ḷā '
sheath ', H. khol m.; -- G. khoḷiyū n. ' quilt '; M. khoḷ m.f. '
pillowcase, mattress cover '.(CDIAL 3944)

64   kollaṉ blacksmith. Ma. kollan blacksmith, artificer.
To. kwala·l Kota smithy. Ka. kolime, kolume, kulame, kulime,
kulume, kulme fire-pit, furnace; (Bell.; U.P.U.) konimi
blacksmith; (Gowda) kola id. Koḍ. Kollë blacksmith. Te.
kolimi furnace. Go. (SR.) kollusānā to mend implements;
(Ph.) kolstānā, kulsānā to forge; (Tr.) kōlstānā to repair (of
ploughshares); (SR.) kolmi smithy (Voc. 948). Kuwi (F.)
kolhali to forge. (DEDR 2133)
[The motifs on m 439, m440 and m1393 to m1395 seem to
be identical; on one side three or more (perhaps five) tiger
heads emanating from a body are shown; on another side a
group of animals surrounding a lizard (gharial): two short-
horned bulls facing each other, a rhinoceros, an elephant, a
tiger looking back and a monkey (?) with face turned
backwards.] kolimi-titti = bellows used for a furnace (Te.lex.)
kollu- to neutralize metallic properties by oxidation (Ta.lex.)
kol brass or iron bar nailed across a door or gate; kollu-t-taṭi-
y- āṇi large nail for studding doors or gates to add to their
strength (Ta.lex.) kollan--kammālai < + karma śālā, kollan--
paṭṭarai, kollan-ulai-k-kūṭam blacksmith's workshop, smithy

(Ta.lex.) cf. ulai smith's forge or furnace (Nālat.i, 298); ulai-k-kaḷam smith's forge; ulai-k-kuṟaṭu smith's tongs; ulai-t-turutti smith's bellows; ulai-y- āṇi-k-kōl smith's poker, beak-iron (Ta.lex.) [kollulaive_r-kan.allār: naiṭata. nāṭṭup.); mitiyulaikkollan- mur-ioṭiṟṟaṉṉa:perumpā) (Ta.lex.) Temple; smithy: kol-l-ulai blacksmith's forge (kollulaik kūṭattiṉā I : Kumara. Pira. Nītiner-i. 14)(Ta.lex.) cf. kolhuār sugarcane milkl and boiling house (Bi.); kolhār oil factory (P.)(CDIAL 3537). kulhu 'a hindu caste, mostly oilmen' (Santali) kolsār = sugarcane mill and boiling house (Bi.)(CDIAL 3538).

66   Grapheme (standard device, generally shown in front of the heifer): G.sāghārɔ m. 'lathe'; M. sāgāḍī f. 'lathe' (CDIAL 12859). kaṭa churning; kaṭaccal turning; kaṭaccil turning and polish- ing (wood, etc.), churning. Ko. karv- (kard-) to churn; karc uḷy lathe. To. kar- (karQ-) to churn. Ka. kaḍe, kaḍi to churn, stir, rub together (as two pieces of wood to excite fire), turn in a lathe; kaḍe, kaḍa, kaḍaha, kaḍeta churning (DEDR 1141)

67   seṇi (f.) [Class. Sk. śreṇi in meaning "guild"; Vedic= row] 1. a guild Vin iv.226; J i.267, 314; iv.43; Dāvs ii.124; their number was eighteen J vi.22, 427; VbhA 466. ° -- pamukha the head of a guild J ii.12 (text seni --). -- 2. a division of an army J vi.583; ratha -- ° J vi.81, 49; seṇimokkha the chief of an army J vi.371 (cp. senā and seniya).(Pali) śréṇi (metr. often śrayaṇi --) f. ' line, row, troop ' RV. [Same as *śrayaṇī -- (for ' line ~ ladder ' cf. *śreṣṭrī --

2)? -- √śri] Pa. sēṇi -- f. ' guild, division of army '; Pk. sēṇi --
f. ' row, collection '; S. sīṇa f. ' the threads of the loom
between which the warp runs '; Bi. senī ' the broad flat metal
plates in a tobacconist's shop '.(CDIAL 12718)

[68] Tu. eraka molten, cast (as metal); eraguni to melt (DEDR
866) erka = ekke (Tbh. of arka) aka (Tbh. of arka) copper
(metal); crystal (Ka.lex.) cf. eruvai = copper (Ta.lex.) eraka,
er-aka = any metal infusion (Ka.Tu.); erako molten cast
(Tu.lex.)

[69] New evidence for sources of and trade in bronze age tin,
in: Alan D. Franklin, Jacqueline S. Olin, and Theodore A.
Wertime, The Search for Ancient Tin, 1977, Seminar
organized by Theodore A. Wertime and held at the
Smithsonian Institution and the National Bureau of
Standards, Washington, D.C., March 14-15, 1977.

[70] karī′ra2 (Uṇ. ká) m. ' Capparis aphylla (a thorny plant
eaten by camels) ' ŚBr., n. ' its fruit ' Suśr. 2. karibha -- m. '
Ficus religiosa (?) ' lex. [Same as karīra -- 1?] 1. Pa. karīra --
m. ' Capparis aphylla ', karēri -- m. ' C. trifoliata '; Pk. karīra -
- m. ' C. aphylla ', L. kaler m., P. karīr m., B. karir; Or. karira '
C. spinosa '; H. karīr, karīl, lā m. ' C. aphylla ', OG. kaïra, G.
kerrɔ m., rī f., karīr n. ' its fruit ' (← M. or Sk.?), M. karīr m., n.
' its fruit '.2. L. karīh, rĩh, rī, rīṭā m. ' C. aphylla ', awāṇ. krĩh,
P. karĩh m. (the fruit is pickled and the bud used as a
vegetable: in this connexion esp. cf. karī′ra -- 1). Some

forms perh. X karavīra -- : L. karvīlā, lū m. ' C. horrida (of which fruit is made into pickles) '; H. karwīl m. ' C. aphylla '. -- Sh. (Lor.) kawīr, kabīr ' caper plant '.(CDIAL 2805).

71 karabhá m. ' young elephant ' BhP. 2. kalabhá -- ' young elephant or camel ' Pañcat. [Poss. a non -- aryan kar -- ' elephant ' also in karéṇu -- , karin -- EWA i 165] 1. Pk. karabha -- m., bhī -- f., karaha -- m. ' camel ', S. karahu, ho m., P. H. karhā m., Marw. karhau JRAS 1937, 116, OG. karahu m., OM. karahā m.; Si. karaba ' young elephant or camel '. 2. Pa. kalabha -- m. ' young elephant ', Pk. kalabha -- m., bhiā -- f., kalaha -- m.; Ku. kalṛo ' young calf '; Or. kālhuṛi ' young bullock, heifer '; Si. kalam̐bayā ' young elephant '.Addenda: karabhá -- : OMarw. karaha ' camel '.(CDIAL 2797)

karin (adj.) [fr. kara] "one who has a hand," an elephant (cp. hatthin) (Pali) Mhvs 24, 34; 25, 68; Dāvs iv.2. In cpds. kari. gajjita the cry of the elephant, an elephant's trumpeting Dāvs v.56; -- vara an excellent elephant Mhbv 4, 143; Dāvs iv.2. (Pali) karin m. ' elephant '. [See karabhá --]Pa. karin -- m., Pk. kari -- , iṇa -- m., iṇī -- , iṇiyā -- f.; <-> Si. kiriyā ← Pa. (CDIAL 2803) करी [karī] m (S Having a hand.) An elephant.करीबल [karībala] n (S) The elephant-branch of an army; the elephant-force.(Marathi)

கரிணி kariṇi , n. < karinī. (பிங்.) 1. Female elephant; பெண்யானை. 2. Elephant; யானை. (Tamil) కరము [karamu] karamu. [Skt.] n. The hand. చేయి చేయ⁹. An elephant's trunk;

కరి⁹ [kari] kari. [Skt. from కరము.] n. An elephant. (Telugu) kari 'having a trunk, an elephant' (Ka.)

iva 'elephant' (Ta.) *இபம்²* ipam, n. < ibha. Elephant; *யானை. திசையிபச் செவி (கலிங். புதுப்.* 331).(Ta.) ఇభము [ibhamu] ibhamu. (Skt of elephant. Gr. elephas.] An elephant. ibhayāna. n. A graceful woman, i. e., a woman with an elephant's easy and luxurious rolling gait. ibhi. n. A she-elephant ibhyuḍu. A ruler, rich man. (A. ii. 125.) (Telugu) ibha m. ' elephant ' Mn. Pa. ibha -- m., Pk. ibha -- , iha -- , Si. iba Geiger EGS 22: rather ← Pa. (CDIAL 1587)

72   Vikalpa: kaḍru 'buffalo' (G.); kaḍa buffalo (Santali) kaṭrā bull calf; kaṭhrā young buffalo bull; kaṭiyā buffalo heifer (H.); kaṭra buffalo calf (WPah.); kaṭai buffalo calf (Gaw.); kaṭrā young buffalo (P.)(CDIAL 245). kaṭādamu = a he-buffalo (Te.lex.)17 kōṛi buffalo (Kond.a); kaḍru (Pe.Mand.); kōru pl. kōrka (Kui); kōḍru, kōdru, gōḍru, kōḍrū (Kuwi)(DEDR 2256). kaḍa, kaḍru, kaṛa 'a buffalo bull' kaḍi 'a female buffalo calf' (Santali) Or. kaṛā ' castrated male buffalo ', kaṛāi ' young buffalo cow that has not calved ', kaṛhi ' lamb that has not borne '; Bi. kāṛā m., ṛī f. ' buffalo calf ', H. kāṛā m. (CDIAL 2658)

goraka. [Tel.] n. A wild buffalo. An iron arrow ఇనుపబాణము.   goraka-kaṭṭe. n. A javelin, or slender spear.(Telugu)

The following glosses, kārā in Urdu, Telugu, Tamil

and karā, kaṛa in Kurku and Santali of the linguistic area indicate an ancient form, kārā to denote 'buffalo'. Rebus: khār 1 खार् । लोहकारः m. (sg. abl. khāra 1 खार; the pl. dat. of this word is khāran 1 खारन्, which is to be distinguished from khāran 2, q.v., s.v.), a blacksmith, an iron worker (cf.bandūka-khār, p. 111b, l. 46; K.*Pr. 46; H. xi, 17); a farrier (El.). This word is often a part of a name, and in such case comes at the end (W. 118) as in Wahab khār, Wahab the smith (H. ii, 12; vi, 17). khāra-basta खार-बस॒त । चर्मप्रसेविका f. the skin bellows of a blacksmith. -büṭhü -ब&above;टू&below; । लोहकारभित्तिः f. the wall of a blacksmith's furnace or hearth. -bāy -बाय् । लोहकारपत्नी f. a blacksmith's wife (Gr.Gr. 34). -dŏkuru -द्रकुरु&below; । लोहकारायोघनः m. a blacksmith's hammer, a sledge-hammer. -gȧji -ग&above;जि&below; or -güjü -ग&above;जू&below; । लोहकारचुल्लिः f. a blacksmith's furnace or hearth. -hāl -हाल् । लोहकारकन्दुः f. (sg. dat. -höjü -हा&above;जू&below;), a blacksmith's smelting furnace; cf. hāl 5. -kūrü -कूरू&below; । लोहकारकन्या f. a blacksmith's daughter. -koṭu -क&above;टु&below; । लोहकारपुत्रः m. the son of a blacksmith, esp. a skilful son, who can work at the same profession. -küṭü -क&above;टू&below; । लोहकारकन्या f. a blacksmith's daughter, esp. one who has the virtues and qualities properly belonging to her father's profession or caste. -më̆tsü 1 -म्य&above;च&dotbelow;&below; । लोहकारमृत्तिका f. (for 2, see [khāra 3]), 'blacksmith's earth,' i.e. iron-ore. -nĕcyuwu -न्यचिवु&below; । लोहकारात्मजः m. a blacksmith's son. -nay -नय् । लोहकारनालिका f. (for khāranay 2, see [khārun]), the trough into which the blacksmith allows melted iron to flow after smelting. -tsaně -च्&dotbelow;ज । लोहकारशान्ताङ्गाराः f.pl. charcoal used by blacksmiths in their furnaces. -wān वान् । (Kashmiri)

காரா kār-ā n. < கரு-மை + ஆ&sup8;. [T. kārāvu, U. kārā.] Buffalo; எருமை. செங்கண் வன்கட் காரா (தஞ்சைசவா. 380).(Tamil) kār-āvu. [Tel.] n. A wild cow. forest cattle. kaarenumu n. wild buffalo (female) (Telugu) गौर gaur, adj. (f. -ī), White, pale; of fair complexion, fair;—yellow;—red, pale red;—s.m. A kind of buffalo, the Bos gaurus (Urdu) kaṛa, kaḍa 'a buffalo bull' (Santali) Kur. kaṛā young male buffalo; kaṛī young female buffalo; kaṛrū, kaḍrū buffalo calf (male or female). Ko. kaṛc ng buffalo calf between two and three years; kaṛc kurl cow calf between two and three years; ? To. kar pen for calves from 6 months to 1-2 years.Ko. (Ph.) kāṛā young buffalo (Voc.648). Konḍa (BB) gṛālu calf. Kui (K.)grāḍu, (W.) ḍrāḍu (pl. ḍrāṭka)id.; (W.) gāṛo a bullock or buffalo not trained to the plough; kṛai young female buffalo or goat. Br. xarās bull, bullock; xaṛ ram.(DEDR 1123). Gaw. kaṭái 'buffalo calf', Bshk. kaṭōr, Sh. (Lor.) k *l tu (ṭ?); K. kaṭh, dat. ṭas m. 'ram, sheep in general, (con- temptuous) son'; L. kaṭṭā m., ṭī f. 'buffalo calf'; P. kaṭṭā m., ṭī f. 'yearling buffalo', kaṭṭū m. 'young buffalo bull', kaṭṛā m., ṛī f. 'young buffalo'; WPah. khaś. rudh. marm. katru 'buffalo calf', bhal. kaṭṭā m., ṭī f. 'buffalo calf', kaṭru n. 'bear cub'; Ku. kāṭo 'young buffalo bull', kaṭyāro 'young buffalo'; H. kaṭiyā f. 'buffalo heifer', kaṭrā

m. 'buffalo calf', kaṭhrā m. 'young buffalo bull' (CDIAL 2645). Vikalpa: ran:gā 'buffalo'; Rebus: ran:ga 'pewter or alloy of tin (ran:ku), lead (nāga) and antimony (an~jana)'(Santali)

73   sal 'place, as in dancing place'; kamar sal 'a smithy'; paura sal 'a liquor shop'; paṭhsal 'a school house'; ak sal 'a place where sugarcane is pressed'; kaṭ sal 'a carpenter or joiner's workshop'; lagṛẽ sal 'a place where the lagṛẽ dance is danced'; piarsalare kamarko salakata 'blacksmiths have opened a smithy in Piarsala'; dare baṭareko salakata 'they have set up a forge under a tree'. சாலை¹ cālai, n. < śālā. Sacrificial hall; யாகசாலை. திருத்திய சாலை புக் கனன் (கம்பரா. திருவவ. 84). School; பள்ளிக் கூடம். கறையறு கல்விகற்குங் காமர்சாலையும் (குசே லோ. குசே. வைகுந். 23). Cow shed; பசுக்கொட்டில். ஆத்துறுசாலைதோறும் (கம்பரா. ஊர்தேடு. 101). Large public hall; பெரிய பொதுமண்டபம். Loc. Royal palace; அரசன் அரண்மனை. (பிங்.). House, mansion; வீடு. விதுரன்சாலைக் கரும்புது விருந்தாமருந்தே (அழகர்கல. 5). Sālā (f.) [cv. Vedic śālā, cp. Gr. kali/a hut, Lat. cella cell, Ohg. halla, E. hall] a large (covered & enclosed) hall, large room, house; shed, stable etc., as seen fr. foll. examples: aggi° a hall with a fire Vin i.25, 49=ii.210; āsana° hall with seats DhA ii.65; udapāna° a shed over the well Vin i.139; ii.122; upaṭṭhāna° á service hall Vin i.49, 139; ii.153, 208, 210; S ii.280;v.321; J i.160; kaṭhina° a hall for the kaṭhina Vin ii.117. kīḷa playhouse J vi.332; kutūhala° a common room D i.179= Siv.398. kumbhakāra potter's hall

DhA i.39; gilāna° sick room, hospital S iv.210; Vism 259; jantāghāra° (large) bath room Vin i.140; ii.122; dāna° a hall for donations J i.262; dvāra° hall with doors M i.382; ii.66; pāniya° a water -- room Vinii.153; bhatta° refectory Vism 72; yañña° hall of sacrifice PugA 233; rajana° dyeing workshop Vism 65; ratha° car shed DhA iii.121; hatthi° an elephant stable Vin i.277, 345; ii.194; Ji.187. (Pali) śā´lā f. ' shed, stable, house ' AV., śālám adv. ' at home ' ŚBr., śālikā -- f. ' house, shop ' lex.Pa. Pk. sālā -- f. ' shed, stable, large open -- sided hall, house ', Pk. sāla -- n. ' house '; Ash. sal ' cattleshed ', Wg. šāl, Kt. šål, Dm. šâl; Paš.weg. sāl, ar. šol ' cattleshed on summer pasture '; Kho. šal ' cattleshed ', šeli ' goatpen '; K. hal f. ' hall, house '; L. sālh f. ' house with thatched roof '; A. xāl, xāli ' house, workshop, factory '; B. sāl ' shed, workshop '; Or.sāḷa ' shed, stable '; Bi. sār f. ' cowshed '; H. sāl f. ' hall, house, school ', sār f. ' cowshed '; M. sāḷ f. ' workshop, school '; Si. sal -- a, ha ' hall, market -- hall '.upaśala -- , *pariśālā -- Add., *pratiśālā -- , *praśālā -- ; aśvaśālā -- , āpānaśālā -- , *kaṇikaśālā -- , karmaśālā -- , *karmāraśālā -- , *kōlhuśālā -- , *khaṇḍuśālā -- , *gāvaśāla -- , gōśālā -- , cathuśāla -- , candraśālā -- , citraśālā -- , chā´ttriśālā -- , jyōtiḥśālā -- , dānaśālā -- , *dhānyaśālā -- , *nayaśālā -- , nayaśālin -- , *nītiśālā -- , paṇyaśālā -- , parṇaśālā -- , *pituḥśālā -- , *prapāśālā -- , bhāṇḍaśālā -- , *bhusaśālā -- , *bhrāṣṭraśālikā -- , *yantraśālā -- , lēkhaśālā -- , *lōhaśālā -- , *vaidyaśālā -- , *śvaśuraśālā -- , hastiśālā --

.Addenda: śā'lā -- : †*āhanaśālā -- , †dharmaśālā -- . (CDIAL 12414)

74   baṭi to turn on the ground to any extent, or roll; uaurbaṭi, to upset or overthrow by shoving or pushing; mabaṭi to overturn by cutting, to fell trees; baṭi-n rflx. v., to lay oneself down; ba-p-aṭi repr. V., to throw each other; baṭi-o to be overturned, overthrown; ba-n-at.i vrb.n., the extent of the overturning, falling down or rolling; baṭi-n rlfx.v., to lie down; baṭi-aṛagu to bring or send down a slope by rolling; baṭi bar.a to roll again and again or here and there; baṭi-bur to turn over by rolling (Mundari)

75   kottukkāran- head of a company of labourers (Ta.); gottugār-a headman (Ka.)(DEDR 2093). goṭ Another name for the Sohrae festival; goṭ gai on the first day of the goṭ. Puja or Sohrae in the evening all the cattle of the village are driven over an egg and the animal which treads on it is called the goṭ gai (Santali)

76   arká— 1 m. 'flash, ray, sun' RV. [√arc] Pa. Pk. akka— m. 'sun', Mth. āk; Si. aka 'lightning', inscr. vid—äki 'lightning flash'. •அற்கன் aṟkaṉ n. < arka. Sun; சூரியன். அற்கன் மேல்வரு மெழிலிகளென (கந்தபு. கயமுகன்வ. 35 Rebus: akka, aka (Tadbhava of arka) metal (Ka.); akka metal (Te.) arka = copper (Skt.) aka-sāla, aga-sāla, aka-sāliga, aka-sāle a gold or silversmith; aka-sa_like the business of a gold or silver smith; akka-sāle, aka-sāle the workshop of a goldsmith; a goldsmith; akka-sāliti a woman of the goldsmith caste (Ka.); akka-c-cālai a shop where metals

are worked (Ta.)(Ka.lex.) •அருக்கம்[1] arukkam •, n. < arka. (நாநார்த்த.) 1. Copper; செம்பு.

[77] Vikalpa: Ta. koṭiṟu pincers. Ma. koṭil tongs. Ko. koṟ hook of tongs. / Cf. Skt. (P. 4.4.18) kuṭilikā- smith's tongs.(DEDR 2052).

[78] konḍu मूलिकादिघर्षणवस्तु m. a washerman's dressing iron (El. kunḍh); a scraper or grater for grating radishes, or the like; usually ° -- , the second member being the article to be grated, as in the following: -- kånḍi-mujü घर्षिता मूलिका f. grated radish, but mujĕ-konḍu, a radish-grater (cf. mujü). (Kashmiri) *khuṭṭa1 ' peg, post '. 2. *khuṇṭa -- 1. [Same as *khuṭṭa -- 2? -- See also kṣōḍa -- .]1. Ku. khuṭī ' peg '; N. khuṭnu ' to stitch ' (der. *khuṭ ' pin ' as khilnu from khil s.v. khī́la --); Mth. khuṭā ' peg, post '; H. khūṭā m. ' peg, stump '; Marw. khuṭī f. ' peg '; M. khuṭā m. ' post '.2. Pk. khuṁṭa -- , khoṁṭaya -- m. ' peg, post '; Dm. kuṇḍa ' peg for fastening yoke to plough -- pole '; L. khūḍī f. ' drum -- stick '; P. khuṇḍ, ḍā m. ' peg, stump '; WPah. rudh. khuṇḍ ' tethering peg or post '; A. khũṭā ' post ', ṭi ' peg '; B. khũṭā, ṭi ' wooden post, stake, pin, wedge '; Or. khuṇṭa, ṭā' pillar, post '; Bi. (with -- ḍa --) khũṭrā, rī ' posts about one foot high rising from body of cart '; H. khũṭā m. ' stump, log ', ṭī f. ' small peg ' (→ P.khũṭā m., ṭī f. ' stake, peg '); G. khūṭ f. ' landmark ', khũṭo m., ṭī f. ' peg ', ṭũ n. ' stump ', ṭiyũ n. ' upright support in frame of wagon ', khũṭrũn. ' half -- burnt piece of fuel '; M. khũṭ m. '

stump of tree, pile in river, grume on teat ' (semant. cf. kīla --
1 s.v. *khila -- 2), khūṭā m. ' stake ', ṭī f. ' wooden pin ',
khūṭalṇē ' to dibble '.Addenda: *khutta -- 1. 2. *khuṇṭa -- 1:
WPah.ktg. khv́ndɔ ' pole for fencing or piling grass round '
(Him.I 35 nd poss. wrong for ṇḍ); J. khuṇḍā m. ' peg to
fasten cattle to '. (CDIAL 3893) Vikalpa: pacar = a wedge
driven ino a wooden pin, wedge etc. to tighten it (Santali.lex.)
pasra = a smithy, place where a black-smith works, to work
as a blacksmith; kamar pasra = a smithy; pasrao lagao akata
se ban:? Has the blacksmith begun to work? pasraedae =
the blacksmith is at his work (Santali.lex.)

[79]   Gypsum. 2.6 cm. Long 1.6 cm. Dia. Tell Suleimeh
(level IV), Iraq; IM 87798; (al-Gailani Werr,1983, p. 49 No.
7). [Drawing by Larnia Al-GailaniWerr. Cf. Dominique Collon
1987, First impressions: cylinder seals in the ancient Near
East, London: 143, no. 609]

[80]   In Pl. 275: Omananda Saraswati 1975. Ancient
Seals of Haryana (in Hindi). Rohtak." (I. Mahadevan,
'Murukan' in the Indus Script, The Journal of the Institute of
Asian Studies, March 1999).   B.B. Lal, 1960. From
Megalithic to the Harappa: Tracing back the graffiti on
pottery. Ancient India, No.16, pp.4-24.

[81]   ḍhākaḷ f. ' old decaying stump ', ḍhākē̃ n. ' stout
stake ', ḍhākaḷ, kūḷ ' old and decaying, bare of leaves &c.
(M.) (CDIAL 5524)

[82] kuthi'smelting furnace'; koṭe 'forged metal' (Santali) •Tu.
koḍapuni to forge, hammer; koḍapāvuni to weld, forge

together; Kuwi (Isr.) koṭoli mallet; Pali koṭṭeti to beat, smash, pound; Nahali koṭṭo- to pound, beat.   (DEDR 2063) Pa. koṭṭēti 'hews, breaks, crushes', Pk. koṭṭēi; Kho. (Lor.) kotik (= —ṭ—?) 'to crush (testicles to castrate)'; Ku. koṭyūno 'to dig up with a hoe'; K. kuṭun 'to pound, crush'; S. kuṭaṇu 'to pound, bruise'; kuttáyati 'crushes, grinds' AVPariś., 'pounds' VarBṛS. 2. *kōṭṭayati. [√kuṭṭ] 1. Pk. kuṭṭēi 'beats, pounds'; Gy. arm. eur. kur— 'to beat', SEeur. kuṛ— JGLS new ser. iv 293; Wg. (Lumsden); S. kuṭaṇu 'to pound, bruise'; L. kuṭṭaṇ 'to beat, pound, ram', P. kuṭṭṇā, WPah. pāḍ. kŏṭaṇ, bhad. bhal. kuṭṇū, khaś. kuṭṭnū, Ku. kuṭṇo, N. kuṭnu; A. kuṭiba 'to cut into small pieces, gnaw, punctuate'; B. kuṭā 'to beat, pound, cut up for cooking'; Or. kuṭibā 'to beat, pound' (CDIAL 3241) கொட்டுக்கன்னார் koṭṭu-k-kaṉṉār , n. < கொட்டு² +. Braziers who work by beating plates into shape and not by casting; செம் படிக்குங் கன்னார். (W.)

83   talka sole of foot; tala, tola sole of shoe (Santali) talka = palm of the hand, ti talka (Santali.lex.) ti = the hand, arm (Santali.lex.) Rebus: talika = inventory, a list of articles, number, to count, to number; hor.ko talkhaetkoa = they are counting the people; mi~hu~ merom reak talikako hataoeda = they are taking the number of the cattle (Santali.lex.)

84   pajhaṛ = to sprout from a root; ; pagra = a cutting of sugar-cane used for planting (Santali) Grapheme: panje, panjho = the hand opened out; a claw, a paw; the five on a dice in play; paslī the hollow of the hand (G.) pañjali = with

outstretched hands, as token of reverence (Skt. prāñjali)(Pali.lex.) pañjā = the paw, the palm; the image of a hand worshipped and taken in procession during the Mohurrum festival (Te.)

85   pasra = a smithy, place where a black-smith works, to work as a blacksmith; kamar pasra = a smithy; pasrao lagao akata se ban:? Has the blacksmith begun to work? pasraedae = the blacksmith is at his work (Santali.lex.) pasra 'smithy' (Santali) pasra mered, pasāra mered = syn. of koțe mered = forged iron, in contrast to dul mered, cast iron (Mundari.)

86   kol, kolhe 'the koles, an aboriginal tribe of iron smelters akin to that of the Santals' (Santali) kor.a 'a boy, a young man' (Santali) kulhu 'a hindu caste, mostly oil men'; kulhu 'an oil press' (Santali) *kōlhu ' machine for pressing sugarcane or oilseeds '. Pk. kolluga -- , kolhua -- m. ' sugarcane press ', S. kolū m., P. kolhū, kuhulū m. ' oilpress, sugarcane press '; WPah. bhal. kō`lū m. ' oilpress ', N. kol; Or. kohliā, kolihā, liā ' sugarcane press '; Bi. kolh, hū, (Gaya) kelhū ' oilpress ', Mth. kōlh, Bhoj. kōlhu; H. kolhū, kolū m. ' sugarcane press, oilpress '; G. kohlu m. ' sugarcane press '. -- Deriv.: B. Or. kalu ' oil -- man (by caste) ', H. kolū m.*kōlhuvagāra -- , *kōlhuśālā -- .Addenda: *kōlhu -- : WPah.ktg. kóllhu m. ' sugar -- cane or oil press '. (CDIAL 3536). *kōlhuvagāra— 'mill house'. [*KŌLHU—, AGĀRA—] P.kolhār m. 'oil factory'; Bi. kolhuār 'sugarcane mill and boiling house'. (CDIAL 3537) *kōlhuśālā— 'pressing house

for sugarcane or oilseeds'. [*KŌLHU—, ŚALĀ—] Bi. kolsār 'sugarcane mill and boiling house'. (CDIAL 3538).

87   kul 'the tiger, felis tigris' (Santali) कोला [kōlā] m (Commonly कोल्हा) A jackal. कोल्हें [kōlhēṃ] n A jackal. Without reference to sex. Pr. अडलें कोल्हें मंगळ गाय Even the yelling jackal can sing pleasantly when he is in distress. कोल्हें लागलें Applied to a practical joke. केल्हेटेकणें or कोल्हेटेकण [kēlhēṭēkaṇē or ṅkōlhēṭēkaṇa] n Gen. in obl. cases with बस or ये, as कोल्हेटेकण्यास बसणें To sit cowering; to sit as a jackal.कोल्हेटेकण्यास येणें To be arrived at or to be approaching the infirmities of age. 2 To be approaching to setting;--used of the sun or the day, when the sun is conceived to be about that distance from the horizon as a jackal, when he rests on his hinder legs, is from the ground. कोल्हेभूंक [kōlhēbhūṅka] or -भोंक f (कोल्हा & भुंकणें To bark.) The yelling of jackals. 2 Early dawn; peep of day. कोल्हेहूक [kōlhēhūka] f The yelling of jackals. 2 fig. Assailing or setting upon with vehement vociferations. (Marathi)

88   Vikalpa: aḍaru twig; aḍiri small and thin branch of a tree; aḍari small branches (Ka.); aḍaru twig (Tu.)(DEDR 67). aḍar = splinter (Santali); rebus: aduru = native metal (Ka.) Vikalpa: kūdī, kūṭī bunch of twigs (Skt.lex.)

89   karaṭi, karuṭi, keruṭi fencing, school or gymnasium where wrestling and fencing are taught (Ta.);garaḍi, garuḍi fencing school (Ka.); garaḍi, garoḍi (Tu.); gariḍi, gariḍī id.,

fencing (Te.) (DEDR1262).

90   kharādī 'turner' (G.) कातारी or कांतारी [kātārī or kāntārī] m (कातणें) A turner. (Marathi) karaḍo, karāḍī 'a goldsmith's tool' (G.)

91   [√rī] Pk. rīi -- f. ' path, fashion '; Or. ria ' shallow narrow channel for catching fish in dry season '; G. rī f. ' method, manner '.Addenda: rītí -- 1: Md. rī ' a discharge ' or prob. der. rīyatē or riyáti. (CDIAL 10751) Rebus: rītí 'brass'.

92 सांगड [sāṅgaḍa] m f (संघट्ट S) f A body formed of two or more (fruits, animals, men) linked or joined together. A float composed of two canoes or boats bound together: also a link of two pompions &c. to swim or float by (Marathi) saṁghāṭayati ' joins together ' Sarvad., ' causes to collect ' Kathās. [√ghaṭ] Or. saṅghāṛibā ' to mix up many materials, stir boiling curry, tie two cattle together and leave to graze '. (CDIAL 12860) सांगडणें [sāṅgaḍaṇēṃ] v c (सांगड) To link, join, or unite together (boats, fruits, animals). 2 Freely. To tie or bind up or unto. (Marathi) सांगडणी [sāṅgaḍaṇī] f (Verbal of सांगडणें) Linking or joining together. saṁghāṭa m. ' fitting and joining of timber ' R. [√ghaṭ] Pa. nāvā -- saṅghāṭa -- , dāru -- s ' raft '; Pk. saṁghāḍa -- , ḍaga -- m., ḍī -- f. ' pair '; Ku. sīgāṛ m. ' doorframe '; N. saṅar, siṅhār ' threshold '; Or.saṅghāri ' pair of fish roes, two rolls of thread for twisting into the sacred thread, quantity of fuel sufficient to maintain the cremation fire '; Bi. sīghārā ' triangular packet of betel '; H. sīghāṛā m. ' piece of cloth folded in triangular shape '; G.

sāghāṛɔ m. ' lathe '; M. sāgaḍ f. ' a body formed of two or more fruits or animals or men &c. linked together, part of a turner's apparatus ', m.f. ' float made of two canoes joined together ' (LM 417 compares saggarai at Limurike in the Periplus, Tam. śaṅgaḍam, Tu. jaṅgala ' double -- canoe '), sāgāḍā m. ' frame of a building ', ḍī f. ' lathe '; Si. saṅgaḷa ' pair ',haṅguḷa, aṅg ' double canoe, raft '. Addenda: saṃghāṭa -- : Md. aṅgoḷi ' junction '? (CDIAL 12859)

[93] can:katam = to scrape (Ta.), san:kad.a (Tu.), san:kaṭam = to scrape (Skt.) sàngīn सं;गीन् adj. c.g. stony, made of stone; firm, solid, strong (Śiv. 1778; Rām. 131, sangīn-bunā, with firm foundations); severe, excessive; grave, serious (K.Pr. 138). (Kashmiri) संगीन [saṅgīna] a (P) Built or made of stone. 2 Hard, firm, solid, compact; opp. to flimsy and fragile. 3 fig. Firm, decided, definite, peremptory;-as speech, a measure. 4 Complete, entire, full, perfect. See सांग. सांग [sāṅga] a (S स & अंग) That is with all its members, parts, wings, appendages, and appertaining particulars; complete,

[94]   Rajesh P. N. Rao*, Nisha Yadav, Mayank N. Vahia, Hrishikesh Joglekar,R. Adhikari, Iravatham Mahadevan, 2009, Entropic Evidence for Linguistic Structure in the Indus Script, Science 23 April 2009; R. P. N. Rao, N. Yadav, M. N. Vahia, H. Joglekar, R. Adhikari, and I. Mahadevan, 2009 http://www.sciencemag.org/cgi/rapidpdf/1170391v1.pdf: A Markov model of the Indus script, PNAS 106, 13685-13690

95   http://www.pnas.org/content/106/33/13685.full.pdf+html

96   Kenoyer, J. Mark and Richard H. Meadow, Inscribed objects from Harappa excavations 1986-2007, in: Parpo, Asko, BM Pande and Petteri Koskikallio, 2010, Corpus of Indus Seals and Inscriptions 3.1 Supplement to Mohenjo-daro and Harapa, Helsinki, Suomalainen Tiedeakatemia, pp. xliv, lvi; fn.1

97   see Kenoyer & Meadow, p. xlviii)." (ibid., p.xv; fn. 47)

98   ibid., p. lvi

99   Ute Frank, 2010, From the Oxus to the Indus: two compartmented seals from Mohenjo-daro (Pakistan), in: Parpo, Asko, BM Pande and Petteri Koskikallio, 2010, Corpus of Indus Seals and Inscriptions 3.1 Supplement to Mohenjo-daro and Harapa, Helsinki, Suomalainen Tiedeakatemia, pp. xvii to xliii; p. xxxv, p. xxxvii

100   Samir S. Patel, Insider: The Indus Enigma, in: Archaeology, Volume 63 Number 2, March/April 2010.

101   Emeneau, 1956; Kuiper, 1948; Masica, 1971; Przyludski, 1929; Southworth, 2005.

102   cf. Epigraphia, 8 slide shows of Corpus of Indus inscriptions.   http://sites.google.com/site/kalyan97/epigraphica-sarasvati

103   kapṓta m. ' pigeon, dove ' RV., aka -- m. ' small do. ' MBh. Pa. kapōta -- m., tī -- f. ' pigeon ', taka -- m., tikā -- f. ' small do. ', Aś. kapota -- m., Pk. kavōya -- , ōḍa -- m., Ḍ. kaū m., Ash. kewī́k, Kt.kawéki, Pr. kowroṭī́, Paš. kawayā́, Kal. rumb. kohóu obl. hólūna, urt. kɔhɔ̄r, Kho. kowór; L. P. kovī

m. ' small dove ', P. kgr. kuvī m.; Si. (DhpAGp. 18832) kovo -

- , vu -- ' dove ', kobō (b due to Tam. influence? H. Smith JA

1950, 188). -- Early loan from Ir. in Wg. kuptə ' white dove ',

Gaw. kōpotá ' pigeon ' Morgenstierne BSOS viii 668.

*kapōtra -- , kā′pōta -- . (CDIAL 2753) *kapōtra ' pigeon '.

[Cf.Pahl. kapōtar: kapóta --] (CDIAL 2754) Tu. puda dove,

Ta. purā, pura, puravam, puravu dove, pigeon. Ma. pirāvu,

prāvu id. Ka. horasu a kind of pigeon; (PBh.) porasu pigeon.

pigeon.Te. burra- piṭṭe a sort of pigeon. (DEDR 4334) Kuwi

(Ṭ.) piṛska sparrow; (Isr.) prīskapoṭa a kind of bird. (DEDR

4190) Konḍa poṭi bird. Pe. poṭi id. Manḍ. puṭi id. Kui poṭa id.

Kuwi (F.) pōta, (S.) potha, (Su. P.) poṭṭa, (Isr.) poṭa id.

(DEDR 4489)

Potam.   A wild wood-pigeon.
Varieties of wild wood-pigeons.
Barge potam. } Turtur Cambayensis, the little
Thikri potam. }   brown dove.
Pondhər potam.
Mala potam. }
Kudbur potam. } The Ring dove.
Tilai potam. }
Kēndrō potam.   The spotted dove, Turtur
     Suratensis.

Bhosko potam.
Kisār potam. } The Imperial pigeon, Carpo-
Gadru gum. }   phaga sylvatica.
Toyo dedger potam. } Cf. barge potam.
Sandi kakar potam. }
Note. The Green pigeon (hubar), Crocopus
     chlorigaster, and the Blue Rock pigeon,
     (parwa) Columba intermedia, are not in-
     cluded among the pigeons by Santals.

Santali glosses.

104   ಸೃಔ mosale 'wild crocodile or alligator. S. gharyālu

m. ' long -- snouted porpoise '; N. ghariyāl ' crocodile'
(Telugu)'; A. B. ghãriyāl ' alligator ', Or. ghariāḷa, H. gharyāl,
ghariār m. (CDIAL 4422) கரவு karavu, n. < கரா. cf. grāha.
Alligator; முதலை. கரவார்தடம் (திவ். திருவாய். 8, 9, 9). கரா
karā, n. prob. grāha. 1. A species of alligator; முதலை.
கராவதன் காலினைக்கதுவ (திவ். பெரியதி. 2, 3, 9). 2. Male
alligator; ஆண்முதலை. (பிங்.) கராம் karām n. prob. grāha. 1.
A species of alligator ; முதலைவகை. முதலையு மிடங்கருங்
கராமும் (குறிஞ்சிப். 257). 2. Male alligator; ஆண் முதலை.
(திவா.)

105   Pali: ayakāra 'iron-smith'.] Both ayaskāma and
ayaskāra are attested in Panini (Pan. viii.3.46; ii.4.10).
WPah. bhal. kamīṇ m.f. labourer (man or woman) ; MB.
kāmiṇā labourer (CDIAL 2902) N. kāmi blacksmith (CDIAL
2900).

106   khār 1 खार् । लोहकारः m. (sg. abl. khāra 1 खार; the pl.
dat. of this word is khāran 1 खारन्, which is to be
distinguished from khāran 2, q.v., s.v.), a blacksmith, an iron
worker (cf. bandūka-khār, p. 111b, l. 46; K.Pr. 46; H. xi, 17);
a farrier (El.). This word is often a part of a name, and in
such case comes at the end (W. 118) as in Wahab khār,
Wahab the smith (H. ii, 12; vi, 17). khāra-basta खार-बस्ऱ्त ।
चर्मप्रसेविका f. the skin bellows of a blacksmith. -būṭhü -
ब&above;ऴ&below; । लोहकारभित्तिः f. the wall of a blacksmith's
furnace or hearth. -bāy -बाय् । लोहकारपत्नी f. a blacksmith's
wife (Gr.Gr. 34). -dŏkuru; । लोहकारायोघनः m. a blacksmith's

hammer, a sledge-hammer.-gȧji -ग&above;जि&below; or -güjü; । लोह्कारचुल्लिः f. a blacksmith's furnace or hearth. -hāl -हाल् । लोह्कारकन्दुः f. (sg. dat. -höjü -हा&above;जू&below;), a blacksmith's smelting furnace; cf. hāl 5. -kūrü; । लोह्कारकन्या f. a blacksmith's daughter. -koṭu; । लोह्कारपुत्रः m. the son of a blacksmith, esp. a skilful son, who can work at the same profession. -küṭü; । लोह्कारकन्या f. a blacksmith's daughter, esp. one who has the virtues and qualities properly belonging to her father's profession or caste. -më̆tsü लोह्कारमृत्तिका f. (for 2, see [khāra 3]), 'blacksmith's earth,' i.e. iron-ore. -nĕcyuwu -न्यचिवु&below; । लोह्कारात्मजः m. a blacksmith's son. -nay -नय् । लोह्कारनालिका f. (for khāranay 2, see [khārun]), the trough into which the blacksmith allows melted iron to flow after smelting. -tsañĕ लोह्कारशान्ताङ्गाराः f.pl. charcoal used by blacksmiths in their furnaces. -wān लोह्कारापणः m. a blacksmith's shop, a forge, smithy (K.Pr. 3). -waṭh -वठ् । आघाताधारशिला m. (sg. dat. -waṭas -वटि), the large stone used by a blacksmith as an anvil. (Kashmiri) kāruvu = mechanic, artisan, Viśvakarma, the celestial artisan (Te.); కారువు [kāruvu] kāruvu. [Skt.] n. An artist, artificer. An agent; gāre = affix of noun denoting one who does it, e.g. samagāre = cobbler (Tu.); garuva (Ka.); gar_uva = an important man (Te.) cf. –ka_ra suffix. 'worker' (Skt.) kāri— m. 'artisan, worker' Pāṇ. 2. f. 'action, work' Bhaṭṭ. [√KṚ 1] 1. P.kārī m. 'worker'. 2. Kt. kår 'work', Wg.kọ̄, Pr. kǟ; S. kāri f. 'work, occupation, use'; L. kār f. 'work'; P. kārī f. 'remedy';

Or. kāri 'work'. (CDIAL 3064) karuvu n. Melting: what is melted (Te.)

Ta. ayil iron. Ma. ayir, ayiram any ore. Ka. aduru native metal. Tu. ajirda karba very hard iron (DEDR 192).

107 कारु [kāru] m (S) An artificer or artisan. 2 A common term for the twelve बलुतेदार q. v. Also कारुनारु m pl q. v. in नारुकारु. (Marathi) कारिगर, कारिगार, कारागीर, कारेगार, कारागार [kārigara, kārigāra, kārāgīra, kārēgāra, kārāgāra] m (P) A good workman, a clever artificer or artisan. 2 Affixed as an honorary designation to the names of Barbers, and sometimes of सुतार, गवंडी, & चितारी. 3 Used laxly as adj and in the sense of Effectual, availing, effective of the end. बलुतें [balutēṃ] n A share of the corn and garden-produce assigned for the subsistence of the twelve public servants of a village, for whom see below. 2 In some districts. A share of the dues of the hereditary officers of a village, such as पाटील, कुळकरणी &c.

बलुतेदार or बलुता [balutēdāra or balutā] or त्या m (बलुतें &c.) A public servant of a village entitled to बलुतें. There are twelve distinct from the regular Governmentofficers पाटील, कुळकरणी &c.; viz. सुतार, लोहार, महार, मांग (These four constitute पहिली or थोरली कास or वळ the first division. Of three of them each is entitled to चार पाचुंदे, twenty bundles of Holcus or the thrashed corn, and the महार to आठ पाचुंदे); कुंभार, चाम्हार, परीट, न्हावी constitute दुसरी orमधली कास or वळ, and are entitled, each, to तीन पाचुंदे; भट, मुलाणा, गुरव, कोळी

form तिसरी or धाकटी कास or वळ, and have, each, दोन पाचुंदे. Likewise there are twelve अलुते or supernumerary public claimants, viz. तेली, तांबोळी, साळी, माळी, जंगम, कळवांत, डवऱ्या, ठाकर, घडशी, तराळ, सोनार, चौगुला. Of these the allowance of corn is not settled. The learner must be prepared to meet with other enumerations of the बलुतेदार (e. g. पाटील, कुळ-करणी, चौधरी, पोतदार, देशपांड्या, न्हावी, परीट, गुरव, सुतार, कुंभार, वेसकर, जोशी; also सुतार, लोहार, चाम्हार, कुंभार as constituting the first-class and claiming the largest division of बलुतें; next न्हावी, परीट, कोळी, गुरव as constituting the middle class and claiming a subdivision of बलुतें; lastly, भट, मुलाणा, सोनार, मांग; and, in the Konkaṇ, yet another list); and with other accounts of the assignments of corn; for this and many similar matters, originally determined diversely, have undergone the usual influence of time, place, and ignorance. Of the बलुतेदार in the Indápúr pergunnah the list and description stands thus:--First class, सुतार, लोहार, चाम्हार, महार; Second, परीट, कुंभार, न्हावी, मांग; Third, सोनार, मुलाणा, गुरव, जोशी, कोळी, रामोशी; in all fourteen, but in no one village are the whole fourteen to be found or traced. In the Pandharpúr districts the order is:-- पहिली or थोरली वळ (1st class); महार, सुतार, लोहार, चाम्हार, दुसरी or मधली वळ(2nd class); परीट, कुंभार, न्हावी, मांग, तिसरी or धाकटी वळ (3rd class); कुळकरणी, जोशी, गुरव, पोतदार; twelve बलुते and of अलुते there are eighteen. According to Grant Duff, the बलतेदार are सुतार, लोहार, चाम्हार, मांग, कुंभार, न्हावी, परीट, गुरव, जोशी, भाट, मुलाणा; and the अलुते are सोनार, जंगम, शिंपी, कोळी,

तराळ or वेसकर, माळी, डवऱ्यागोसावी, घडशी, रामोशी, तेली, तांबोळी, गोंधळी. In many villages of Northern Dakhaṇ the महार receives the बलुतें of the first, second, and third classes; and, consequently, besides the महार, there are but nine बलुतेदार. The following are the only अलुतेदार or नारू now to be found;-- सोनार, मांग, शिंपी, भट गोंधळी, कोर- गू, कोतवाल, तराळ, but of the अलुतेदार & बलुते- दार there is much confused intermixture, the अलुतेदार of one district being the बलुतेदार of another, and vice versâ. (The word कास used above, in पहिली कास, मध्यम कास, तिसरी कास requires explanation. It means Udder; and, as the बलुतेदार are, in the phraseology of endearment or fondling, termed वासरें (calves), their allotments or divisions are figured by successive bodies of calves drawing at the कास or under of the गांव under the figure of a गाय or cow.) (Marathi)

kruciji 'smith' (Old Church Slavic)

[108] सवा हात लेखणीचा का0 A term of ironical commendation for a clerk.कारकुनी [kārakunī] f (कारकून) The office or business of Kárkún. 2 Remuneration to a Kárkún for service rendered. 3 The profits or fees (of Kárkúns) on services done, articles bought &c. 4 Any extra cess laid to pay Kárkún-service. 5 fig. Economizing; careful and thrifty management. कारकुनी [kārakunī] a (कारकून) Relating to Kárkún--mode of writing &c. कारकुनीकावा [kārakunīkāvā] m कारकुनीमत n The astuteness, chicanery, or trickery pertaining to the Writerclass. Hence Craftiness or wiliness gen.

[109] CL Fabri, 1935, The punch-marked coins: a survival of the

Indus civilization The Punch-Marked Coins: A Survival of the Indus Civilization, *The Journal of the Royal Asiatic Society of Great Britain and Ireland*, No. 2 (Apr., 1935), pp. 307-318
Royal Asiatic Society of Great Britain and Ireland
http://www.jstor.org/stable/25201111

[110] Ta. koṭṭakai shed with sloping roofs, cow-stall; marriage pandal; koṭṭam cattle-shed; koṭṭil cow-stall, shed, hut; (STD) koṭambe feeding place for cattle. Ma. koṭṭil cowhouse, shed, workshop, house. Ka. koṭṭage, koṭige, koṭṭige stall or outhouse (esp. for cattle), barn, room. Koḍ. koṭṭï shed. Tu.koṭṭa hut or dwelling of Koragars; koṭya shed, stall. Te. koṭṭāmu stable for cattle or horses; koṭṭāyi thatched shed. Kol. (Kin.) koṛka, (SR.) korkā cowshed; (Pat., p. 59) konṭoḍi henhouse. Nk. khoṭa cowshed. Nk. (Ch.) koṛka id. Go. (Y.) koṭa, (Ko.) koṭam (pl. koṭak) id. (Voc. 880); (SR.) koṭkashed; (W. G. Mu. Ma.) koṛka, (Ph.) korka, kurka cowshed (Voc. 886); (Mu.) koṭorla, koṭorli shed for goats (Voc. 884). Malt. koṭa hamlet. / Influenced by Skt. goṣṭha-

Ta. koṭi banner, flag, streamer; kōṭu summit of a hill, peak, mountain; kōṭai mountain; kōṭar peak, summit of a tower; kuvaṭu mountain, hill, peak;kuṭumi summit of a mountain, top of a building, crown of the head, bird's crest, tuft of hair (esp. of men), crown, projecting corners on which a door swings.Ma. koṭi top, extremity, flag, banner, sprout; kōṭu end; kuvaṭu hill, mountain-top; kuṭuma, kuṭumma narrow point, bird's crest, pivot of door used as hinge, lock of hair worn as caste distinction; koṭṭu head of a bone. Ko. koṛy flag on temple; koṭ top tuft of hair (of Kota boy, brahman), crest of bird; kuṭ clitoris.To. kwïṭ tip, nipple, child's back lock of hair. Ka. kuḍi pointed end, point, extreme tip of a creeper, sprout, end, top, flag, banner; guḍi point, flag, banner;kuḍilu sprout, shoot; kōḍu a point, the peak or top of a hill; koṭṭu a point, nipple, crest, gold ornament worn by women in their plaited hair; koṭṭa state of being extreme; koṭṭa-kone the extreme point; (Hav.) koḍi sprout; Koḍ. koḍi top (of mountain, tree, rock, table), rim of pit or tank, flag. Tu. koḍi point, end, extremity, sprout, flag; koḍipuni to bud, germinate; (B-K.) koḍipu, koḍipel; a sprout; koḍirè the top-leaf; koṭṭu cock's comb, peacock's tuft. Te.koḍi tip, top, end or point of a flame; koṭṭa-kona the very end or extremity. Kol. (Kin.) koṛi point. Pa. kūṭor cock's comb. Go. (Tr.) koḍḍī tender tip or shoot of a plant or tree; koḍḍi (S.) end, tip, (Mu.) tip of bow; (A.) koḍi point (Voc. 891). Malt. qoṛgo comb of a cock; ? qóru the end, the top (as of a tree). Cf. 2081 Ta. konṭai and 2200 Ta Ta. konṭai and 2200 Ta. kōṭu.(DEDR 2058)

111   cf. PS Vermaak, 2008, Guabba, the Meluhhan village in Mesopotamia, Journal of Semitics, 17/2, pp. 553-570.

112   Mohenjodaro. Silver seal. Mackay 1938: Vol. 1, p. 348, Vol. 2, Pl. XC,1; XCVI, 520. Altyn-depe. Silver seal. Pictograph of ligatured animal with three heads. ·Ras-al-Junyz Copper seal. ·Harappa, raised script,on eight inscribed copper tablets H94-2198 (After Fig. 4.14 in JM

Kenoyer, 1998). Figures can be seen at
http://sites.google.com/site/kalyan97/seafaring-meluhhan

113   Wilson, Thomas (Curator, Department of Prehistoric Anthropology, U.S. National Museum) 1896,The Swastika: The Earliest Known Symbol, and Its Migrations; with Observations on the Migration of Certain Industries in Prehistoric Times. In Annual report of the Board of Regents of the Smithsonian Institution. Washington DC http://fax.libs.uga.edu/J84xSl3x1/

114   dula दुल । युग्मम् m. a pair, a couple, esp. of two similar things (Rām. 966) (Kashmiri) Vikalpa: 1. saṁghāṭa m. ' fitting and joining of timber ' R. [√ghaṭ] Pa. nāvā -- saṅghāṭa -- , dāru -- s ' raft '; Pk. saṁghāḍa -- , ḍaga -- m., ḍī -- f. ' pair ' (CDIAL 12859) 2. barea = two (Ka.); Rebus: baṛea = blacksmith (Santali)

115   miṇḍāl 'markhor' (Tōrwālī) meḍho a ram, a sheep (G.)(CDIAL 10120) miṇḍ 'ram' (Pktl.); mēḍha (G.) cf. mēṣa = goat (Skt.lex.) மேடம்¹ mēṭam, n. < mēṣa. 1. Sheep, ram; ஆடு. (பிங்.) 2. Aries of the zodiac; ராசிமண்டலத்தின் முதற்பகுதி. (பிங்.) 3. The first solar month. See சித்திரை¹, 2. மேடமாமதி (கம்பரா. திருவவதா. 110) ēḍika. [Tel. of Tam ஈடு.] n. A ram (Telugu) मेंढा [mēṇḍhā] m (मेष S through H) A male sheep, a ram or tup. (Marathi) meṇḍa The Ved. (Sk.) word for ram is meṣa] 1. a ram D i.9; J iv.250, 353 (°visāṇa -- dhanu, a bow consisting of a ram's horn). -- °patha Npl. "ram's road" Nd1 155=415. -- °yuddha ram fight D i.6. -- 2. a

groom, elephant -- driver in cpd. hatthi° elephants' keeper J iii.431; v.287; vi.489. (Pali)

116   kodiyum 'heifer' (G.) kodiyum; खोंड [khōṇḍa] m A young bull, a bullcalf. (Marathi) [kōḍe] kōḍe. [Tel.] n. A bullcalf. *-దూడ. A young bull. kāru-kōḍe. [Tel.] n. A bull in its prime. [kōḍiya] G. godhɔ m. ' bull ', dhũ n. ' young bull ', OG. godhalu m. ' entire bull ', G. godhliyũ n. ' young bull ' (CDIAL 4315). Te. kōḍiya, kōḍe young bull; adj. male (e.g. kōḍe dūḍabull calf), young, youthful; kōḍek;ḍu a young man. Kol. (Haig) kōḍē bull. Nk. khoṛe male calf. Konda kōḍi cow; kōṛe young bullock. Pe.kōḍi cow. Mand. kūḍi id. Kui kōḍi id., ox. Kuwi (F.) kōḍi cow; (S.) kajja kōḍi bull ; (Su. P.) kōḍi cow (DEDR 2199) cf. koṛa 'a boy, a young man' (Santali)

117   damya ' tameable ', m. ' young bullock to be tamed ' Mn. [~ *dāmiya -- . -- √dam] Pa. damma -- ' to be tamed (esp. of a young bullock) '; Pk. damma -- ' to be tamed '; S. ḍamu ' tamed '; -- ext. -- ḍa -- : A. damrā ' young bull ', dāmuri ' calf '; B. dāmṛā ' castrated bullock '; Or. dāmaṛī ' heifer ', dāmaṛiā ' bullcalf, young castrated bullock ', dāmuṛ, ṛi ' young bullock '. Addenda: damya -- : WPah.ktg. dām m. ' young ungelt ox '.(CDIAL 6184)

118   Glyph: *ḍaṅgara1 ' cattle '. 2. *ḍaṅgara -- . [Same as ḍaṅ- gara -- 2 s.v. *ḍagga -- 2 as a pejorative term for cattle] 1. K. ḍangur m. ' bullock ', L. ḍaṅgur, (Ju.) ḍ̠āgar m. ' horned cattle '; P. ḍaṅgar m. ' cattle ', Or. ḍaṅgara; Bi. ḍ̠āgar

' old worn -- out beast, dead cattle ', dhūr ḍāgar ' cattle in general '; Bhoj. ḍāṅgar ' cattle '; H. ḍāgar, ḍāgrā m. ' horned cattle '.2. H. dāgar m. = prec. (CDIAL 5526)

119   meṛed (Mundari); meḍ 'iron' (Ho) meṛed, mẽṛed iron; enga meṛed soft iron; sanḍi meṛed hard iron; ispāt meṛed steel; dul meṛed cast iron; i meṛed rusty iron, also the iron of which weights are cast; bica meṛed iron extracted from stone ore; bali meṛed iron extracted from sand ore; meṛed-bica = iron stone ore, in contrast to bali-bica, iron sand ore (Mu.lex.)

120   Rebus: ḍāṅgar 'blacksmith' (H.); dhā~gar., dhā~gar blacksmith; digger of wells (H.) Nepali. डाङ्रे ḍāṅre , or ḍāgre, adj. Large; lazy; working with- out thoroughness or seriousness; -- s. A partic. kind of bird, the mainā; -- a contemptuous term for a blacksmith डाङ्रो ḍāṅro , or ḍāgro, s. A term of contempt used for a blacksmith (kāmi). [v.s.v. ḍāṅre.] ḍān:ro = a term of contempt for a blacksmith (N.)(CDIAL 5524).   ṭhākur = blacksmith (Mth.) (CDIAL 5488). ठाकूर [ṭhākūra] m (ठक्कुर S through H) A tribe or an individual of t. They inhabit woods and wilds (esp. of N. Konkaṇ). 2 A chief among certain castes of Rájpúts, Bhíls &c., a title or compellation of respect. 3 The Supreme God: also an idol or a god. 4 A family priest among certain tribes of Shúdras. ठाकूरजी [ṭhākūrajī] m (ठक्कुर S) A name for the Deity. Among Byrágís. ठाकूरद्वार [ṭhākūradvāra] n sometimes ठाकूरदारा m (ठाकूर The Deity, द्वार A door.) Among Byrágís. A

temple or idol-house: also the adytum or penetralia.ठकूरदारा मांडून बसणें To make an outlay or great display (of sanctity or piety). ṭhakkaru, ṭhakkaruḍu = a deity; an idol; an honorific title same as ṭhākūru = a father; a religious preceptor (Te.lex.) ṭhākur blacksmith (Mth.)(CDIAL 5488).

121   baṭhi furnace for smelting ore (the same as kuṭhi) (Santali) bhaṭa = an oven, kiln, furnace; make an oven, a furnace; iṭa bhaṭa = a brick kiln; kun:kal bhaṭa a potter's kiln; cun bhaṭa = a lime kiln; cun tehen dobon bhaṭaea = we shall prepare the lime kiln today (Santali); bhaṭṭha_ (H.) bhart = a mixed metal of copper and lead; bhart-i_ya_ = a barzier, worker in metal; bhaṭ, bhrāṣṭra = oven, furnace (Skt.) me~r.he~t bat.i = iron (Ore) furnaces. [Synonyms are: mẽt = the eye, rebus for: the dotted circle (Santali.lex) baṭha [H. baṭṭhī (Sad.)] any kiln, except a potter's kiln, which is called coa; there are four kinds of kiln: cunabat.ha, a lime-kin, it.abat.ha, a brick-kiln, e_re_bat.ha, a lac kiln, kuilabaṭha, a charcoal kiln; trs. Or intrs., to make a kiln; cuna rapamente ciminaupe baṭhakeda? How many limekilns did you make? baṭha-sen:gel = the fire of a kiln; baṭi [H. Sad. baṭṭhi, a furnace for distilling) used alone or in the cmpds. Arkibut.i and bat.iora, all meaning a grog-shop; occurs also in ilibaṭi, a (licensed) rice-beer shop (Mundari.lex.) bhaṭi = liquor from mohwa flowers

(Santali)

122   Yale tablet.YBCE.5447; dia. c. 2.5 cm. Possibly from Ur. Buchanan, studies Landsberger, 1965, p. 204; A seal impression was found on an *inscribed tablet (called Yale tablet) dated to the tenth year of Gungunum, King of Larsa, in southern Babylonia--that is, 1923 BCE according to the most commonly accepted ('middle') chronology of the period. The design in the impression closely matches that in a stamp seal found on the Failaka island in the Persian Gulf, west of the delta of the Shatt al Arab, which is formed by the confluence of the Tigris and Euphrates rivers.

123   batak = a duck (G.) vartikā = quail (RV.); wuwrc partridge (Ash.); barti = quail, partridge (Kho.); vaṭṭaka_ quail (Pali); vaṭṭaya (Pkt.) (CDIAL 11361).

124   khonḍu । खण्डितः, विकलावयवः adj. (f. khünḍü 1, sg. dat. khanjĕ 1 खंज्य), broken, divided into parts; hence, deprived of a part or limb or member, maimed, mutilated; unevenly formed, irregularly angled. (Kashmiri)

125   baṭa = a quail, or snipe, coturuix coturnix cot; bonḍe baṭa = a large quail; dak baṭa = the painted

stripe, rostraluta benghalensis bengh; guṇḍri baṭa = a small type, coloured like a guṇḍri (quail); kũk baṭa = a medium-sized type; kheḍra baṭa = the smallest of all; laṇḍha baṭa = a small type (Santali.lex.) baṭai (Nag.); baṭer (Has.); [H. baṭai or bat.er perdix olivacea; Sad. baṭai] coturnix coromandelica, the blackbreasted or rain-quail; two other kinds of quail are called respectigely: hur.in bat.ai and gerea baṭai (Mundari.lex.) baṭer = quail (Ku.B.); baṭara, batara = the grey quail (Or.)(CDIAL 11350).

126   MBh. Pa. kanaka -- n., Pk. kaṇaya -- n., MB. kanayā ODBL 659, Si. kanā EGS 36.(CDIAL 2717) కనకము [kanakamu] kanakamu. [Skt.] n. Gold. (Telugu) கனகம் kaṉakam, n. < kanaka. 1. Gold; பொன். காரார்வண்ணன் கனகமனையானும் (தேவா. 502, 9 (Tamil) kanaka (nt.) [cp. Sk. kanaka; Gr. knh_kos yellow; Ags. hunig=E. honey. See also kañcana] gold, usually as uttatta° molten gold; said of the colour of the skin Bu i.59; Pv iii.32; J v.416; PvA 10 suvaṇṇa).-- agga gold -- crested J v.156; -- chavin of golden complexion J vi.13; -- taca (adj.) id. J v.393; -- pabhā golden splendour Bu xxiii.23; -- vimāna a fairy palace of gold VvA 6; PvA 47, 53; -- sikharī a golden peak, in °rājā king of the golden peaks (i. e. Himālayas): Dāvs iv.30. (Pali) Vikalpa: kaṉ 'copper work' (Ta.)

127   Vikalpa: khareḍo = a currycomb (G.) Rebus: kharādī ' turner' (G.) kharkhara खर॒ऽखर । अश्वादिकण्डूयनयन्त्रम् m. a

curry-comb (K.Pr. 15) (Kashmiri) Vikalpa: खोरें [khōrēṃ] n A sort of hoe or dung and rubbish scraper. Pr. खोरें माती आपल्याकडे उसपणें (Earth dug out by a hoe comes towards one's self.) Used where a man's working or doing is for selfish ends. 2 A narrow valley; a rude hollow between hills. खोरें लावणें See खोरणें लावणें under खोरणें. खोरणें [khōraṇēṃ] n A sort of scraper or rubbish-hoe. 2 A stick kept as a fire-raker. खो0 लावणें To make large demands (upon one's benevolence &c.); to draw away (his money) by shovelsfull. (Marathi) kṣurapra ' sharp -- edged like a razor ' BhP., m. ' sharp- edged arrow ' MBh., ' sharp -- edged knife ' Pañcat., ' a sort of hoe ' lex. [Cf. *prakṣurikā -- . -- kṣurá+?] Pa. khurappa -- m. ' arrow with a horseshoe head '; Pk. khurappa -- , ruppa -- m. ' a kind of arrow, knife for cutting grass '; S. khurpo m. ' a pot -- scraper '; P. khurpā m., pī f. ' pot -- scraper, grubber for grass '; N. khurpo ' sickle ', pi ' weeding knife '; B. khurpā ' spud for grubbing up grass ' (Xkhanítra -- q.v.), Or. khurapa, pā, pi, rupā, pi;; Bi. khurpā ' blade of hoe ', pī ' small hoe for weeding '; Mth. khurpā, pī ' scraper '; H. khurpā m. ' weeding knife ', pī f. ' small do. '; G. kharpɔ m. ' scraper ', pī f. ' grubber ' (X kāpvũ in karpī f. ' weeding tool '); M. khurpẽ n. ' curved grubbing hoe ',pī f. ' grub -- axe '. -- Deriv. H. khurapnā, rupnā ' to scrape up grass '; G. kharapvũ ' to cut, dig, remove with a scraper '; M. khurapṇẽ ' to grub up '. (CDIAL 3730) Ta. kurappam currycomb. Ma. kurappam, kurappan id. Ka. korapa, gorapa id. Te. kurapamu, korapamu, gorapamu id. / ? Cf. Turner, CDIAL, no. 3730, kṣurapra- ('scraper'-meanings). (DEDR 1771).

Glyph: kāmsako, kāmsiyo = a large sized comb (G.) Vikalpa: kaṅghā m. ' large comb (P.)

Rebus: kaṁsa = bronze (Te.) kaŋsa [cp. Sk. kaŋsa; of uncertain etym., perhaps of Babylonian origin, cp. hirañña] 1. bronze Miln 2; magnified by late commentators occasionally into silver or gold. Thus J vi.504 (silver) and J i.338; iv.107; vi.509 (gold), considered more suitable to a fairy king. -- 2. a bronze gong Dh 134 (DhA iii.58). -- 3. a "bronze," i. e. a bronze coin worth 4 kahāpaṇas Vin iv.255, 256. See Rhys Davids, Coins and Measures §§ 12, 22. -- "Golden bronze" in a fairy tale at Vv 54 is explained by Dhammapāla VvA 36 as "bells." -- It is doubtful whether brass was known in the Ganges valley when the earlier books were composed; but kaŋsa may have meant metal as opposed to earthenware. (Pali) Vikalpa: kan:g = brazier, fireplace (K.)(IL 1332) Portable brazier ka~_guru, ka~_gar (Ka.) whence, large brazier = kan:gar (K.)

128   Rebus: kaṁsá1 m. ' metal cup ' AV., m.n. ' bell -- metal ' Pat. as in S., but would in Pa. Pk. and most NIA. lggs. collide with kā´ṁsya -- to which L. P. testify and under which the remaining forms for the metal are listed. 2. *kaṁsikā -- .1. Pa. kaṁsa -- m. ' bronze dish '; S. kañjho m. ' bellmetal '; A. kāh ' gong '; Or. kãsā ' big pot of bell -- metal ';

OMarw. kāso (= kā -- ?) m. ' bell -- metal tray for food, food ';
G. kāsā m. pl. ' cymbals '; -- perh. Woṭ. kasóṭ m. ' metal pot '
Buddruss Woṭ 109. 2. Pk. kaṁsiā -- f. ' a kind of musical
instrument '; A. kāhi ' bell -- metal dish '; G. kāśī f. ' bell --
metal cymbal ',kāśiɔ m. ' open bellmetal pan ' kā´ṁsya -- ; -
- *kaṁsāvatī -- ? Addenda: kaṁsá -- 1: A. kāh also ' gong '
or < kā´ṁsya – (CDIAL 2576). kāṁsya ' made of bell -- metal
' KātyŚr., n. ' bell -- metal ' Yājñ., ' cup of bell -- metal ' MBh.,
aka -- n. ' bell -- metal '. 2. *kāṁsiya -- .[kaṁsá -- 1] 1. Pa.
kaṁsa -- m. (?) ' bronze ', Pk. kaṁsa -- , kāsa -- n. ' bell --
metal, drinking vessel, cymbal '; L. (Jukes) kājā adj. ' of
metal ', awāṇ. kāsā ' jar ' (← E with -- s-- , not ñj); N. kāso '
bronze, pewter, white metal ', kas -- kuṭ ' metal alloy '; A. kāh
' bell -- metal ', B. kāsā, Or. kāsā, Bi. kāsā; Bhoj. kās ' bell --
metal ',kāsā ' base metal '; H. kās, kāsā m. ' bell -- metal ',
G. kāsũ n., M. kāsẽ n.; Ko. kāśẽ n. ' bronze '; Si. kasa ' bell -
- metal '. 2. L. kāihã m. ' bell -- metal ', P. kāssī, kāsī f., H.
kāsī f.*kāṁsyakara -- , kāṁsyakāra -- , *kāṁsyakuṇḍikā -- ,
kāṁsyatāla -- , *kāṁsyabhāṇḍa -- .Addenda: kāṁsya -- : A.
kāh also ' gong ', or < kaṁsá -- . (CDIAL 2987).*kāṁsyakara
' worker in bell -- metal '. [See next: kāṁsya -- , kará -- 1] L.
awāṇ. kasērā ' metal worker ', P. kaserā m. ' worker in
pewter ' (both ← E with -- s --); N. kasero ' maker of brass
pots '; Bi. H. kaserā m. ' worker in pewter '. (CDIAL 2988).
kāṁsyakāra m. ' worker in bell -- metal or brass ' Yājñ. com.,
kaṁsakāra -- m. BrahmavP. [kā´ṁsya -- , kāra -- 1] N. kasār

' maker of brass pots '; A. kãhār ' worker in bell -- metal '; B. kāsāri ' pewterer, brazier, coppersmith ', Or. kāsārī; H. kasārī m. ' maker of brass pots '; G.kãsārɔ, kas m. ' coppersmith '; M. kāsār, kās m. ' worker in white metal ', kāsārḍā m. ' contemptuous term for the same '. (CDIAL 2989)

129   kũdār, kũdāri (B.); kundāru (Or.); kundau to turn on a lathe, to carve, to chase; kundau dhiri = a hewn stone; kundau murhut = a graven image (Santali) kunda a turner's lathe (Skt.)(CDIAL 3295).

130   aṭaruka 'to burst, crack, sli off,fly open; aṭarcca ' splitting, a crack'; aṭarttuka 'to split, tear off, open (an oyster) (Ma.); a ḍ aruni 'to crack' (Tu.) (DEDR 66)

131   Glyph: M. ḍagar f. ' little hill, slope '.S. ṭakuru m. ' mountain ' N. ṭākuro, ri ' hill top '. P. ṭekrā m., rī f. ' rock, hill '; H. ṭekar, krā m. ' heap, hillock '; G. ṭekrɔ m., rī f. ' mountain, hillock '.6. K. ṭēg m. ' hillock, mound '.7. G. ṭũk ' peak '.8. M. ṭũg n. ' mound, lump '. -- Ext. -- r -- : Or. ṭuṅguri ' hillock '; M. ṭũgar n. ' bump, mound ' (see *uṭṭungara --); -- -- l -- : M. ṭũgal, gūl n.9. K. ḍaki f. ' hill, rising ground '. -- Ext. -- r -- : K. ḍakürü f. ' hill on a road '.10. Ext. -- r -- : Pk. ḍaggara -- m. ' upper terrace of a house '; 11. Ku. ḍãg, ḍāk ' stony land '; B. ḍāṅ ' heap ', ḍāṅgā ' hill, dry upland '; H. ḍãg f. ' mountain -- ridge '; M. ḍãg m.n., ḍāgaṇ, gāṇ, ḍãgāṇ n. ' hill -- tract '. -- Ext. -- r -- : N. ḍaṅgur ' heap '.12. M. ḍũg m. ' hill, pile ', gā m. ' eminence ', gī f. ' heap '. -- Ext. -- r -- : Pk. ḍumgara -- m. ' mountain '; Ku. ḍũgar, ḍũgrī; N. ḍuṅgar ' heap '; Or. ḍuṅguri ' hillock ', H. ḍũgar m., G. ḍũgar m., ḍũgrī f. 13. S.ḍũgaru m. '

hill ', H. M. ḍõgar m. 14. Pa. tuṅga -- ' high '; Pk. tuṁga -- ' high ', tuṁgīya -- m. ' mountain '; K. tŏng, tŏngu m. ' peak ', P. tuṅg f.; A. tuṅg ' importance '; Si. tuṅgu ' lofty, mountain '. -- Cf. uttuṅga -- ' lofty ' MBh. 15. K. thŏngu m. ' peak '. 16. H. ḍāg f. ' hill, precipice ', ḍāgī ' belonging to hill country '. Addenda: *ṭakka -- 3. 12. *ḍuṅga -- : S.kcch. ḍūṅghar m. ' hillock '. (CDIAL 5423). unc An eminence, a mount, a little hill (Marathi). ṭākuro = hill top (N.); ṭāngī = hill, stony country (Or.); ṭān:gara = rocky hilly land (Or.); ḍān:gā = hill, dry upland (B.); ḍā~g = mountain-ridge (H.)(CDIAL 5476). Marathi. डांग [ḍāṅga] m n (H Peak or summit of a hill.)

[132] ḍān:ro = a term of contempt for a blacksmith (N.)(CDIAL 5524). ṭhākur = blacksmith (Mth.) (CDIAL 5488).ḍāṅgar 'blacksmith' (H.); Nepali. डांड्रे ḍāṅre , or ḍāgre, adj. Large; lazy; working with- out thoroughness or seriousness; -- s. A partic. kind of bird, the mainā; -- a contemptuous term for a blacksmith डांड्रो ḍāṅro , or ḍāgro, s. A term of contempt used for a blacksmith (kāmi). [v.s.v. ḍāṅre.] ḍhā~gar., dhā~gar blacksmith; digger of wells (H.)

133   Pa. kōḍ (pl. kōḍul) horn; Ka. kōḍu horn, tusk, branch of a tree; kōṟ horn Tu. kōḍů, kōḍu horn Ko. kṟ (obl. kṭ-)((DEDR 2200) Paš. kōṇḍā'bald', Kal. rumb. kōṇḍa 'hornless'.(CDIAL 3508). Kal. rumb.khōṇḍ a' half' (CDIAL 3792).

134	koṭiyum = a wooden circle put round the neck of an animal; koṭ = neck (G.) Vikalpa: kaḍum 'neck-band, ring'; rebus: khāḍ 'trench, firepit' (G.) Vikalpa: khaḍḍā f. hole, mine, cave (CDIAL 3790) kanduka, kandaka ditch, trench (Tu.); kandakamu id. (Te.); kanda trench made as a fireplace during weddings (Konda); kanda small trench for fireplace (Kui); kandri a pit (Malt)(DEDR 1214) khaḍḍa— 'hole, pit'. [Cf. *gaḍḍa— and list s.v. kartá—1] Pk. khaḍḍā— f. 'hole, mine, cave', ḍaga— m. 'one who digs a hole', ḍōlaya— m. 'hole'; Bshk. (Biddulph) "kād" (= khaḍ?) 'valley'; K. khŏḍ m. 'pit', khŏḍü f. 'small pit', khoḍu m. 'vulva'; S. khaḍa f. 'pit'; L. khaḍḍ f. 'pit, cavern, ravine'; P. khaḍḍ f. 'pit, ravine', ḍī f. 'hole for a weaver's feet' (→ Ku. khaḍḍ, N. khaḍ; H. khaḍ, khaḍḍā m. 'pit, low ground, notch'; Or. khãḍi 'edge of a deep pit'; M. khaḍḍā m. 'rough hole, pit'); WPah. khaś. khaḍḍā 'stream'; N. khāṛo 'pit, bog', khāṛi 'creek', khāṛal 'hole (in ground or stone)'. — Altern. < *khāḍa—: Gy. gr. xar f. 'hole'; Ku. khāṛ 'pit'; B. khāṛī 'creek, inlet', khāṛal 'pit, ditch'; H. khāṛī f. 'creek, inlet', khaṛ—har, al m. 'hole'; Marw. khāṛo m. 'hole'; M. khāḍ f. 'hole, creek', ḍā m. 'hole', ḍī f. 'creek, inlet'. 3863 khātra— n. 'hole' HPariś., 'pond, spade' Uṇ. [√khan] Pk. khatta— n. 'hole, manure', aya— m. 'one who digs in a field'; S. khātru m. 'mine made by burglars', ṭro m. 'fissure, pit, gutter made by rain'; P. khāt m. 'pit, manure', khāttā m. 'grain pit', ludh.

khattā m. (→ H. khattā m., khatiyā f.); N. khāt 'heap (of stones, wood or corn)'; B. khāt, khātṛū 'pit, pond'; Or. khāta 'pit', tā 'artificial pond'; Bi. khātā 'hole, gutter, grain pit, notch (on beam and yoke of plough)', khattā 'grain pit, boundary ditch'; Mth. khātā, khattā 'hole, ditch'; H. khāt m. 'ditch, well', f. 'manure', khātā m. 'grain pit'; G. khātar n. 'housebreaking, house sweeping, manure', khātriyũ n. 'tool used in housebreaking' (→ M. khātar f. 'hole in a wall', khātrā m. 'hole, manure', khātryā m. 'housebreaker'); M. khāt n.m. 'manure' (deriv. khatāviṇẽ 'to manure', khāterẽ n. 'muck pit'). — Un- expl. ṭ in L. khāṭvā m. 'excavated pond', khāṭī f. 'digging to clear or excavate a canal' (~ S. khāṭī f. 'id.', but khāṭyāro m. 'one employed to measure canal work') and khaṭṭaṇ 'to dig'. (CDIAL 3790) •gaḍa— 1 m. 'ditch' lex. [Cf. *gaḍḍa—1 and list s.v. kartá—1] Pk. gaḍa— n. 'hole'; Paš. gaṛu 'dike'; Kho. (Lor.) gōḷ 'hole, small dry ravine'; A. garā 'high bank'; B. gaṛ 'ditch, hole in a husking machine'; Or. gaṛa 'ditch, moat'; M. gaḷ f. 'hole in the game of marbles'. 3981 *gaḍḍa— 1 'hole, pit'. [G. < *garda—? — Cf. *gaḍḍ—1 and list s.v. kartá—1] Pk. gaḍḍa— m. 'hole'; WPah. bhal. cur. gaḍḍ f., paṅ. gaḍḍrī, pāḍ. gaḍōr 'river, stream'; N. gaṛ— tir 'bank of a river'; A. gārā 'deep hole'; B. gāṛ, ṛā 'hollow, pit'; Or. gāṛa 'hole, cave', gāṛiā 'pond'; Mth. gāṛi 'piercing'; H. gāṛā m. 'hole'; G. garāḍ, ḍɔ m. 'pit, ditch' (< *gradda— < *garda—?); Si. gaḍaya 'ditch'. — Cf. S. giḍi f. 'hole in the ground for fire during Muharram'. — X khānī—: K. gān m.

'underground room'; S. (LM 323) gāṇ f. 'mine, hole for keeping water'; L. gāṇ m. 'small embanked field within a field to keep water in'; G. gāṇ f. 'mine, cellar'; M. gāṇ f. 'cavity containing water on a raised piece of land' WPah.ktg. gāṛ 'hole (e.g. after a knot in wood)'. (CDIAL 3947) 3860 *khāḍa— 'a hollow'. [Cf. *khaḍḍa— and list s.v. kartá—1] S. khārī f. 'gulf, creek'; P. khāṛ 'level country at the foot of a mountain', rī f. 'deep watercourse, creek'; Bi. khārī 'creek, inlet'; G. khāṛi , rī f., rɔ m. 'hole'. — Altern. < *khaḍḍa—: Gy. gr. xar f. 'hole'; Ku. khāṛ 'pit'; B. khārī 'creek, inlet', khāṛal 'pit, ditch'; H. khārī 'creek, inlet', khaṛ—har, al m. 'hole'; Marw. khāṛo m. 'hole'; M. khāḍ f. 'hole, creek', ḍā m. 'hole', ḍī f. 'creek, inlet'.

135   खोंडा [khōṇḍā] m A कांबळा of which one end is formed into a cowl or hood. खोंडी [khōṇḍī] f An outspread shovelform sack (as formed temporarily out of a कांबळा, to hold or fend off grain, chaff &c. (Marathi) khŏdrang, khudrang ख्वद्ːरंग adj. c.g. self-coloured; as subst. m. N. of a kind of blanket having the natural colour of the wool (L. 37). khudürü और्णशाटकविशेषः f. a kind of coarse woollen blanket. (Kashmiri) Pa. kotthalī -- f. ' sack (?) '; Pk. kotthala -- m. ' bag, grainstore ' (kōha -- m. ' bag ' < *kōtha?); K. kŏthul, lu m. ' large bag or parcel ', kothüjü f. ' small do. '; S. kothirī f. ' bag '; Ku. kuthlo ' large bag, sack '; B. kūthlī ' satchel, wallet '; Or. kuthali, thuli, kothali, thili '

wallet, pouch '; H. kothlā m. ' bag, sack, stomach (see *kōttha --) ', lī f. ' purse '; G.kothlɔ m. ' large bag ', lī f. ' purse, scrotum '; M. kothḷā m. ' large sack, chamber of stomach (= peṭā ċā k) ', ḷẽ n. ' sack ', lī f. ' small sack '; -- X gōṇī′ -- : S. gothirī f. ' bag ', L. gutthlā m.(CDIAL 3511) Ta. kaṇṭāḷam travelling sack placed on a bullock, pack-saddle. Ka. kaṇṭale, kaṇṭāḷa, kaṇṭāḷe, kaṇṭle double bag carried across a beast. Te. kaṇṭalamu, kaṇṭlamubullock-load consisting of two bags filled with goods. / Cf. Mar. kaṇṭhāḷī a bag having opening in the middle (DEDR 1174)

gōṇī′ f. ' sack ' Pāṇ., gōṇikā -- f. ' blanket ' BHS ii 215. [← Drav. EWA i 345 with lit.] Pa. gōṇa -- saṁthata -- ' covered with a woollen rug ', gōṇaka -- m. ' woollen rug with a long fleece '; NiDoc. goni ' sack '; Gy. pal. gŏ́ni ' bag, purse ', eur. gono m. ' sack '; Ash.gō˜ ' carpet ', Wg. gŏ̆́ŏī, gŏ̆ē, Dm. gūni; Paš. gōṇī ' saddlebag '; K. guna f. ' pair of large saddlebags usu. of goat's hair for carrying grain '; S. guṇī f. ' coarse sackcloth '; L. gūṇī′f. ' sack '; P. gūṇ f. ' hair cloth, hempen sacking ', gūṇī f. ' sack '; B. gun ' sacking '; Or. goṇī ' sackcloth, sack, corn measure, ragged garment '; Bi. gon ' grain sack '; H. gon f. ' sack '; G. gū̆ṇi f. ' sacking, sack '; M. goṇ f. ' sack ', ṇī f. ' sackcloth ', ṇā m. ' large grain sack '.Addenda: gōṇī′ -- : WPah.ktg.

gōṇ f. (obl. -- i) ' sack for corn '; <-> Md. (RTMV1) gōṇi ' sack ' ← Ind. (CDIAL 4275) gōṇamu. [Tel. of Tam. కోణమము.] n. A waist cloth or modesty piece. [gōṇi] gōṇi. [Skt.] n. A sack, sackcloth. a sackful. [Tel.] gōtamu. [Tel.] n. A sack, a bag. (Telugu)

136   koḍ = place where artisans work (G.) कोंडण [kōṇḍaṇa] f A fold or pen. (Marathi) koṭṭil cowhouse, shed, workshop, house; Malt. koṭa hamlet. / Influenced by Skt. goṣṭha-. (DEDR 2059). kūṭam = workshop (Tamil); கோட்டம் kōṭṭam,n. <kōṣṭha. 1. Room, enclosure; அறை. சுடும ணோாங்கிய நெடு நிலைக் கோட்டமும் (மணி. 6, 59). 2. Temple; கோயில். கோழிச் சேவற் கொடியோன் கோட்டமும் (சிலப். 14, 10). koṭe meṛed = forged iron (Mu.) meḍ 'iron' (Ho.) dul meṛed, cast iron (Mu.) koṭe 'forged metal' (Santali) கொட்டுக்கன்னார் koṭṭu-k-kaṉṉār , n. < கொட்டு² +. Braziers who work by beating plates into shape and not by casting; செம் படிக்குங் கன்னார். (W.)

[137] [cp. kara] one who does, handles or deals with: ayakāra iron -- smith Miln 331. ayo° DhA i.148 (v. l. ayo°). -kāra a worker in iron Miln 331. (Pali) khār 1 खदरf ᛁ लांह्कदरm m. (sg. abl. khāra 1 खदर; the pl. dat. of this word is khāran 1 खदरनf, which is to be distinguished from khāran 2, q.v., s.v.), a blacksmith, an iron worker (cf. bandūka-khār, p. 111b, l.

46;K.Pr. 46; H. xi, 17); a farrier (El.). This word is often a part of a name, and in such case comes at the end (W. 118) as in Wahab khār, Wahab the smith (H. ii, 12; vi, 17) (Kashmiri) [138] Gy. pal.kam ' work, esp. smith's work ', arm. kam ' work, thing, booty '; kárman1 n. ' act, work ' RV. Pa. kamma nom. sg. n., Aś. shah. kramaṁ, man. kramane dat., kāl. dh. jau. gir. kaṁma -- , NiDoc. kaṁa, Pk. kamman -- , ma -- n., mā -- f.; Ash. kŕem, käm, kləm, Niṅg. ṣlam, Kaṭ. kam, Dm. Tir. kram, Paš. lauṛ. lām m., uzb.ṣam, gul. kuṛū´m, nir. lagh. lām, ar. plōm, Shum. lām, Gaw. lam, Woṭ. kam, Kal. krum, Kho. korum (obl. kormo), Bshk. lām, Mai. Tor. kām, Sv. kəram, Phal. kram, Sh. gil. krǫm m. (→ Ḍ. krom m.), koh. kom, pales. kōm, K. kam m., kömü f., S. kamu m., L. P. kamm m., WPah. bhad. kamm n., Ku. N. A. B. kām, Or. kāma, Mth. Bhoj. kām, Aw. lakh. kāmu, H. Marw. kām m.; G. kām n. ' work ', kāmū n. ' an office, administration '; M. kām n., Ko. kāman., Si. kama. (CDIAL 2892) Si. (SigGr) kamuṇa ' artisan ' (CDIAL 2893). Pk. kammasālā -- f.; L. kamhāl f. ' hole in the ground for a weaver's feet '; Si. kamhala ' workshop ', kammala ' smithy ' (CDIAL 2896). karmā´ra m. ' blacksmith ' RV. [EWA i 176 < stem *karmar -- ~ karman -- , but perh. with ODBL 668 ← Drav. cf. Tam. karumā ' smith, smelter ' whence meaning ' smith ' was transferred also to karmakāra --]

Pa. kammāra -- m. ' worker in metal '; Pk. kammāra -- , aya -- m. ' blacksmith ', A. kamār, B. kāmār; Or. kamāra ' blacksmith, caste of non -- Aryans, caste of fishermen '; Mth.

kamār ' blacksmith ', Si. kaṁburā.*karmāraśālā -- . Addenda: karmā´ra -- : Md. kaṅburu ' blacksmith ' (CDIAL 2898)*karmāraśālā ' smithy '. [karmā´ra -- , śā´lā --]Mth. kamarsārī; -- Bi. kamarsāyar? (CDIAL 2899). [karmakāra] n a blacksmith, an ironsmith; (rare) an ironmonger. (Bengali)

[139] Akkadian, reign of Shar-kali-sharri. Mesopotamia. Cuneiform inscription in Old Akkadian. Serpentine; Diam. 2.6 cm (1 in.); H. 3.9 cm Musée du Louvre, Département des Antiquités Orientales, Paris AO 22303.
http://www.metmuseum.org/special/First_Cities/images/135BR3.R.jpg

[140] Fig. 20 in Michael Pieter Kovink, 2008, The Indus script -- a positional-statistical approach, USA, Gilund Press, ISBN 978-0-6151-8239-1showing varieties of fish signs and positional sequencing on epigraphs.

[141] beḍa hako (ayo) 'fish' (Santali); beḍa 'either of the sides of a hearth' (G.) Indian mackerel Ta. ayirai, acarai, acalai loach, sandy colour, Cobitis thermalis; ayilai a kind of fish. Ma. ayala a fish, mackerel, scomber; aila, ayila a fish; ayira a kind of small fish, loach (DEDR 191) Munda: So. Ayo `fish'. Go. ayu `fish'. Go <ayu> (Z), <ayu?u> (Z),, <ayu?> (A) {N} ``^fish''. Kh. kaDOG `fish'. Sa. Hako `fish'. Mu. hai(H) ~ haku(N) ~ haikO(M) `fish'. Ho haku `fish'. Bj. hai `fish'. Bh.haku `fish'. KW haiku ~ hakO |Analyzed hai-kO, ha-kO (RDM). Ku. Kaku`fish'.@(V064,M106) Mu. ha-i, haku `fish' (HJP). @(V341) ayu>(Z), <ayu?u> (Z) <ayu?>(A) {N} ``^fish''. #1370. <yO>\\<AyO>(L) {N} ``^fish''. #3612. <kukkulEyO>,,<kukkuli-yO>(LMD) {N} ``prawn''. !Serango

dialect. #32612. <sArjAjyO>,,<sArjAj>(D) {N} ``prawn". #32622. <magur-yO>(ZL) {N} ``a kind of ^fish". *Or.<>. #32632. <ur+GOl-Da-yO>(LL) {N} ``a kind of ^fish". #32642.<bal.bal-yO>(DL) {N} ``smoked fish". #15163. Vikalpa: Munda: <aDara>(L) {N} ``^scales of a fish, sharp bark of a tree".#10171. So<aDara>(L) {N} ``^scales of a fish, sharp bark of a tree".

[142] a~s = scales of fish (Santali); rebus: aya = iron (G.); ayah, ayas = metal (Skt.) aduru native metal (Ka.); ayil iron (Ta.) ayir, ayiram any ore (Ma.); ajirda karba very hard iron (Tu.)(DEDR 192). Ta. ayil javelin, lance, surgical knife, lancet.Ma. ayil javelin, lance; ayiri surgical knife, lancet. (DEDR 193). aduru = gan.iyinda tegadu karagade iruva aduru = ore taken from the mine and not subjected to melting in a furnace (Ka. Siddhānti Subrahmaṇya' Śastri's new interpretation of the AmarakoŚa, Bangalore, Vicaradarpana Press, 1872, p.330); adar = fine sand (Ta.); ayir – iron dust, any ore (Ma.) Kur. adar the waste of pounded rice, broken grains, etc. Malt. adru broken grain (DEDR 134). Ma. aśu thin, slender;ayir, ayiram iron dust.Ta. ayir subtlety, fineness, fine sand, candied sugar; ? atar fine sand, dust. அய.ர³ ayir, n. 1. Subtlety, fineness; நணசம. (த_வ_.) 2. [M. ayir.] Fine sand; நணமணல. (மலசலப. 92.) ayiram, n. Candied sugar; ayil, n. cf. ayas. 1. Iron; 2. Surgical knife, lancet; Javelin, lance; ayilavaṉ, Skanda, as bearing a javelin (DEDR 341).Tu. gadarů a lump (DEDR

1196) kadara— m. 'iron goad for guiding an elephant' lex. (CDIAL 2711). अयस्कठिन [ayaskaṭhina] a as hard as iron; extremely hard (Bengali) अयोगू: A blacksmith; Vāj.3.5. अयस् a. [इ-गतौ-असुन्] Going, moving; nimble. n. (-यः) 1 Iron (एति चलति अयस्कान्तसंनिकर्षं इति तथात्वम्; नायसोल्लिख्यते रत्नम् Śukra 4.169. अभितप्तमयो$पि मार्दवं भजते कैव कथा शरीरिषु R.8.43. -2 Steel. -3 Gold. -4 A metal in general. ayaskāṇḍa 1 an iron-arrow. -2 excellent iron. -3 a large quantity of iron. -क_नत_(अयसक_नत_) 1 'beloved of iron', a magnet, load-stone; 2 a precious stone; °मजण_ a loadstone; ayaskāra 1 an iron-smith, blacksmith (Skt.Apte) ayas-kāntamu. [Skt.] n. The load-stone, a magnet. ayaskārudu. n. A black smith, one who works in iron. ayassu. n. ayō-mayamu. [Skt.] adj. made of iron (Te.) áyas— n. 'metal, iron' RV. Pa. ayō nom. sg. n. and m., aya— n. 'iron', Pk. aya— n., Si. ya. AYAŚCŪRṆA—, AYASKĀṆḌA—, *AYASKŪṬA—. Addenda: áyas—: Md. da 'iron', dafat 'piece of iron'. ayaskāṇḍa— m.n. 'a quantity of iron, excellent iron' Pān. gaṇ. viii.3.48 [ÁYAS—, KAAˊṆḌA—]Si.yakaḍa 'iron'.*ayaskūṭa— 'iron hammer'. [ÁYAS—, KUUˊṬA—1] Pa. ayōkūṭa—, ayak m.; Si. yakuḷa'sledge —hammer', yavuḷa (< ayōkūṭa) (CDIAL 590, 591, 592). cf. Lat. aes , aer-is for as-is ; Goth. ais , Thema aisa; Old Germ. e7r , iron ;Goth. eisarn ; Mod. Germ. Eisen.

ಆದುರು aduru. 3. Native metal. ಗದಿರುತ್ತ ತಾಗದು ಳದಗದೆ ಇದುದ ಆದುದು (ಅೞ್ತ 81. 330). (Tě. ಆಇದು, sparkle; —dear, costly; T. ಅೞೂ, fine sand; ಅೂೂ, iron; beauty; ಆೂ, splendour; M. ಅೂೂೂ, iron dust, any ore).

143   kala stag, buck (Ma.); kal a.r. Nilgiri ibex (Ko.); kalai

stag, buck, male black monkey (Ta.); kalan:kompu stag's horn (Ta.)(DEDR 1312) (capra sibirica hemalayanus)

144   kallan mason (Ma.); kalla glass beads (Ma.); kalu stone (Kond.a); xal id., boulder (Br.)(DEDR 1298).

[145] kár, kãr 'neck' (Kashmiri) Kal. gr̆ä ' neck '; Kho. goḷ ' front of neck, throat '. gala m. ' throat, neck ' MBh. (CDIAL 4070) körü 1 का&above;रू॒ । शिरोधिः f. (for 2, see kôru 2; cf. also kārun), the neck (El.kár and kãr; Gr.Gr. 13; K.Pr. 156, kãr; YZ. 64; W. 12; Śiv. 52, 971, 1363). -mārüñü - ग्रीवातिर्यक्करणम् f.inf. to bend the neck; to bow the head or nod in acquiescence; to nod the head in a pleased sort of way (K.Pr. 77). Cf. nigayĕ-ko, s.v. nigay. kāri-holu वक्रग्रीवः adj. (f. -hüjü -), crooked necked, wry-necked (by nature or from rheumatism, etc.). -pàti 1 प&above;ति&below; । पुष्पविशेषः m. N. of a certain wild flower, described as dark in colour, with small tooth-shaped shoots at the back (pàti) (Rām. 649, 655). -pàti ग्रीवायाः पश्चाद्भागे adv. on the back or nape of the neck (Rām. 1615). -thodu उद्धुरकन्धरः adj. (f. -thüzü -), 'high in the neck,' one who carries his head high in public, one who occupies an honourable position and knows it (cf. Śiv. 971, 1363). (Kashmiri)

[146] L. (Ju.) sãgh m. ' throat ', sãghṛī f. ' enlarged uvula ', awāṅ. sagh ' throat '; P. saṅgh, ghā m. ' throat, front part of neck, gullet '; WPah. (Joshi) śāgī f. ' throat '.*śaṅkhahanu -- . Addenda: śaṅkha --2: WPah.kṭg. śáṅgɔ m. ' throat ', śaṅge f.

' neck, throat '. (CDIAL 12264).

[147] sāk 'a conch'; sāk ghonga 'a shell used as a conch'; sāk rokoc 'a shell used as a conch (Santali); sāk 'one who sells coral beads'; sāk mala 'coral beads (Santali) Grapheme: sāk 'a goose' (Santali) śaṅkhá1 m. (n. lex.) ' conch -- shell ' AV., śaṅkhaka- m.n. MBh. Pa. saṅkha -- m. ' conch, mother -- of -- pearl '; Pk. saṁkha -- m.n. ' conch ', khiyā -- f. ' small do. '; S. saṅghī f. ' a kind of bracelet '; B. sākh ' conch -- shell ', sākhā, kā, sēkhā ' conch bracelet ', Or. saṅkhā; OAw. sāṁkha m. ' conch -- shell ', H. saṅkh m., Si. sak -- a, ha. -- Lws. in S. saṅkhu m. ' conch ', Ku. sākh, sāk. śāṅkhika -- , *śāṅkhinī -- ; śaṅkhakāra -- , śaṅkhadāraka -- .Addenda: śaṅkhá -- 1 [a < non -- apophonic IE. O (Gk. ko/gxos) T. Burrow BSOAS xxxviii 69] WPah.ktg. śáṅkkh m. ' conch ' ← H.; Md. sangu ← Ind.; A. śāk (phonet. x --) ' bracelet made of shells ' AFD 187. (CDIAL 12263). śaṅkhakāra -- , aka -- m. ' shell -- worker ' lex. [śaṅkhá -- 1, kāra -- 1] B. sāk(h)āri ' maker of conch -- shell bracelets '; Or. saṅkhāri ' shell -- worker '; -- or < śaṅkhadāraka -- . śaṅkhadāraka -- m. ' shell -- cutter ' lex. [śaṅkhá -- 1, dāra -- 1] (CDIAL 12265).

[148] kamari the work of a blacksmith, the money paid for blacksmith work; nunak ato reak in kamarieda I do the blacksmith work for so many villages (Santali) kārmāra = metalsmith who makes arrows etc. of metal (RV. 9.112.2: jaratībhih oṣadhībhih parṇebhih śakunānām ka_rmāro

aśmabhih dyubhih hiraṇyavantam icchatī) kammar a, kammāra, kammagāra, karmāra, karmakāra, kammagāra, kambāra = one who does any business; an artisan, a mechanic; a blacksmith (Ka.)

[149] Kho. krəm ' back ' NTS ii 262 with (?) (CDIAL 3145)[Cf. Ir. *kamaka -- or *kamraka -- ' back ' in Shgh. čủmč ' back ', Sar. čomǰ EVSh 26] (CDIAL 2776) cf. Sang. kamak ' back ', Shgh. čomǰ (< *kamak G.M.) ' back of an animal ', Yghn. kama ' neck ' (CDIAL 14356). kár, kār[149] 'neck' (Kashmiri) Kal. gr̆ä ' neck '; Kho. goḷ ' front of neck, throat '. gala m. ' throat, neck ' MBh. (CDIAL 4070) Rebus: khār, khar 'blacksmith' (Kashmiri) kôru 2 कोरु॒ । अशोभनाङ्गः adj. (f. körü 2 कारू॒; for 1, see s.v.), one-eyed (= kônu 4, q.v.) (L.V. 2); crooked limbed, deformed (of a person). (Kashmiri)

[150] Generally D ii.126, A v.263; a silversmith Sn 962= Dh 239; J i.223; a goldsmith J iii.281; v.282. The smiths in old India do not seem to be divided into black -- , gold -- and silver -- smiths, but seem to have been able to work equally well in iron, gold, and silver, as can be seen e. g. from J iii.282 and VvA 250, where the smith is the maker of a needle. They were constituted into a guild, and some of them were well -- to -- do as appears from what is said of Cunda at D ii.126; owing to their usefulness they were held in great esteem by the people and king alike J iii.281.--kula a smithy M i.25

151   A. putalā ' image ', putalī ' doll, pupil of eye '; B. putul, putlo ' image ', putli ' doll, pupil of eye '; Or. putuḷā, pit, putuḷi, pit ' doll, pupil of eye ', puttaḷi ' doll '; Bi.putlā, ī ' doll '; OMth. putari ' doll, pupil of eye '; Mth. putrā ' doll '; OAw. putarī f. ' wooden image '; H. pū˘tlā m., ī f. ' doll '; G. putḷũ n. ' small image ', ī f. ' doll, pupil of eye '(CDIAL 8269).

152 Kuwait National Museum. French Archaeological Expedition in Kuwait. Several inscriptions at Failaka mention the Dilmunite god Enzak and his temple or Mesopotamian deities. [Remi Boucharlat, Archaeology and Artifacts of the Arabian Peninsula, in: Jack M. Sasson (ed.), Civilizations of the Ancient Near East, pp. 1335-1353].

153Vikalpa: kōḷ 'planet' (Ta.). Rebus: kol = metal (Ta.)

154   मेढा [mēḍhā] menda A twist or tangle arising in thread or cord, a curl or snarl. (Marathi) (CDIAL 10312). [dial., cp. Prk. mĕṇṭha & miṇṭha: Pischel, Prk. Gr. § 293. The Dhtm (156) gives a root meṇḍ (meḍ) in meaning of "koṭilla," i. e. crookedness. (Pali) Vikalpa: ḍhompo = knot on a string (Santali) Rebus: ḍhompo = ingot (Santali)

155   [dial., cp. Prk. mĕṇṭha & miṇṭha: Pischel, Prk. Gr. § 293. The Dhtm (156) gives a root meṇḍ (meḍ) in meaning of "koṭilla," i. e. crookedness. (Pali) Vikalpa: ḍhompo = knot on a string (Santali) Rebus: ḍhompo = ingot (Santali)

156   jasta = zinc (Hindi) sattva, yasada (Jaina Pkt.) Kashmiri. Grierson lex. zasath ज़स॒थ् or zasuth ज़सुथ् । त्रपु m. (sg. dat. zastas ज़स्तस्), zinc, spelter, pewter (cf. Hindī jast).

jasti jasti । त्रपुधातुविशेषनिर्मितम् adj. c.g. made of zinc or pewter. jasth जस्थ । त्रपु m. (sg. dat. jastas जस्तस्), zinc, spelter; pewter. jastuvu जस्तुवु&below; । त्रपूद्रवः adj. (f. jastüvü, made of zinc or pewter. satavu, satuvu, sattu = pewter, zinc (Ka.) dosta = zinc (Santali) jasada, yasada, yasadyaka, yasatva = zinc (Jaina Pali) ruhi-tutiya (Urdu) tuttha (Arthas'a_stra) totamu, tutenag (Te.) oriechalkos (Gk.)

[157] KC Aryan, 1991, Indian Folk Bronzes New Delhi
http://www.purpleonion.nl/background/tribal_bronzes

[158] Vikalpa: In Turi language (North Munda) the word for set of five is 'hand'. The word is *ti.* Related Munda language Bonda has the word tiram to denote 5. Pram is the Khmer word for five.

[159] cf. Konda mandi earthen pan, a covering dish. Pe. mandi cooking pot. Kui mandi brass bowl. Kuwi (S.) mandi basin; (Isr.) mandi plate, bowl.(DEDR 4678) Ta. muntai a small vessel; montai a small earthen vessel, a small wooden vessel; (Koll.) monne a kind of pot. Ma. monta cruse, goglet; mōnta brass ewer to draw water, water-vessel of kings. Ka. munde a jar-like brass vessel. Te. munta small pitcher. Pa. (p. 97) mutta basin. Konda muta small pitcher or pot. Pe. muta metal vessel. Kui mūta small brass pot. Kuwi mūnta (F.) water pot of brass, (Isr.) small metal jug, pot, vessel.(DEDR 4965)

[160] *mr̥ndati: WPah.ktg. mandnõ ' to rub, smear, thrash,

crush ' (Him.I 172 if not < márdati with rd > ṇḍ), J. minṇu ' to rub, pinch '; -- (X mánthati) WPah.ktg. máṇḍhṇõ ' to rub oneself '. Gy. wel. mōr -- ' to rub, polish, grind '; Dm. man -- ' to rub '; Paš.laur. kur. muṇḍ -- , dar. muṇ -- , weg. muṛ -- , gul. muṇḍal -- tr. ' to break ' (IIFL iii 3, 123 < múṇṭati), laur. maṇḍ -- ' to rub, smear ', kur. māṇ -- ' to thresh, smear ', chil. mēṇ -- ' to crush ', ar. māṛ -- ' to rub '; Gaw. mīṇḍemím ' I crush, thresh, grind, wash (clothes) '; Phal. māṇḍ -- ' to knead '; K. maṇḍun ' to rub, trample, wash (woollen cloth by kneading it with the feet) '; S. manaṇu ' to shampoo, make clothes ready for steaming '; WPah. (Joshi) minṇu ' to rub '; Ku. minaṇo ' to beat, rub '; Mth. mīrab ' to knead, grind, shampoo '; H. mī̃rnā, mī̃ḍ° ' to rub with the hands, clean '; M. mãḍṇẽ ' to smear vessels '; Si. mañḍinavā, maḍin°, maḍan° ' to rub, press, clean rice from the husk ', (inscr.) mäñḍä absol. ' to crush ', maḍavanavā ' to prepare a field for planting by buffaloes treading it ' (pret. maṇḍā < *mañḍvā). -- X mánthati (L. mandhaṇ, P.maddhṇā: cf. H. mã̄ḍhnā in 1) or poss. < mṛddhá -- : L.awān. middhaṇ, pp. middhā ' to crush '; P. middhṇā, pp. middhā ' to stir up, mix, knead (mortar), rumple, tumble (clothes, paper, &c.), spoil by treading on (crops) '. -- X mṛśáti q.v. Addenda: márdati. 1. A. māriba also ' to knead (dough) ' AFD 331 (CDIAL 9890)

[161] Kol. me·g- (me·kt-) to purify with cowdung solution. Nk. mēgh- (mēkt-) to apply. Go. (Tr.) maṛhuttānā to paint cattle for the Pola or the Diwali festival (Voc. 2748); ? mācānā (Tr.) to plaster mud on a wall or dam, (SR. M.) to smear; (G. Mu.

Ma. Y.) māc- to plaster (Voc. 2773); (SR.) miṭānā to apply (Voc. 2823); (Hislop III, p. 132) mitus- to apply (sacred mark); (ASu.) miṭṭūs- to apply saffron powder on the forehead. Koṇḍa miṛis- (-t-) to rub and clean utensils with ashes, etc. Kuwi (S.) mrispi kīnai to polish; (Isr.) mṇek- (-h-) to make clean filling holes, etc. Br. miring to plaster. Ta. meṛ uku (meṛuki-) to cleanse floor with cowdung solution, smear as the body with sandal paste, gloss over, varnish; n. cowdung, wax, gum, soft waxy pill, mass; meṛukku smearing with cowdung water as the floor, cowdung, substance or solution used to smear any surface; meṛukkam ground or floor prepared by being smeared with cowdung water. Ma. meṛu, meṛuku wax; meṛukuka to anoint, wax, varnish, daub a place with cowdung; meṛukku anointing, varnish, daubing, polishing. Ir. mëkku wax. PālKu., Ālku. (Zvelebil 1980 on Ir.) mëkku id. Ko. mek bee's-wax; mek- (meky-) to cleanse floor with cowdung water. To. mösk- (mösky-) to smear with dung of buffaloes as a ritual purification; mösk wax. Koḍ. mukk- (mukki-) to smear (mud, manure on ground). (DEDRF 5082)

[162] cf. bangaru, bangaramu ' gold' (Te.) बांगडी [bāṅgaḍī] f A bracelet of glass (sometimes of metal or wood) worn by females. (Marathi). bhagaṇa 'a bangle (IA 19)(IEG) bangan 'bangle' (cf. K ālibangan, 'black bangle', name of a site on River Sarasvati basin) Vikalpa: kācā 'glass' (Santali); rebus: kācār 'maker of glass bangles' (M.)

[163] http://www.patentstorm.us/patents/6293993-description.html

[164] posta 'red thread employed to make borders of cloth' (Santali) pōta2 m. ' cloth ', pōtikā -- f. lex. 2. *pōtta -- 2 (sanskrit- ized as pōtra -- 2 n. ' cloth ' lex.). 3. *pōttha -- 2 ~ pavásta<-> n. ' covering (?) ' RV., ' rough hempen cloth ' AV. T. Chowdhury JBORS xvii 83. 4. pōntī -- f. ' cloth ' Divyāv. 5. *pōcca -- 2 < *pōtya -- ? (Cf. pōtyā = pōtānāṁ samūhaḥ Pāṇ.gaṇa. -- pṓta -- 1?). [Relationship with prōta -- n. ' woven cloth ' lex., plōta -- ' bandage, cloth ' Suśr. or with pavásta -- is obscure: EWA ii 347 with lit. Forms meaning ' cloth to smear with, smearing ' poss. conn. with or infl. by pusta -- 2 n. ' working in clay ' (prob. ← Drav., Tam. pūcu &c. DED 3569, EWA ii 319)] 1. Pk. pōa -- n. ' cloth '; Paš.ar. pōwok ' cloth ', pōg ' net, web ' (but lauṛ. dar. pāwāk ' cotton cloth ', Gaw. pāk IIFL iii 3, 150). 2. Pk. potta -- , °taga -- , °tia -- n. ' cotton cloth ', pottī -- , °tiā -- , °tullayā -- , puttī -- f. ' piece of cloth, man's dhotī, woman's sāṛī ', pottia -- ' wearing clothes '; S. potī f. ' shawl ', potyo m. ' loincloth '; L. pot, pl. °tã f. ' width of cloth '; P. potṛā m. ' child's clout ', potṇā ' to smear a wall with a rag '; N. poto ' rag to lay on lime -- wash ', potnu ' to smear '; Or. potā ' gunny bag '; OAw. potaï ' smears, plasters '; H. potā m. ' whitewashing brush ', potī f. ' red cotton ', potiyā m. ' loincloth ', potṛā m. ' baby clothes '; G. potn. ' fine cloth, texture ', potũ n. ' rag ', potī f., °tiyũ n. ' loincloth ', potṛī f. ' small do. '; M. pot m. ' roll of coarse cloth ', n. ' weftage or texture of cloth ', potrẽ n. ' rag for smearing cowdung '.3. Pa. potthaka -- n. ' cheap rough hemp cloth ',

potthakamma -- n. ' plastering '; Pk. pottha -- , °aya -- n.m. ' cloth '; S. potho m. ' lump of rag for smearing, smearing, cloth soaked in opium '. 4. Pa. ponti -- ' rags '. 5. Wg. pōč ' cotton cloth, muslin ', Kt. puč; Pr. puč ' duster, cloth ', pū´čuk ' clothes '; S. poco m. ' rag for plastering, plastering '; P. poccā m. ' cloth or brush for smearing ',pocṇā ' to smear with earth '; Or. pucāra, pucurā ' wisp of rag or jute for whitewashing with, smearing with such a rag '. (CDIAL 8400) [165] போத்தி pōtti போற்றி pōrri , < id. n. 1. Praise, applause, commendation; புகழ்மொழி. (W.) 2. Brahman temple-priest of Malabar; கோயிற் பூசைசெய்யும் மலையாளநாட்டுப் பிராமணன். (W.) 3. See போத்தி, 1.--int. Exclamation of praise; துதிச்சொல்வகை. பொய்தீர் காட்சிப் புரையோய் போற்றி (சிலப். 13, 92) (Tamil) potR `" Purifier "'N. of one of the 16 officiating priests at a sacrifice (the assistant of the Brahman (RV. Br. ŚrS. Hariv.)

[166]   kolli = a fish (Ma.); koleji id. (Tu.)(DEDR 2139). kōlā flying fish, exocaetus, garfish, belone (Ta.) kōlān, kōli needle-fish (Ma.)(DEDR 2241). Vikalpa: cūḷi = scales of fish (Ma.)(DEDR 2740). cūḷai = kiln; cuḷḷai = furnace (Ta.)

     Grapheme: xolā = tail (Kur.); qoli = id. (Malt.)(DEDR 2135).

     kulullu, 'fish-man; kuliltu, 'fish-woman'; fish-garbed figure: apkallu, 'sage' (in fish-guise); Apkallu is shown in two ligatures: one with wings and one with fish (Contextual glyphs relate to tree and water). Masked as Enki, half-fish and half-priest; from a relief of Assurnasirpal II (883--859 BC) from Calah. Gypsum. Height ca. 2.5 m. After Jeremias 1929: 353, fig. 183; cf. Asko Parpola, 1984, Deciphering the Indus Script, Cambridge Univ. Press, Fig. 10.19, p. 190). Lishtar notes: "The apkallu were also known as the priests of Enki…Enki's organized world…in which wealth can be brought to the Land as a whole. " (Lishtar, Understanding Enki and the world order).

http://www.gatewaystobabylon.com/essays/essayenkiworld.html

Apkallu, priest of Enki

Grapheme: kōli = a stubble of jōḷa (Ka.) kōle a stub or stump of corn (Te.)(DEDR 2242). (cf. Ear of corn held in Apkallu's right hand).

•Glyphs: giant ear of corn, eagle wings, antelope

•Source: Apkalu Angel, Fig. of Apkallu from Nimrud, ancient Mesopotamia (north-west palace, room Z, 875-860 BCE), Waw Allap, ISBN: AS-33

http://www.gorgiaspress.com/bookshop/pc-339-35-apkalu-angel.aspx

http://www.ashmol.ox.ac.uk/ash/amocats/anet/pdf-files/ANET-26Bronze1MesV.pdf

[167] kol 'working in iron, blacksmith (Ta.); kollan-blacksmith (Ta.); kollan blacksmith, artificer (Ma.)(DEDR 2133) kolme = furnace (Ka.) kole.l 'temple, smithy' (Ko.); kolme smithy' (Ka.) kol = pañcalōha (five metals); kol metal

(Ta.lex.) pañcalōha = a metallic alloy containing five metals: copper, brass, tin, lead and iron (Skt.); an alternative list of five metals: gold, silver, copper, tin (lead), and iron (dhātu; Nānārtharatnākara. 82; Mangarāja's Nighaṇṭu. 498)(Ka.) kol, kolhe, 'the koles, an aboriginal tribe if iron smelters speaking a language akin to that of Santals' (Santali)

168   Vikalpa: gaṇḍe = a fish (Te.) gāḍ गाड़ । मीनः f. a fish (K.Pr. 14, 38, 63, 14, 15, 168, 258; H. i, 8, 9) (Kashmiri) gaḍa— 4 m. 'young of the fish Ophiocephalus lata or Cyprinus garra', aka— m. lex. B. gaṛ, gaṛai 'species of gilt—head fish'; Or. gaṛiśa, śā 'the fish O. lata', gaḷa 'a kind of fish'.(CDIAL 3970) Rebus:Tu. kandŭka, kandaka ditch, trench. Te. kandakamu id. Konḍa kanda trench made as a fireplace during weddings. Pe. kanda fire trench. Kui . kanda small trench for fireplace. Malt. kandri a pit. (DEDR 1214) Vikalpa: kolli = a kind of fish (Ma.); koleji (Tu.)(DEDR 2139). gullo (Tu.), golla-dondu (Te.), kōlān = needle-fish (Ma.) kōla (Ta.) Rebus : kol 'pancaloha'; kollan 'smith' (Ta.) Vikalpa: ḍhāḷ = a slope; the inclination of a plane; ḍhaḷavum = to incline, to lean over (G.); rebus: ḍhāḷako = a large metal ingot (G.)

169   Tu. kōḍi corner; kōṇṭu angle, corner, crook. Nk. kōnta corner (DEDR 2054b) G. khūṭṛī f. 'angle'

170   koḍ 'artisan's workshop' (Kuwi) koḍ = place where artisans work (G.) ācāri koṭṭya 'smithy' (Tu.) कोंडण [kōṇḍaṇa]

f A fold or pen. (Marathi) B. kõdā 'to turn in a lathe';
Or.kūnda 'lathe', kūdibā, kūd 'to turn' (→ Drav. Kur. kūd '
lathe') (CDIAL 3295) A. kundār, B. kũdār, ri, Or. kundāru; H.
kũderā m. 'one who works a lathe, one who scrapes', rī f.,
kũdernā 'to scrape, plane, round on a lathe'; kundakara— m.
'turner' (Skt.)(CDIAL 3297).

171   कोंदण [kōndaṇa] n (कोंदणें) Setting or infixing of
gems.(Marathi)

खোদকার [khōdakāra] n an engraver; a carver.
खोदकारি n. engraving; carving; interference in other's work.
खोदाই [khōdai] n engraving; carving. खोदाइ করা v. to
engrave; to carve. খোদানো v. & n. en graving; carving.
খোদিতি [khōdita] a engraved. (Bengali) खोदकाम [
khōdakāma] n Sculpture; carved work or work for the
carver. खोदगिरी [khōdagirī] f Sculpture, carving, engraving:
also sculptured or carved work. खोदणावळ [khōdaṇāvaḷa] f
(खोदणें) The price or cost of sculpture or carving. खोदणी [
khōdaṇī] f (Verbal of खोदणें) Digging, engraving &c. 2 fig. An
exacting of money by importunity. v लाव, मांड. 3 An
instrument to scoop out and cut flowers and figures from
paper. 4 A goldsmith's die. खोदणें [khōdaṇēṃ] v c & i (H) To
dig. 2 To engrave. खोद खोदून विचारणें or -पुसणें To question
minutely and searchingly, to probe. खोदाई [khōdāī] f (H)
Price or cost of digging or of sculpture or carving. खोदींव [
khōdīṃva] p of खोदणें Dug. 2 Engraved, carved, sculptured.
(Marathi)

172   pattar 'trough'; rebus: . patthara -- m. ' stone; pattar 'merchants, guild (smiths)' (The word may, thus, denote a lapidary).(CDIAL 8857).

173 N. sutāri ' bodkin, awl '; Bi. H. sutārī ' bodkin ' (or < 2.).2. H. sutālī f. ' large needle, bodkin '.(CDIAL 13565) sūtradhāra m. ' carpenter ' MBh. [Cf. sūtrakāra -- m. R. -- sū´tra -- , dhāra --] Pk. Suttahāra -- m. ' carpenter ', mg. śuttadhālī -- f., S. sūṭaharu m., N. sutār, A. xutār, B. chutār, Or. chutāra, (dial.) sutāra; OH. sūtahāra m., H. sutār m. ' carpenter, wheelwright, head workman '; OG. sūtahāra m., G. sut(h)ār m. ' carpenter ', M. sutār m. (CDIAL 13563) ā´rā f. ' shoemaker's awl ' RV.Pa. Pk. ārā -- f. ' awl '; Ash. arċū´ċ ' needle '; K. örü f. ' shoemaker's awl ', S. āra f., L. ār f.; P. ār f. ' awl, point of a goad '; N. āro ' awl '; A. āl ' sharp point, spur '; B. ārā ' awl ', Or. āra, āri, Bi. ār, araī, aruā, (Patna) arauā spike at the end of a driving stick ', Mth. aruā, (SETirhut) ār ' cobbler's awl '; H. ār f. ' awl, goad ', ārī f. ' awl ', araī ' goad ', ārām. ' shoemaker's awl or knife '; G. M. ār f. ' pointed iron spike '; M. ārī, arī ' cobbler's awl '.(CDIAL 1313).

174   kuṇḍa n. ' clump ' e.g. darbha-- kuṇḍa-- Pāṇ. [← Drav. (Tam. koṇṭai ' tuft of hair ', Kan. goṇḍe ' cluster ', &c.) T. Burrow BSOAS xii 374] Pk. kuṁḍa-- n. ' heap of crushed sugarcane stalks ' (CDIAL 3266) Ta. koṇṭai tuft, dressing of hair in large coil on the head, crest of a bird, head (as of a nail), knob (as of a cane), round top. Ma. koṇṭa tuft of hair.

Ko.goṇḍ knob on end of walking-stick, head of pin; koṇḍ knot of hair at back of head. To. kwïḍy Badaga woman's knot of hair at back of head (< Badaga koṇḍe). Ka. koṇḍe, goṇḍe tuft, tassel, cluster. Koḍ. koṇḍe tassels of sash, knob-like foot of cane-stem. Tu. goṇḍè topknot, tassel, cluster. Te. koṇḍe, (K. also) koṇḍi knot of hair on the crown of the head. Cf. 2049 Ta. koṭi. / Cf. Skt. kuṇḍa- clump (e.g. darbha-kuṇḍa-), Pkt. (DNM) goṇḍī- = mañjarī-; Turner, CDIAL, no. 3266; cf. also Mar. gōḍā cluster, tuft. (DEDR 2081)

175   Woṭ. šen ' roof ', Bshk. šan, Phal. šān(AO xviii 251, followed by Buddruss Woṭ 126, < śar(a)ṇa --); WPah. (Joshi) śannī f. ' small room in a house to keep sheep in '. Addenda: śaraṇá -- 2. 2. *śarṇa --WPah. kṭg.śónni f. ' bottom storey of a house in which young of cattle are kept '. śaraṇá ' protecting ', n. ' shelter, home ' RV. 2. *śarṇa -- . [√śar] 1. Pa. Pk. saraṇa -- n. ' protection, shelter, house '; Ḍ. šərón m. ' roof ' (← Sh.?), Dm. šaran; P. saraṇ m. ' protection, asylum ', H. saran f.; G. sarṇũ n. ' help '; Si.saraṇa ' defence, village, town '; -- < *śarāṇa -- or poss. *śāraṇa -- : Kho. šarān ' courtyard of a house ', Sh. šarāṇŭ m. ' fence '. (CDIAL 12326)

176   A gloss in Telugu explains such a group, lexeme clusters which can, semantically, be interpreted as an 'animal specie'. pasaramu, pasalamu = an animal, a beast, a brute, quadruped (Te.lex.)

177   Ka. kaṇḍi, kiṇḍi, gaṇḍi chink, hole, opening. Tu.

kaṇḍi, khaṇḍi, gaṇḍi hole, opening, window; kaṇḍeriyuni to make a cut. Te. gaṇḍi, gaṇḍika hole, orifice, breach, gap, lane (DEDR 1176). kandhi = a lump, a piece (Santali.lex.)

178   Ta. kaṇ eye, aperture, orifice, star of a peacock's tail. Ma. kaṇ, kaṇṇu eye, nipple, star in peacock's tail, bud. Ko. kaṇ eye. To. koṇ eye, loop in string. Ka. kaṇ eye, small hole, orifice. Koḍ. kaṇṇï id. Te. kanu, kannu eye, small hole, orifice, mesh of net, eye in peacock's feather. Kol. kan (pl. kaṇḍl) eye, small hole in ground, cave. Ga. (Oll.) kana (pl. kaṇul) hole; (S.) kanu (pl. kankul)eye. Go. (Tr.) kan (pl. kank) id.; (A.) kaṛ (pl. kaṛk) id. Konda kaṇ id. Pe. kaṅga (pl. -ŋ, kaṅku) id. Manḍ. kan (pl. -ke) id. Kui kanu (pl. kan-ga), (K.) kanu (pl. kaṛka) id. Kuwi (F.) kannū (pl. kar&nangle;ka), (S.) kannu (pl. kanka), (Su. P. Isr.) kanu (pl. kaṇka) id. (DEDR 1159a). Pa. kanḍp- (kanḍt-) to look for, seek. Ga. (Oll.) kandp- (kandt-) to search. Ta. kāṇ (kāṇp-, kaṇṭ-) to see, consider, investigate, appear, become visible; n. sight, beauty Te. kanu (allomorph kān-), kāncu to see (DEDR 1443)

B. kan ' eye of corn, particle ', kanā ' piece of dust, cummin seed ', kanī ' atom, particle '; Or.kana, ṇā ' particle of dust, eye of seed, atom ', kaṇi ' particle of grain '; OAw. kana ' drop (of dew) ' M. kaṇ m. ' grain, atom, corn ', kaṇī f. ' hard core of grain, pupil of eye, broken bit ', kaṇē n. ' very small particle ' (CDIAL 2661)

179   Pa.kandi (pl. -l) necklace, beads. Ga. (P.) kandi (pl. -l) bead, (pl.) necklace; (S.2)kandiṭ bead (DEDR 1215). kandil, kandīl = a globe of glass, a lantern (Ka.lex.)

180   A. putalā ' image ', putalī ' doll, pupil of eye '; B. putul, putlo ' image ', putli ' doll, pupil of eye '; Or. putuḷā, pit, putuḷi, pit ' doll, pupil of eye ', puttaḷi ' doll '; Bi.putlā, lī ' doll '; OMth. putari ' doll, pupil of eye '; Mth. putrā ' doll '; OAw. putarī f. ' wooden image '; H. pū̆tlā m., lī f. ' doll '; G. putḷũ n. ' small image ', lī f. ' doll, pupil of eye '(CDIAL 8269).

181   Ta. po (-pp-, -tt-) to perforate, puncture, make a hole; poy (-v-, -t-) to be hollowed; n. tubularity, hole, hollow or recess in tree; poku (-pp-, -tt-) to make a hole, perforate; pokkaṇai hole in a tree, stone, or ground, cleft in rock; pokku hollow in a tree, defect, fault, blemish; pokkai little hole, crack, having a part deformed, blemish; potir (-pp-, -tt-) to pierce; potu (-v-, -nt-) to be perforated; (-pp-, -tt-) to bore, pierce; potumpu hole, hollow in a tree, pit, cave;pottu hole, rat-hole, hollow in a tree, rent or puncture, defect; pottal, pottai hole, orifice, defect; pottilam hole in a tree; pōttu, pontar, pontu hole, hollow;pōṉ cave. Ma. pottu hole in the ground, cavity, hollow hand; pōtu a hole as in worm-eaten wood. Ko. pok-va·yṇ man whose teeth are all gone (cf. Ta.pokku-vāy, pokkai-vāy toothless mouth). Ka. bokke any round, small hole made by rats, etc.; hodaru hollow of a tree, hole in the ground; bokka a toothless man; (Hav.) bokku

toothless. Tu. boṅku hollow, void, empty; (B-K.) poguḷu a hole, usually in a mud dam across a watercourse; (B-K.) bokku, bokkubāyimouth without teeth. Te. bokka hole, orifice, aperture, pit; (Telangana dial., K.) pokka hole; botta hole, leak; bonda hole, bore; bokki toothless. Kol. pokkaditch, grave; (Pat., p. 115) pokor hollow; bogga small hole, perforation. Nk. Pokka hole, cave; bogga hole. Pa. botta id.; potpa, poppa a chisel. Ga. (P.)boŋga hole. Go. (Tr. W. Ph.) pohpī, (Ma.) poʔpi chisel (Voc. 2432); (D. G. Mu. Ma.) būka hole (Voc. 2585); (Ma.) bokka id. (Voc. 2614); (S.) boŋa id. (Voc. 2620); (Koya Su.) boḍga id. Konḍa (BB) pot- (-t-) to bore, perforate. Pe. pot- (-t-) id. Kui pospa (post-) to pierce, bore a hole, mortise; n. act of piercing, mortising; pondo hole; ? bojo wood dust resulting from dry rot. Kuwi (F.) pōthali to hollow out; (S.) poth'nai to hole; (Isr.) pot- (-h-) to make a hole (in wood, etc.). Kur. pattnā to pierce, perforate, tap with a chisel; pattā chisel to dig a hole in a piece of wood. Malt. pattre to pierce. / Cf. Skt. (lex.) bhūka- hole; also Turner, CDIAL, nos. 8391, *pōka- hollow; 9263(6), bōkkha- toothless; 9624, *bhōkkha- hollow. (DEDR 4452) *bhōkka ' hollow '. 2. *bhōṅka -- 2. 3. *bhōṅga -- . [See list s.v. *pōka --]1. Ku. bhokro, bhokāro ' hollow, concave '; G. bhok n. ' hole ', bhokvũ ' to pierce ', bhokārũ n. ' hollowness '; M. bhok n. ' hole ', bhokū m. 'perforation, bhokṇẽ ' to pierce ', bhoksā m. ' rude gap '; Si. boku ' hollow, oval '.2. N. bhwāṅ ' hole ', H. bhõk m. ' stab '; G. bhõk m. ' hole '; M.

bhõk m. ' hollowness '.3. M. bhõgaḷ, bhõgḷā ' hollow, loose ',
bhõgḷī f. ' hollow of a tube '. (CDIAL 9624).

¹⁸² póta -- 1, aka -- m. ' young of animal or plant ' MBh.
2. *pōtara -- . 3. *pōtala -- , pōtalaka -- m. ' young animal '
BHSk., gō -- pōtalikā -- f. ' heifer ' Pat. 4. *pōtāla -- . 5. *pōtta
-- 1. 6. *pōṭṭa -- 3. 7. *pōna -- 1. 8. *pōttha -- 1. 9. *phōta -- .
10. *phōtta -- 2. [Variety of form points to non -- Aryan origin
(scarcely with Wackernagel AiGr ii 2, 591 < putrá --): prob.
with T. Burrow BSOAS xii 386 ← Drav. Tam. pōttu &c. DED
3748. -- Cf. pōṭā -- f. ' female slave ', pōṭaka -- m. ' servant '
KātyŚr. com. -- See also *pōṅga -- 2] 1. Pa. pōta -- , aka --
m. ' young of an animal ' H. poṭā m. ' young of animal,
unfledged bird '. Ku. potho ' any young animal ', K. āwali --
pūt ' goat's kid ' pōtalaka -- m. ' young animal ' BHSk., gō --
pōtalikā -- f. ' heifer ' Pat. 4. *pōtāla -- . 5. *pōtta -- 1. 6.
*pōṭṭa -- 3. 7. *pōna -- 1. 8. *pōttha -- 1. 9. *phōta -- . 10.
*phōtta -- 2. [Variety of form points to non -- Aryan origin
(scarcely with Wackernagel AiGr ii 2, 591 < putrá --): prob.
with T. Burrow BSOAS xii 386 ← Drav. Tam. pōttu &c. DED
3748. -- Cf. pōṭā -- f. ' female slave ', pōṭaka -- m. ' servant '
KātyŚr. com. -- See also *pōṅga -- 2] (CDIAL 8399) Ta. pōttu
sapling, tender branch or shoot of tree; pōtu flower bud,
freshness, beauty.Te. bōda young of bird. Pa. pottid twig.
Konḍa bōdel bride, young lady. Kui podeli sapling, young
green branch; bōda child. Kuwi pōde (F. S.) girl, (Su.)
woman, girl; (Isr.) pōti small girl; pōdi pōti small children,

young boys and girls; (F.) pōdipōda boys and girls. / (DEDR 4587) Poati 'to be with young, applied to animals'; paotiakanae 'she is in calf'. (Santali)

183   jaṇḍ khaṇḍ = ivory (Jat.ki) khaṇḍi_ = ivory in rough (Jat.ki_); gaṭī = piece of elephant's tusk (S.)

184   kaṇḍ = altar, furnace (Santali) *लोहकारकन्दुः* f. a blacksmith's smelting furnace (Grierson Kashmiri lex.) payĕn-kōda *पयन्‌-कौँद / परिपाककन्दुः* f. a kiln (a potter's, a lime-kiln, and brick-kiln, or the like); a furnace (for smelting)]. kāndavika = a baker; kandu = an iron plate or pan for baking cakes etc. (Ka.lex.)

185   khaḍgá1 m. ' rhinoceros ' MaitrS. 2. khāḍga- ' coming from a rhinoceros ' ŚāṅkhŚr., khaḍga -- m. ' rhinoceros horn ' lex. 3. *khāḍgin -- . [Of non -- Aryan origin: cf. gaṇḍá -- 4 EWA i 318] 1. Pa. Pk. khagga -- m. ' rhinoceros ', Si. kagayā; <-> OAw. khagahā. 2. Ku. N. khāg, khāgo ' rhinoceros horn '; B. khāg ' rhinoceros horn, boar's tusk ', H. khāg, khāg m. ' rhinoceros horn, boar's tusk, cock's spur '. -- Altern. < khaḍgá -- 2: P.khaggā m. ' leaf of Aloe perfoliata ', B. khāg, khāgṛā ' reed for pens ', Or. khagaṛā ' the reed Saccharum spontaneum '.3. Pk. Khaggi -- ' rhinoceros '.(CDIAL 3786).

186   kangar 1 कंगर् m. a large portable brazier (El.). kāgürü काँग्; or kāgürü काँग; or kāgar काँग्‍ ॄ ॄ ॄ । हसब्तिका f. (sg.

dat. kāgrĕ काँग्र्य or kāgarĕ काँगर्य, abl. kāgri काँग्रि), the portable brazier, or kāngrī, much used in Kashmīr (K.Pr. kángár, 129, 131, 178; kángrí, 5, 128, 129). For particulars see El. s.v. kángri; L. 7, 25, kangar; and K.Pr. 129. The word is a fem. dim. of kang, q.v. (Gr.Gr. 37). kāgri-khŏphürü काँग्रि-ख्वफृ॰; । भग्रा काष्ठाङ्गारिका f. a worn-out brazier. -khôru -खोरु; । काष्ठाङ्गारिका<-> र्धभागः m. the outer half (made of woven twigs) of a brazier, remaining after the inner earthenware bowl has been broken or removed; see khôru. -kŏnḍolu - क्रंड&above;लु&below; । हसन्तिकापात्रम् m. the circular earthenware bowl of a brazier, which contains the burning fuel. -köñü -काञू; । हसन्तिकालता f. the covering of woven twigs outside the earthenware bowl of a brazier (Kashmiri)

187   pṛṣa ' *drop ' (in cmpd. ' speckled '). [Cf. pŕṣat- ' spotted ' AV., ' ghee ' (in pŕṣadvant -- RV.), n. ' drop of water ' Hariv. and Ir. *pṛšaka -- in Pers.pušk, Par. p&omacrtodtod; rk ' dung of sheep or goats '(CDIAL 8363). pṛdāku m. (pṛdākū´ -- f. AV.) ' snake ' RV., pṛdāku -- m. ' tiger, panther ' lex. [If with H. W. Bailey BSOAS xi 782 orig. meaning is ' spotted ', both may be same word and the latter not necessarily ← Ir. (Psht. pṛāng, &c.): see EWA ii 335 with lit.] L. parṛā m., ṛī f. ' leopard ' (< *praḍā --). -- Kho. purdùm < *pṛdhūma -- Belvalkar Vol 94 with (?). (CDIAL 8362).

188   pasra = a smithy, a place where a blacksmith works; to do a blacksmith's work; kamar pasrat.hene sen akantalea = our man has gone to the smithy; pasrao lagao (or ehop)

akata = he (the blacksmith) has started his work (Santali);
pasra (Mundari) (Santali.lex.Bodding) pasra, pasāra (Sad.;
Or. Pasrā, a blacksmith's implements) = a blacksmith's
forge; the place where a brazier (tenṭera, malaṛa) makes his
bowls, armlets; ne pāl ṭapuakana pasarate idiime = this
ploughshare is blunt, take it to the smithy; the set of a
blacksmith working in his forge; pasra o = of the blacksmith's
work in the forge; panasra = the length of a blacksmith's
work n the forge; pasraili = rice beer offered for sale; pasra
meṛed,,pasāra meṛed, = syn. of koṭe meṛed = forged iron, in
contrast to dul meṛed, cast iron (Mundari.lex.)

189   prasāra— m. 'extension' Suśr., 'trader's shop' Nalac.
[Cf. prasārayati 'spreads out for sale' Mn. — √SṚ] Paš. lāsar
'bench—like flower beds outside the window' IIFL iii 3, 113;
K. pasār m. 'rest' (semant. cf.prasaratil in Ku. N. Aw.); P.
puhārā m. 'breaking out (of fever, smallpox, &c.)'; Ku. pasāro
'extension, bigness, ex- tension of family or property,
lineage, family, household'; N. pasār 'extension'; B. pasār
'extent of practice in business, popularity', Or. pasāra; H.
pasārām.'stretching out, expansion' (→ P. pasārā m.;
S.pasāro m. 'expansion, crowd'), G. pasār, rɔ m.,M.pasārā;
— K. pasôru m. 'petty shopkeeper'; P. pahārā m.
'goldsmith's workshop'; A. pohār 'small shop'; — ← Center:
S. pasāru m. 'spices'; P. pasār—haṭṭā m. 'druggist's shop';
— X paṇyaśālā—:Ku. pansārī f. 'grocer's shop'.(CDIAL
8835).

[190] Vikalpa: Ta. akai (-v-, -nt-) to flourish, sprout; (-pp-, -tt-) to sprout, rise; to raise; akaippu rising, elevation. Ma. aka germ, bud, shoot; akekka to bud; ava bud, esp. the fruit-like sprout of Artocarpus; avekka to sprout. Ka. age seedling, shoot from the root of a plant or tree, sprout. Koḍ. age paddy seedling. Tu. agge the shoot of a branch. Kur. akhuā seed-bud, sprout, shoot; akrārnā to germinate, shoot, sprout. (DEDR 15) Rebus: agasāle 'goldsmithy' (Te.)

[191] U. 16397; Gadd, PBA 18 (1932), pp. 10-11, pl. II, no. 11

[192] mūh metal ingot (Santali) mūhā = the quantity of iron produced at one time in a native smelting furnace of the Kolhes; iron produced by the Kolhes and formed like a four-cornered piece a little pointed at each end; mūhā mēṛhēt = iron smelted by the Kolhes and formed into an equilateral lump a little pointed at each end; kolhe tehen me~ṛhe~t mūhā akata = the Kolhes have to-day produced pig iron (Santali.lex.)

[193] kal Nilgiri ibex (Ko.)(DEDR 1312) Rebus: kallan mason (Ma.); kalla glass beads (Ma.); kalu stone (Konṇḍa) (DEDR 1298).

[194] L. Legrain, 1936, Ur excavations, Vol. 3, Archaic Seal Impressions.

[195] byucu बिचु; । वृश्००्चिकः m. (sg. dat. bicis बिचिस्), a scorpion. bici-zöṭsü bici-zöṭsü । परोपतापनस्वभावः adj. c.g. scorpion - natured, malignant, malicious, spiteful, maleficent. -ṭŏph -ट्वफ् । वृश्००्चिकदंशः f. (sg. dat. -ṭŏpi -ट्वपि), the sting of

a scorpion; met. a secret malignant act. (Kashmiri) vŕścika
m. (vŕścana -- m. lex.) ' scorpion ' RV., ' cater- pillar covered
with bristles ' lex. [Variety of form for ' scorpion ' in MIA. and
NIA. due to taboo? <-> √vraśc?] Pa. vicchika -- m. ' scorpion
', Pk. vicchia -- , viṁchia -- m., Sh.koh. bičh m. (< *vŕści -- ?),
Ku. bichī, A. bisā (also ' hairy caterpillar ': -- ī replaced by m.
ending -- ā), B. Or. bichā, Mth. bīch, Bhoj. Aw.lakh. bīchī, H.
poet. bīchī f., bīchā m., G. vīchī, vīchī m.; -- *vicchuma -- :
Paš.laur. ućúm, dar. učum, S. vichū m., (with greater
deformation) L.mult. vaṭhūhã, khet. vaṭṭhūha; -- Pk. vicchua -
- , viṁchua -- m., L. vichū m., awāṇ. vicchū, P. bicchū m., Or.
(Sambhalpur) bichu, Mth. bīchu, H. bicchū, bīchū m., G.
vīchu m.; -- Pk. viccu -- , ua -- , viṁcua -- m., K. byucu m. (←
Ind.), P.bhaṭ. biccū, WPah.bhal. biććū m., cur. biccū, bhiḍ.
biććoṭū n. ' young scorpion ', M. vīčũ, vīčū m. (vīčḍā m. '
large scorpion '), vīčvī, ćvīṇ, čīṇ f., Ko. viccu, viṁcu,iṁcu. --
N. bacchiũ ' large hornet '? (Scarcely < *vapsi -- ~ *vaspi --
).vŕścikapattrikā -- .Addenda: vŕścika -- : Garh. bicchū, chī '
scorpion ', A. also bichā (phonet. -- s --) AFD 218. (CDIAL
12081)

196   bica, bica-diri (Sad. bicā; Or. bicī) stone ore; meṛeḍ
bica, stones containing iron; tambabica, copper-ore stones;
samṛobica, stones containing gold (Mundari.lex.)

197   Ta. kūti pudendum muliebre. Ma. kūti posteriors,
membrum muliebre. To. ku·Qy anus, region of buttocks in
general. Tu. kūdi anus, posteriors, membrum muliebre.

(DEDR 1888)

198   Glyph (seven women): bahula_ = Pleiades (Skt.)bagaḷā = name of a certain godess (Te.) bagaḷā ,bagaḷe, vagalā (Ka.); baka , bagaḷḷā , vagaḷā (Te.) bakkula = a demon, uttering horrible cries, a form assumed by the Yakkha Ajakalāpaka, to terrify the Buddha (Pali.lex.) bahulā f. pl. the Pleiades VarBṛS., likā -- f. pl. lex. [bahulá --] Kal. bahul the Pleiades , Kho. ból, (Lor.) boul, bolh, Sh. (Lor.) b*lle (CDIAL 9195) bahulegal. = the Pleiades or Kṛittikā-s (Ka.lex.) bahula_ (VarBr.S.); bahul (Kal.) six presiding female deities: vahulā the six presiding female deities of the Pleiades (Skt.); vākulai id. (Ta.)(Ta.lex.) Pleiades: bahulikā pl. pleiades; bahula born under the pleiades; the pleiades (Skt.lex.) bahule, bahulegal. the pleiades or kr.ttikās (Ka.)(Ka.lex.) Image: female deities of the pleiades: vākulēyan- < va_kulēya Skanda (Ta.lex.) பாகுளி pākuḷi, n. perh. bāhulī. Full moon in the month of Puraṭṭāci; புரட்டாசி மாதத்துப் பௌர்ணமி. அதைப் பாகுளி யென்று (விநாயகபு. 37, 81).

Glyph (twig on head on seven women): adaru 'twig'; rebus: aduru 'native metal'. Thus, the seven women ligatured with twigs on their heads can be read as: bahulā + adaru; rebus: bangala 'goldsmith's portable furnace' + aduru 'native metal'.

bāhulēya Kārttikēya, son of S'iva; bāhula the month

kārttika (Skt.Ka.)(Ka.lex.) வாகுலை vākulai, n. < Vahulā. The six presiding female deities of the Pleiades. Rebus: bagalo = an Arabian merchant vessel (G.lex.) bagala = an Arab boat of a particular description (Ka.); bagalā (M.); bagarige, bagarage = a kind of vessel (Ka.) bagalo = an Arabian merchant vessel (G.lex.) cf. m1429 seal.

bāhuḷyamu. [Skt. from బహుళము.] n. Abundance.

Vikalpa: Rebus: bhāgaḷiyo = a bazaar shopkeeper (G.lex) bakāḷa (Ka.); baāla = a shopkeeper with contemptuous implications (M.)(Ka.lex.) bakāl = [Ar. bakkāl, a greengrocer fr. bakcū, vegetable] a petty shopkeeper; a ānia (so called in contempt); bakālu = fresh vegetables (G.lex.)

Vikalpa: ban:gala = n. An oven. కుంపటి°.kumpaṭi = an:gāra śakaṭī = a chafing dish a portable stove, a goldsmith's portable furnace (Te.lex.) cf. ban:garu, ban:garamu = gold (Te.lex.)

199   kuṭika— 'bent' MBh. [√kuṭ 1] Ext. in H. kuṛuk f. 'coil of string or rope'; M. kuḍċā m. 'palm contracted and hollowed', kuḍapṇē 'to curl over, crisp, contract'. CDIAL 3231 kuṭilá— 'bent, crooked' KātyŚr., aka— Pañcat., n. 'a partic. plant' lex. [√kuṭ 1] Pa. kuṭila— 'bent', n. 'bend'; Pk. kuḍila— 'crooked', illa— 'humpbacked', illaya— 'bent' DEDR 2054 Ta. koṭu curved, bent, crooked; koṭumai crookedness,

obliquity; koṭukki hooked bar for fastening doors, clasp of an ornament. A pair of curved lines: dol 'likeness, picture, form' [e.g., two tigers, two bulls, sign-pair.] Kashmiri. dula दुल l युग्मम् m. a pair, a couple, esp. of two similar things (Rām. 966). Rebus: dul meṛed cast iron (Mundari. Santali) dul 'to cast metal in a mould' (Santali) pasra meṛed, pasāra meṛed = syn. of koṭe meṛed = forged iron, in contrast to dul meṛed, cast iron (Mundari.lex.)

[200] Vikalpa: Ta. kulavu (kulavi-) to bend, curve; n. bend, curve. Kuiklōnga (klōngi-) to be contracted, drawn in, bent up; klōpka(< klōk-p-; klōkt-) to contract, draw up, depress. Kur.xolkhnā, xolxnā to cause one to bend the head;xolkhrnā, xolxrnā to bend the head, bow, stoop. Malt. qolġrubelow, beneath, underneath; kolge to curve, bend; kolgro bent, curved. DEN 29 (Pfeiffer for Kur. Malt.) (DEDR 2136) *kōla4 ' curved, crooked '. [Cf. kaula -- m. ' worshipper of Śakti according to left -- hand ritual ', khōla -- 3 ' lame ' s.v. khōra -- 1. Prob. < *kaura -- (IE. *qou -- lo -- cf. WP i 371?) in Khot. kūra -- ' crooked ' BSOS ix 72 and poss. Sk. kōra -- m. ' movable joint ' Suśr.] Ash. kṓlə ' curved, crooked '; Dm. kōla ' crooked ', Tir. kṓolə; Paš. kōlā´ ' curved, crooked ', Shum. kolā´nṭa; Kho. koli ' crooked ', (Lor.) also ' lefthand, left '; Bshk. kōl ' crooked ', Tor. kōl (Grierson Tor 161 < kuṭila -- : rejected by Morgenstierne AO xii 181), Phal. kūulo; Sh. kōlu̱ ' curved, crooked '. (CDIAL 3533).

[201]   bhaṭa 'furnace' (G.) baṭa = kiln (Santali); baṭa = a kind of iron (G.) bhaṭṭha -- m.n. ' gridiron (Pkt.) baṭhu large

cooking fire' baṭhī f. 'distilling furnace'; L. bhaṭṭh m. 'grain—parcher's oven', bhaṭṭhī f. 'kiln, distillery', awāṇ. bhaṭh; P. bhaṭṭh m., ṭhī f. 'furnace', bhaṭṭhā m. 'kiln'; S. bhaṭṭhī keṇī 'distil (spirits)'. (CDIAL 9656)

[202] Ta. koṭi creeper, umbilical cord. Ma. koṭi creeper, what is long and thin, umbilical cord, etc. Ko koṛy creeper; koc binding (for firewood, etc.) made from plant. To. kwïṛy creeper. Koḍ. koḍi ele betel leaf. Pe. goḍi creeper. Maṇḍ. kuṛi id. Cf. 1678, esp. Kur. kuḍḍā. Ta. koṭi banner, flag, streamer; kōṭu summit of a hill, peak, mountain; kōṭai mountain; kōṭar peak, summit of a tower; kuvaṭu mountain, hill, peak;kuṭumi summit of a mountain, top of a building, crown of the head, bird's crest, tuft of hair (esp. of men), crown, projecting corners on which a door swings.Ma. koṭi top, extremity, flag, banner, sprout; kōṭu end; kuvaṭu hill, mountain-top; kuṭuma, kuṭumma narrow point, bird's crest, pivot of door used as hinge, lock of hair worn as caste distinction; koṭṭu head of a bone. Ko. koṛy flag on temple; koṭ top tuft of hair (of Kota boy, brahman), crest of bird; kuṭ clitoris.To. kwïṭ tip, nipple, child's back lock of hair. Ka. kuḍi pointed end, point, extreme tip of a creeper, sprout, end, top, flag, banner; guḍi point, flag, banner;kuḍilu sprout, shoot; kōḍu a point, the peak or top of a hill; koṭṭu a point, nipple, crest, gold ornament worn by women in their plaited hair; koṭṭa state of being extreme; koṭṭa-kone the extreme point; (Hav.) koḍi sprout; Koḍ. koḍi top (of mountain, tree, rock,

table), rim of pit or tank, flag. Tu. koḍi point, end, extremity, sprout, flag; koḍipuni to bud, germinate; (B-K.) koḍipu, koḍipelů a sprout; koḍirè the top-leaf; koṭṭu cock's comb, peacock's tuft. Te.koḍi tip, top, end or point of a flame; koṭṭa-kona the very end or extremity.Kol.(Kin.)koṛi point. Pa. kūṭor cock's comb. Go. (Tr.) koḍḍī tender tip or shoot of a plant or tree; koḍḍi (S.) end, tip, (Mu.) tip of bow; (A.) koḍi point (Voc. 891). Malt. qorgo comb of a cock; ? qóru the end, the top (as of a tree).(DEDR 2049) Cf. 2081 Ta. koṇṭai and 2200 Ta. kōṭu. (DEDR 2050)

203   kharādī 'turner' (G.) कातारी or कांतारी [kātārī or kāntārī] m (कातणें) A turner. (Marathi) karaḍo, karāḍī 'a goldsmith's tool' (G.)

204   ḍhākaḷ f. ' old decaying stump ', ḍhākẽ n. ' stout stake ', ḍhākaḷ, kūḷ ' old and decaying, bare of leaves &c. (M.) (CDIAL 5524)

205   bha_rat.iyum, bhārvaṭiyo, bhāroṭiyo = a beam (G.lex.) bāri = bamboo splits fastened lengthwise to the rafters of a roof from both sides (Tu.lex.) bārapaṭṭe = chief beam lying on pillars (Te.lex.) bharaṇum a piece in architecture; placed at the top of a pillar to support a beam (G.)

206   kol 'working in iron, blacksmith (Ta.); kollan-blacksmith (Ta.); kollan blacksmith, artificer (Ma.)(DEDR 2133) kolme = furnace (Ka.) kole.l 'temple, smithy' (Ko.); kolme smithy' (Ka.) kol = pan~calo_ha (five metals); kol

metal (Ta.lex.) pan~caloha = a metallic alloy containing five metals: copper, brass, tin, lead and iron (Skt.); an alternative list of five metals: gold, silver, copper, tin (lead), and iron (dhātu;Nānārtharatnākara 82; Mangarāja's Nighaṇṭu. 498)(Ka.) kol, kolhe, 'the koles, an aboriginal tribe if iron smelters speaking a language akin to that of Santals' (Santali)

[207] skandhá m. ' shoulder, upper part of back ' AV., ' trunk of tree, mass (esp. of an army) ' MBh., skándhas<-> n. ' branching top of a tree ' RV. [Absence of any trace of initial s -- in Kafiri and Dardic supports possibility of IA. *kandha- beside sk (unnecessarily assumed in ODBL 438 for NIA. k -- which is dissim. from kh<-> before dh as prob. in Aś. agi -- k(h)aṁdha --)] Pa. khandha -- m. ' shoulder, back, tree -- trunk ', aka<-> m. ' division, chapter '; Pk. khaṁdha -- , ka m. ' shoulder, tree trunk, wall '; Ash. kándä ' stem, trunk ', Kt. kə́nē, Wg. kaná; Paš.lauṛ. xānd ' shoulder ', ar. kandī́, kuṛ. kōn (obl. kānda); Shum. kandam ' my shoulder '; Gaw. kandík ' shoulder '; Bshk. kān (with rising tone) ' shoulder, upper part of back '; Tor. kan ' shoulder ', Sv. kandike, Phal. kān, kan; S. kandhu m. ' neck, back of neck ', dhom. ' back of neck, edge ', dhī f. ' bank of river ', dhī pāso ' neighbourhood '; L.awāṇ. khaddhā ' multitude ', P. khandhā m. ' mass, multitude, flock of sheep or goats, herd of buffaloes ', ludh. kannhā m. ' shoulder ', (Ambala) kandhā m.; Ku. kād, kādho, kāno ' shoulder ', gng. kāni ' neck '; N.

kādh,kād ' shoulder, back ' (whence khãduwā, dilo ' heavy,
solid ', kãdheuli, khãde ' stick carried by coolies across
shoulders to take the weight of a load '); A. kāndh, kān '
shoulder ', kandhā, kanā ' large bundle of reeds &c. carried
on the shoulder ', kādhi ' pent house, veranda, eaves '; B.
kādh ' shoulder ', kādhā ' edge, bank '; Or. kāndha, kādhā '
shoulder '; Bi. kānhe ' on the shoulder ', (Patna) khandh, dhā
' large area of cultivated land '; Mth. kānh,kanhā ' shoulder ',
Bhoj. kānh, Aw.lakh. kādh; H. kādh, dhā m. ' shoulder ',
kandh m. ' tree trunk, thick branch '; G. khādhi, kā f. '
shoulder '; M. khād, dā m. ' shoulder, back of neck ', f. ' large
bough '; Ko. khāndhu m. ' shoulder '; Si. kaňda ' shoulder,
tree trunk, collection, mass ', kaňdu' mountain ' (< -- aka --).
-- With metath. K. nakh, dat. khas m. ' shoulder '? <-> Bshk.
khan m. ' hill ', Tor. Mai. khān, Chil. Gau. kān (→ Par.
khándiIlFL i 265) poss. all < skandhá -- , but prob. like Tor.
(Grierson) khaṇḍ ' hill ', Phal. khāṇ, khaṇ, Sh.koh. khŭṇ m.,
gur. khonn, pales. khõṇə, jij. khõṇ rather < khaṇḍá -- AO xviii
240. -- X maṇi -- 2 q.v. S.kcch. kandh m. ' back of neck ',
kandho m. ' shoulder '; WPah.ktg. kannh m. ' shoulder ', kc.
kānh, jaun. kānn m.; ktg. (kc.) khándɔ m. ' big box along the
wall of living room for grain '. (CDIAL 13627)

208   [bāhú --] Pk. bāhulaga -- m. arm ; Gy. pal. Baúlă
bracelet ; L. bôhlī, mult. bāhvlī, (Ju.) b̤ālhī f. ' action of the
arms in swimming , b̤ūhlī f. sleeve ; P. bāhulī f. sleeve , ludh.
bauhlī f.; Ku. baũlī hand, arm , baũlo sleeve , gng. bɔ̃ l_; N.
bāulo sleeve , li ' small do. ; Or. bāhuḷa armour for the arms

; M. bāhulā, bāvlā m. region of the shoulder joint (CDIAL 9233)

209   kammaṭṭam, kammiṭṭam coinage, mint (Ma.); kammatia coiner (Ka.)(DEDR 1236) kammaṭa = coinage, mint (Ka.M.) kampaṭṭa-k-kūṭam mint; kampaṭṭa-k-kāran-coin-maker.

210 . [Vikalpa: Line ger-a (Te.), gira_ (Or.); rebus: Battle keral. (Ka.); ceru (Ta.) qeru]

211 ḍhangar 'trough for feeding one animal' पात्र pātra, (I.) s. Vessel, cup, plate; receptacle. [lw. Sk. id.] (Nepali) pātramu A utensil, ఉపకరణము. Hardware. metal vessels. (Telugu) பத்தல் pattal, n. பத்தர்¹ pattar 1. A wooden bucket; மரத்தாலான நீரிறைக்குங் கருவி. தீம்பிழி யெந்திரம் பத்தல் வருந்த (பதிற்றுப். 19, 23).

212 பத்தர்² pattar , n. < T. battuḍu. A caste title of goldsmiths; தட்டார் பட்டப்பெயருள் ஒன்று. பட்டடை¹ paṭṭaṭai , n. prob. படு¹- + அடை¹-. 1. [T. paṭṭika, K. paṭṭaḍe.] Anvil; அடைகல். (பிங்.) சீரிடங்காணி னெறிதற்குப் பட்ட டை (குறள், 821). 2. [K. paṭṭaḍi.] Smithy, forge; கொல்லன் களரி பத்தல் pattal , n. 1. A wooden bucket; மரத்தாலான நீரிறைக்குங் கருவி. தீம்பிழி யெந்திரம் பத்தல் வருந்த (பதிற்றுப். 19, 23). பத்தர்¹ pattar , n. 1. See பத்தல், 1, 4, 5. 2. Wooden trough for feeding animals; தொட்டி. பன்றிக் கூழ்ப்பத்தரில் (நாலடி, 257).

pattar-ai community; guild as of workmen (Ta.); pattar merchants; perh. vartaka (Skt.)

Patthara [cp. late Sk. prastara. The ord. meaning of Sk. pr. is "stramentum"] 1. stone, rock S i.32. -- 2. stoneware Miln 2. (Pali) Pa. Pk. patthara -- m. ' stone ', S. patharu m., L. (Ju.) pathar m., khet. patthar, P. patthar m. (→ forms of Bi. Mth. Bhoj. H. G. below with atth or ath), WPah.jaun. pātthar; Ku. pāthar m. ' slates, stones ', gng. pāth*lr ' flat stone '; A. B. pāthar ' stone ', Or. pathara; Bi. pāthar, patthar, patthal ' hailstone '; Mth. pāthar, pathal ' stone ', Bhoj. pathal, Aw.lakh. pāthar, H. pāthar, patthar, pathar, patthal m., G. patthar, pathrɔ m.; M. pāthar f. ' flat stone '; Ko. phāttaru ' stone '; Si. patura ' chip, fragment '; -- S. pathirī f. ' stone in the bladder '; P. pathrī f. ' small stone '; Ku. patharī ' stone cup '; B. pāthri ' stone in the bladder, tartar on teeth '; Or. pathurī ' stoneware '; H. patthrī f. ' grit ', G. pathrī f. *prastarapaṭṭa -- , *prastaramṛttikā -- , *prastarāsa -- .Addenda: prastará -- : WPah.kṭg. pátthər m. ' stone, rock '; pəthreuṇõ ' to stone '; J. pāthar m. ' stone '; OMarw. pātharī ' precious stone '. (CDIAL 8857)

paṭṭarai 'workshop' (Ta.) pattharika [fr. patthara] a merchant Vin ii.135 (kaŋsa°).(Pali) cf. Pattharati [pa+tharati] to spread, spread out, extend J i.62; iv.212; vi.279; DhA i.26; iii.61 (so read at J vi.549 in cpd °pāda with spreading feet, v. l. patthaṭa°). -- pp. patthaṭa (q. v.). பத்தர்&sup5; pattar, n. perh. vartaka. Merchants; வியாபாரிகள். (W.) battuḍu. n. The caste title of all the five castes of artificers as vaḍla b*, carpenter.

213   http://www.ling.hawaii.edu/faculty/stampe/aa.html

See http://kalyan97.googlepages.com/mleccha1.pdf

214   Possehl, Gregory, 2006, Shu-ilishu's cylinder seal, Expedition, Vol. 48, No. 1
http://www.penn.museum/documents/publications/expedition/PDFs/48-1/What%20in%20the%20World.pdf

215   Translation based on
http://www.valmikiramayan.net/sundara/sarga30/sundara_30_frame.htm
See: Narayana Iyengar, 1938, Vanmeegarum Thamizhum;
http://tashindu.blogspot.com/2006_12_01_archive.html In this work, Narayana Iyengar cites that the commentator interpret mānuṣam vākyam as the language spoken in Kosala.

216   See http://www.scribd.com/doc/2232617/lexicon linked at
http://sites.google.com/site/kalyan97/indus-writing

217   Witzel, Michael, 1999, Substrate Languages in Old Indo-Aryan (R_gvedic, Middle and Late Vedic, Electronic Journal of Vedic Studies (EJVS) 5-1 (1999) pp.1-67.
http://www.ejvs.laurasianacademy.com/ejvs0501/ejvs0501article.pdf

218   cf. Steve Farmer, Richard Sproat, and Michael Witzel, 2005, The Collapse of the Indus-Script Thesis: The Myth of a Literate Harappan Civilization, EJVS 11-2 Dec. 13, 2005.

219http://huntingtonarchive.osu.edu/Makara%20Site/makara/index.html

220   http://tinyurl.com/gonsh

221 কুঁদন, কোঁদন [kuṅdana, kōṅdana] n act of turning (a thing) on a lathe; act of carving; act of rushing forward to

attack or beat; act of skip ping or frisking; act of bragging. (Bengali)কুঁদ [kuṅda] n a (turner's) lathe; a variety of multi-petalled jasmine.কুঁদ¹ [kuṅda¹] v to turn (a thing) on a lathe, to shape by turning on a lathe; to carve; to rush forward to attack or beat; to skip, to frisk; to brag.

222 kottamu, kottama. [Tel.] n. A pent roofed chamber or house as distinguished from 'midde' which is flat-roofed. Pounding in a mortar. A stable for elephants or horses, or cattle A. i. 43. [koṭṭāmu] koṭṭāmu. [Tel.] n. A pent roofed house. [koṭṭaruvu] koṭṭaruvu. [Tel.] n. A barn, a grain store. [koṭāru], [Tel.] n. A store, a granary. A place to keep grain, salt, &c. కొఠారు [koṭhāru] Same as [koṭhī] koṭhī. [H.] n. A bank. A mercantile house or firm (Telugu) kốṣṭha2 n. ' pot ' Kauś., ' granary, storeroom ' MBh., ' inner apartment ' lex., aka -- n. ' treasury ', ikā f. ' pan ' Bhpr. [Cf. *kōttha -- , *kōtthala -- : same as prec.?] Pa. kottha -- n. ' monk's cell, storeroom ', aka<-> n. ' storeroom '; Pk. koṭṭha -- , kuṭ, koṭṭhaya -- m. ' granary, storeroom '; Sv. dāntar -- kuṭha ' fire -- place '; Sh. (Lor.) kōti (ṭh?) ' wooden vessel for mixing yeast '; K. kōṭha m. ' granary ', kuṭhu m. ' room ', kuṭhü f. ' granary, storehouse '; S. koṭho m. ' large room ', ṭhī f. ' storeroom '; L. koṭhā m. ' hut, room, house ', ṭhī f. ' shop, brothel ', awāṇ. koṭhā ' house '; P. koṭṭhā, koṭhā m. ' house with mud roof and walls, granary ', koṭṭhī, koṭhī f. ' big well -- built house, house for married women to prostitute themselves in '; WPah. pāḍ. kuṭhī ' house '; Ku. koṭho ' large

square house ', gng. kōṭhi ' room, building '; N. koṭho ' chamber ', ṭhi ' shop '; A. koṭhā, kŏṭhā ' room ', kuṭhī ' factory '; B. koṭhā ' brick -- built house ', kuṭhī ' bank, granary '; Or. koṭhā ' brick -- built house ', ṭhī ' factory, granary '; Bi. koṭhī ' granary of straw or brushwood in the open '; Mth. koṭhī̆ grain -- chest '; OAw. koṭha 'storeroom '; H. koṭhā m. ' granary ', ṭhī f. ' granary, large house ', Marw. koṭho m. ' room '; G. koṭhɔ m. ' jar in which indigo is stored, warehouse ', ṭhī f. ' large earthen jar, factory '; M. koṭhā m. ' large granary ', ṭhī f. ' granary, factory '; Si. koṭa ' storehouse '. -- Ext. with -- ḍa -- : K. kūṭhürü f. ' small room '; L. koṭhṛī f. ' small side room '; P. koṭhṛī f. ' room, house '; Ku. koṭherī ' small room '; H. koṭhrī f. ' room, granary '; M. koṭhḍī f. ' room '; -- with -- ra -- : A. kuṭharī ' chamber ', B. kuṭhrī, Or. koṭhari; -- with -- lla -- : Sh. (Lor.) kotul (ṭh?) ' wattle and mud erection for storing grain '; H. koṭhlā m., lī f. ' room, granary '; G. koṭhlɔ m. ' wooden box ' kōṣṭhapāla -- , *kōṣṭharūpa -- , *kōṣṭhāṁśa -- , kōṣṭhāgāra -- ; *kajjalakōṣṭha -- , *duvārakōṣṭha-, *dēvakōṣṭha -- , dvārakōṣṭhaka -- .Addenda: kṓṣṭha -- 2: WPah.kṭg. kóṭṭhi f. ' house, quarters, temple treasury, name of a partic. temple ', J. koṭhā m. ' granary ', koṭhī f. ' granary, bungalow '; Garh. koṭhu ' house surrounded by a wall '; Md. koḍi ' frame ', <-> koři ' cage ' (X kōṭṭa --). -- with ext.: OP. koṭhārī f. ' crucible ', P. kuṭhālī f., H.kuṭhārī f.; -- Md. koṭari ' room '.(CDIAL 3546)

kōṣṭhapāla m. ' storekeeper ' W. [kṓṣṭha -- 2, pāla --] M. koṭhvaḷā m. (CDIAL 3547) 3550 kōṣṭhāgāra n. ' storeroom, store ' Mn. [kŏṣṭha -- 2, agāra --] Pa. koṭṭhāgāra -- n. ' storehouse, granary '; Pk. koṭṭhāgāra -- , koṭṭhāra -- n. ' storehouse '; K. kuṭhār m. ' wooden granary ', WPah. bhal. kóṭhār m.; A. B. kuṭharī ' apartment ', Or. koṭhari; Aw. lakh. koṭhār ' zemindar's residence '; H. kuṭhiyār ' granary '; G. koṭhār m. ' granary, storehouse ', koṭhāriyũ n. ' small do. '; M. koṭhār n., koṭhārē n. ' large granary ', -- rī f. ' small one '; Si. koṭāra ' granary, store '.kŏṣṭhāgārika -- .Addenda: kŏṣṭhāgāra -- : WPah.ktg. kəthā´r, kc. kuṭhār m. ' granary, storeroom ', J. kuṭhār, kṭhār m.; -- Md. kořāru ' storehouse ' ← Ind. (CDIAL 3550). kŏṣṭhāgārika m. ' storekeeper ' BHSk. [Cf. kŏṣṭhā- gārin -- m. ' wasp ' Suśr.: kŏṣṭhāgāra --] Pa. koṭṭhāgārika -- m. ' storekeeper '; S. koṭhārī m. ' one who in a body of faqirs looks after the provision store '; Or. koṭhārī ' treasurer '; Bhoj. koṭhārī ' storekeeper ', H. kuṭhiyārī m. Addenda: kŏṣṭhāgārika -- : G. koṭhārī m. ' storekeeper '. kŏṣṭhin -- see kuṣṭhin -- Add2. (CDIAL 3552) Ta. koṭṭakai shed with sloping roofs, cow-stall; marriage pandal; koṭṭam cattle-shed; koṭṭil cow-stall, shed, hut; (STD) koṭambe feeding place for cattle. Ma. koṭṭil cowhouse, shed, workshop, house. Ka. koṭṭage, koṭige, koṭṭige stall or outhouse (esp. for cattle), barn, room. Koḍ. koṭṭï shed. Tu.koṭṭa hut or dwelling of Koragars; koṭya shed, stall. Te. koṭṭāmu stable for cattle or horses; koṭṭāyi thatched shed. Kol. (Kin.) koṛka, (SR.) korkācowshed; (Pat., p. 59) konṭoḍi henhouse. Nk. khoṭa cowshed. Nk. (Ch.) koṛka id. Go. (Y.) koṭa, (Ko.) koṭam (pl. koṭak) id. (Voc. 880); (SR.) koṭka shed;

(W. G. Mu. Ma.) koṛka, (Ph.) korka, kurka cowshed (Voc. 886); (Mu.) koṭorla, koṭorli shed for goats (Voc. 884). Malt. koṭa hamlet. / Influenced by Skt. goṣṭha-. (DEDR 2058) கொட்டகை koṭṭakai, n. < gōṣṭhaka. [T. koṭṭamu, K. koṭṭage, Tu. koṭya.] Shed with sloping roofs, cow-stall, marriage-pandal; பந்தல் விசேடம். கொட்டகைத் தூண்போற் காலிலங்க (குற்றா. குற. 84, 4). கொட்டம் koṭṭam, n. House; வீடு. ஒரு கொட்டம் ஒழிச்சுக் குடுத்துருங்கோ (எங்களூர், 47). கோட்டம்² kōṭṭam, n. < kōṣṭha. 1. Room, enclosure; அறை. சுடும ணோாங்கிய நெடு நிலைக் கோட்டமும் (மணி. 6, 59). 2. Temple; கோயில். கோழிச் சேவற் கொடியோன் கோட்டமும் (சிலப். 14, 10).

kottha (m. nt.) [Sk. koṣṭha abdomen, any cavity for holding food, cp. kuṣṭa groin, and also Gr. ku/tos cavity, ku/sdos pudendum muliebre, ku/stis bladder = E. cyst, chest; Lat. cunnus pudendum, Ger. hode testicle] anything hollow and closed in (Cp. gabbha for both meanings) as -- 1. the stomach or abdomen Miln 265, Vism 357; Sdhp 257. -- 2. a closet, a monk's cell, a storeroom, M i.332; Th 2, 283 (?)=ThA, 219; J ii.168. <-> 3. a sheath, in asi° Vin iv.171. -- aṭṭhi a stomach bone or bone of the abdomen Vism 254, 255. -- abbhantara the intestinal canal Miln 67; -- âgāra (nt.) storehouse, granary, treasury: in conn. with kosa (q. v.) in formula paripuṇṇa -- kosa -- koṭṭhâgāra (adj.) D i.134, expld at DA i.295 as threefold, viz. dhana° dhañña° vattha°, treasury, granary, warehouse; PvA 126, 133; -- âgārika a storehouse -- keeper, one who hoards up wealth Vin i.209; DhA i.101; -- āsa [=koṭṭha +aṇsa] share, division, part; °koṭṭhāsa (adj.) divided into, consisting of. K. is a prose word only and in all Com. passages is used to explain bhāga: J i.254; 266; vi.368; Miln 324; DhA iv.; 108 (=pada), 154; PvA 58, 111, 205 (kāma°=kāmaguṇā); VvA 62; anekena k° -- ena infinitely PvA 221. Koṭṭhaka1 (nt.) "a kind of koṭṭha," the stronghold over a gateway, used as a store -- room for various things, a chamber, treasury, granary Vin ii.153, 210; for the purpose of keeping water in it Vin ii.121=142; 220; treasury J i.230; ii.168; -- store -- room J ii.246; koṭṭhake pāturahosi appeared at the gateway, i. e. arrived at the mansion Vin i.291.; -- udaka -- k a bath -- room, bath cabinet Vin i.205 (cp. Bdhgh's expln at Vin. Texts ii.57); so also nahāna -- k° and piṭṭhi -- k°, bath -- room behind a hermitage J iii.71; DhA ii.19; a gateway, Vin ii.77; usually in cpd. dvāra - - k° "door cavity," i. e. room over the gate: gharaṇ satta -- dvāra -- koṭṭhakapaṭimaṇḍitaṇ "a mansion adorned with seven gateways" J i.227=230, 290; VvA 322. dvāra -- koṭṭhakesu āsanāni paṭṭhapenti "they spread mats in the gateways" VvA 6; esp. with bahi: bahi -- dvārakoṭṭhakā nikkhāmetvā "leading him out in front of the gateway" A iv.206; °e thiṭa or nisinna standing or sitting in front of the gateway S i.77; M i.161, 382; A iii.30. -- bala -- k. a line of infantry J i.179. -- koṭṭhaka -- kamma or the occupation connected with a storehouse (or bathroom?) is mentioned as an example of a low occupation at Vin iv.6; Kern, Toev. s. v.

"someone who sweeps away dirt." (Pali)

[223] http://www.scribd.com/doc/6151815/Sri-Vatsa

[224]   (n.) ariyan, nobleman, gentleman (opp. servant); (adj.) arīyan, well-born, belonging to the ruling race, noble, aristocratic, gentlemanly J v.257; Vv 396. -- f. ayirā lady, mistress (of a servant) J ii.349 (v. l. oyyakā); voc. ayire my lady J v.138 Ariya (adj. -- n.) [Vedic ārya, of uncertain etym. The other Pāli forms are ayira & ayya] 1. (racial) Aryan D ii.87. <-> 2. (social) noble, distinguished, of high birth. -- 3.(ethical) in accord with the customs and ideals of the Aryan clans, held in esteem by Aryans, generally approved. Hence: right, good, ideal. [The early Buddhists had no such ideas as we cover with the words Buddhist and Indian. Ariya does not exactly mean either. But it often comes very near to what they would have considered the best in each]. -- (adj.): D i.70 = (°ena sīlakkhandhena samannāgata fitted out with our standard morality); iii.64 (cakkavatti -- vatta), 246 (diṭṭhi); M i.139 (pannaddhaja); ii.103 (ariyāya jātiyā jāto, become of the Aryan lineage); S ii.273 (tuṇhībhāva); iv.250 (vaddhi), 287 (dhamma); v.82 (bojjhangā), 166 (satipaṭṭhānā), 222 (vimutti), 228 (ñāṇa), 255 (iddhipādā), 421 (maggo), 435 (saccāni), 467 (paññā -- cakkhu); A i.71 (parisā); ii.36 (ñāya); iii.451 (ñāṇa); iv.153 (tuṇhībhāva); v.206 (sīlakkhandha); It 35 (paññā), 47 (bhikkhu sammaddaso); Sn 177 (patha = aṭṭhangiko maggo SnA 216); Dh 236 (bhūmi), 270; Ps ii.212

(iddhi). -- alamariya fully or thoroughly good D i.163 = iii.82 = A iv.363; nâlamariya not at all good, object, ignoble ibid. -- (m.) Vin i.197 (na ramati pāpe); D i.37 = (yaŋ taŋ ariyā ācikkhanti upekkhako satimā etc.: see 3rd. jhāna), 245;iii.111 (°ānaŋ anupavādaka one who defames the noble); M i.17, 280 (sottiyo ariyo arahaŋ); S i.225 (°ānaŋ upavādaka); ii.123 (id.); iv.53 (°assa vinayo), 95 (id.); A i.256 (°ānaŋ upavādaka); iii.19, 252 (id.); iv.145 (dele! see arīhatatta); v.68, 145 sq., 200, 317; It 21, 108; Dh 22, 164, 207; J iii.354 = Miln 230; M i.7, i35 (ariyānaŋ adassāvin: "not recognising the Noble Ones") PvA 26, 146; DhA ii.99; Sdhp 444 (°ānaŋ vaŋsa). <-> anariya (adj. & n.) not Ariyan, ignoble, undignified, low, common, uncultured Ai.81; Sn 664 (= asappurisa SnA 479; DhsA 353); J ii.281 (= dussīla pāpadhamma C.); v.48 (°rūpa shameless), 87; DhA iv.3. -- See also ñāṇa, magga, sacca, sāvaka.   -- âvakāsa appearing noble J v.87. -- uposatha the ideal feast day (as one of 3) A i.205 sq., 212. -- kanta loved by the Best D iii.227. -- gaṇā (pl.) troops of worthies J vi.50 (= brāhmaṇa -- gaṇā, te kira tāda ariyâcārā ahesuŋ, tena te evam āha C.). -- garahin casting blame on the righteous Sn 660. -- citta a noble heart. -- traja a true descendant of the Noble ones Dpvs v.92. -- dasa having the ideal (or best) belief It 93 = 94. -- dhana sublime treasure; always as sattavidha° sevenfold, viz. saddhā°, sīla°, hiri°, ottappa°, suta°, cāga°, paññā° "faith, a moral life, modesty, fear of evil, learning, self -- denial, wisdom" ThA 240; VvA 113; DA ii.34. -- dhamma the national customs of the Aryans (= ariyānaŋ eso dhammo Nd1 71, 72) M i.1, 7, 135; A ii.69; v.145 sq., 241, 274; Sn 783; Dhs 1003. -- puggala an (ethically) model person, Ps i.167; Vinv.117; ThA 206. -- magga the Aryan Path. -- vaŋsa the (fourfold) noble family, i. e. of recluses content with the 4 requisites D iii.224 = A ii.27 = Ps i.84 = Nd2 141; cp. A iii.146. -- vattin leading a noble life, of good conduct J iii.443. -- vatā at Th 1, 334 should be read °vattā (nom. sg. of vattar, vac) "speaking noble words": -- vāsa the most excellent state of mind, habitual disposition, constant practice. Ten such at D iii.269, 291 = A v.29 (Passage recommended to all Buddhists by Asoka in the Bhabra Edict). -- vihāra the best practice S v.326. -- vohāra noble or honorable practice. They are four, abstinence from lying, from slander, from harsh language, from frivolous talk. They are otherwise known as the 4 vacī -- kammantā & represent sīla nos. 4 -- 7. See D iii.232; A ii.246; Vin v.125. -- sangha the communion of the Nobles ones PvA 1. -- sacca, a standard truth, an established fact, D i.189, ii.90, 304 sq.; iii 277; M i.62, 184; iii.248; S v.415 sq. = Vin i.10, 230. It 17; Sn 229, 230, 267; Dh 190; DhA iii.246; KhA 81, 151, 185, 187; ThA 178, 282, 291; VvA 73. -- sāvaka a disciple of the noble ones (= ariyānaŋ santike sutattā a. SnA 166). M i.8, 46, 91, 181, 323; ii.262; iii.134, 228, 272; It 75; Sn 90; Miln 339; DhA i.5, (opp. putthujjana). -- sīlin of unblemished conduct, practising virtue D i.115 (= sīlaŋ ariyaŋ uttamaŋ parisuddhaŋ DA i.286); M ii.167. When the commentators, many centuries afterwards, began to write Pali in S. India & Ceylon, far from the ancient seat of the Aryan clans, the racial sense of the wordariya was scarcely, if at all, present to their minds. Dhammapāla especially was probably a non -- Aryan, and certainly lived in a Dravidian environment. The then current similar popular etmologies of ariya and arahant (cp. next article) also assisted the confusion in their minds. They sometimes therefore erroneously identify the two words and explain Aryans as meaning Arahants (DhA i.230; SnA 537; PvA 60). In other ways also they misrepresented the old texts by ignoring the racial force of the word. Thus at J v.48 the text, speaking of a hunter belonging to one of the aboriginal tribes, calls him anariya -- rūpa. The C. explains this as "shameless", but what the text has, is simply that he looked like a non -- Aryan. (cp ' frank ' in English).

225   http://www.art-andarchaeology.com/india/calcutta/ei524.jpg

226 More examples at

http://www.scribd.com/doc/13001736/Continuing-Legacy-Hieroglyphs-Ancient-Coins

Source: C.J. Brown, 1922, The coins of India, The Heritage of India Series, Association Press, Calcutta.

See: http://www.scribd.com/doc/12921150/Survival-of-Hieroglyphs-on-Punch-Marked-Coins

227 http://www215.pair.com/sacoins/images/maps/Map2_small.jpg

228 Source for the pictures showing use of bow to cut śankha:

[229] Chatterjee, SK, The study of kol, Calcutta Review, 1923, p. 455

[230] Przyluski, Non-aryan loans in Indo-Aryan, in: Bagchi, PC, *Pre-aryan and pre-dravidian,* pp.28-29

[231] Prob. separate from RV. kr̥̄tā -- ' girl ' H. W. Bailey TPS 1955, 65; K. kūrü f. ' young girl ', kash. kōr̥ī, ram. kur̥hī; L. kur̥ā m. ' bridegroom ', kur̥ī f. ' girl, virgin, bride ', awāṇ. kur̥ī f. ' woman '; P. kur̥ī f. ' girl, daughter ', (CDIAL 3295). कारकोळी or ळ्या [kārakōr̥ī or ḷyā] a Relating to the country कार- कोळ--a tribe of Bráhmans (Marathi) —हरिवंश में **कोल** राज्य का नाम दक्षिण के पांडय और केरल के साथ आया है । पर बौद्ध ग्रंथों में कोल राज्य कपिलवस्तु के पूर्व रोहिणी नदी के उस पार बतलाया गया है । शुद्धौदन और सिद्धार्थ दोनों का विवाह इसी वंश में हुआ था । इस कोल वंश के विषय में बौद्धों मे ऐसा प्रसिद्ध कि इक्ष्वाकुवंश के चार पुरुष अपनी कोढ़िन बहन को हिमालय के अंचल में ले गए और उसे एक गुफा में बंद कर आए । कुछ दिनों के उपरांत काशी का एक कोढ़ी राजा भी उसी स्थान पर पहुँचा और काली मिर्च (कौल) खाकर अच्छा हो गया । राजा ने एक दिन देखा कि एक सिंह उस गुफा के द्वार पर रखे हुए पत्थर को हटाना चाहता है । राजा ने सिंह को मारा और गुहा से उसे कन्या का उद्धार करके उसका कुष्ट रोग छुड़ा दिया । उन्ही दोनों के संयोग से कौल वंश की उत्पत्ति हुई । स्कंद पुराण के हिमवत् खंड लिखा में है कि कोल एक म्लेच्छ जाति थी जो हिमालय में शिकार करती हुई घूमा करती थी । १२. एक जगली जाति । उ०—बन हित कोल किरात किसोरी । रची बिरंचि विषय सूख भोरी ।—मानस २ ।६० । **विशेष**— ब्रह्मवैवर्त पुराण में कोल को लेट पुरुष और तीवर स्त्री से उत्पन्न एक वर्णसंकर जाति लिखा है । स्कंदपुराण में इसे म्लेच्छ जाति लिखा है । पद्मपुराण में लिखा है कि जब पवन, पल्लव, कोलि, सर्प आदि सगर के भय से वशिष्ट की शरण में आए, तब उन्होंने उनका सिर आदि मुँडाकर उन्हें केवल संस्कारभ्रष्ट

कर दिया । आजकल जो कोल नाम की एक जंगली जाति है, वह आर्यों से स्वतत्र एक आदिम जाति जान पड़ती है, और छोटा नागपुर से लेकर मिरजापुर के जंगलों तक फैली हुई है । (Hindi *sabdasagara*)

232   http://www.suwanneeriverranch.com/photos/BlackBuckBody.jpg

233http://en.wikipedia.org/wiki/Invasion_of_India_by_Scythian_Tribes#Establishment_of_Mlechcha_Kingdoms_in_Northern_India

234   MBh. trans. PC Roy, vol. I, p. 179

235   MBh. trans. PC Roy, vol. I, p. 179

236   S. Beal, 1973, The Life of Hiuen Tsiang, New Delhi, p 57; cf. NL Dey, Geographical Dictionary of India, p. 113 for an identification of Lamgham (Lampakā) 20 miles north-west of Jalalabad.

237   Matsya Purāṇa 148.8-9; Bhāgavata Purāṇa IX.23.16.

238   Rājataraṅgiṇī , VII. 2762-64.

239   Vāyu Purāṇa 88.122. 136- 43; Brahmāṇḍa Purāṇa 3.48.43-49; 63.119-34.

240   Viṣṇu Purāṇa 4.3.38-41.

241   Harivaṃśa 10.41-45.

242   Sten Konow, CII, vol. II, pp. xx ff; Sten Konow, EI, no. 20 'Taxila Inscription of the Year 136', vol. XIV, pp. 291-2.

243   EJ Rapson, ed., 1922,Cambridge History of India , vol. I, Ancient India, Cambridge, p. 564.

244   FW Thomas, 'Sakastana', JRAS, 1906, p. 216.

245   Rājataraṅgiṇī, 1.107-8.

246   The Buddhist Concepts of Spirits, p 81, Dr B. C. Law.

247   NL Dey, Geographical Dictionary, p. 115.

248   Nāmalingānuśāsana, with commentary ṭīkāsarvasva, of Sarvānanda (ed. Ganapati śāstri).

249   SK Chatterji, 1950, Kirāta-jana-kṛti --The Indo-Mongoloids: Their contributions to the and culture of India, Journal of Royal Asiatic Society of Bengal, Vol. XVI, pp.143-253.

250   WF Leemans, Foreign Trade in the Old Babylonian Period, 1960; 'Trade Relations on Babylonia', Journal of Economic and Social History of the Orient, vol. III, 1960, p.30 ff. 'Old Babylonian Letters and Economic History', Journal of Economic and Social History of the Orient, vol. XI, 1968, pp. 215-26; J. Hansam, 'A Periplus of Magan and Meluhha', Bulletin of the School of Oriental and African Studies, vol. 36, pt. III, 1973, pp. 554-83. Asko and Simo Parpola, 'On the Relationship of the Sumerian Toponym Meluhha and Sanskrit Mleccha', Studia Orientalia,vol. 46, 1975, pp. 205-38.

251   J. Hansam, 'A Periplus of Magan and Meluhha', Bulletin of the School of Oriental and African Studies, vol. 36, pt. III, 1973, pp. 560.

252   WF Leemans, 'Old Babylonian Letters and Economic History', Journal of Economic and Social History of the Orient, vol. XI, 1968, pp. 215-26. P. Aalto, 1971, 'Marginal

Notes on the Meluhha Problem,' Professor KA Nilakanta Sastri Felicitation Volume, Madras, pp. 234-38.

253   ibid., pp. 222-23.

254   Kohl, Phil L., 1979, "The 'World Economy' of West Asia in the Third Millenium BC." In South Asian Archaeology 1977, Naples. Durante, Silvio, 1979, "Marine Shells from Balakot, Shahr-I-Sokhta and Tepe Yahya: Their Significance for Trade Technology in Ancient Indo-Iran." In South Asian Archaeology 1977, Naples.

255   Chris JD Kostman, The Indus Valley Civilization: in search of those elusive centers and peripheries; Originally published in JAGNES, the Journal of the Association of Graduates in Near Eastern Studies.
http://www.adventurecorps.com/centperiph.html

256   http://www.scribd.com/doc/2232617/lexicon

257   After Fig. 2 in P.R.S. Moorey, 1994, Ancient Mesopotamian Materials and Industries, Oxford, Clarendon Press.

258   Source for the archaeological sites distribution maps: Current Science, Vol. 98, No. 6, 25 March 2010, pp 846-852; Spatio-temporal analysis of the Indus urbanization Kavita Gangal, M. N. Vahia and R. Adhikari
http://www.ias.ac.in/currsci/25mar2010/846.pdf

259   Source: Magan and Meluhha See Steinkeller 1984, 265.

260   Jain, 1984, Life in Ancient India as Described in the

Jain Canon and Commentaries (6th century BC - 17th century AD, p. 150.

261   Cowell, 1973, Jatakas Book II, p. 172 ff.

262 F.B.J. Kuiper, 1948, Proto-Munda Words in Sanskrit, Amsterdam, Verhandeling der Koninklijke Nederlandsche Akademie Van Wetenschappen, Afd. Letterkunde, Nieuwe Reeks Deel Li, No. 3, 1948, p.9 http://www.scribd.com/doc/12238039/mundalexemesinSanskrit

263 M.B.Emeneau, India as a Linguistic Area [Lang. 32, 1956, 3-16; LICS, 196, 642-51; repr. In Collected papers: Dravidian Linguistics Ethnology and Folktales, Annamalai Nagar, Annamalai University, 1967, pp. 171-186.

264 M.B.Emeneau, Linguistic Prehistory of India PAPS98 (1954). 282-92; Tamil Culture 5 (1956). 30-55; repr. In Collected papers: Dravidian Linguistics Ethnology and Folktales, Annamalai Nagar, Annamalai University, 1967, pp. 155-171.

265   Swaminatha Iyer, 1975, Dravidian Theories, Madras, Madras Law Journal Office

266   Bryant, Edwin and Laurie L. Patton, 2005, The Indo-Aryan controversy: evidence and inference in Indian history, Routledge, p.197.

267   K. V. Sarma, 1983, "Spread of Vedic Culture in Ancient. South India" in The Adyar Library Bulletin, 1983, 43:1.

268   Emeneau, MB, 1956, India as a linguistic area, in:

Language, 32.3-16

•Kuiper, FBJ, 1967, The genesis of a linguistic area, Indo-Iranian Journal 10: 81-102

•Masica, Colin P., 1976, Defining a linguistic area, South Asia, Chicago, University of Chicago Press

•Franklin Southworth, 2005, Linguistic Archaeology of South Asia, Routledge Curzon

[269]   http://en.wikipedia.org/wiki/Areal_feature

[270]   Emeneau, Murray. 1956. India as a Lingusitic Area. "Langauge" 32: 3-16.

http://en.academic.ru/dic.nsf/enwiki/113093

[271]   Berger, H. Die Burushaski-Sprache von Hunza und Nagar. Vols. I-III. Wiesbaden: Harrassowitz 1988] [Tikkanen (2005)]

[272]   [G.Morgenstierne, Irano-Dardica. Wiesbaden 1973]

[273]   The Munda Languages. Edited by Gregory D. S. Anderson. London and New York: Routledge (Routledge Language Family Series), 2008.

[274] Tentative readings of such glyphs yet to be validated by the cipher code key of Indus script are detailed (including decipherment of inscriptions from scores of small sites) at http://sites.google.com/site/kalyan97/induswriting

[275] Graphemes:

kol 'the name of a bird, the Indian cuckoo' (Santali)

kolo 'a large jungle climber, dioscorea doemonum (Santali)

kulai 'a hare' (Santali)

Grapheme: Ta. kōl stick, staff, branch, arrow. Ma. kōl staff, rod, stick, arrow. Ko. kl stick, story of funeral car. To. kwš stick.Ka. kōl, kōlu stick, staff, arrow. Koḍ. Klï stick. Tu. kōlů, kōlustick, staff. Te. kōla id., arrow; long, oblong; kōlanaelongatedness, elongation; kōlani elongated. Kol. (SR.) kolā, (Kin.) kōla stick. Nk. (Ch.) kōl pestle. Pa. kōl shaft of arrow.Go. (A.) kōla id.; kōlā (Tr.) a thin twig or stick, esp. for kindling a fire, (W. Ph.) stick, rod, a blade of grass, straw; (G. Mu. Ma. Ko.) kōla handle of plough, sickle, knife, etc. (Voc.988); (ASu.) kōlā stick, arrow, slate-pencil; (LuS.) kola the handle of an implement. Konḍa kōl big wooden pestle. Pe. kōlpestle. Manḍ. kūl id. Kui kōḍu (pl. kōṭka) id. Kuwi (F.)kōlū (pl. kōlka), (S. Su.) kōlu (pl. kōlka) id. Cf. 2240 Ta.kōlam (Tu. Te. Go.). / Cf. OMar. (Master) kōla stick. (DEDR 2237). कोलदंडा or कोलदांडा [kōladaṇḍā or kōladāṇḍā] m A stick or bar fastened to the neck of a surly dog. (Marathi)

kola [kōla] f. The bandicoot rat, mus malibaricos (Rajasthani)

Graphemes: డోలు [ḍōlu] ḍōlu. [Tel.] n. A drum.

ḍollu. [Tel.] v. n. To fall, to roll over. పడు, పొరలు. డోలుచు [ḍolucu] or ḍoluṭsu. [Tel.] v. n. To tumble head over heels as dancing girls do (Telugu)

maṇḍa = a branch; a twig; a twig with leaves on it (Te.lex.)

maṇḍhwa, maṇḍua, maṇḍwa 'a temporary shed or booth erected on the occasion of a marriage' (Santali) maṇḍā = warehouse, workshop (Kon.lex.)

maṇḍā = warehouse, workshop (Kon.lex.)

*khōla2 ' cavity, hollow '. 2. *khōlla -- 2. 3. *khōḍa -- . 4. *khōra -- 2. [Cf. Par. khur ' cave ' IIFL i 265]1. Paš. gul. khōl ' ravine '; P. khol f. ' cavity, hollow '; WPah. cur. khol ' stream '; N. kholo ' small river, valley '; Bi. khol, li ' trough in which the share lies when fixed in body of plough '; H. khol, lar m. ' cavity, cave '; -- A. kholiba ' to hollow out ', kholni ' mortice '; Or. kholibā ' to dig '. -- X kōṭará -- q.v.2. Pk. kholla -- n. ' hollow '; L. kholā ' hollow '; Or. khola ' cave '; G. khol f. ' hollowness '; M. khol ' deep '.3. Kho. (Lor.) khōl ' cave, hollow under rock '; P. khor f. ' cavity, hollow '; -- A. khor ' cavity, hole ' or < *khōra -- 2.4. Gy. arm. xor ' deep, hollow, depth ', eur. xor ' deep, depth ', wel. xorō ' deep '; Sh. (Lor.) kōr ' cave '; L. khorī ' enclosure '; P. khorā ' empty '; N. khor ' enclosure, trap ', ro ' crack in skin of foot ', ri ' small pocket of leaves '; A. khor ' cave ' (or < *khōḍa --); B. khor ' sore in foot -- andmouth disease '; H. khorm. ' cave ', f. ' cavity ', rā m. ' pit, cave '; M. khor m. ' glen '. Addenda: *khōla -- 2. 3. khōḍa -- : WPah.ktg. khv́r m. ' lowest storey of house where cattle are kept (often dug into the hillside) ' (but cf. P. kur, kgr. kurh f. ' enclosure for cattle ' Him.I 35); -- perh. also khv́r ' dung, manure '. (CDIAL 3943)

khōll ' to open '. 2. *khull -- ' to be open '.1. Gy. pal. kółăr '

loosens ', eur. wel. xulav -- ' to comb out (hair), part, divide ';
K. khōlun ' to open ', S. kholaṇu, L. awāṇ. khōluṇ; P. kholhṇā
' to open, loose '; WPah. rudh. kholl -- ' to open '; Ku. gng.
khoe ' releases '; N. kholnu ' to open ', B. kholā, khulā, Or.
kholibā, Mth. Aw. lakh. khōlab, H. kholnā, Marw. kholṇo, G.
kholvũ; M. kholṇẽ ' to deepen (a well) '.2. S. khulaṇu intr. ' to
open ', L. awāṇ. khullaṇ ' to be open ', P. khullhṇā, WPah.
cam. khulhṇā, Ku. khulṇo, N. khulnu, B. khulā, H. khulnā, G.
khulvũ, M.khulṇẽ; -- OMarw. khulo adj. ' open '.*utkhōll -- ,
*niṣkhōll -- .Addenda: *khōll -- . 1. S.kcch. kholṇū ' to open ';
WPah.kṭg. (kc.) khólṇõ.2. *khull -- : WPah.kṭg. khúlṇõ ' to be
opened ', khullɔ ' spacious, wide '; J. khulā ' loosened
'.(CDIAL 3945)

276

A pearl merchant of South India settling
price for a pearl using finger gestures under a
handkerchief. Cited in Karl Menninger, 1969, *Number
words and number symbols: a cultural history of numbers*,
MIT Press, p.212. http://tinyurl.com/26ze95s